ESCAPE...

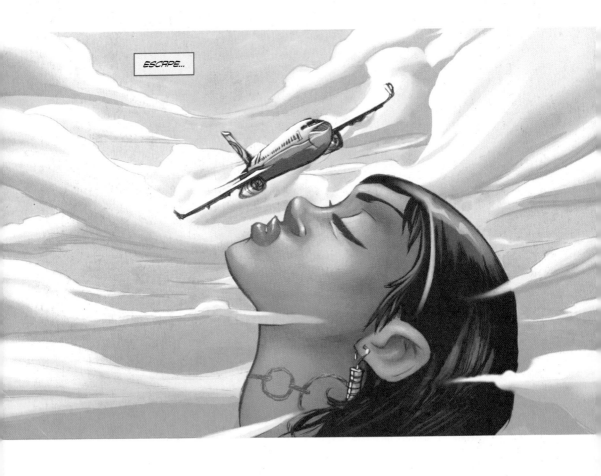

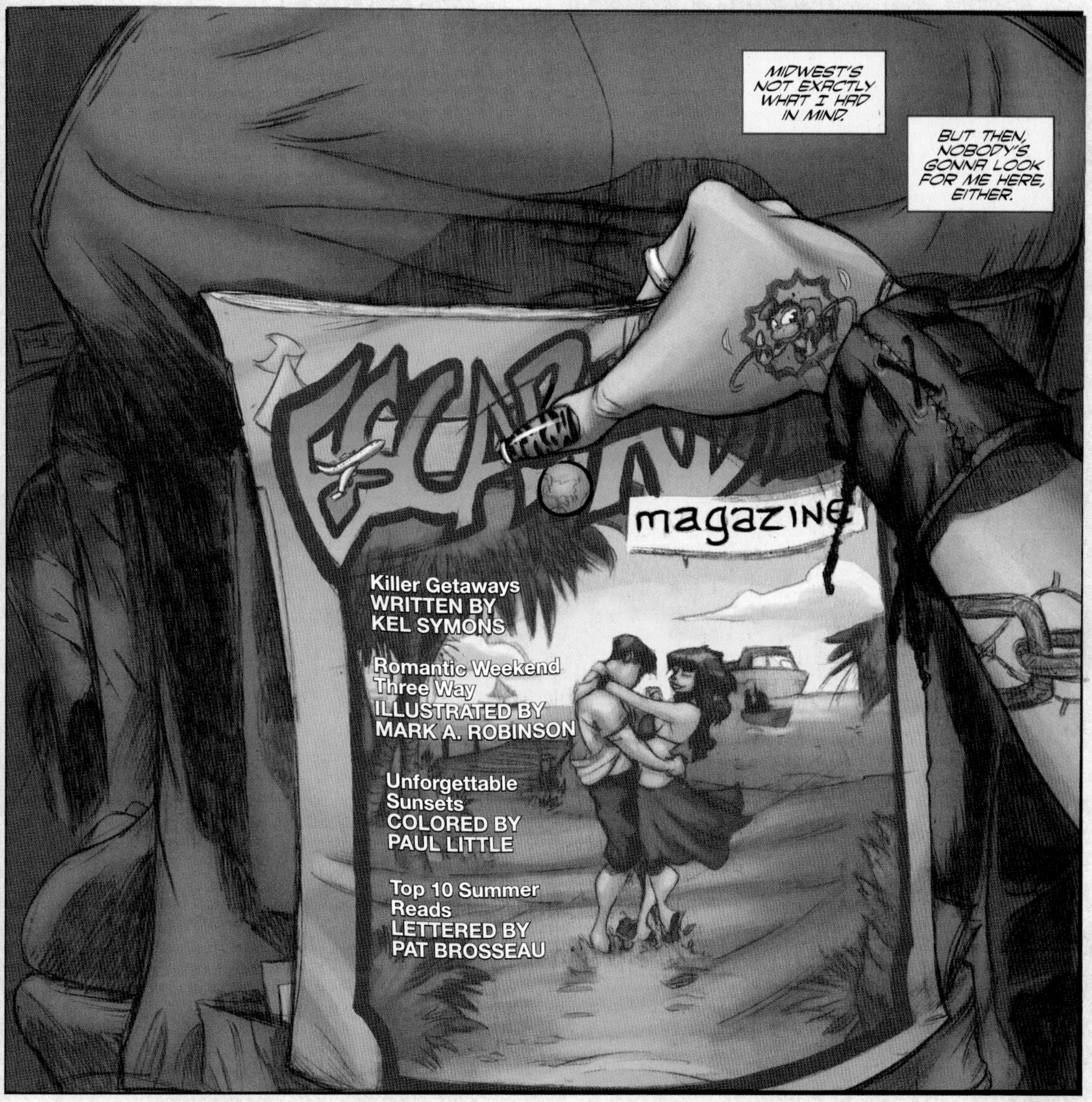
MIDWEST'S NOT EXACTLY WHAT I HAD IN MIND.
BUT THEN, NOBODY'S GONNA LOOK FOR ME HERE, EITHER.
magazine
Killer Getaways
WRITTEN BY
KEL SYMONS
Romantic Weekend
Three Way
ILLUSTRATED BY
MARK A. ROBINSON
Unforgettable
Sunsets
COLORED BY
PAUL LITTLE
Top 10 Summer
Reads
LETTERED BY
PAT BROSSEAU

BOOK ONE
DISAPPEARING ACT
SIGH.
WHAT IS IT THEY SAY?
WHEN THE GOING GETS TOUGH, THE TOUGH GET...
FELICIA! FELICIA!!
TATT
...AS FAR FUCKING AWAY AS POSSIBLE.

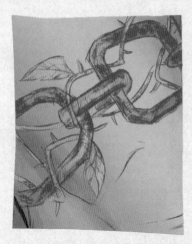

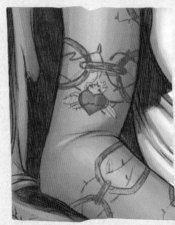

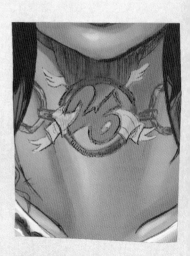

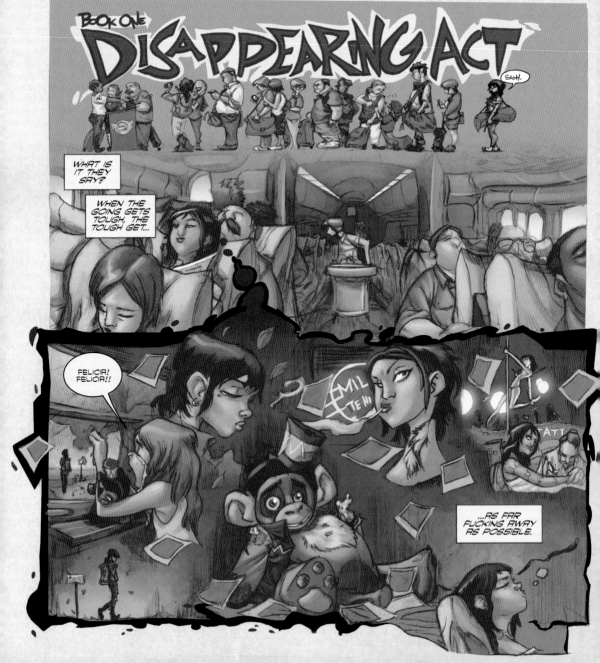

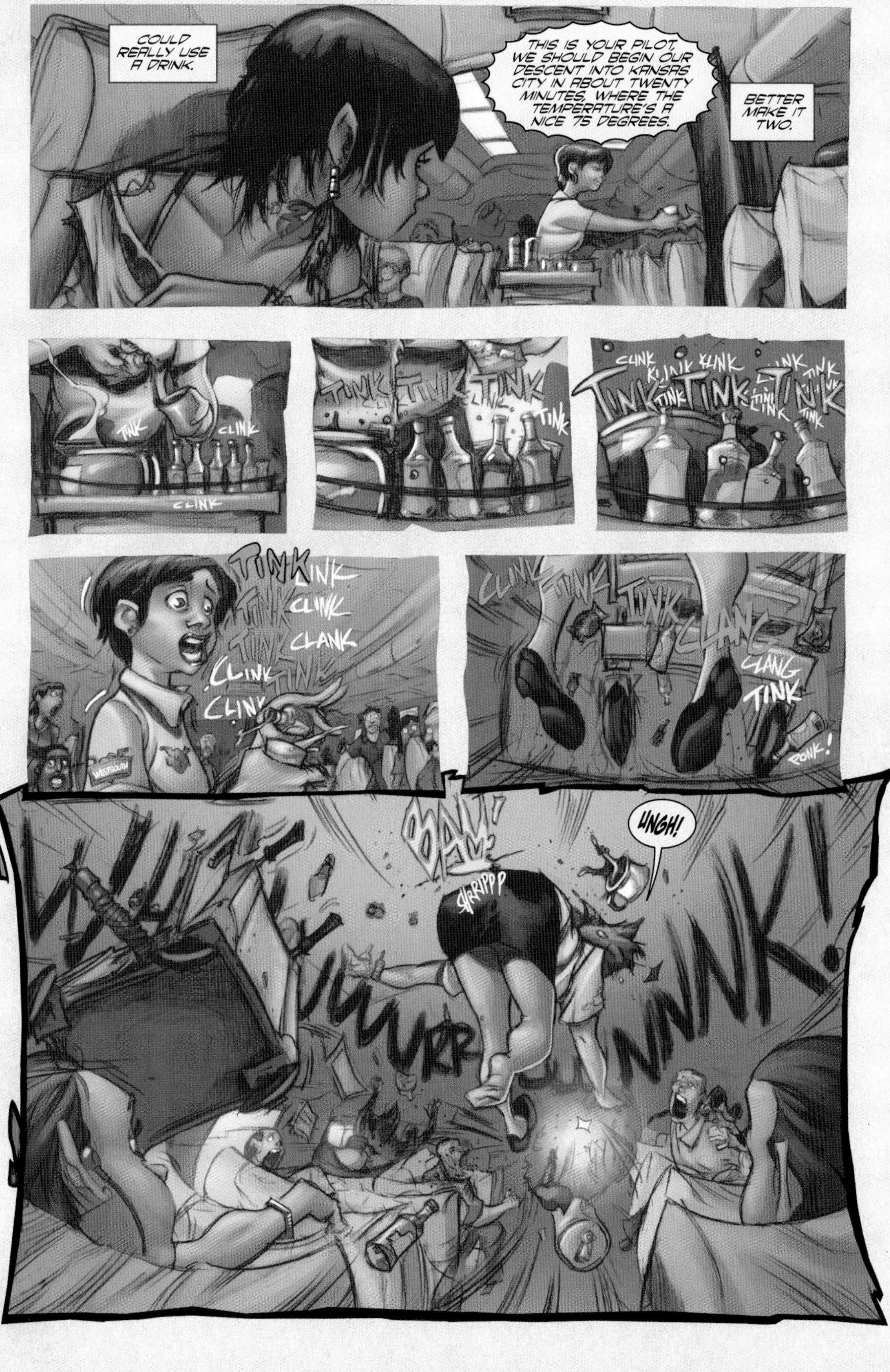
COULD REALLY USE A DRINK.
THIS IS YOUR PILOT, WE SHOULD BEGIN OUR DESCENT INTO KANSAS CITY IN ABOUT TWENTY MINUTES, WHERE THE TEMPERATURE'S A NICE 75 DEGREES.
BETTER MAKE IT TWO.
TINK
CLINK
CLINK
TINK TINK TINK
TINK
TINK TINK TINK
TINK CLINK
CLINK
CLANK
CLINK
CLINK
CLINK TINK TINK
CLANG
CLANG
TINK
PONK!
UNGH!
SHRIPPP
WESTSOUTH

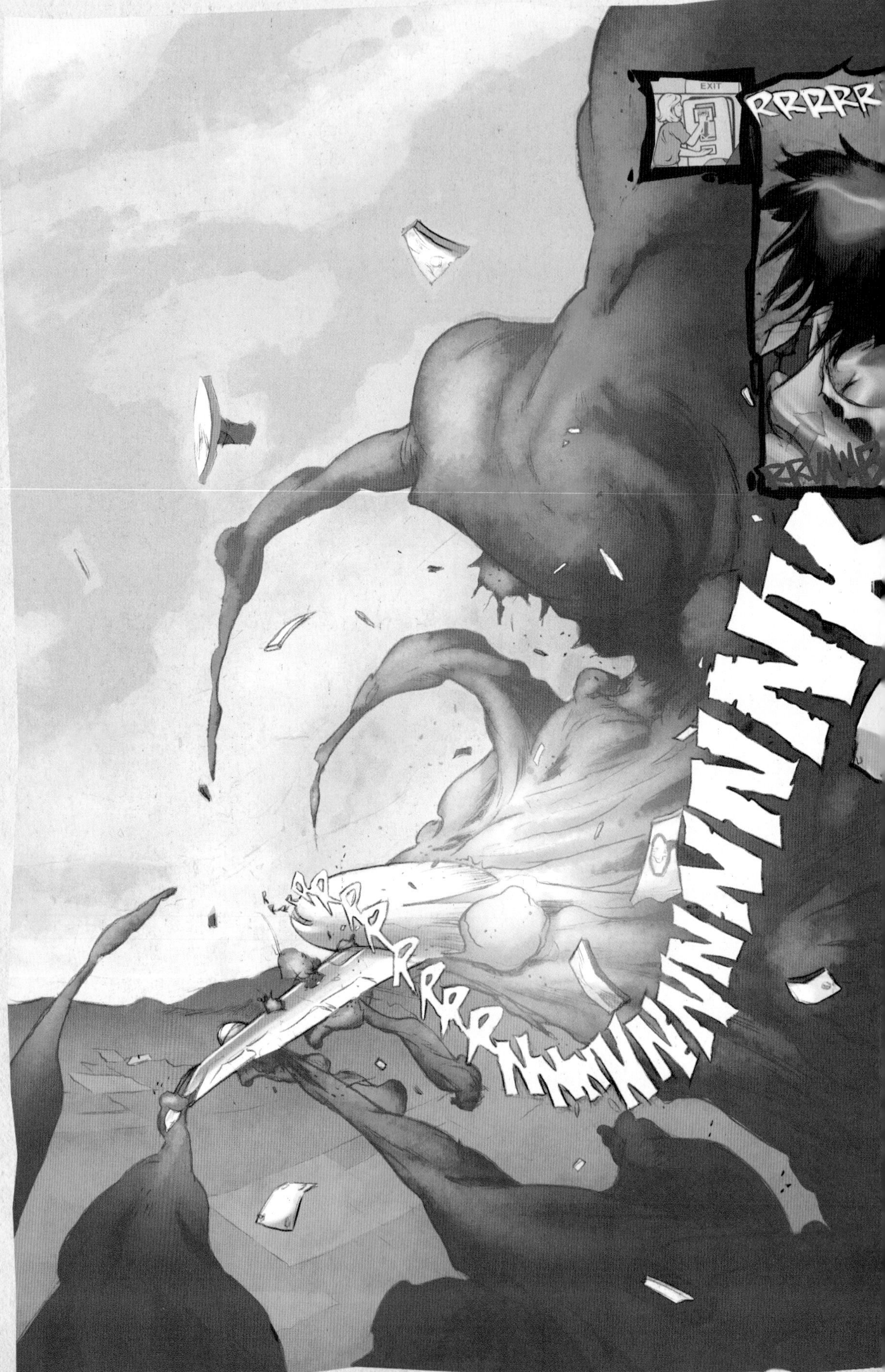
EXIT
RRRRR
RRUMMB
RRRRRRRRNNNNNNNNNNNK

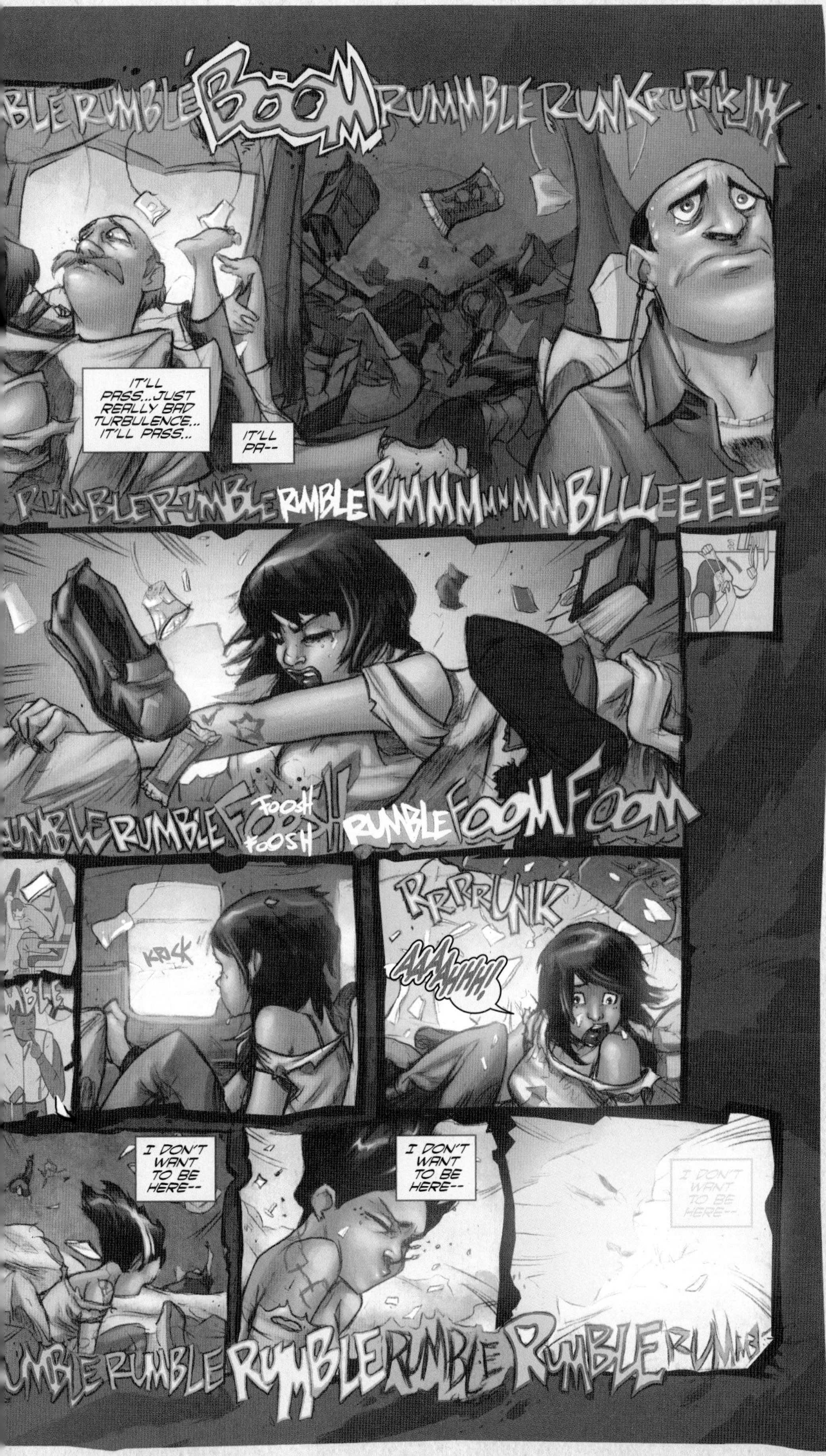
RUMBLE
BOOM
RUMMBLE
IT'LL PASS...JUST REALLY BAD TURBULENCE... IT'LL PASS...
IT'LL PA--
RUMBLE RUMBLE RUMBLE
RUMBLE RUMBLE
FOOSH FOOSH
RUMBLE
FOOM FOOM
RRRRUNK
AAAAHHH!
I DON'T WANT TO BE HERE--
I DON'T WANT TO BE HERE--
I DON'T WANT TO BE HERE--
RUMBLE RUMBLE RUMBLE RUMBLE RUMBLE

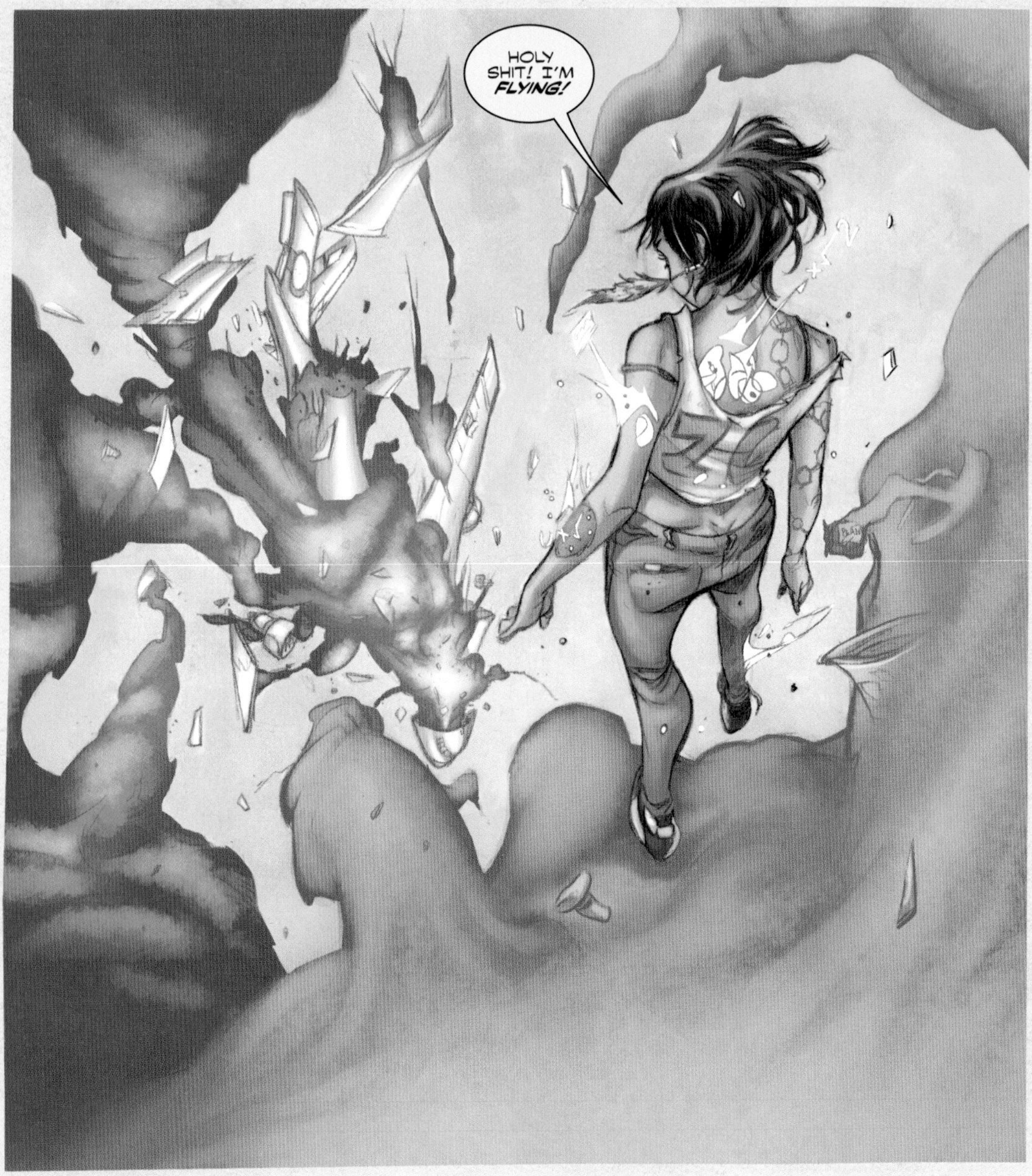
HOLY SHIT! I'M *FLYING!*

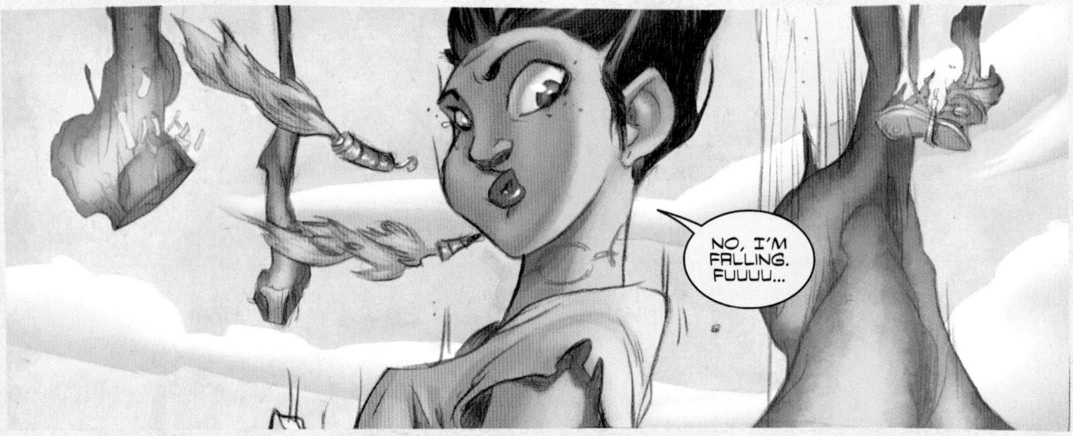
NO, I'M FALLING. FUUUU...

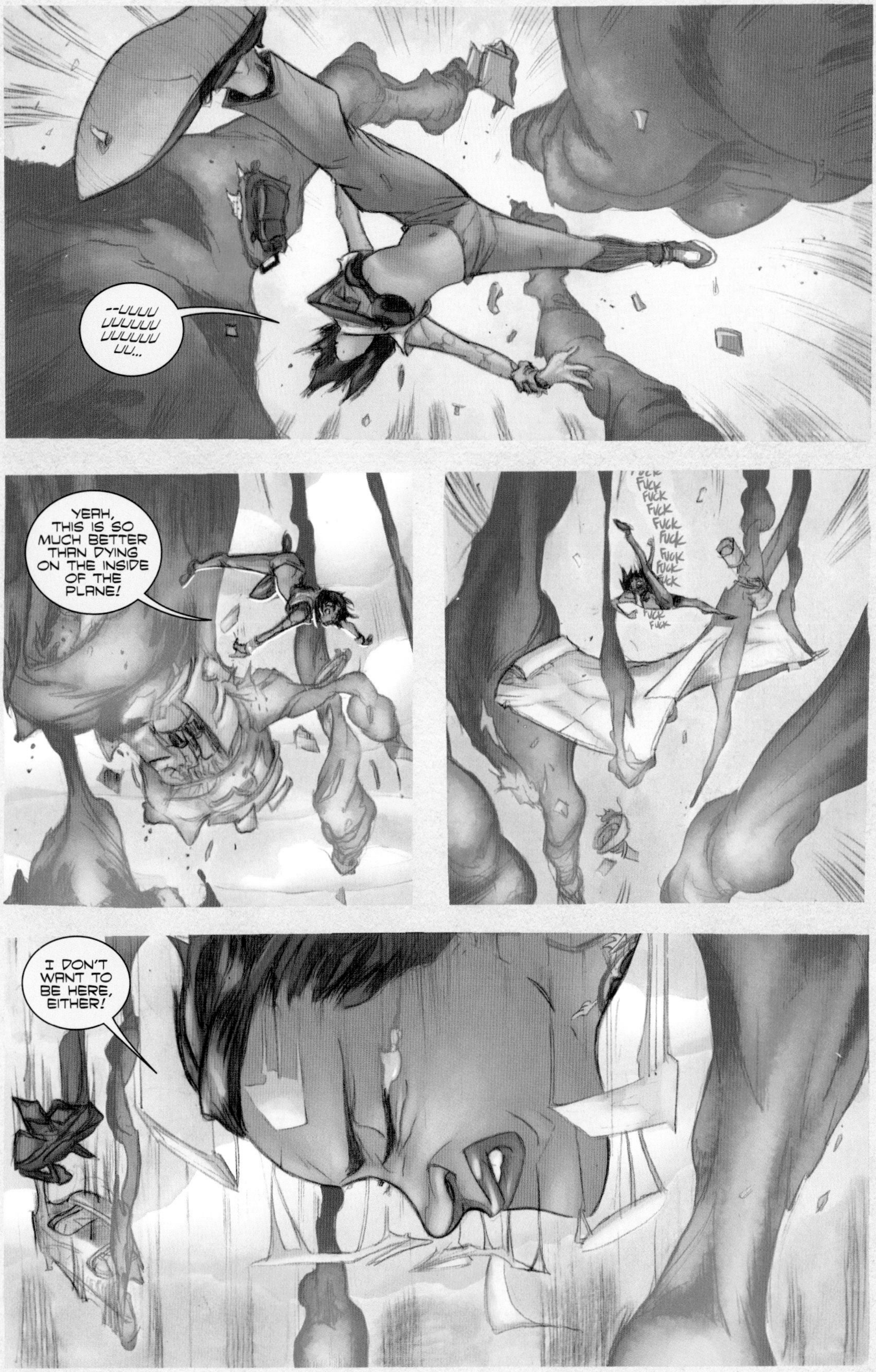
--UUUU UUUUUU UUUUUU UU...
YEAH, THIS IS SO MUCH BETTER THAN DYING ON THE INSIDE OF THE PLANE!
FUCK FUCK FUCK FUCK FUCK FUCK FUCK
FUCK FUCK
I DON'T WANT TO BE HERE, EITHER!

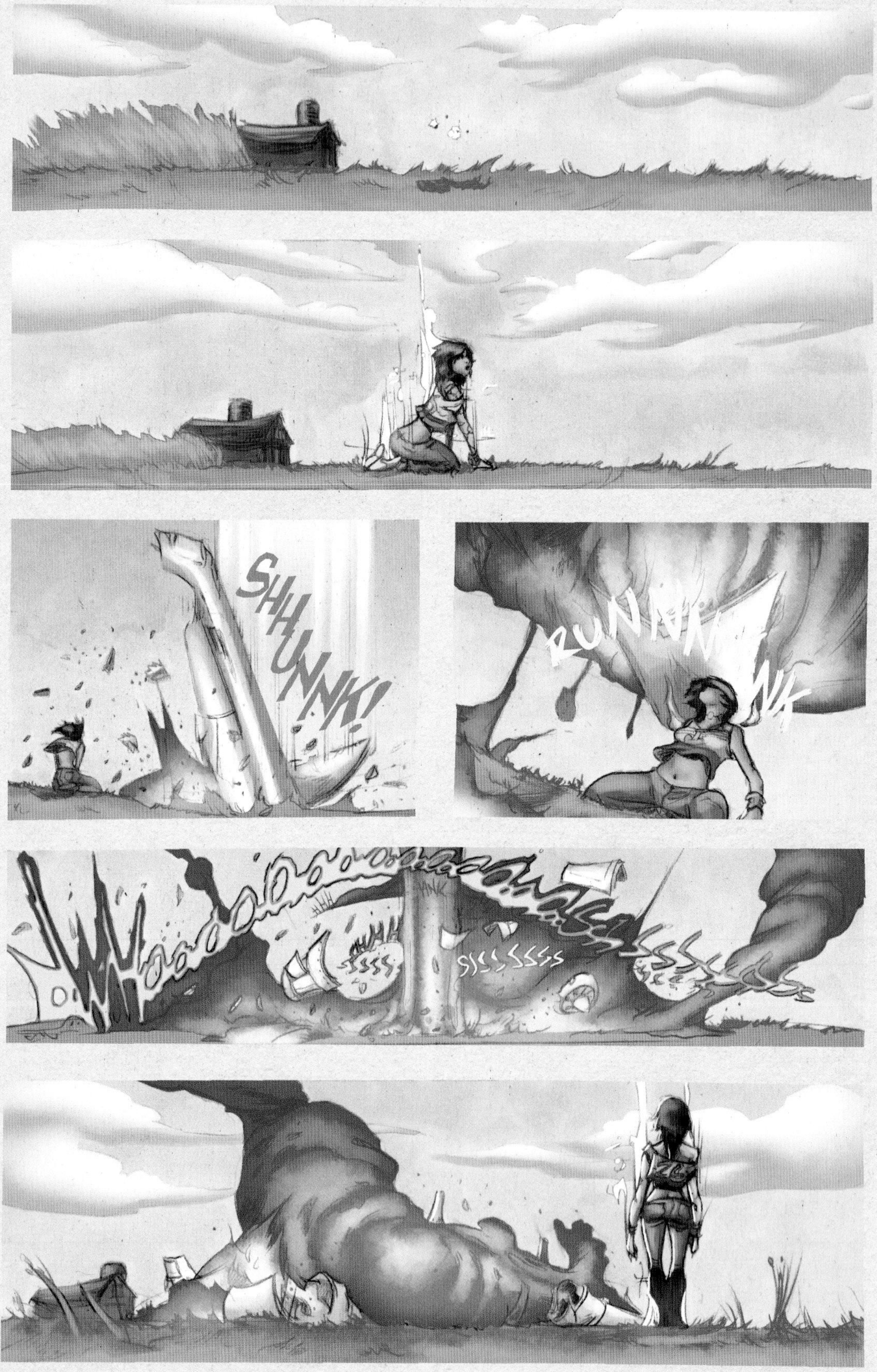
SHHUNNK!

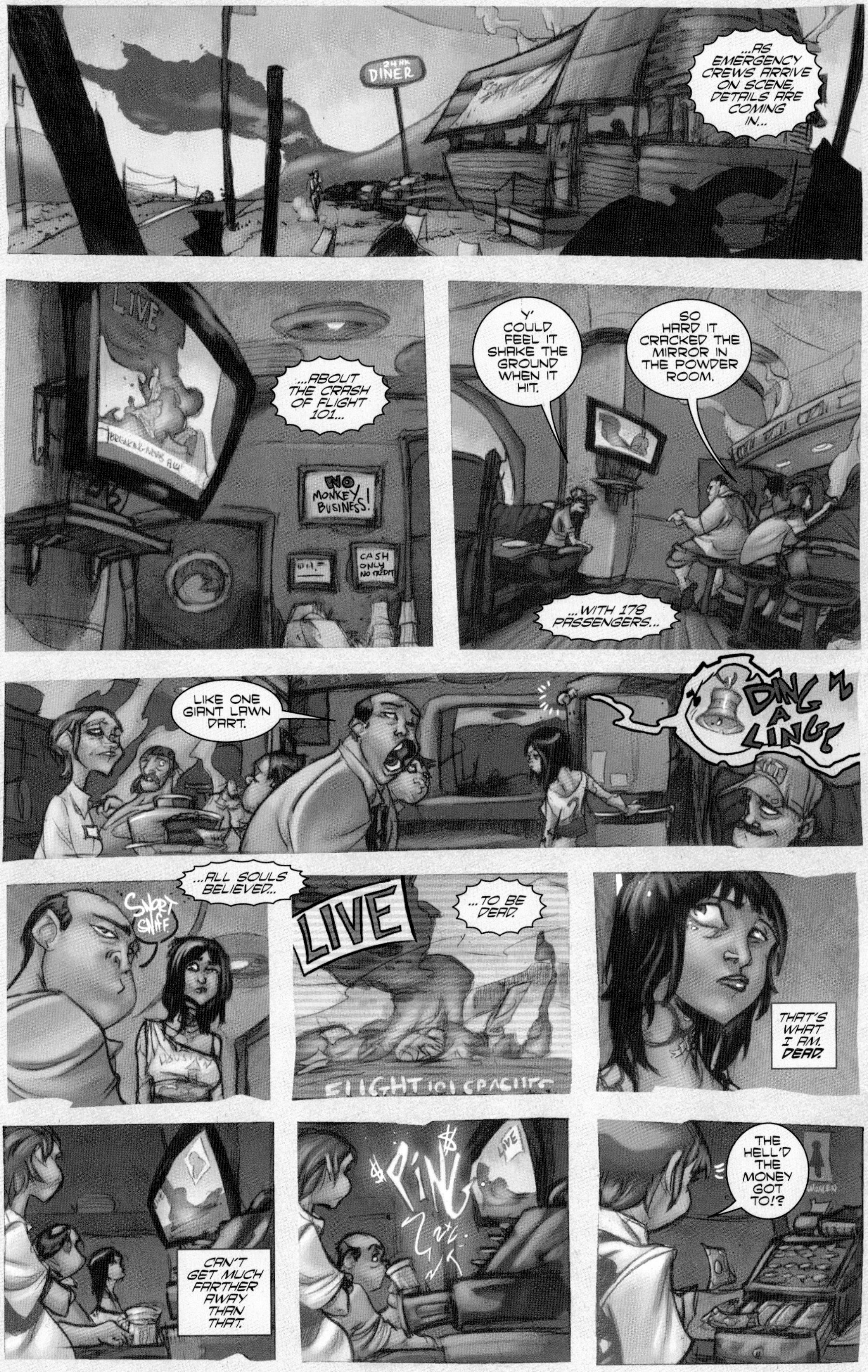
24 HR DINER
...AS EMERGENCY CREWS ARRIVE ON SCENE, DETAILS ARE COMING IN...
LIVE
...ABOUT THE CRASH OF FLIGHT 101...
NO MONKEY BUSINES!
CASH ONLY NO CREDIT
Y' COULD FEEL IT SHAKE THE GROUND WHEN IT HIT.
SO HARD IT CRACKED THE MIRROR IN THE POWDER ROOM.
...WITH 178 PASSENGERS...
LIKE ONE GIANT LAWN DART.
DING A LING!
...ALL SOULS BELIEVED...
SNORT SNIFF.
LIVE
...TO BE DEAD.
THAT'S WHAT I AM. **DEAD.**
CAN'T GET MUCH FARTHER AWAY THAN THAT.
PING
THE HELL'D THE MONEY GOT TO!?
WOMEN

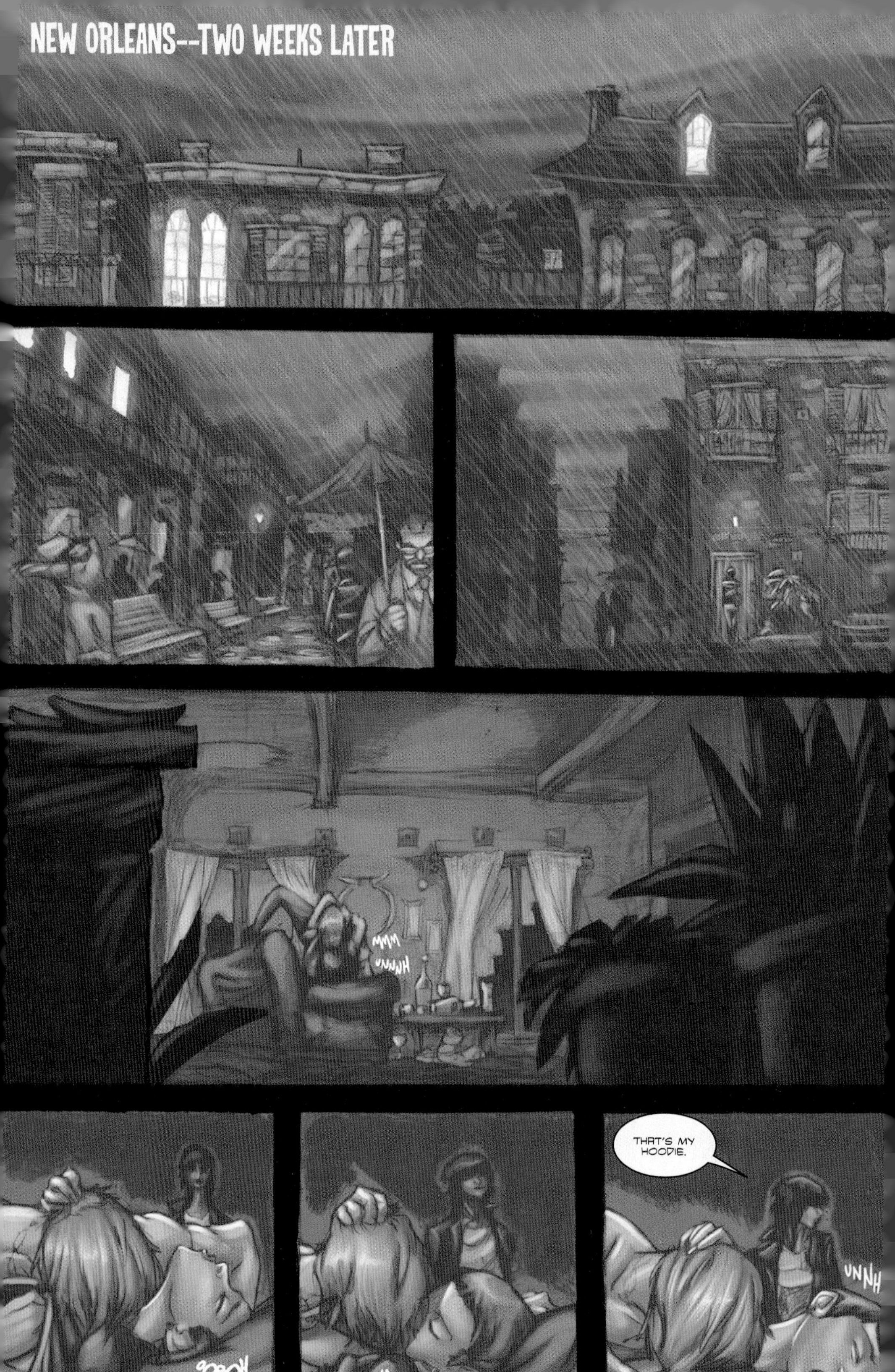
NEW ORLEANS--TWO WEEKS LATER
MMM
UNNH
OOOH
MMMMMMM
THAT'S MY HOODIE.
UNNH

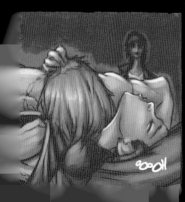

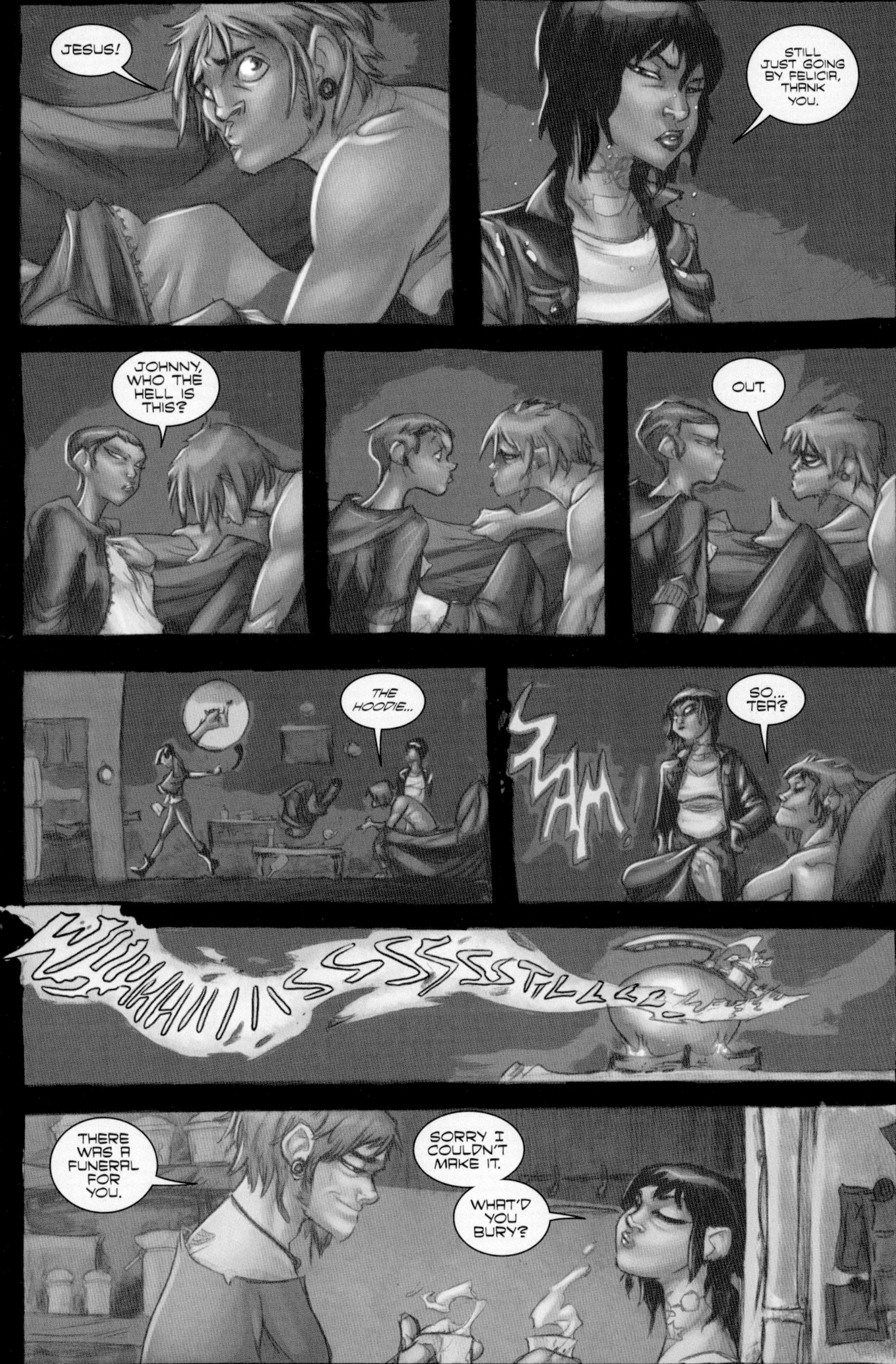
JESUS!
STILL JUST GOING BY FELICIA, THANK YOU.
JOHNNY, WHO THE HELL IS THIS?
OUT.
THE HOODIE...
SO... TEA?
ZAM!
WHHHHHIIISSSSSSSTILLLLL
THERE WAS A FUNERAL FOR YOU.
SORRY I COULDN'T MAKE IT.
WHAT'D YOU BURY?

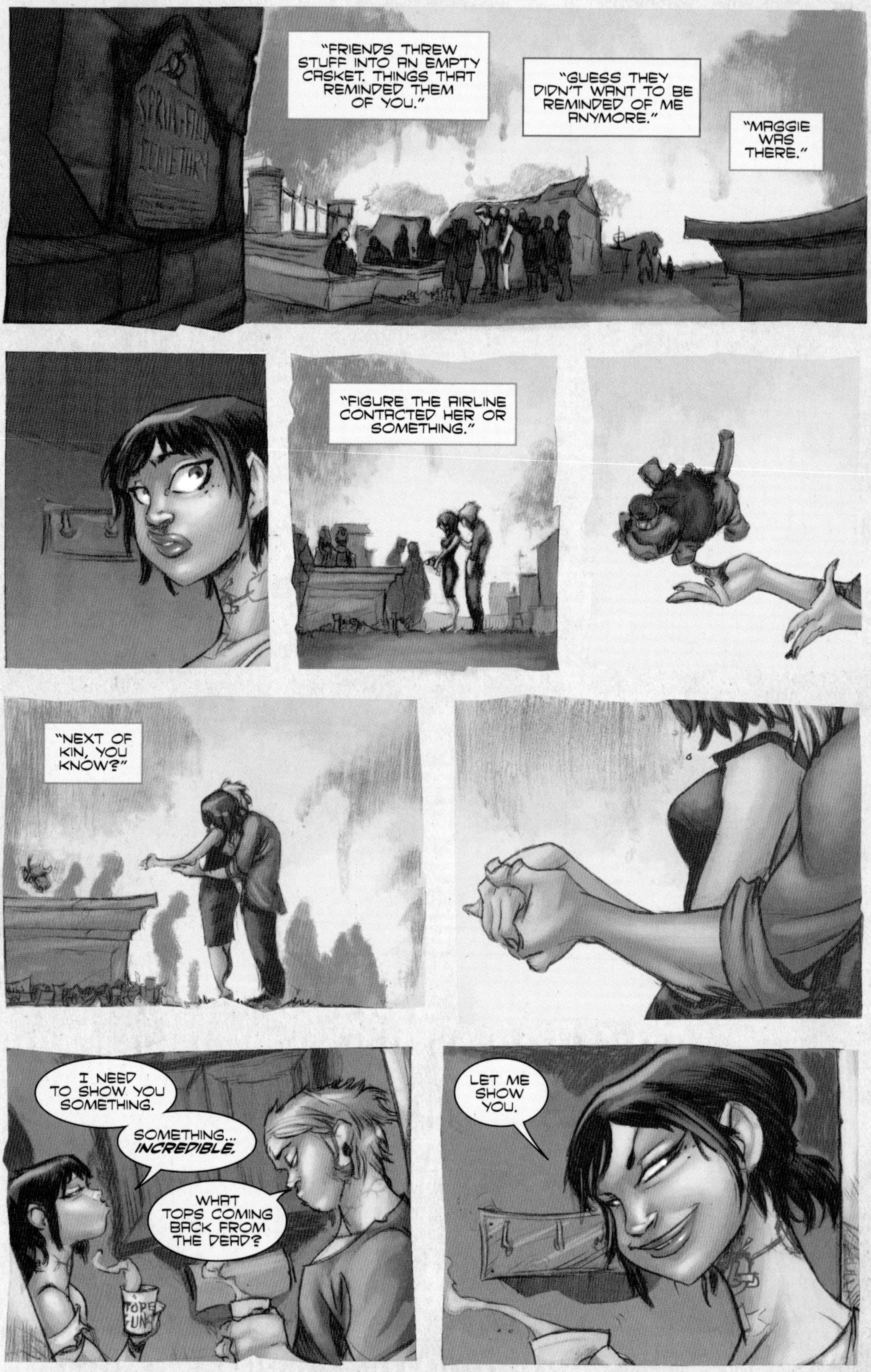
SPRINGFIELD CEMETARY
"FRIENDS THREW STUFF INTO AN EMPTY CASKET. THINGS THAT REMINDED THEM OF YOU."
"GUESS THEY DIDN'T WANT TO BE REMINDED OF ME ANYMORE."
"MAGGIE WAS THERE."
"FIGURE THE AIRLINE CONTACTED HER OR SOMETHING."
"NEXT OF KIN, YOU KNOW?"
I NEED TO SHOW YOU SOMETHING.
SOMETHING... *INCREDIBLE.*
WHAT TOPS COMING BACK FROM THE DEAD?
LET ME SHOW YOU.

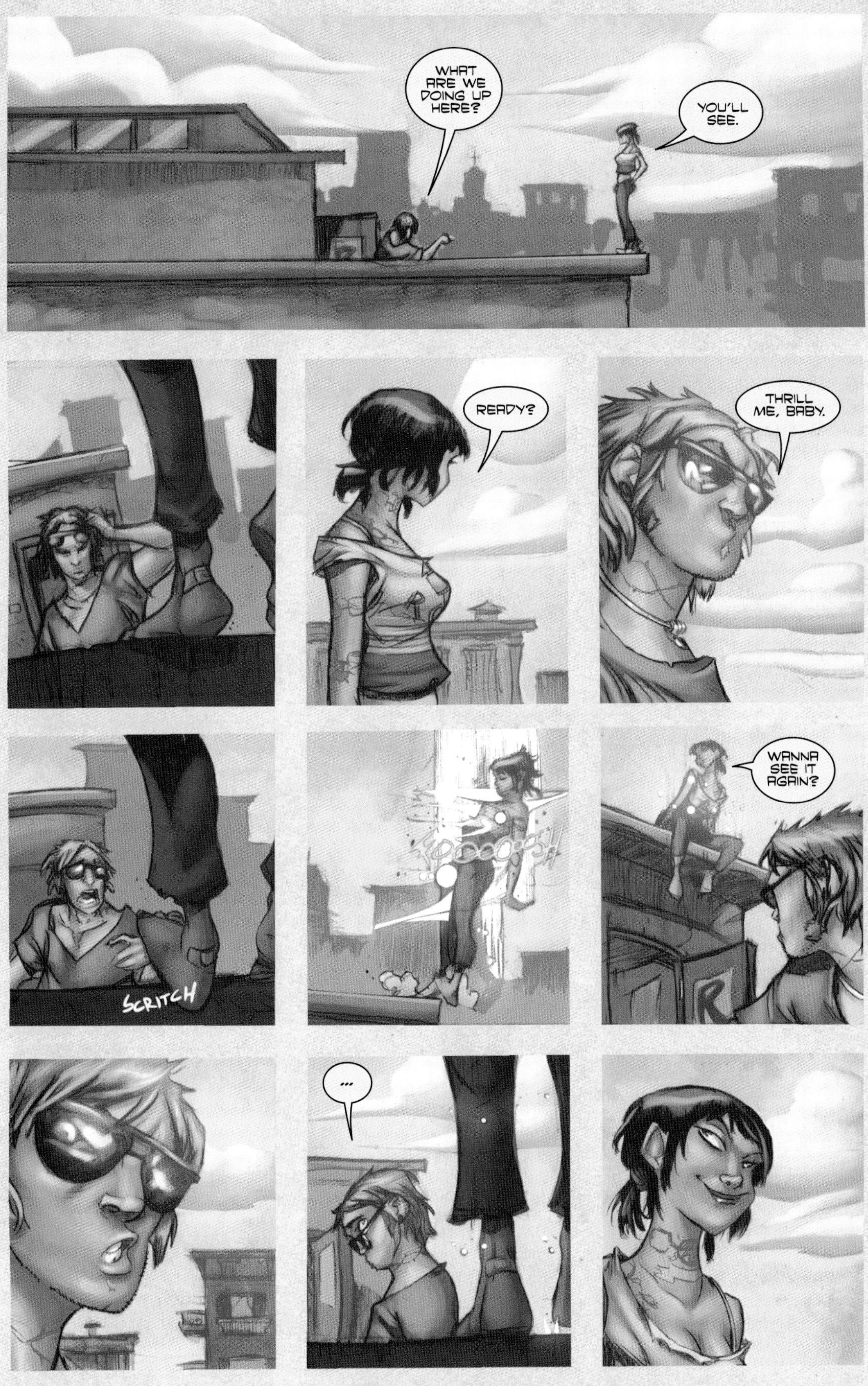
WHAT ARE WE DOING UP HERE?
YOU'LL SEE.
READY?
THRILL ME, BABY.
SCRITCH
FOOOOOOSH
WANNA SEE IT AGAIN?
...

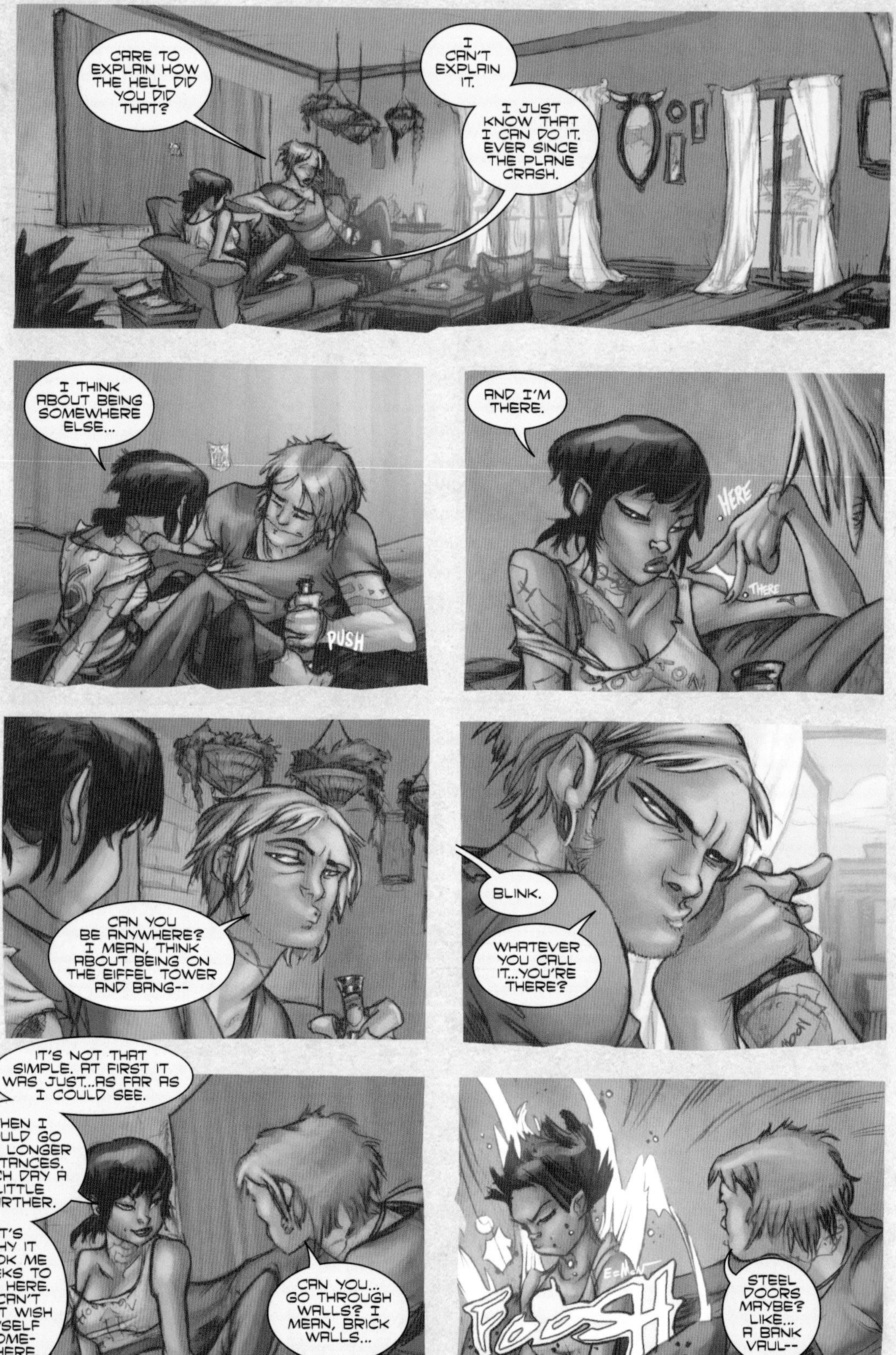
CARE TO EXPLAIN HOW THE HELL DID YOU DID THAT?
I CAN'T EXPLAIN IT.
I JUST KNOW THAT I CAN DO IT. EVER SINCE THE PLANE CRASH.
I THINK ABOUT BEING SOMEWHERE ELSE...
PUSH
AND I'M THERE.
HERE
THERE
CAN YOU BE ANYWHERE? I MEAN, THINK ABOUT BEING ON THE EIFFEL TOWER AND BANG--
BLINK.
WHATEVER YOU CALL IT...YOU'RE THERE?
IT'S NOT THAT SIMPLE. AT FIRST IT WAS JUST...AS FAR AS I COULD SEE.
THEN I COULD GO FOR LONGER DISTANCES. EACH DAY A LITTLE FARTHER.
IT'S WHY IT TOOK ME WEEKS TO GET HERE. I CAN'T JUST WISH MYSELF SOME-WHERE.
CAN YOU... GO THROUGH WALLS? I MEAN, BRICK WALLS...
FOOSH
STEEL DOORS MAYBE? LIKE... A BANK VAUL--

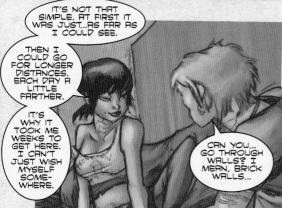

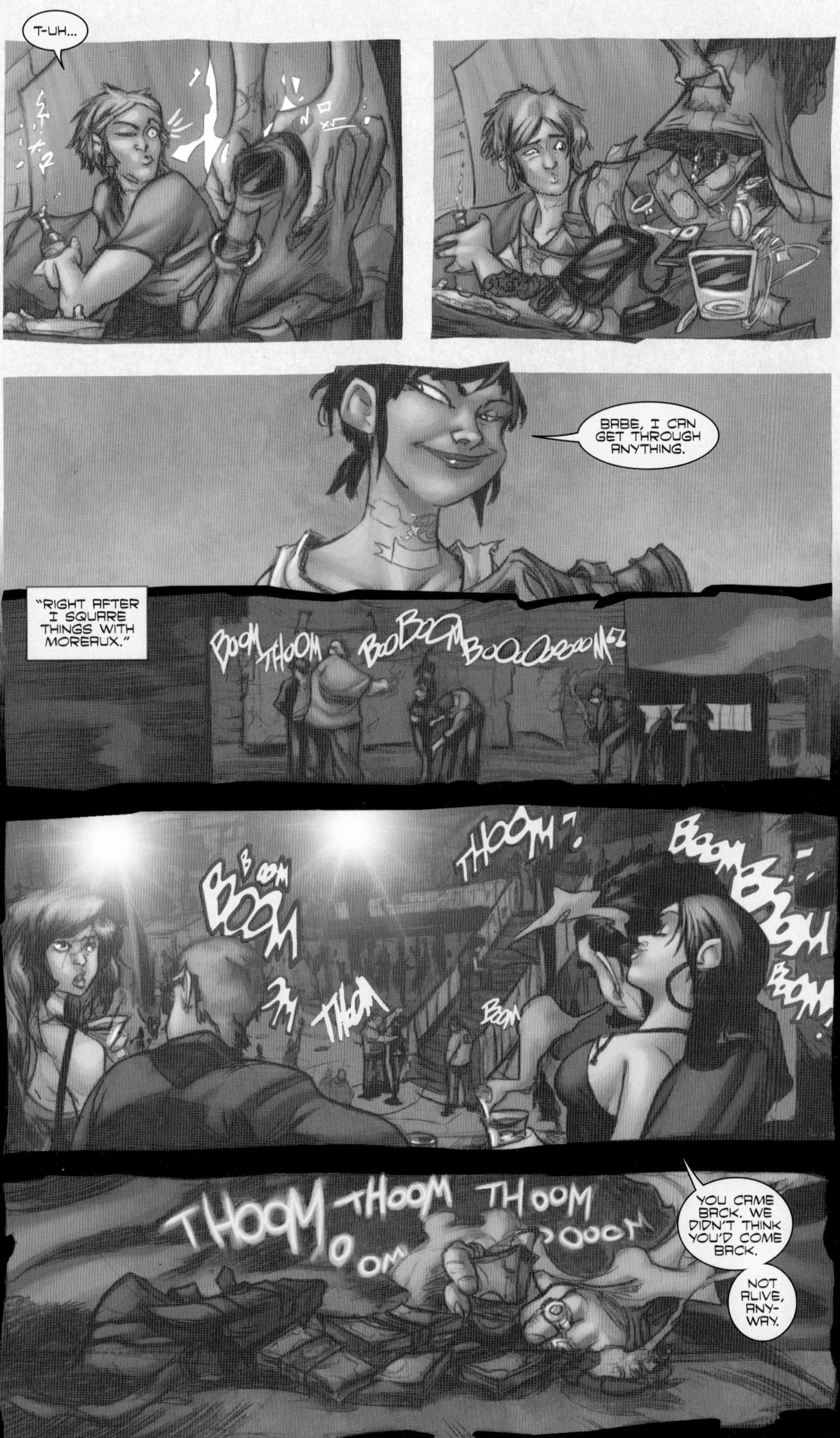
T-UH...
BABE, I CAN GET THROUGH ANYTHING.
"RIGHT AFTER I SQUARE THINGS WITH MOREAUX."
BOOM THOOM BOOBOOM BOOOOBOOOM
BBOOM BOOM
THOOM
BOOMBOOM BOOM
THOOM
BOOM
THOOM THOOM THOOM
YOU CAME BACK. WE DIDN'T THINK YOU'D COME BACK.
NOT ALIVE, ANY-WAY.

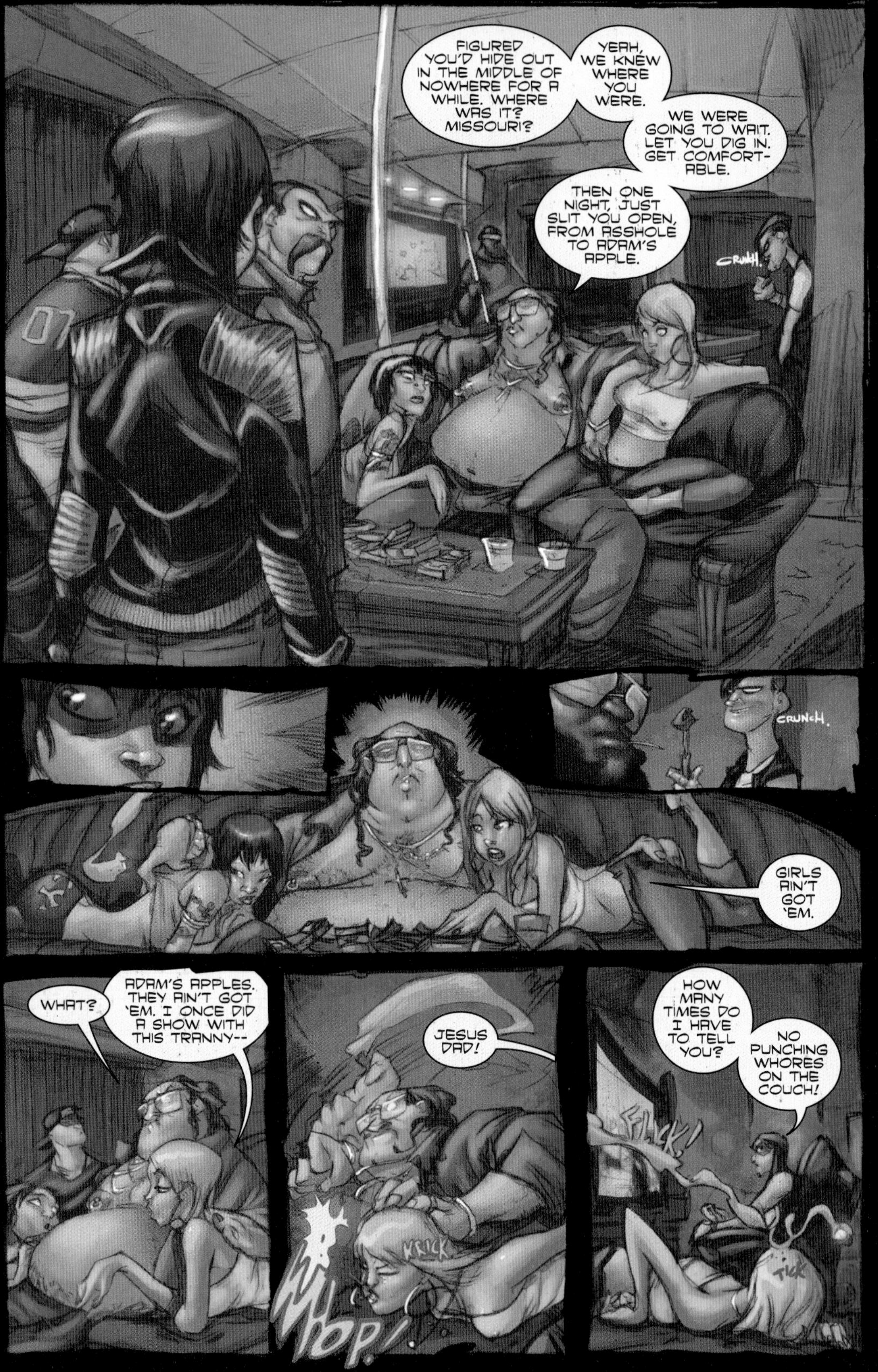

FIGURED YOU'D HIDE OUT IN THE MIDDLE OF NOWHERE FOR A WHILE. WHERE WAS IT? MISSOURI?
YEAH, WE KNEW WHERE YOU WERE.
WE WERE GOING TO WAIT. LET YOU DIG IN. GET COMFORT-ABLE.
THEN ONE NIGHT, JUST SLIT YOU OPEN, FROM ASSHOLE TO ADAM'S APPLE.
CRUNCH.
CRUNCH.
GIRLS AIN'T GOT 'EM.
WHAT?
ADAM'S APPLES. THEY AIN'T GOT 'EM. I ONCE DID A SHOW WITH THIS TRANNY--
JESUS DAD!
WHOP!
HOW MANY TIMES DO I HAVE TO TELL YOU?
NO PUNCHING WHORES ON THE COUCH!

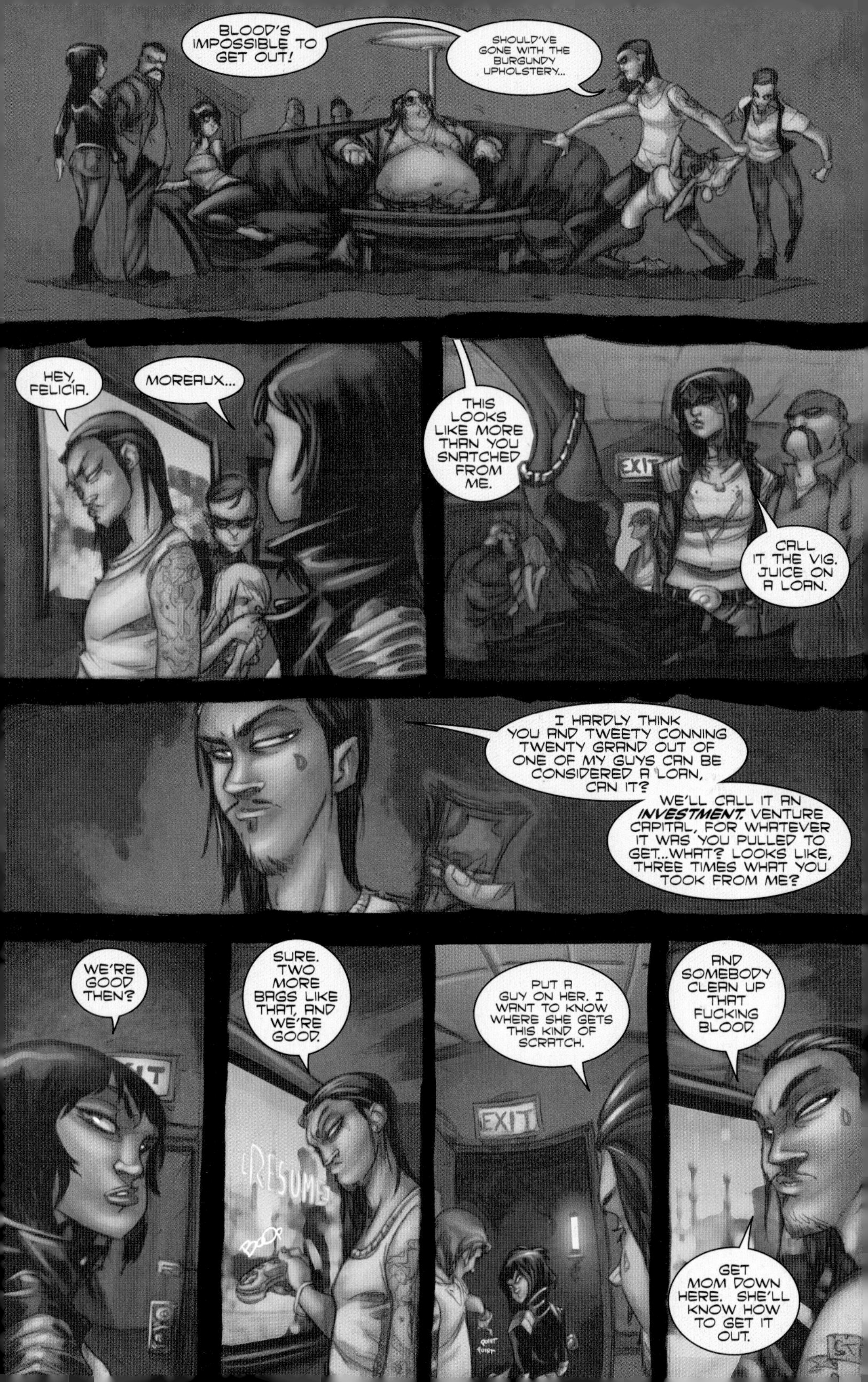
BLOOD'S IMPOSSIBLE TO GET OUT!
SHOULD'VE GONE WITH THE BURGUNDY UPHOLSTERY...
HEY, FELICIA.
MOREAUX...
THIS LOOKS LIKE MORE THAN YOU SNATCHED FROM ME.
CALL IT THE VIG. JUICE ON A LOAN.
I HARDLY THINK YOU AND TWEETY CONNING TWENTY GRAND OUT OF ONE OF MY GUYS CAN BE CONSIDERED A LOAN, CAN IT?
WE'LL CALL IT AN ***INVESTMENT.*** VENTURE CAPITAL, FOR WHATEVER IT WAS YOU PULLED TO GET...WHAT? LOOKS LIKE, THREE TIMES WHAT YOU TOOK FROM ME?
WE'RE GOOD THEN?
SURE. TWO MORE BAGS LIKE THAT, AND WE'RE GOOD.
PUT A GUY ON HER. I WANT TO KNOW WHERE SHE GETS THIS KIND OF SCRATCH.
AND SOMEBODY CLEAN UP THAT FUCKING BLOOD.
GET MOM DOWN HERE. SHE'LL KNOW HOW TO GET IT OUT.

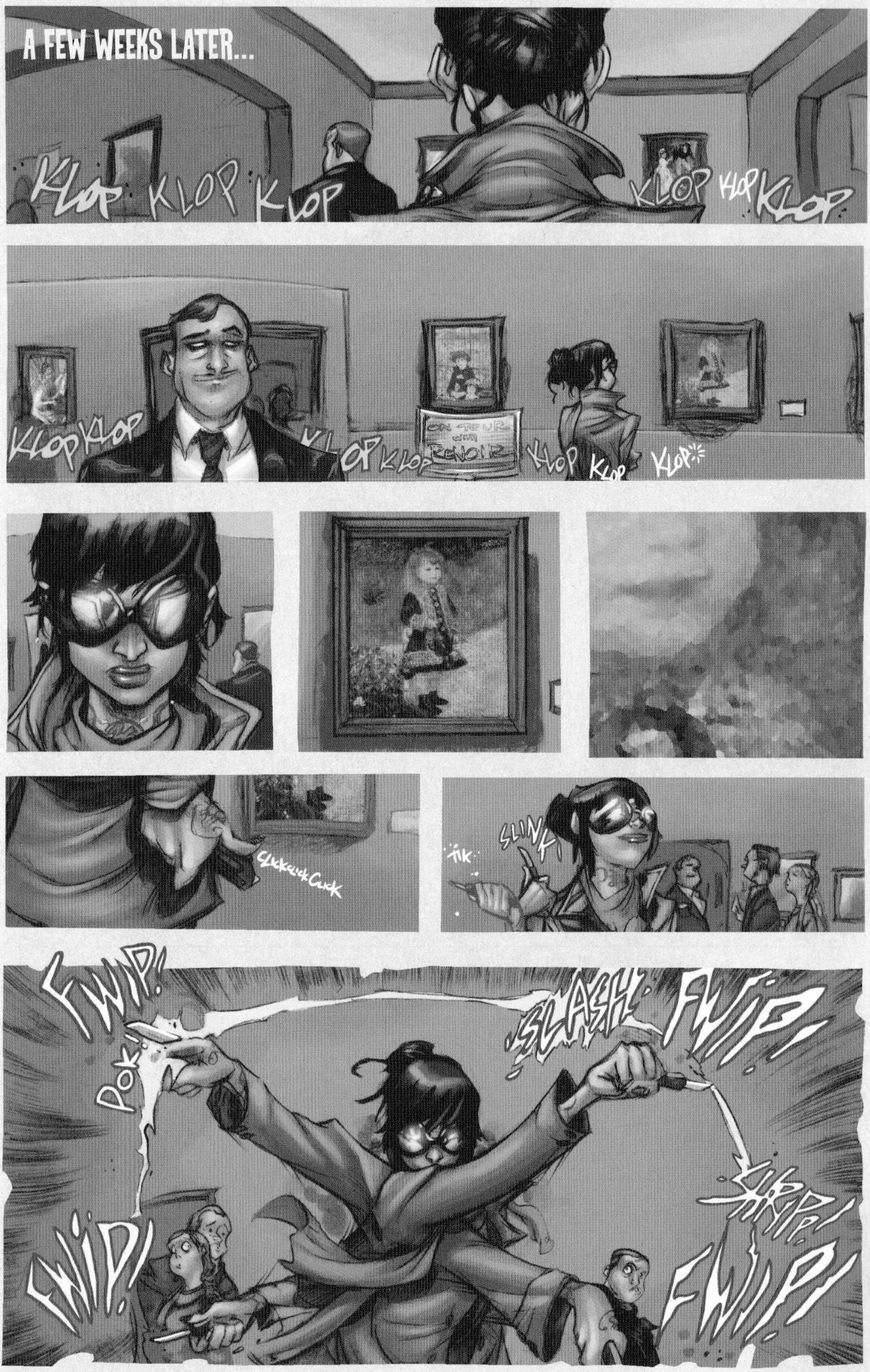
A FEW WEEKS LATER...
KLOP KLOP KLOP
KLOP KLOP KLOP
KLOP KLOP
ON TOUR with RENOIR
KLOP KLOP
KLOP KLOP KLOP
Clickclick Click
TIK
SLINK
FWIP!
POK
SLASH
FWIP!
FWIP!
FWIP!

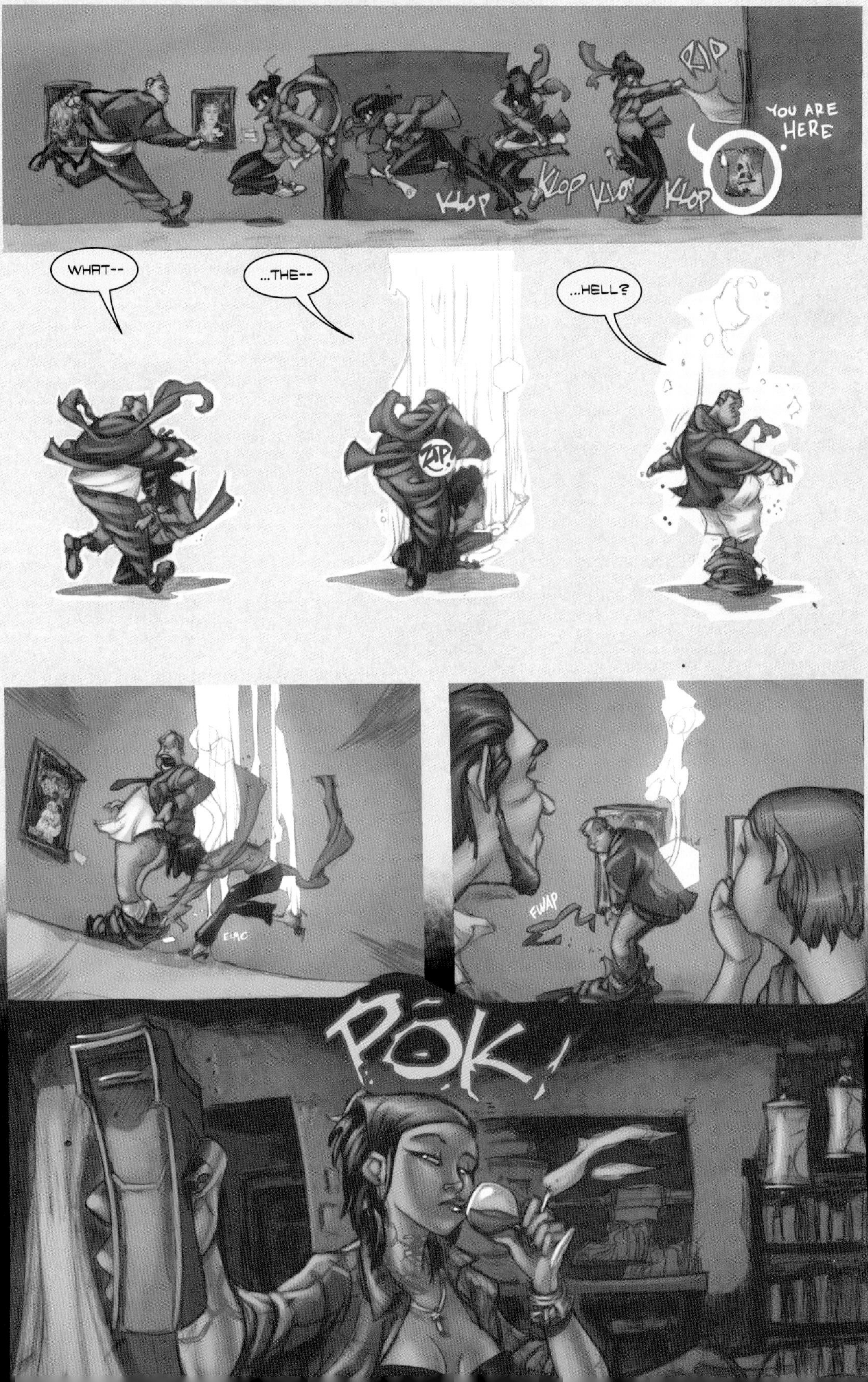

KLOP
KLOP
KLOP
KLOP
RIP
YOU ARE HERE
WHAT--
...THE--
RIP!
...HELL?
E=MC
FWAP
POK!

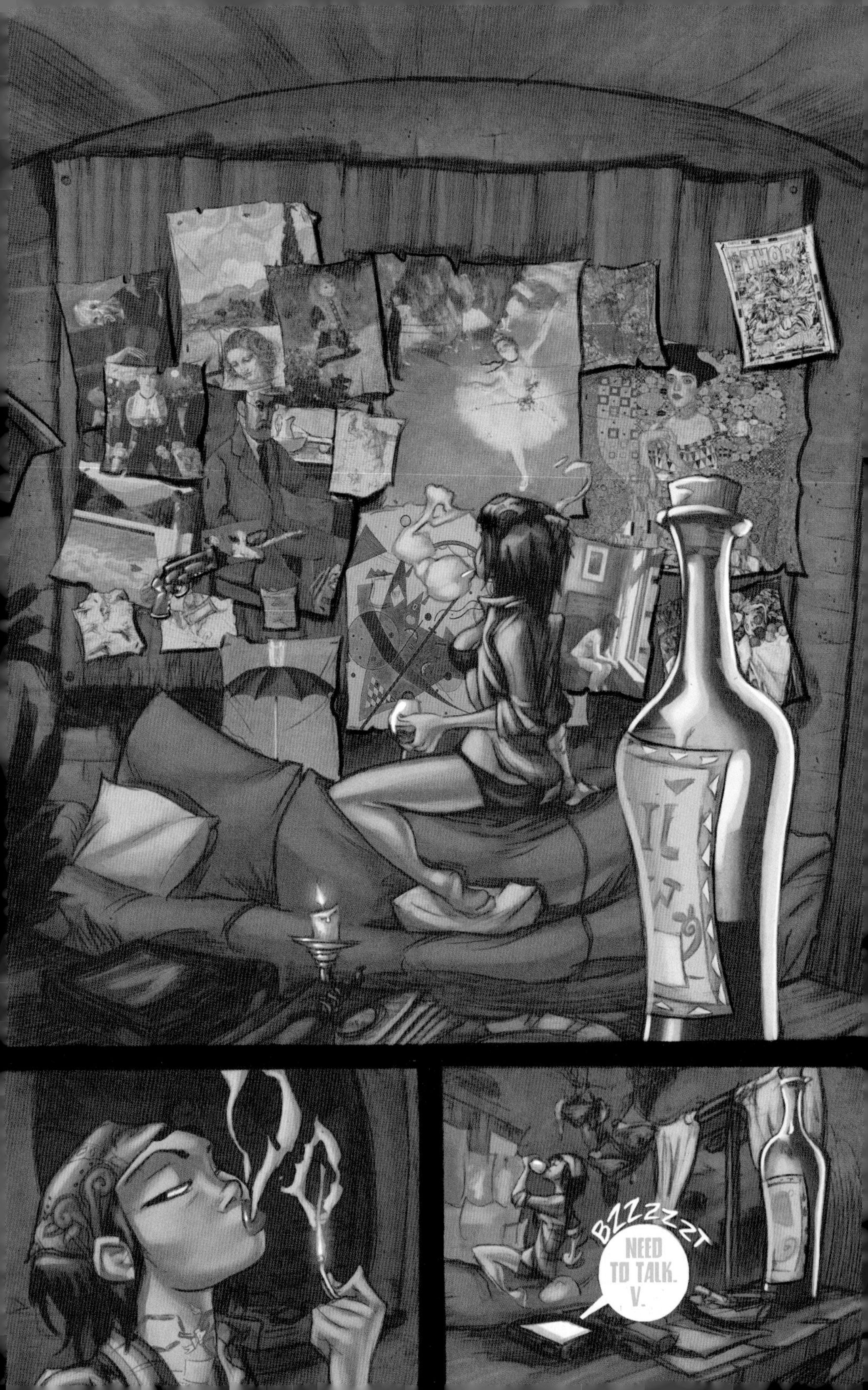
BZZZZZT
NEED TO TALK. V.

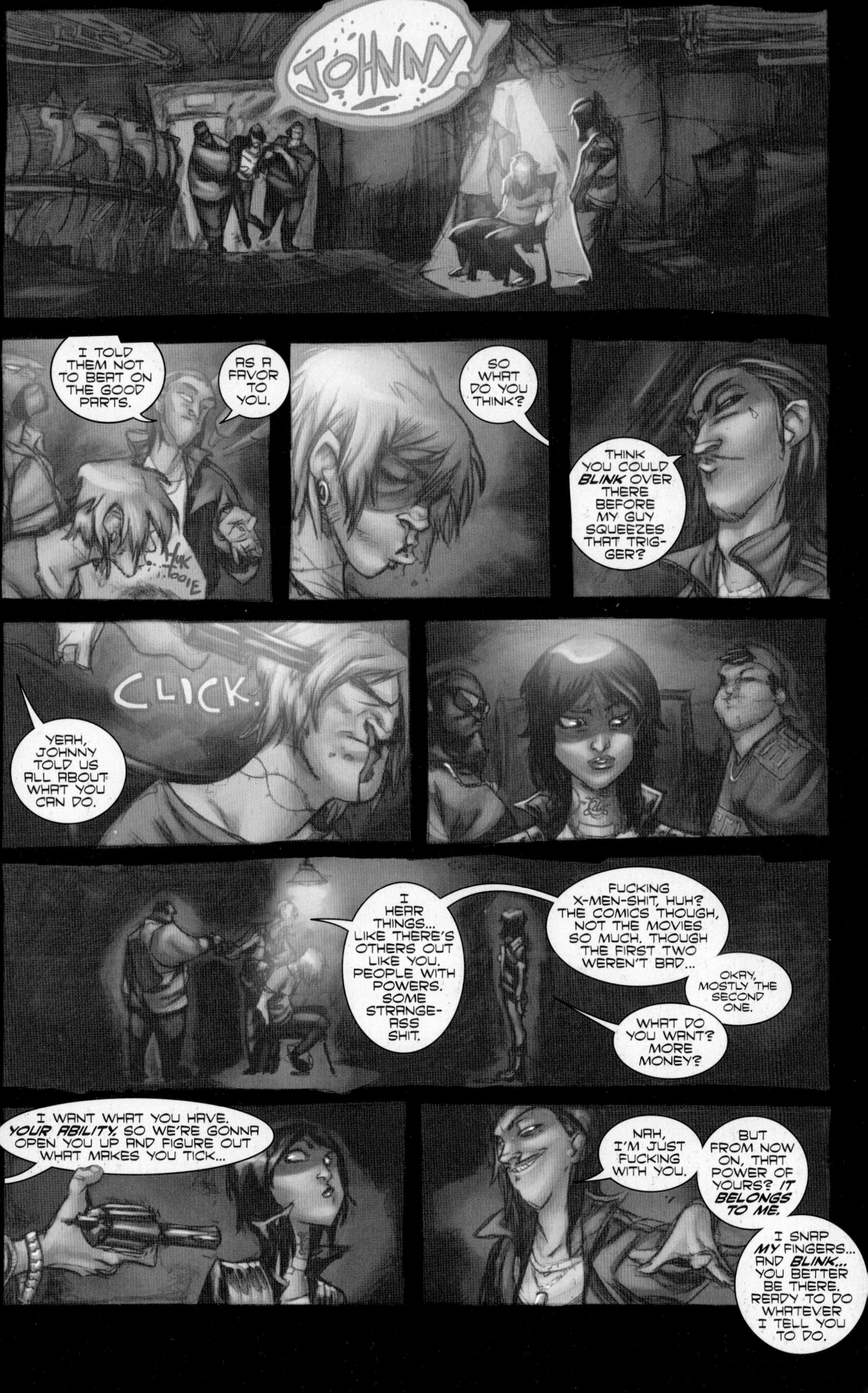
JOHNNY!
I TOLD THEM NOT TO BEAT ON THE GOOD PARTS.
AS A FAVOR TO YOU.
HUK TOOIE
SO WHAT DO YOU THINK?
THINK YOU COULD BLINK OVER THERE BEFORE MY GUY SQUEEZES THAT TRIG-GER?
CLICK.
YEAH, JOHNNY TOLD US ALL ABOUT WHAT YOU CAN DO.
I HEAR THINGS... LIKE THERE'S OTHERS OUT LIKE YOU. PEOPLE WITH POWERS. SOME STRANGE-ASS SHIT.
FUCKING X-MEN-SHIT, HUH? THE COMICS THOUGH, NOT THE MOVIES SO MUCH. THOUGH THE FIRST TWO WEREN'T BAD...
OKAY, MOSTLY THE SECOND ONE.
WHAT DO YOU WANT? MORE MONEY?
I WANT WHAT YOU HAVE. YOUR ABILITY. SO WE'RE GONNA OPEN YOU UP AND FIGURE OUT WHAT MAKES YOU TICK...
NAH, I'M JUST FUCKING WITH YOU.
BUT FROM NOW ON, THAT POWER OF YOURS? IT BELONGS TO ME.
I SNAP MY FINGERS... AND BLINK... YOU BETTER BE THERE. READY TO DO WHATEVER I TELL YOU TO DO.

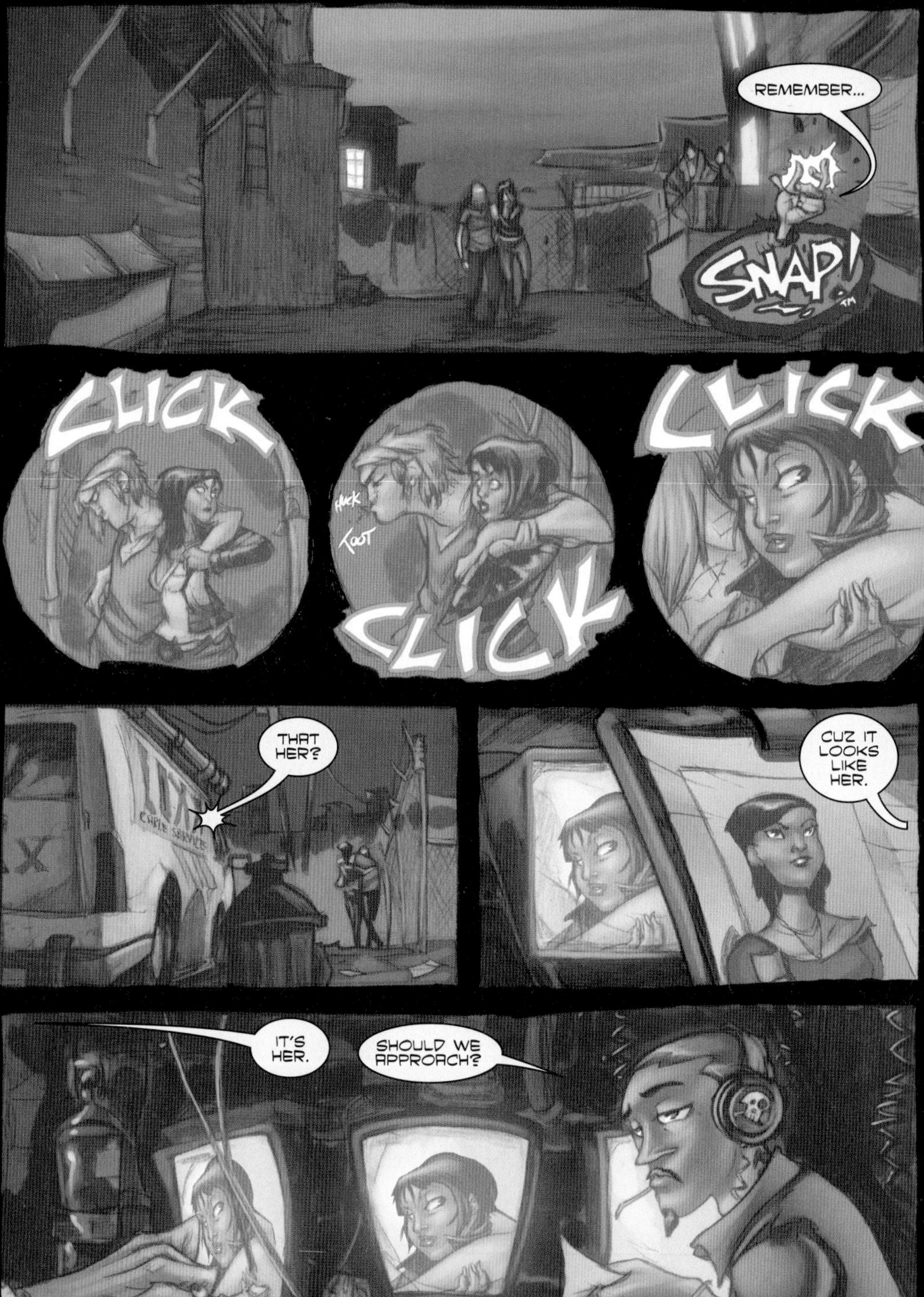
REMEMBER...
SNAP!
CLICK
HACK
TOOT
CLICK
CLICK
THAT HER?
CUZ IT LOOKS LIKE HER.
IT'S HER.
SHOULD WE APPROACH?

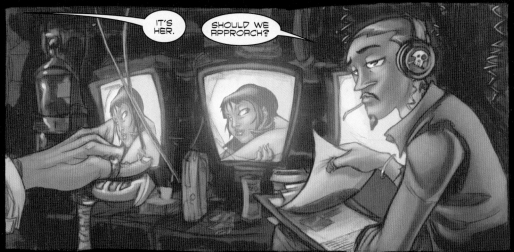

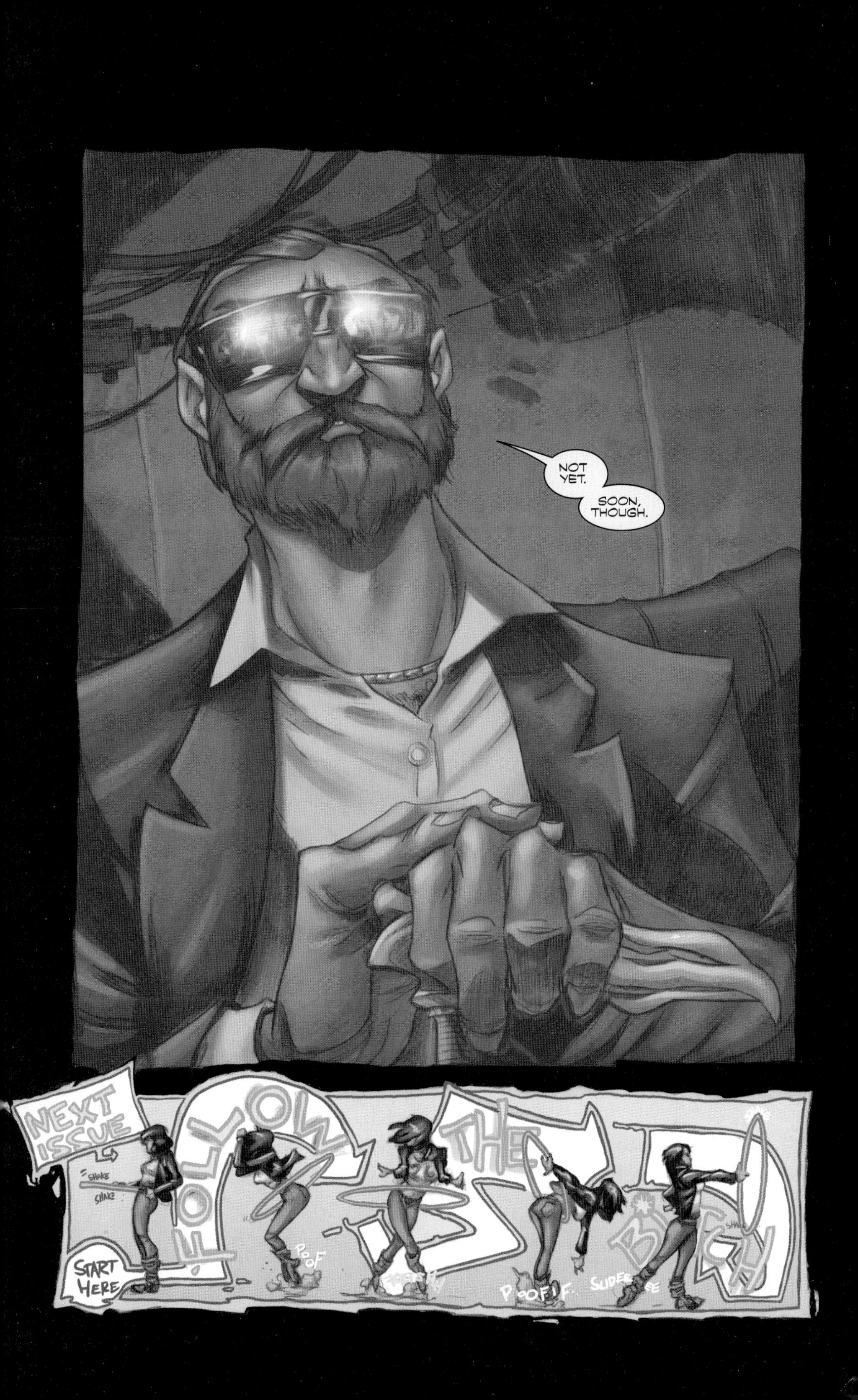
NOT YET.
SOON, THOUGH.
NEXT ISSUE
START HERE
SHAKE
SHAKE
FOLLOW
POOF
THE
SHAKE
SHAKE

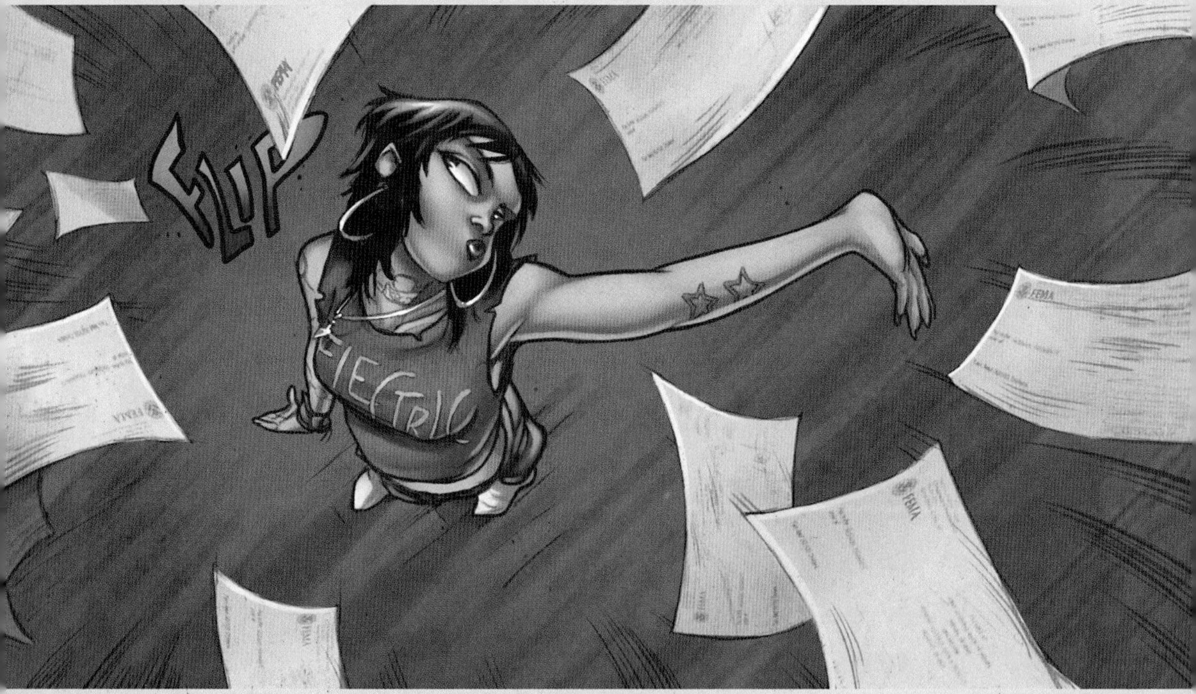
FLIP
ELECTRIC
FEMA

A FEW YEARS AGO...

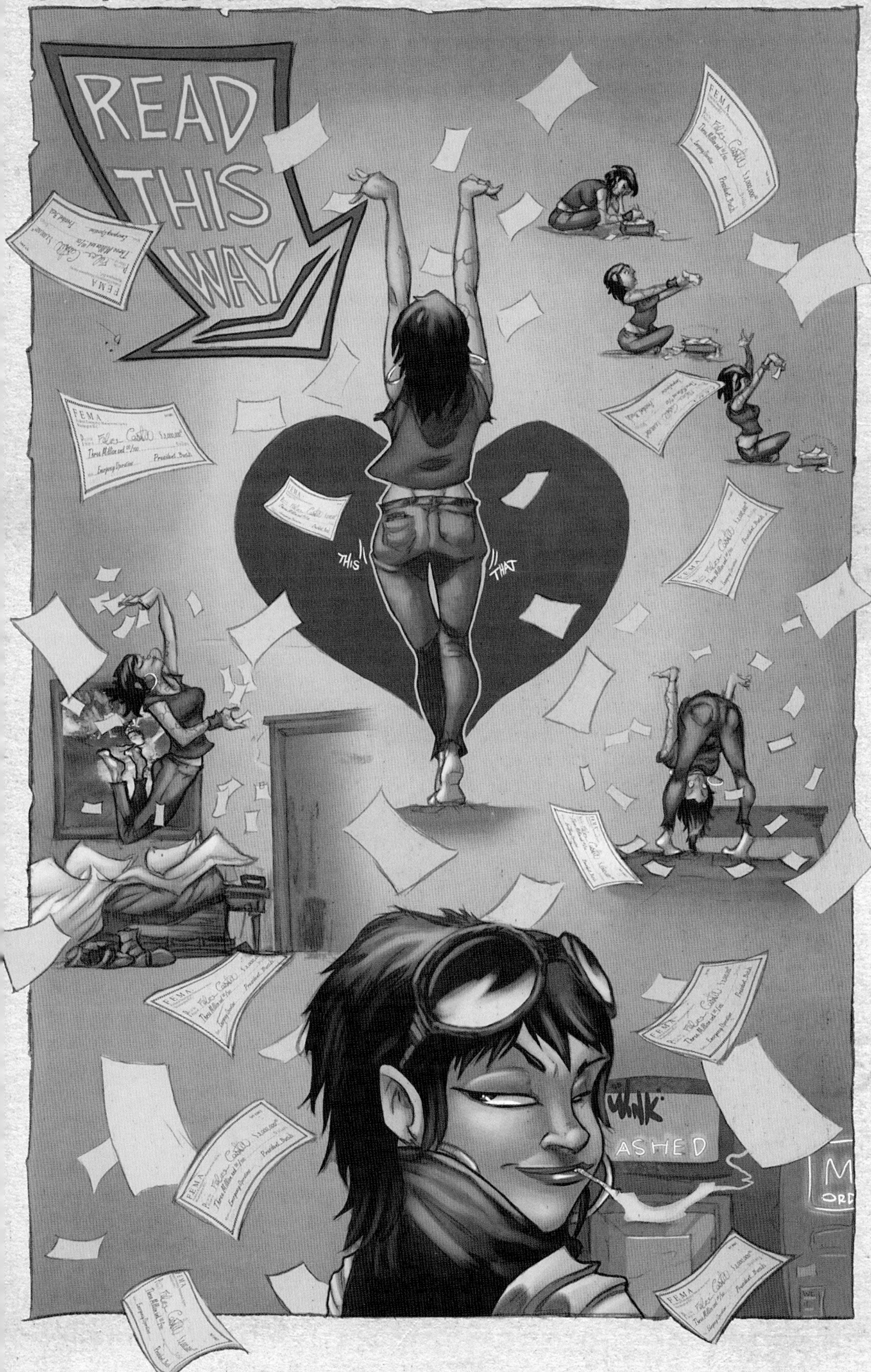
READ THIS WAY
FEMA
THIS
THAT
ASHED
M
ORD

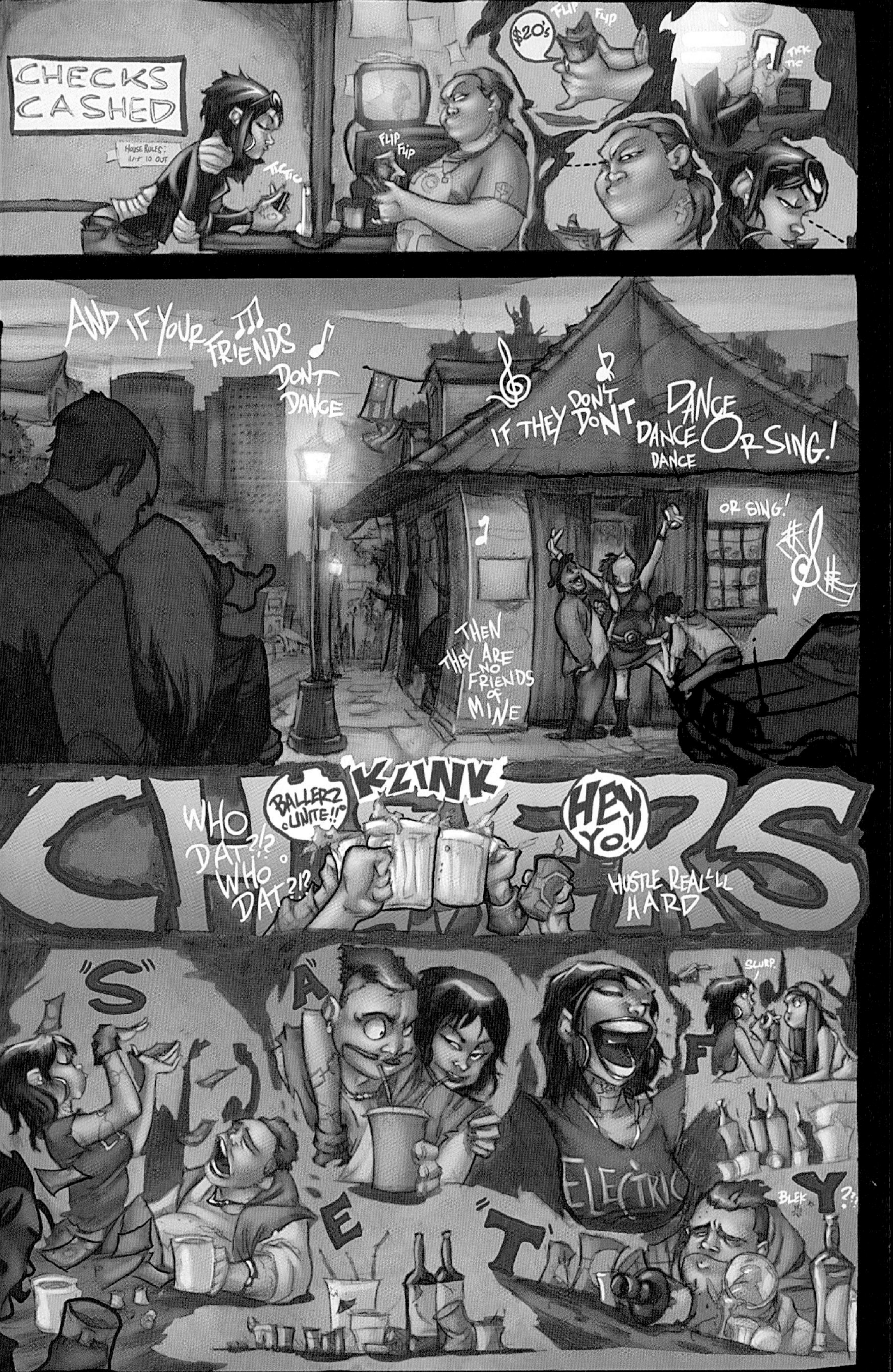
CHECKS CASHED
HOUSE RULES:
TIC TIC
FLIP FLIP
$20's
FLIP FLIP
TICK TIC
AND IF YOUR FRIENDS DON'T DANCE
IF THEY DON'T DON'T DANCE DANCE DANCE OR SING!
OR SING!
THEN THEY ARE NO FRIENDS OF MINE
BALLERZ UNITE!!
KLINK
WHO DAT?!? WHO DAT?!?
HEY YO!!
HUSTLE REAL'LL HARD
"S" "A" F "E" "T" Y
SLURP.
BLEK
??
ELECTRIC

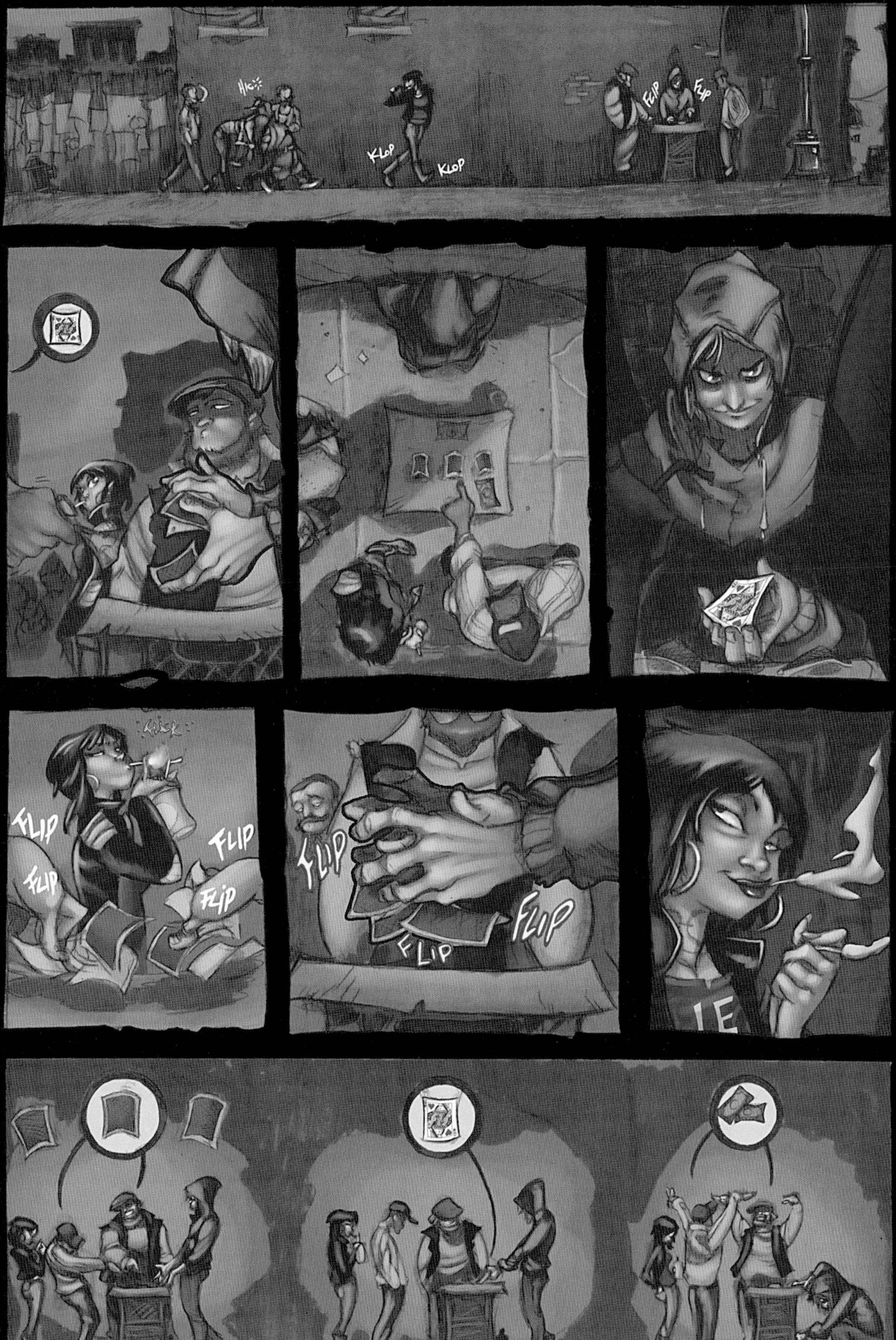
HIC
KLOP
KLOP
FLIP
FLIP
FLIP
FLIP
FLIP
FLIP
FLIP
FLIP
FLIP

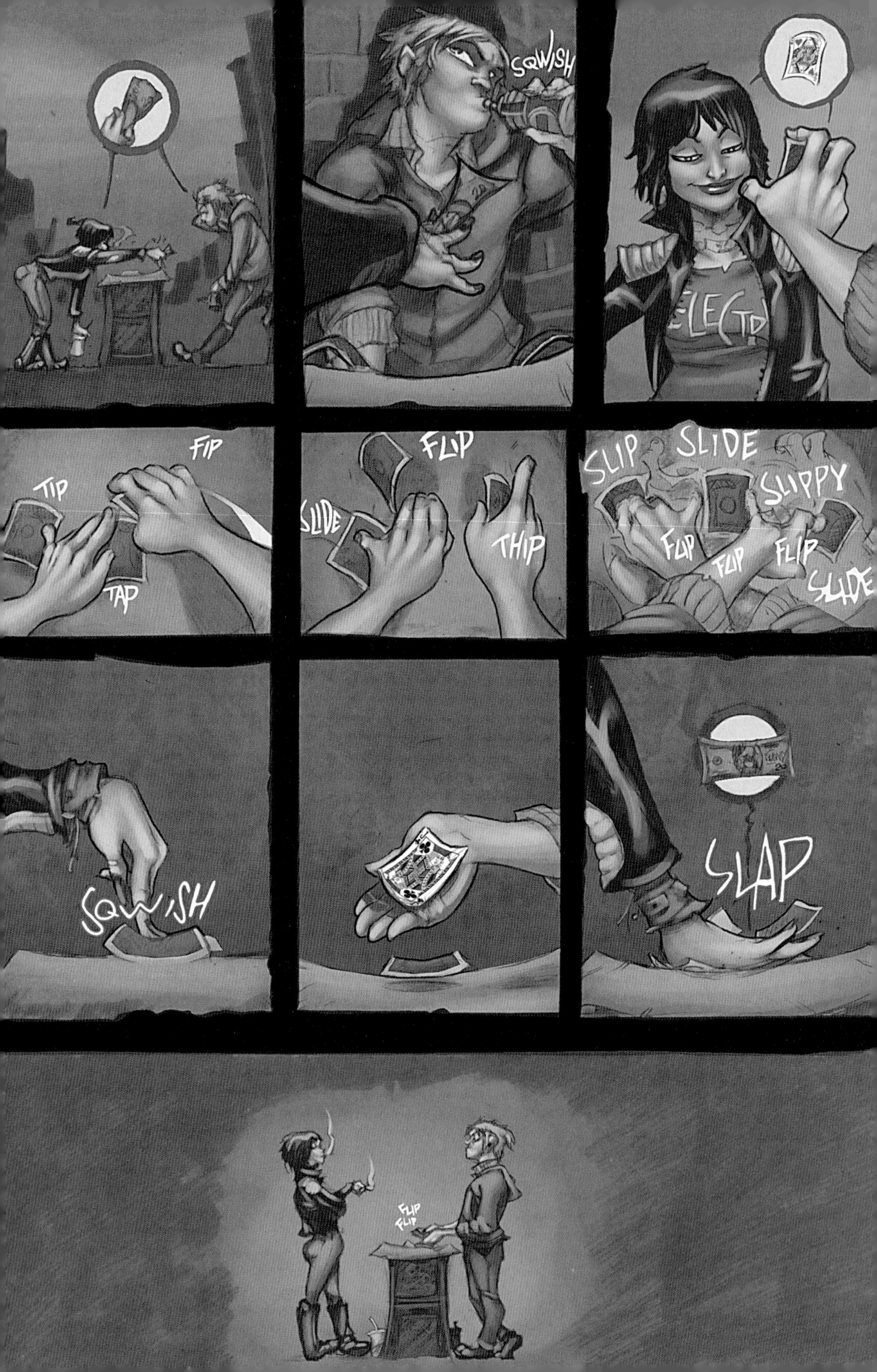
SQWISH
FIP
TIP
TAP
FLIP
SLIDE
THIP
SLIP SLIDE
SLIPPY
FLIP
FLIP
FLIP
SLIDE
SQWISH
SLAP
FLIP
FLIP

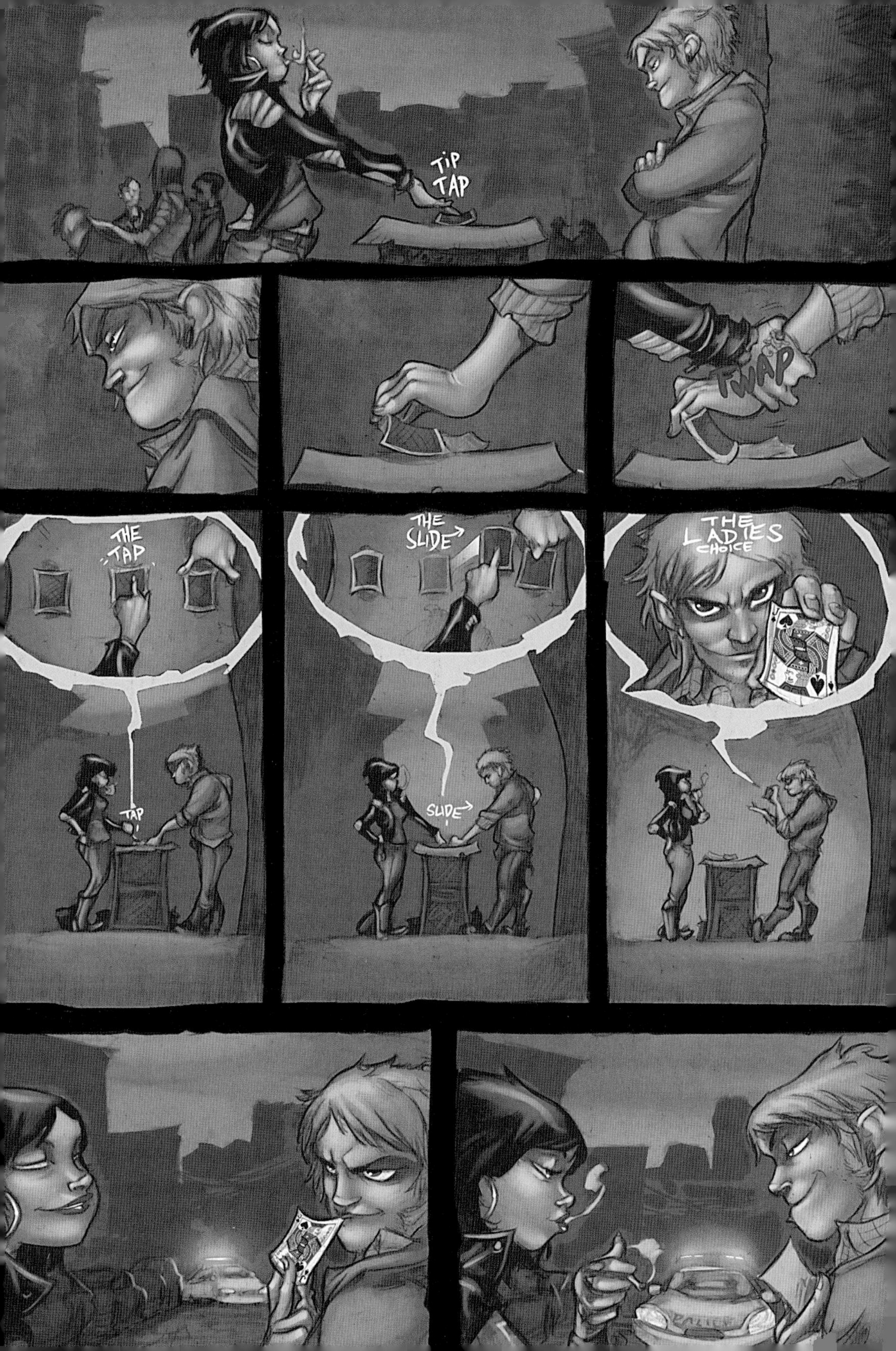
TIP
TAP
TWAP
THE TAP
TAP
THE SLIDE
SLIDE
THE LADIES CHOICE

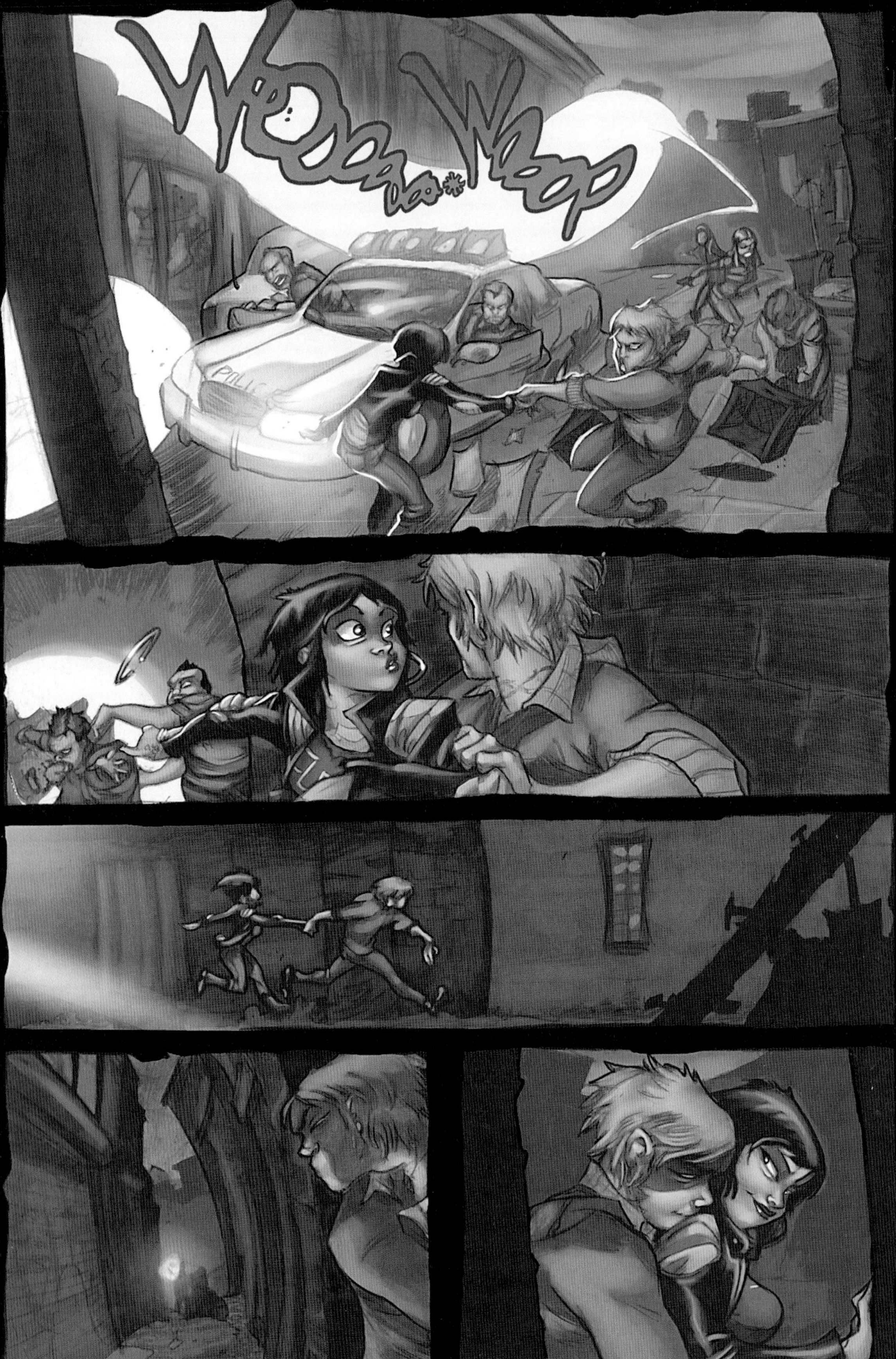
POLICE

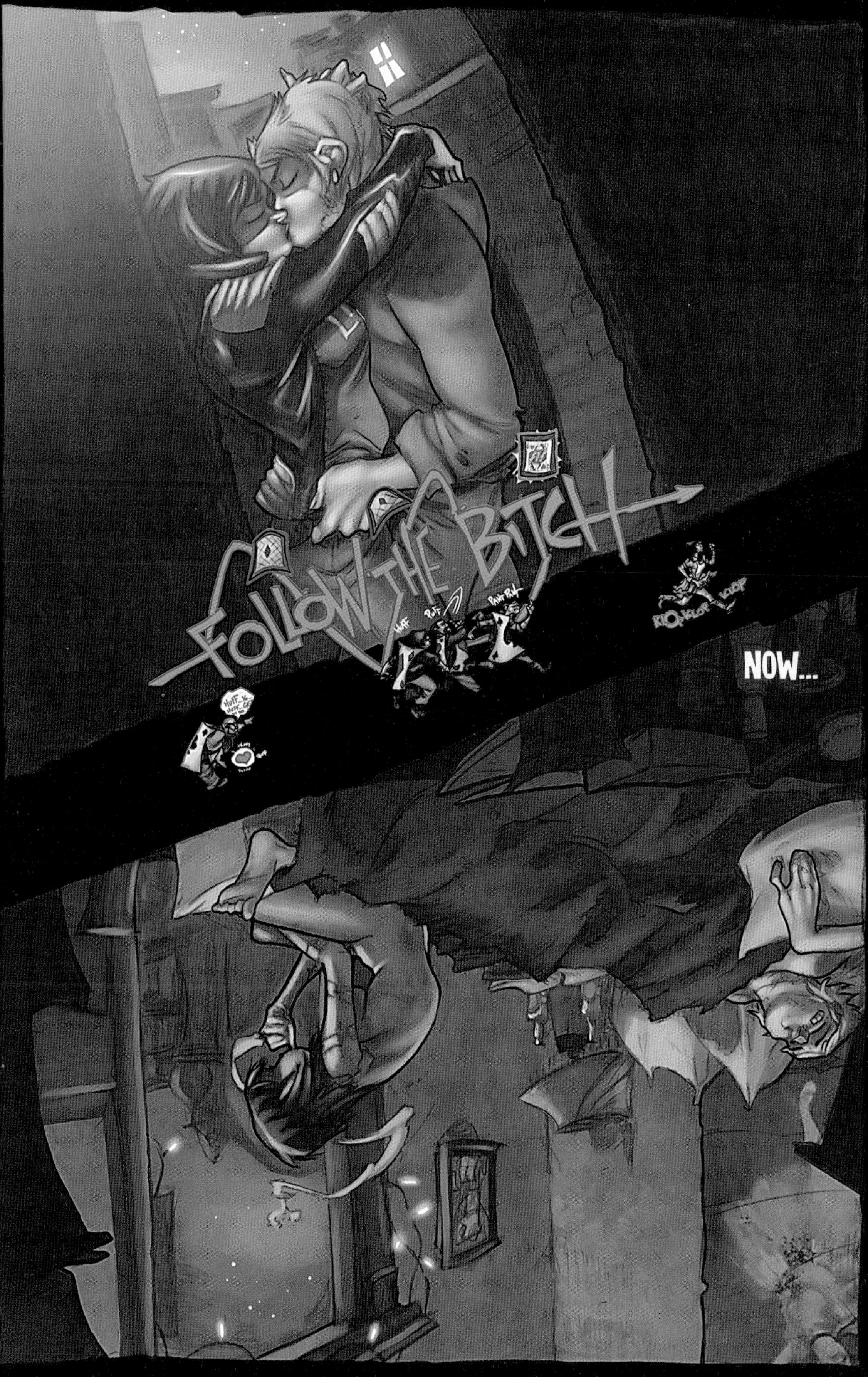
FOLLOW THE BITCH
HUFF
PUFF
PANT PANT
KLOP KLOP KLOP
NOW...

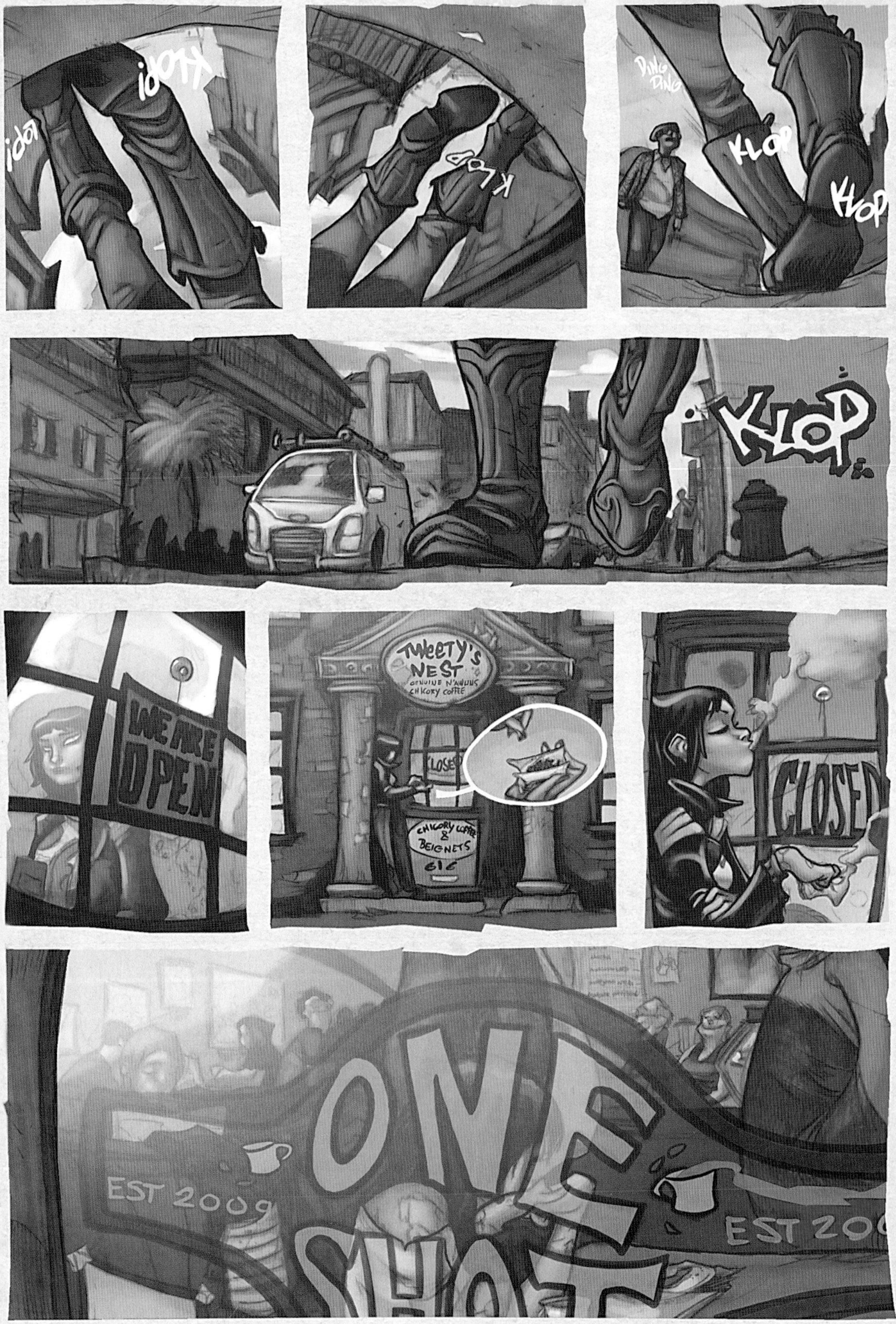
KLOP
KLOP
KLOP
DING DING
KLOP
KLOP
KLOP
WE ARE OPEN
TWEETY'S NEST
GENUINE N'AWLINS CHICORY COFFEE
CLOSED
CHICORY COFFEE & BEIGNETS
CLOSED
ONE SHOT
EST 2009

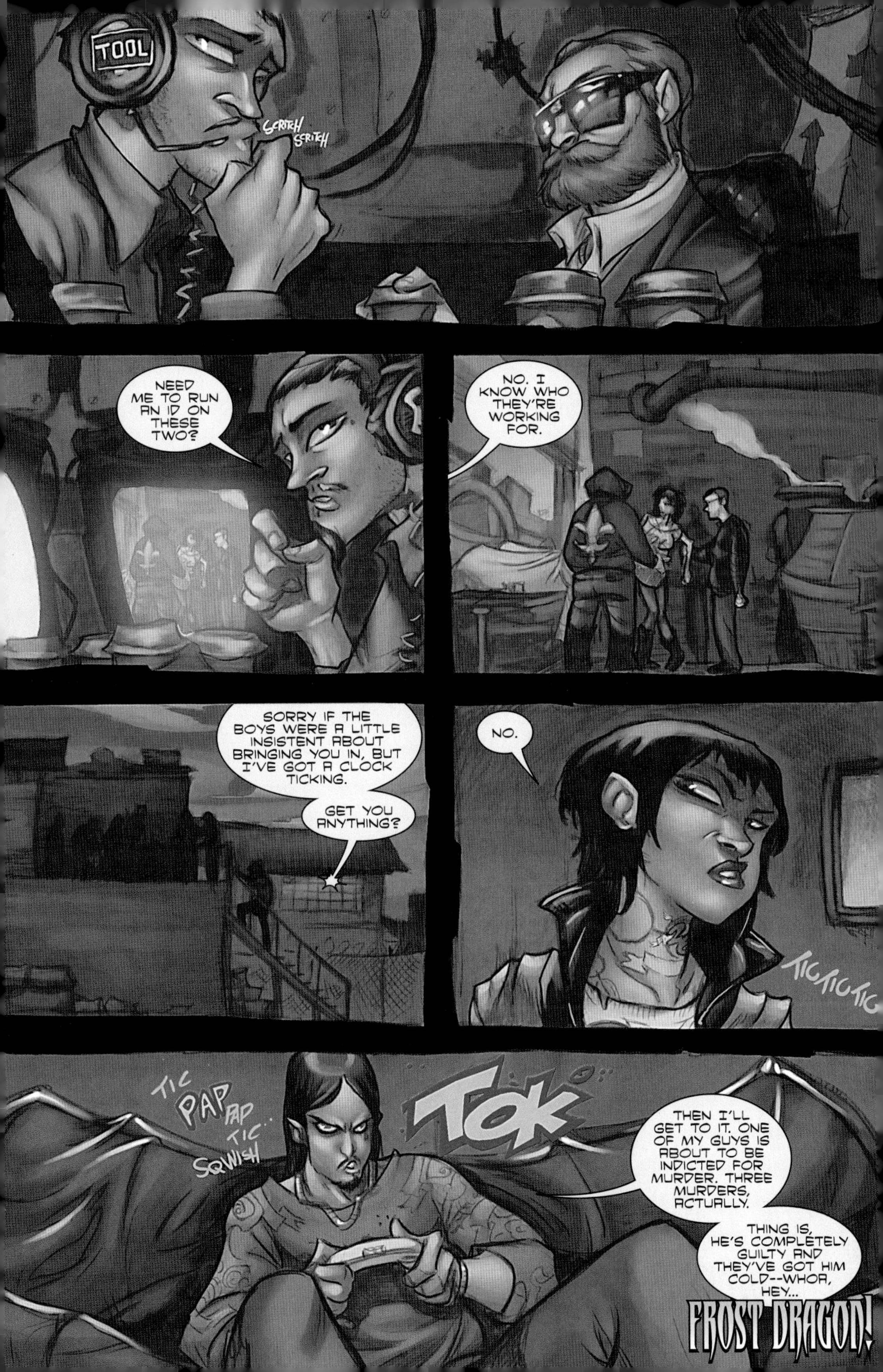
TOOL
SCRITCH SCRITCH
NEED ME TO RUN AN ID ON THESE TWO?
NO. I KNOW WHO THEY'RE WORKING FOR.
SORRY IF THE BOYS WERE A LITTLE INSISTENT ABOUT BRINGING YOU IN, BUT I'VE GOT A CLOCK TICKING.
GET YOU ANYTHING?
NO.
TICTICTIC
TIC PAP PAP TIC.. SQWISH
TOK
THEN I'LL GET TO IT. ONE OF MY GUYS IS ABOUT TO BE INDICTED FOR MURDER. THREE MURDERS, ACTUALLY.
THING IS, HE'S COMPLETELY GUILTY AND THEY'VE GOT HIM COLD--WHOA, HEY...
FROST DRAGON!

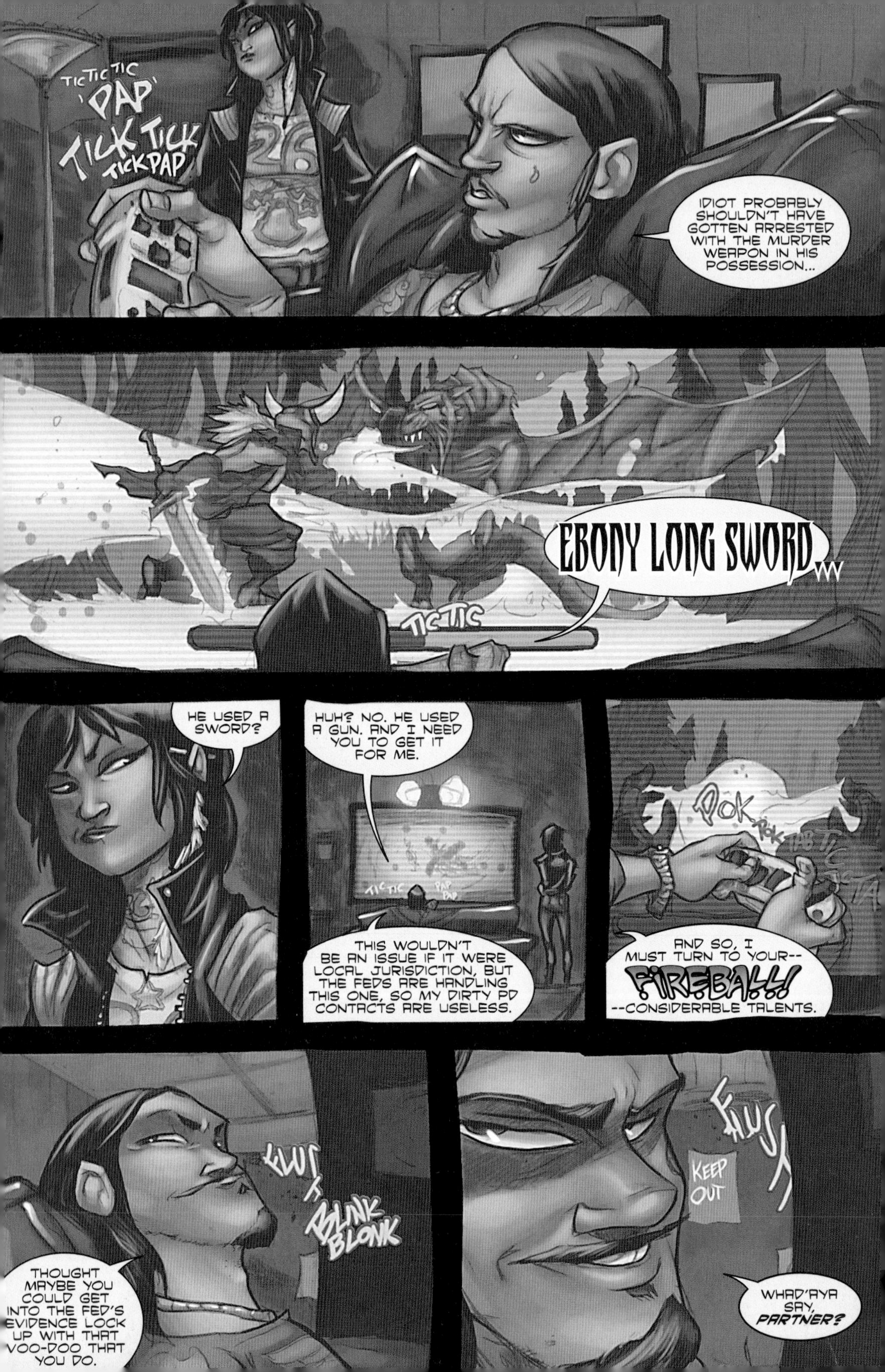
TICTICTIC 'PAP' TICK TICK TICKPAP
IDIOT PROBABLY SHOULDN'T HAVE GOTTEN ARRESTED WITH THE MURDER WEAPON IN HIS POSSESSION...
EBONY LONG SWORD...
TICTIC
HE USED A SWORD?
HUH? NO. HE USED A GUN. AND I NEED YOU TO GET IT FOR ME.
TICTIC PAP PAP
THIS WOULDN'T BE AN ISSUE IF IT WERE LOCAL JURISDICTION, BUT THE FEDS ARE HANDLING THIS ONE, SO MY DIRTY PD CONTACTS ARE USELESS.
POK
AND SO, I MUST TURN TO YOUR--
FIREBALL!
--CONSIDERABLE TALENTS.
FLUSH
BLINK BLONK
THOUGHT MAYBE YOU COULD GET INTO THE FED'S EVIDENCE LOCK UP WITH THAT VOO-DOO THAT YOU DO.
FLUSH
KEEP OUT
WHAD'AYA SAY, PARTNER?

A FEW MONTHS AGO...

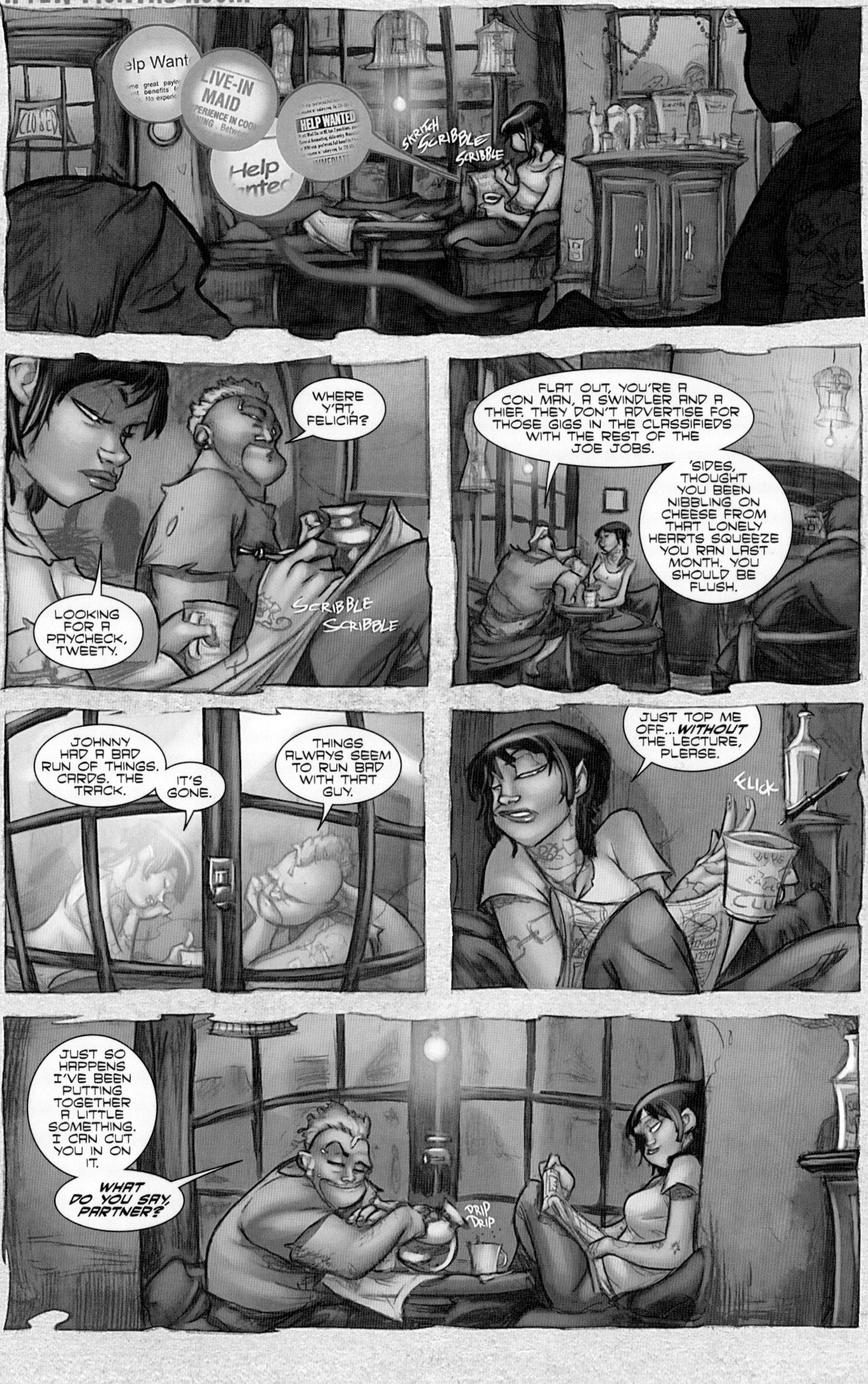
LIVE-IN MAID
HELP WANTED
SKRITCH SCRIBBLE SCRIBBLE
WHERE Y'AT, FELICIA?
LOOKING FOR A PAYCHECK, TWEETY.
SCRIBBLE SCRIBBLE
FLAT OUT, YOU'RE A CON MAN, A SWINDLER AND A THIEF. THEY DON'T ADVERTISE FOR THOSE GIGS IN THE CLASSIFIEDS WITH THE REST OF THE JOE JOBS.
'SIDES, THOUGHT YOU BEEN NIBBLING ON CHEESE FROM THAT LONELY HEARTS SQUEEZE YOU RAN LAST MONTH. YOU SHOULD BE FLUSH.
JOHNNY HAD A BAD RUN OF THINGS. CARDS. THE TRACK.
IT'S GONE.
THINGS ALWAYS SEEM TO RUN BAD WITH THAT GUY.
JUST TOP ME OFF... *WITHOUT* THE LECTURE, PLEASE.
FLICK
JUST SO HAPPENS I'VE BEEN PUTTING TOGETHER A LITTLE SOMETHING. I CAN CUT YOU IN ON IT.
WHAT DO YOU SAY, PARTNER?
DRIP DRIP

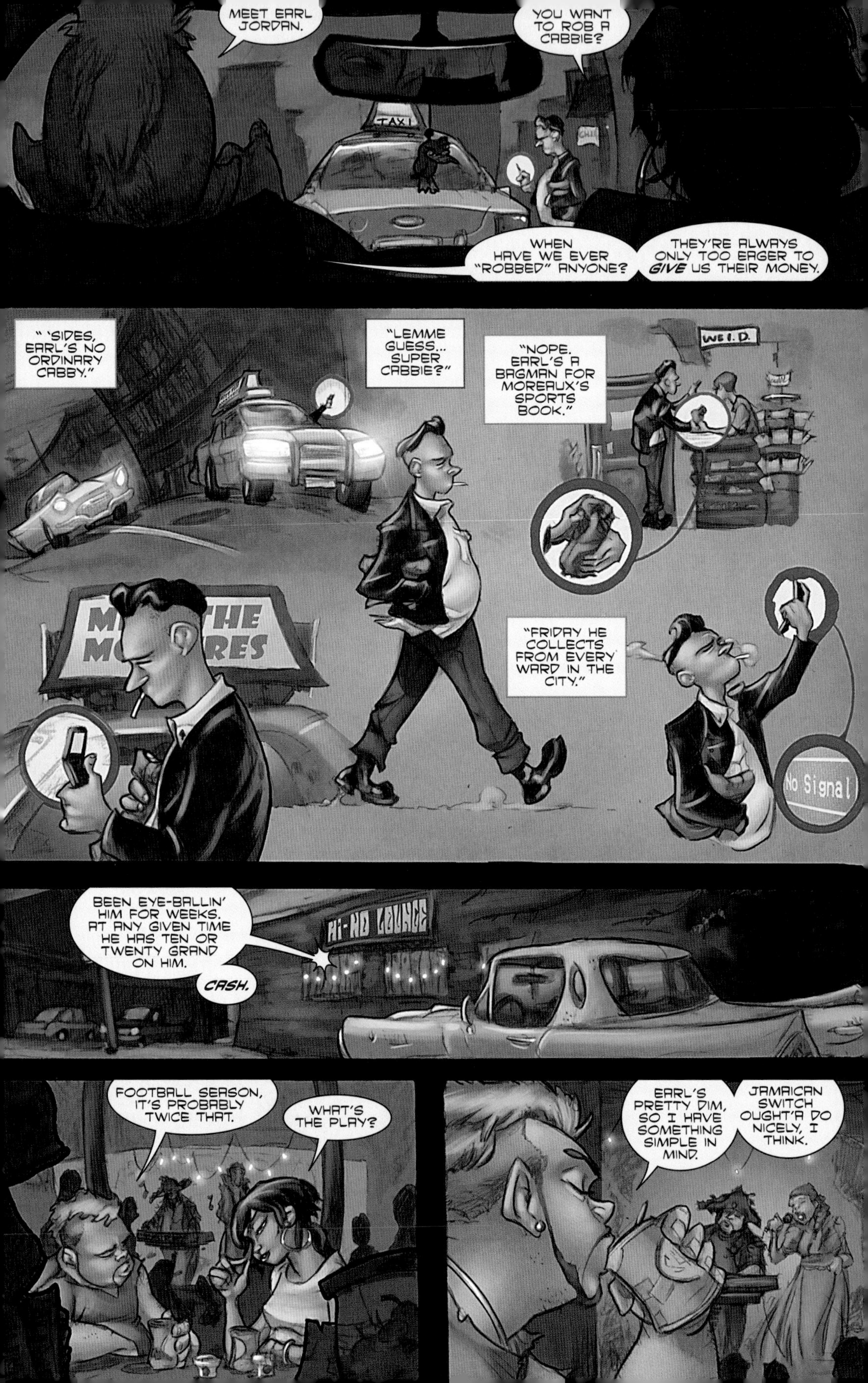
MEET EARL JORDAN.
YOU WANT TO ROB A CABBIE?
WHEN HAVE WE EVER "ROBBED" ANYONE?
THEY'RE ALWAYS ONLY TOO EAGER TO *GIVE* US THEIR MONEY.
" 'SIDES, EARL'S NO ORDINARY CABBY."
"LEMME GUESS... SUPER CABBIE?"
"NOPE. EARL'S A BAGMAN FOR MOREAUX'S SPORTS BOOK."
"FRIDAY HE COLLECTS FROM EVERY WARD IN THE CITY."
No Signal
BEEN EYE-BALLIN' HIM FOR WEEKS. AT ANY GIVEN TIME HE HAS TEN OR TWENTY GRAND ON HIM.
CASH.
HI-NO LOUNGE
FOOTBALL SEASON, IT'S PROBABLY TWICE THAT.
WHAT'S THE PLAY?
EARL'S PRETTY DIM, SO I HAVE SOMETHING SIMPLE IN MIND.
JAMAICAN SWITCH OUGHT'A DO NICELY, I THINK.

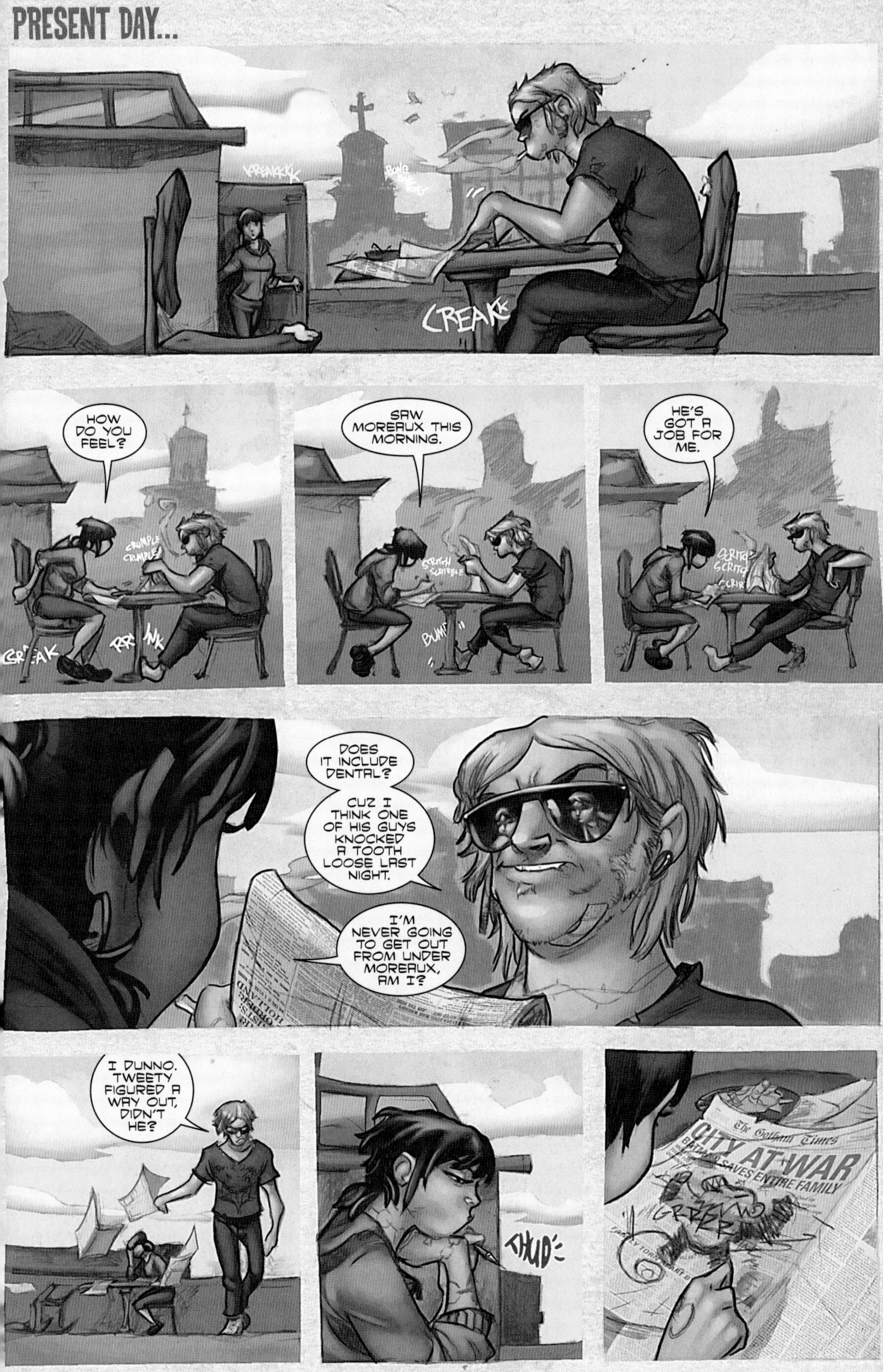
PRESENT DAY...
CREAKK
HOW DO YOU FEEL?
CRUMPLE CRUMPLE
CREAK
SAW MOREAUX THIS MORNING.
SCRITCH SCRIBBLE
BUMP
HE'S GOT A JOB FOR ME.
DOES IT INCLUDE DENTAL?
CUZ I THINK ONE OF HIS GUYS KNOCKED A TOOTH LOOSE LAST NIGHT.
I'M NEVER GOING TO GET OUT FROM UNDER MOREAUX, AM I?
I DUNNO. TWEETY FIGURED A WAY OUT, DIDN'T HE?
THUD
The Gotham Times
CITY AT WAR
BATMAN SAVES ENTIRE FAMILY

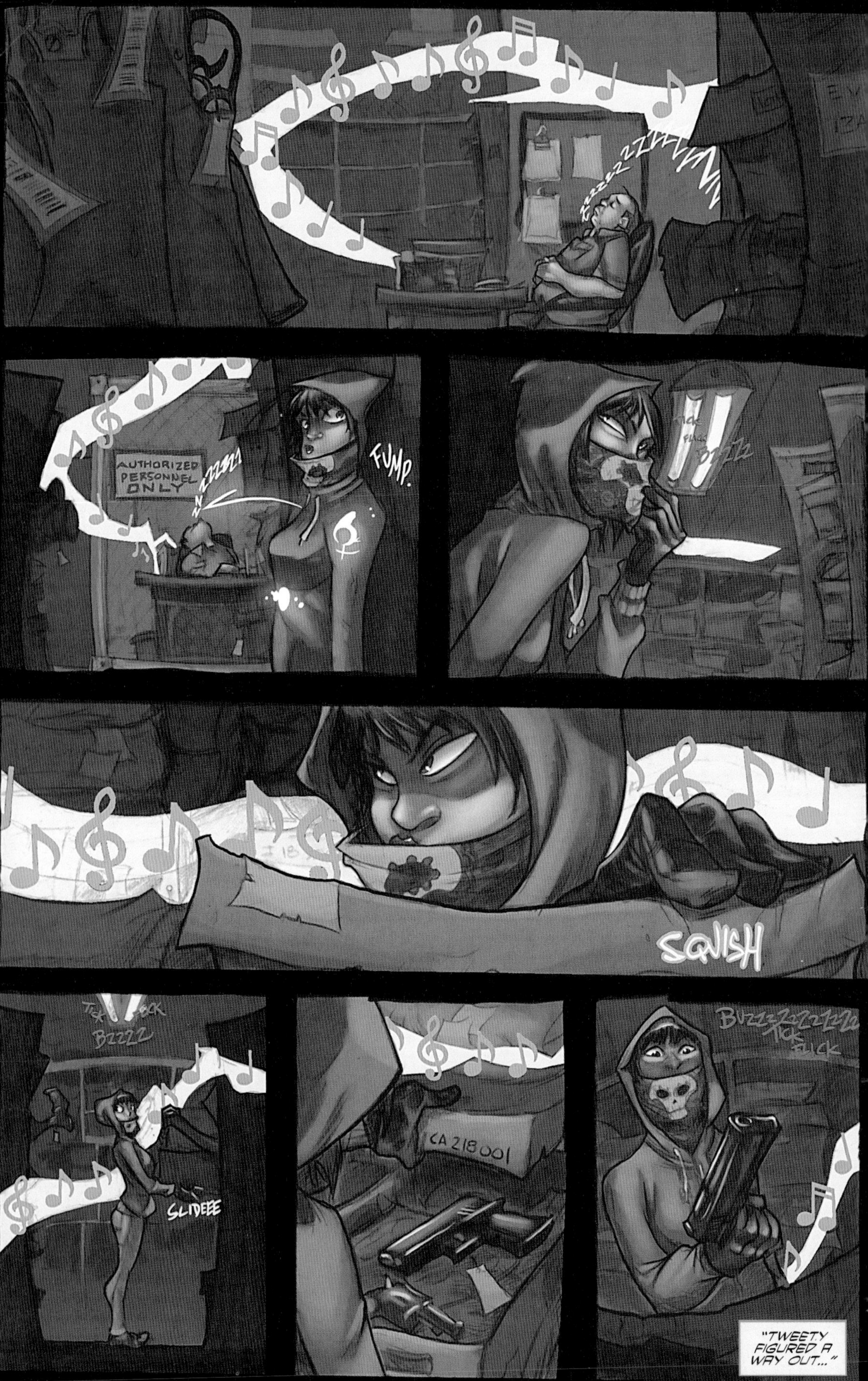
AUTHORIZED PERSONNEL ONLY
FUMP.
SQUISH
SLIDEEE
CA 218001
"TWEETY FIGURED A WAY OUT..."

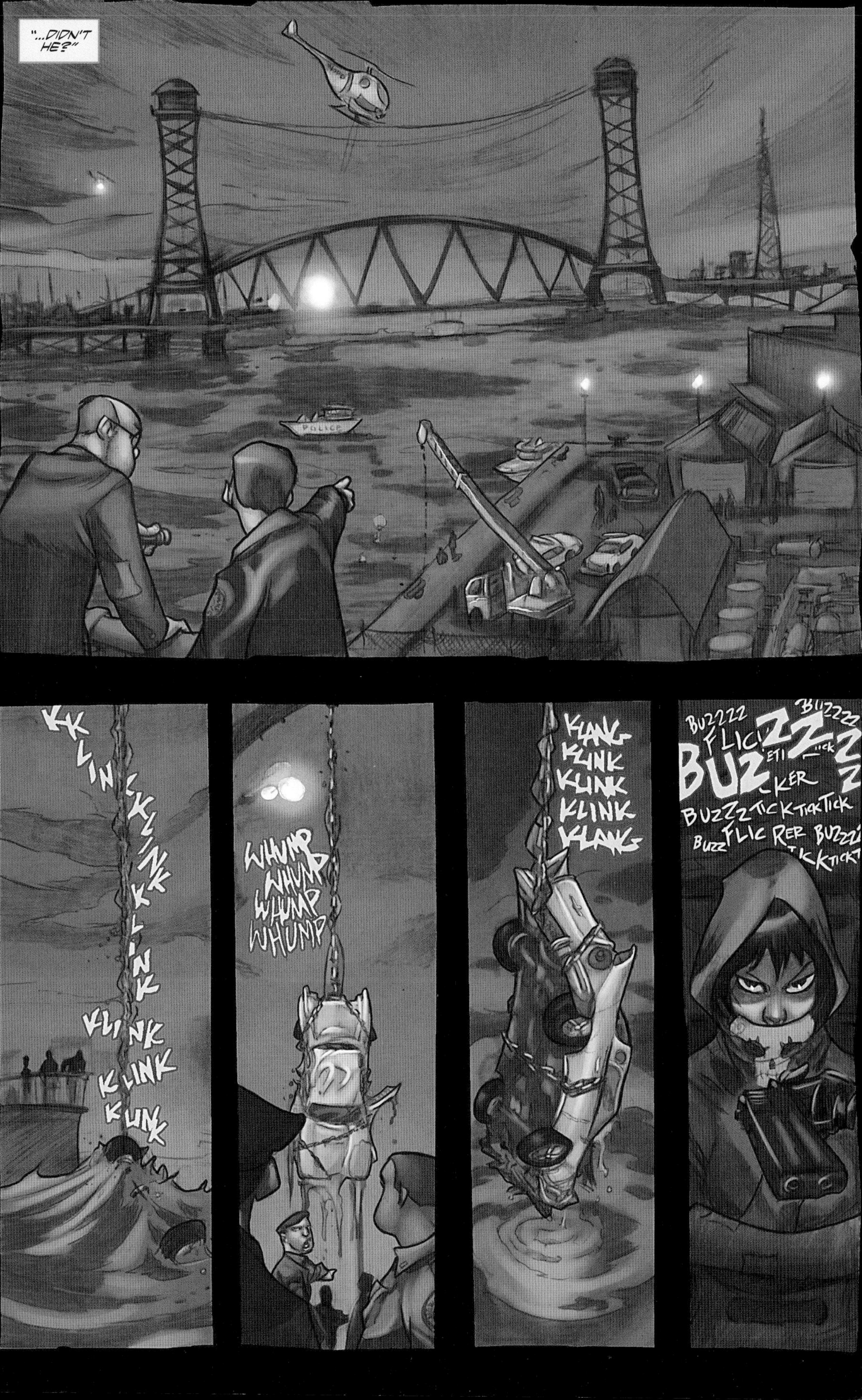
"...DIDN'T HE?"
POLICE
KLINK KLINK KLINK KLINK KLINK KLINK
WHUMP WHUMP WHUMP WHUMP
KLANG KLINK KLINK KLINK KLANG
BUZZZZ BUZZZZ BUZZZ
BUZZZ TICK TICK TICK
BUZZ FLIC RER BUZZZ

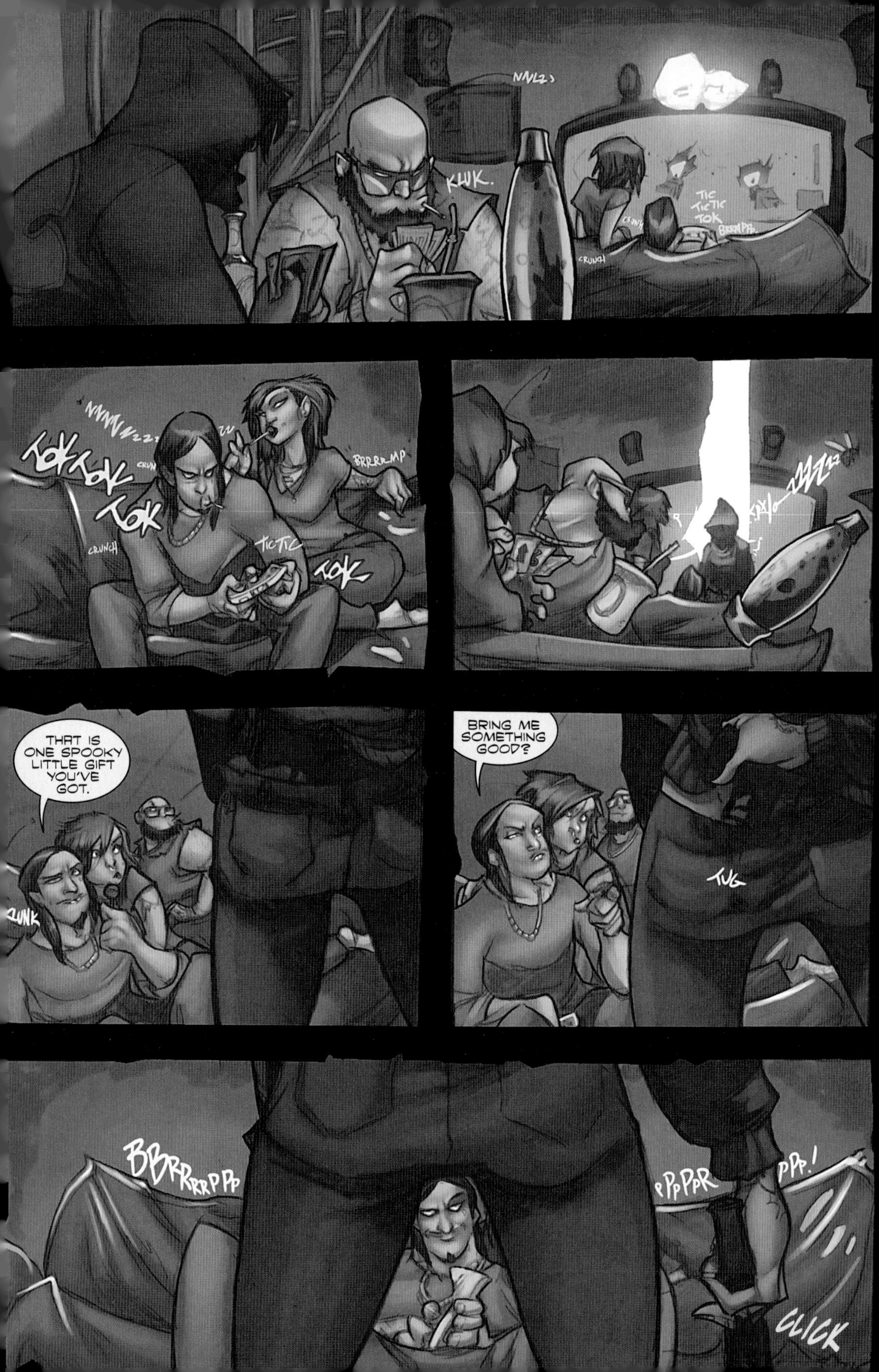
KLUK.
TIC
TIC TIC
TOK
CRUNCH
CRUNCH
TOK TOK
TOK
CRUNCH
CRUNCH
TIC TIC
TOK
BRRRRMP
THAT IS ONE SPOOKY LITTLE GIFT YOU'VE GOT.
BRING ME SOMETHING GOOD?
TUG
BBRRRRPPP
PPPPR
PPP!
CLICK

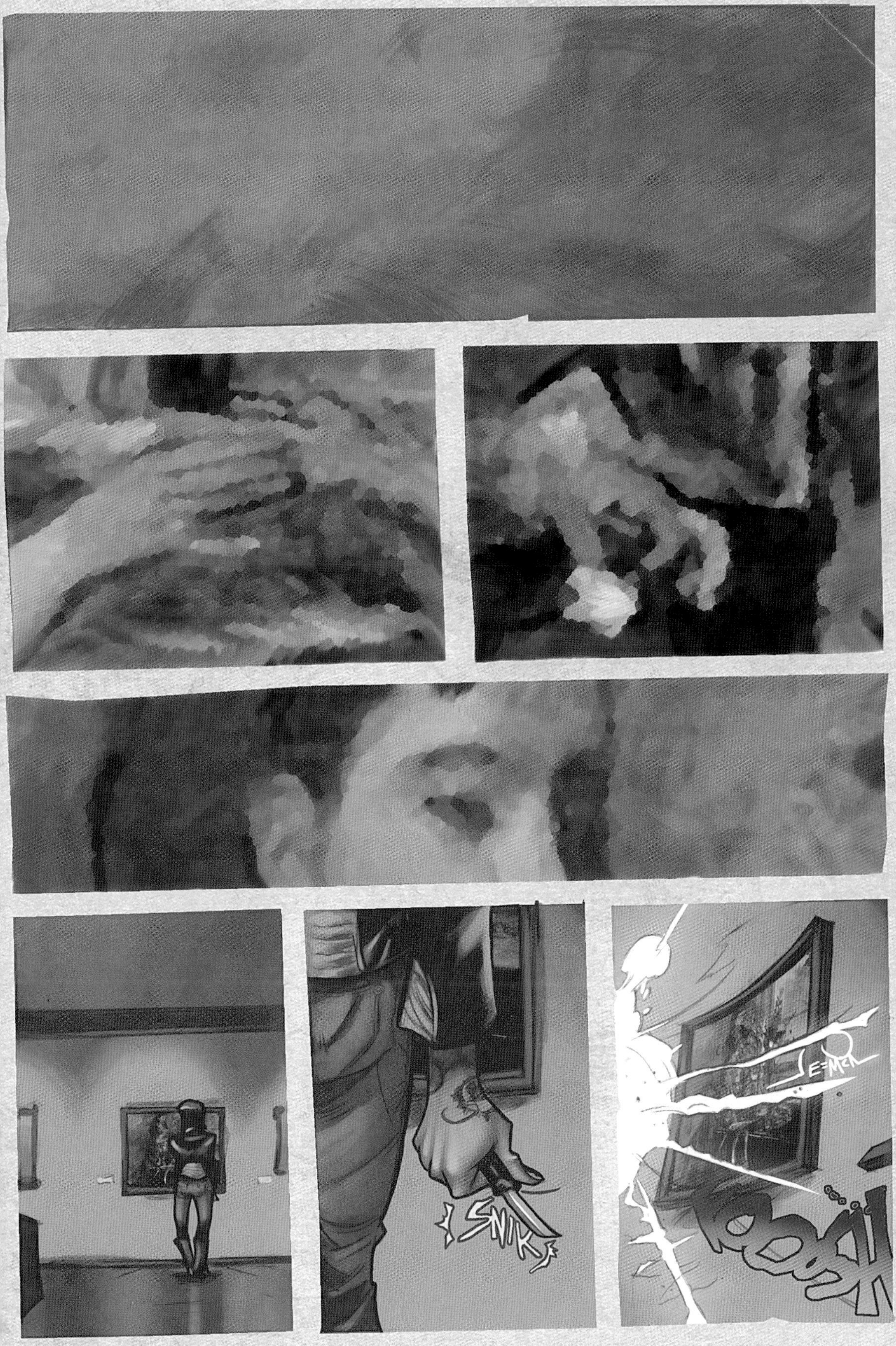
SNIK
E=MC

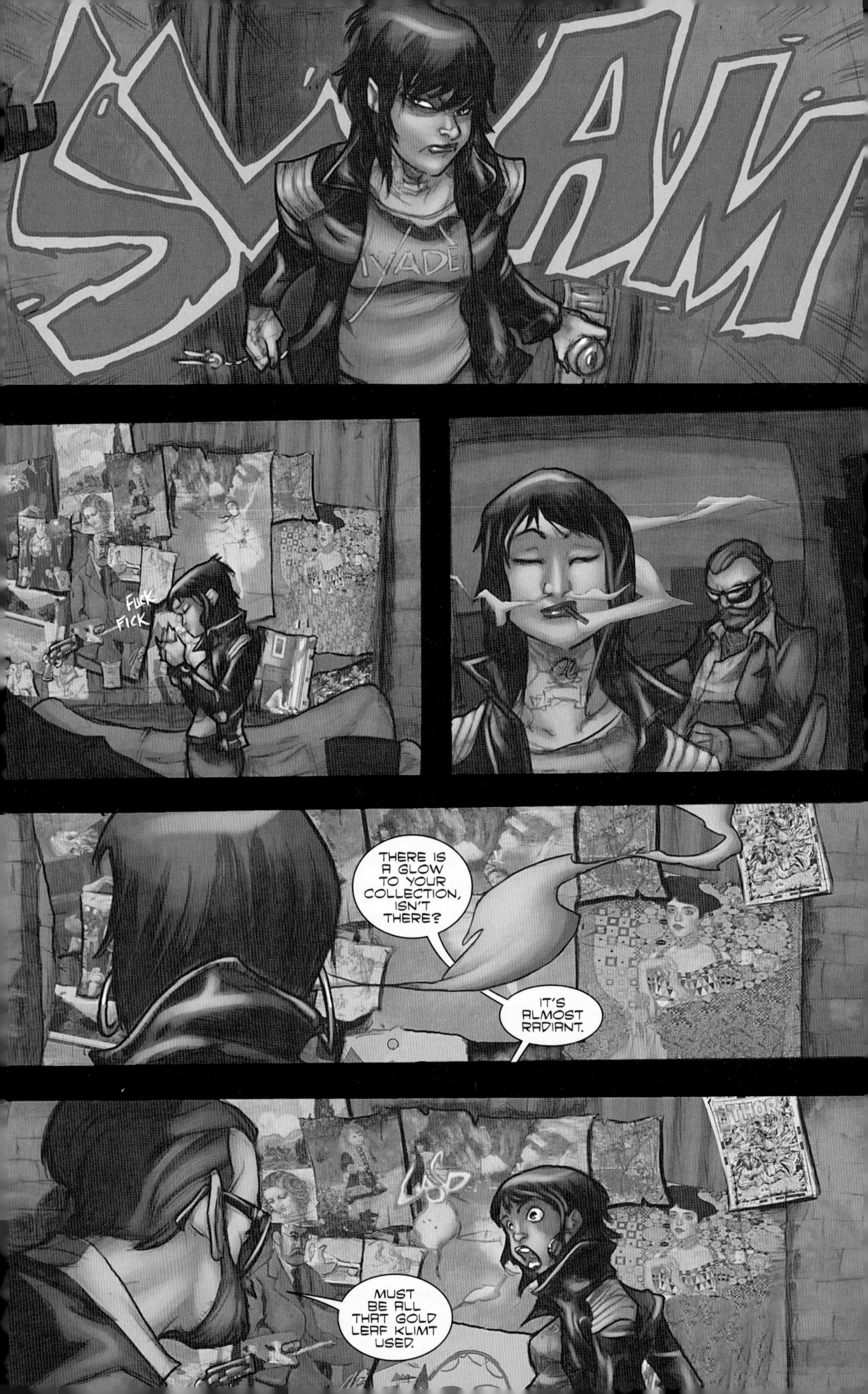
SLAM
FUCK
FICK
THERE IS A GLOW TO YOUR COLLECTION, ISN'T THERE?
IT'S ALMOST RADIANT.
THOR
MUST BE ALL THAT GOLD LEAF KLIMT USED.

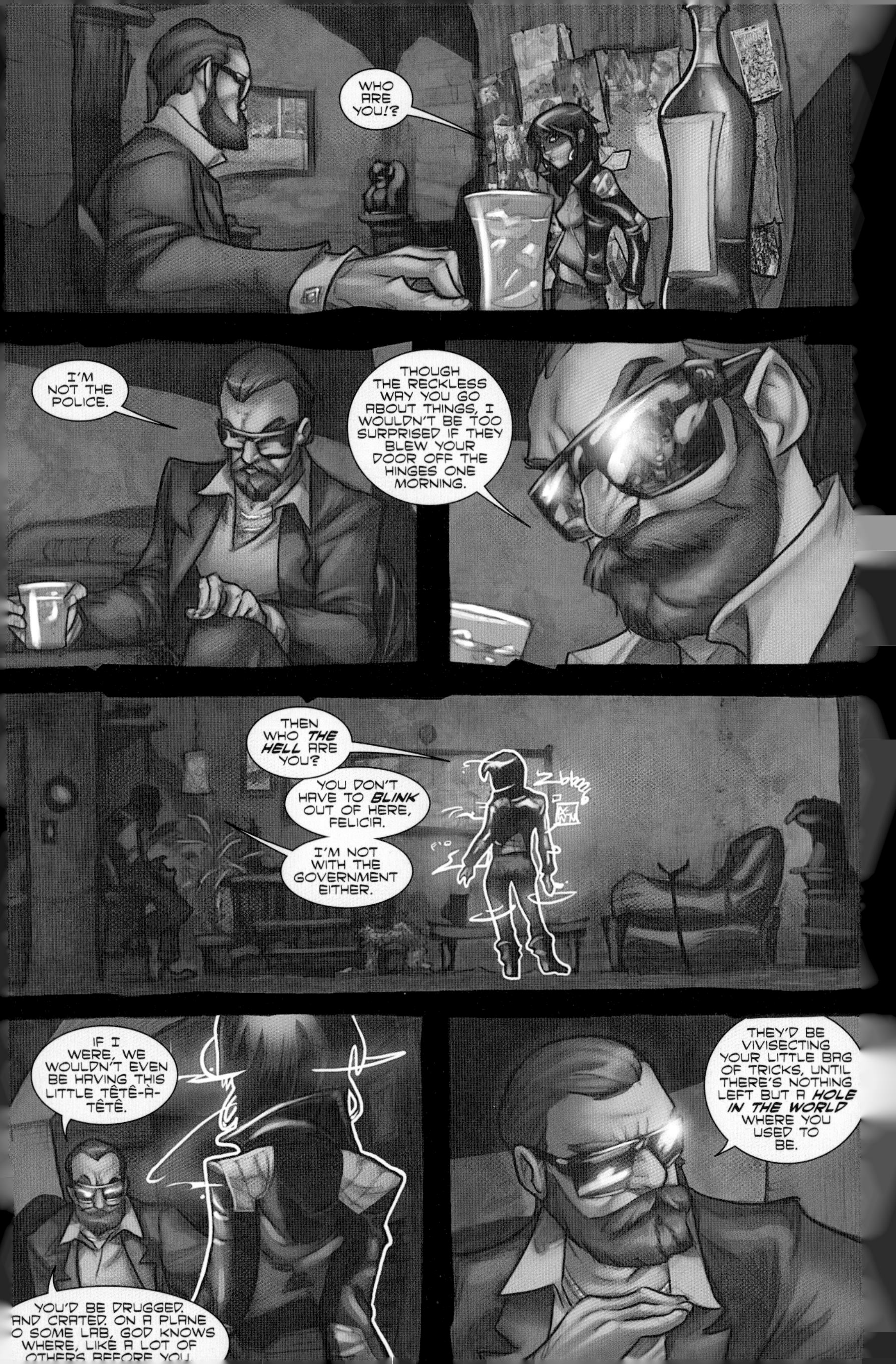
WHO ARE YOU!?
I'M NOT THE POLICE.
THOUGH THE RECKLESS WAY YOU GO ABOUT THINGS, I WOULDN'T BE TOO SURPRISED IF THEY BLEW YOUR DOOR OFF THE HINGES ONE MORNING.
THEN WHO *THE HELL* ARE YOU?
YOU DON'T HAVE TO *BLINK* OUT OF HERE, FELICIA.
I'M NOT WITH THE GOVERNMENT EITHER.
IF I WERE, WE WOULDN'T EVEN BE HAVING THIS LITTLE TÊTE-À-TÊTE.
YOU'D BE DRUGGED. AND CRATED, ON A PLANE O SOME LAB, GOD KNOWS WHERE, LIKE A LOT OF OTHERS BEFORE YOU
THEY'D BE VIVISECTING YOUR LITTLE BAG OF TRICKS, UNTIL THERE'S NOTHING LEFT BUT A *HOLE IN THE WORLD* WHERE YOU USED TO BE.

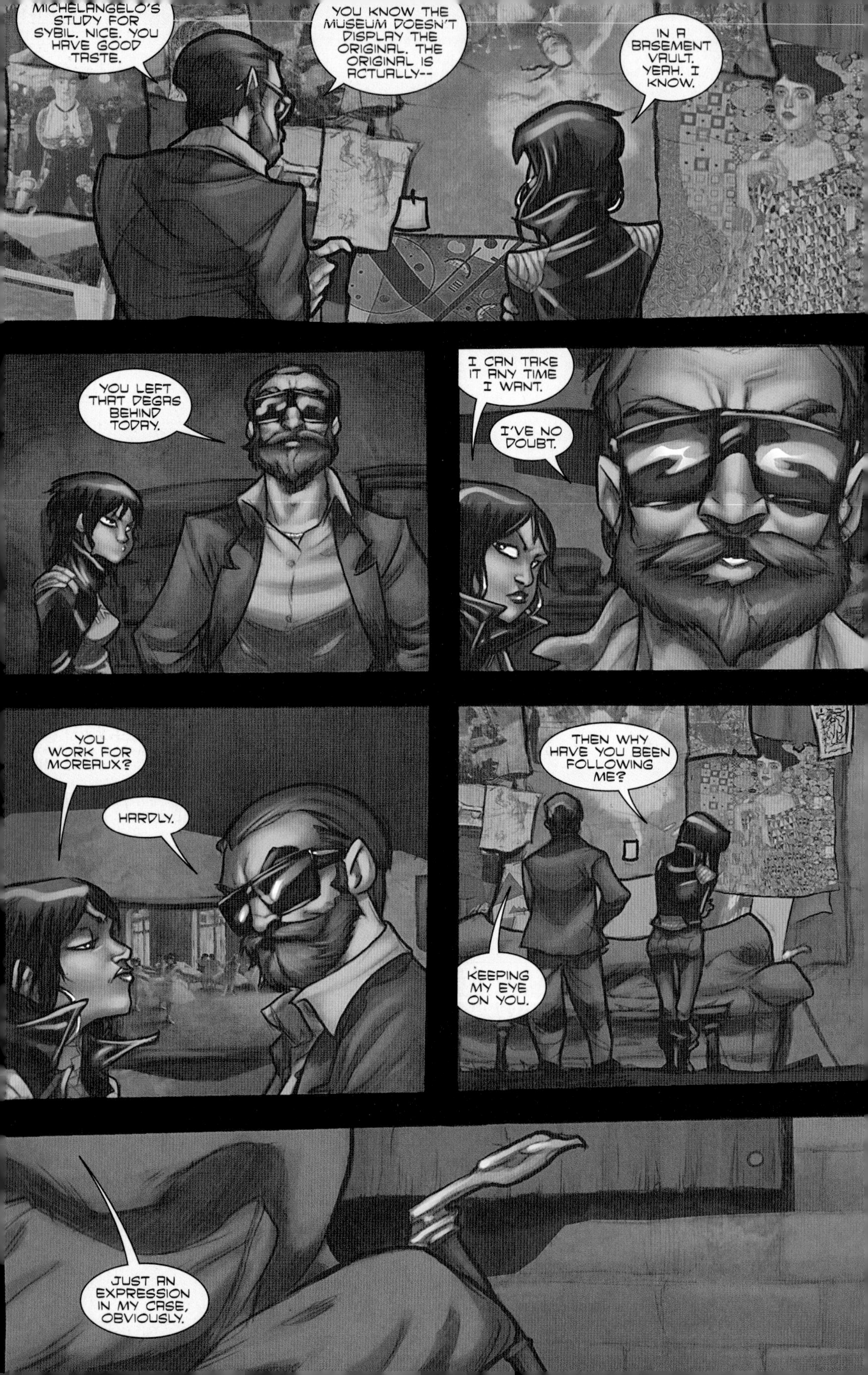
MICHELANGELO'S STUDY FOR SYBIL. NICE. YOU HAVE GOOD TASTE.
YOU KNOW THE MUSEUM DOESN'T DISPLAY THE ORIGINAL. THE ORIGINAL IS ACTUALLY--
IN A BASEMENT VAULT. YEAH. I KNOW.
YOU LEFT THAT DEGAS BEHIND TODAY.
I CAN TAKE IT ANY TIME I WANT.
I'VE NO DOUBT.
YOU WORK FOR MOREAUX?
HARDLY.
THEN WHY HAVE YOU BEEN FOLLOWING ME?
KEEPING MY EYE ON YOU.
JUST AN EXPRESSION IN MY CASE, OBVIOUSLY.

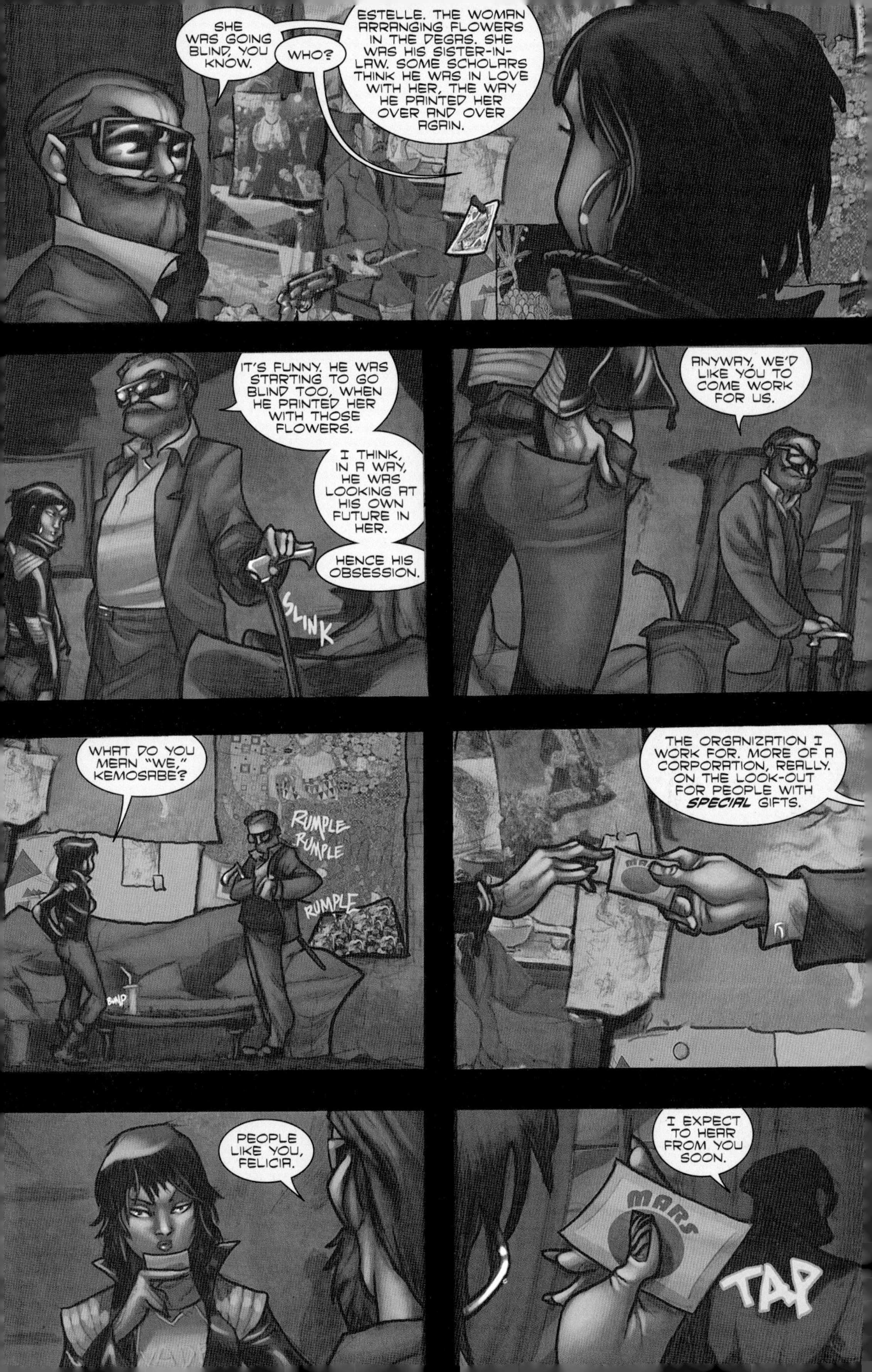
SHE WAS GOING BLIND, YOU KNOW.
WHO?
ESTELLE. THE WOMAN ARRANGING FLOWERS IN THE DEGAS. SHE WAS HIS SISTER-IN-LAW. SOME SCHOLARS THINK HE WAS IN LOVE WITH HER, THE WAY HE PAINTED HER OVER AND OVER AGAIN.
IT'S FUNNY. HE WAS STARTING TO GO BLIND TOO, WHEN HE PAINTED HER WITH THOSE FLOWERS.
I THINK, IN A WAY, HE WAS LOOKING AT HIS OWN FUTURE IN HER.
HENCE HIS OBSESSION.
SHLINK
ANYWAY, WE'D LIKE YOU TO COME WORK FOR US.
WHAT DO YOU MEAN "WE," KEMOSABE?
RUMPLE
RUMPLE
RUMPLE
BUMP
THE ORGANIZATION I WORK FOR. MORE OF A CORPORATION, REALLY. ON THE LOOK-OUT FOR PEOPLE WITH SPECIAL GIFTS.
PEOPLE LIKE YOU, FELICIA.
I EXPECT TO HEAR FROM YOU SOON.
MARS
TAP

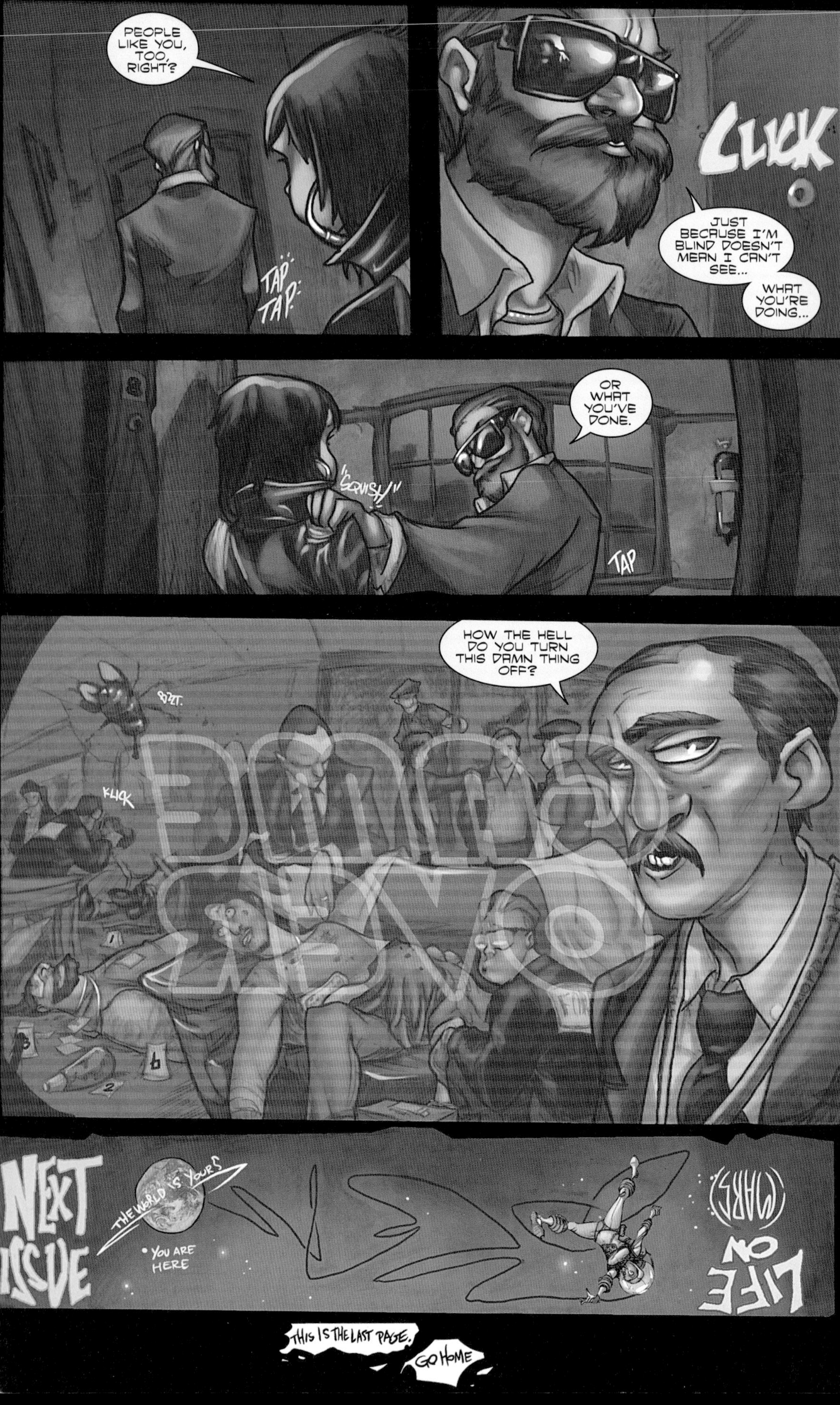
PEOPLE LIKE YOU, TOO, RIGHT?
TAP TAP
CLICK
JUST BECAUSE I'M BLIND DOESN'T MEAN I CAN'T SEE...
WHAT YOU'RE DOING...
OR WHAT YOU'VE DONE.
"SQUISH"
TAP
HOW THE HELL DO YOU TURN THIS DAMN THING OFF?
BZZT.
KLICK
NEXT ISSUE
THE WORLD IS YOURS
YOU ARE HERE
LIFE ON (MARS)
THIS IS THE LAST PAGE.
GO HOME

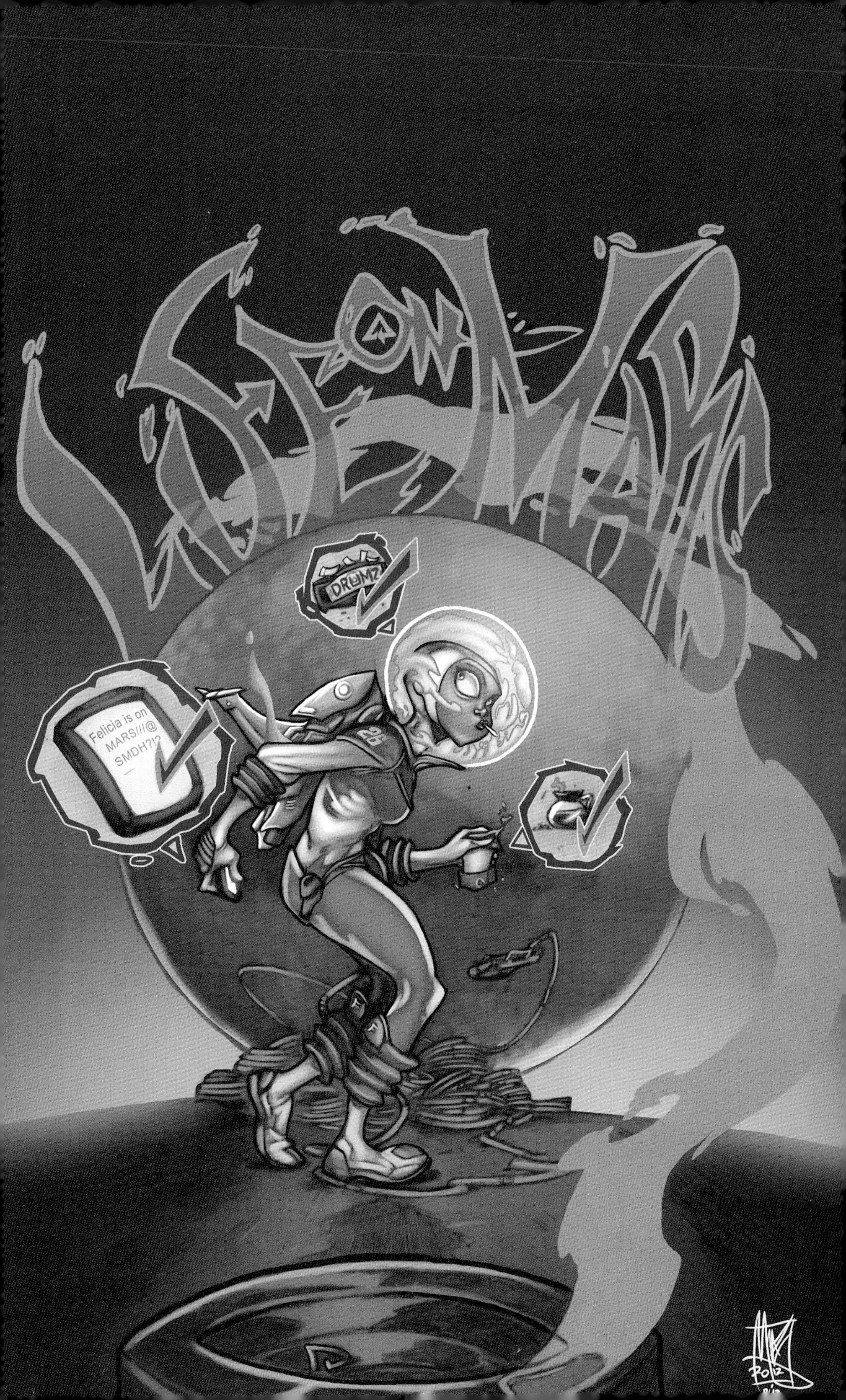

DRUMZ
Felicia is on MARS///@ SMDH?!?

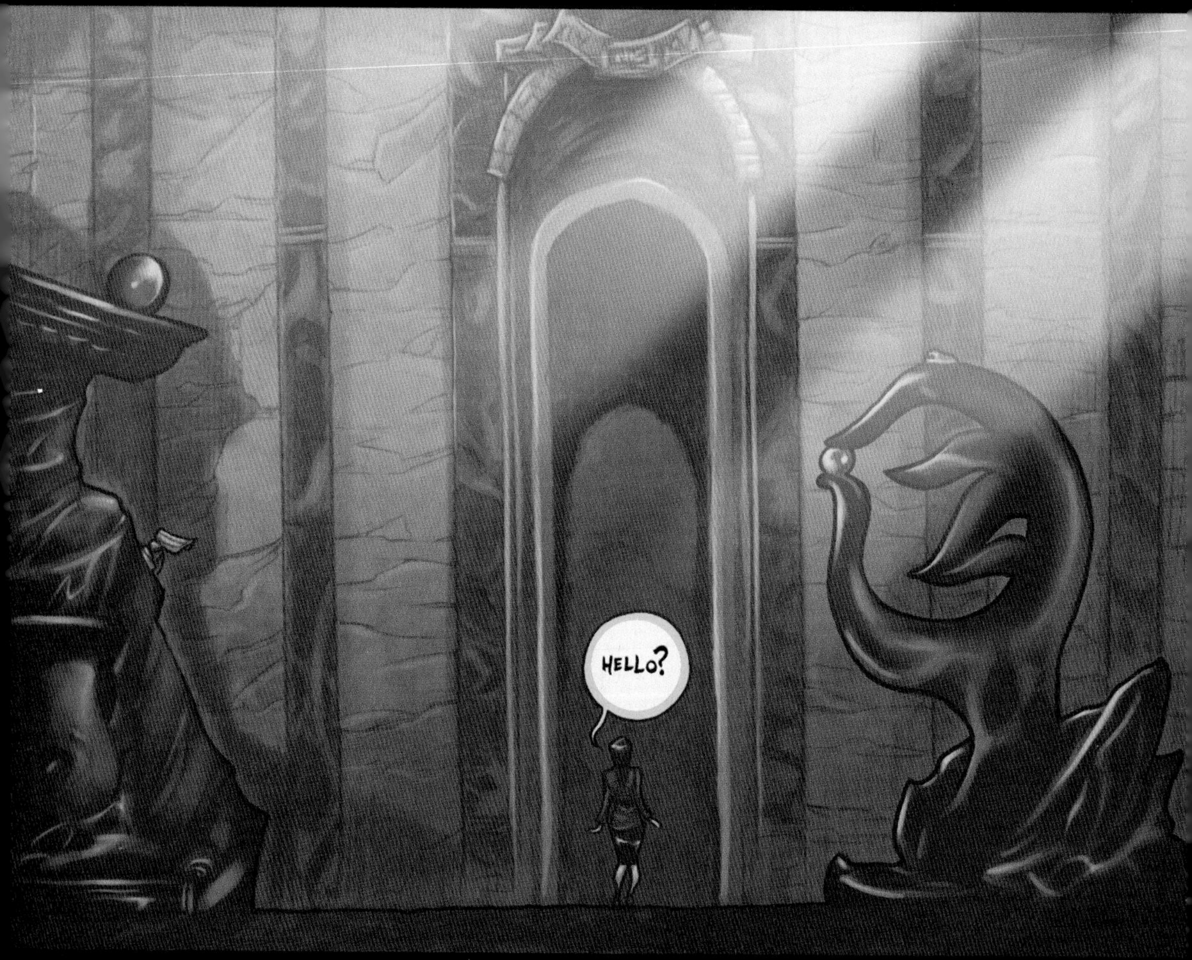
HELLO?

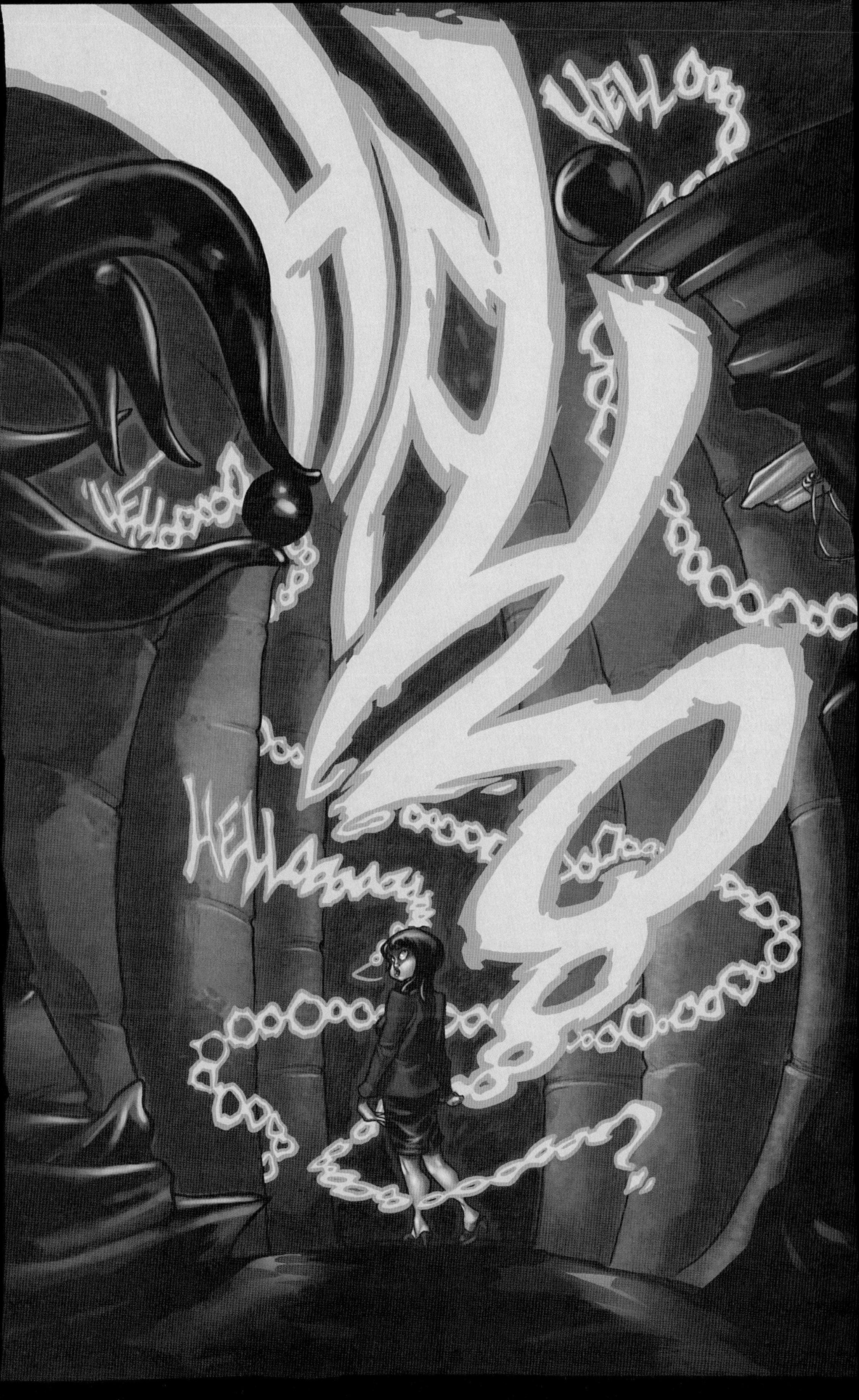
HELLO
HELLOOOO
HELLOOOO

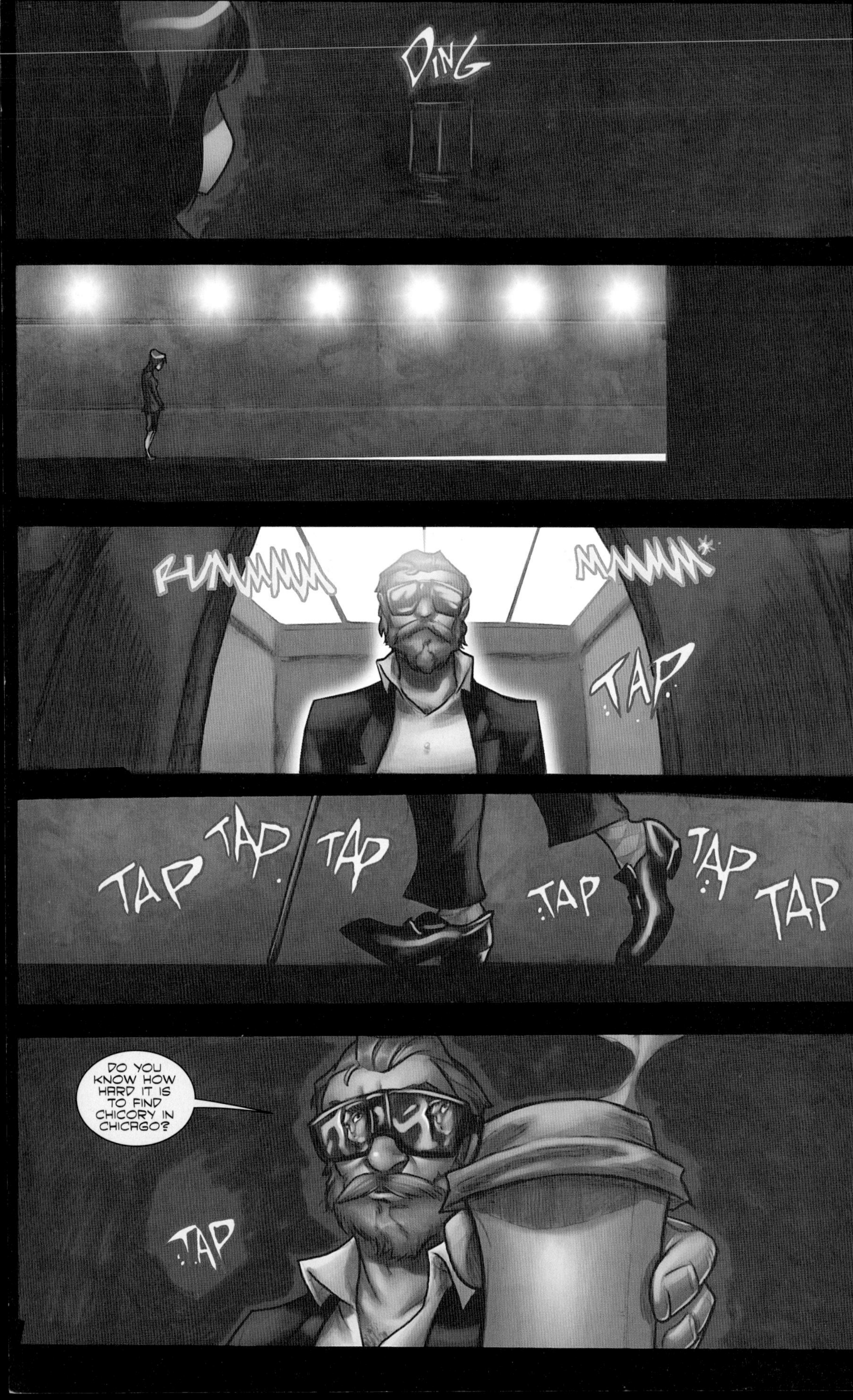
DING
RUMMMM
MMMM*
TAP
TAP TAP TAP
TAP TAP TAP
DO YOU KNOW HOW HARD IT IS TO FIND CHICORY IN CHICAGO?
TAP

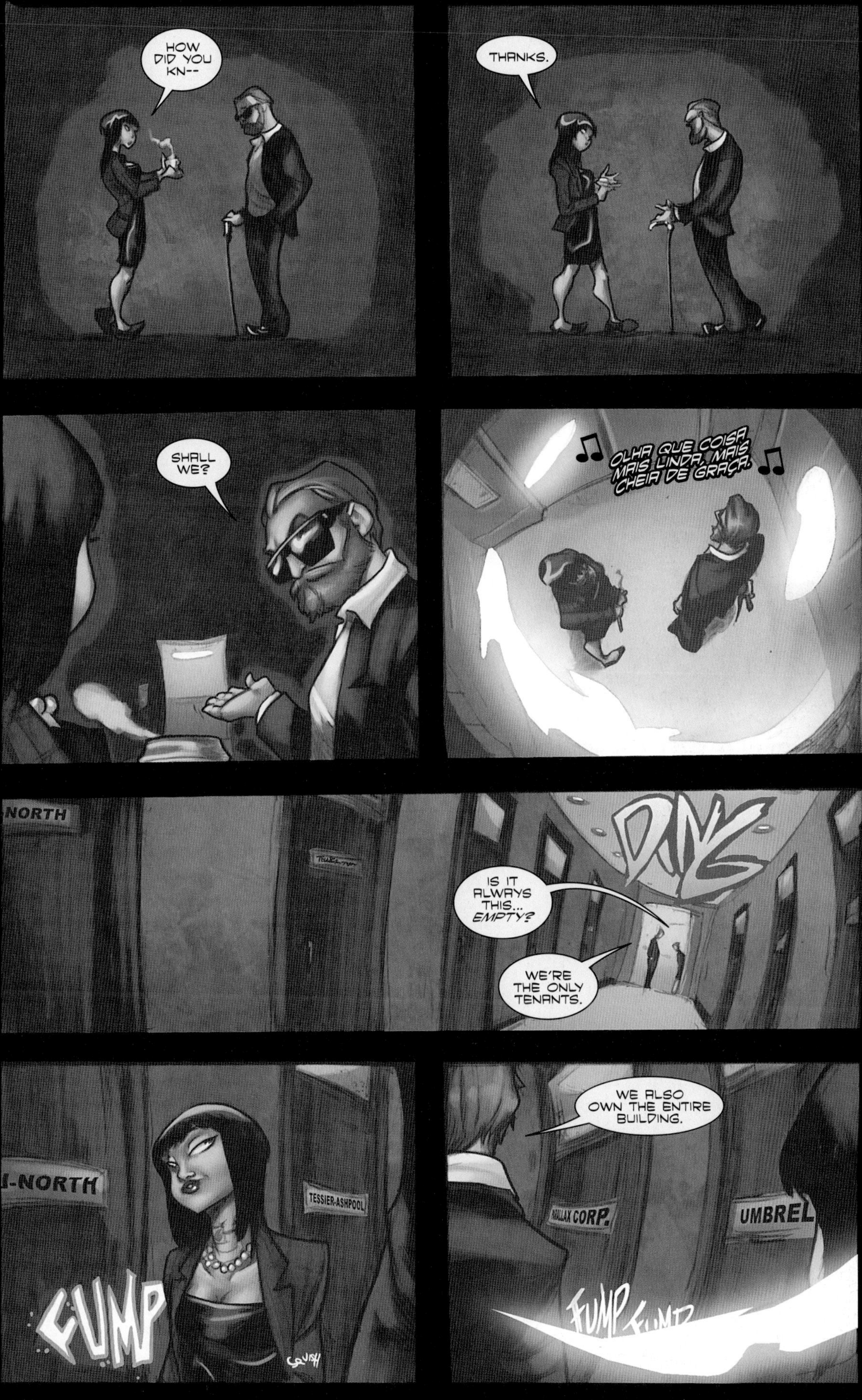
HOW DID YOU KN--
THANKS.
SHALL WE?
OLHA QUE COISA MAIS LINDA, MAIS CHEIA DE GRAÇA.
-NORTH
IS IT ALWAYS THIS... EMPTY?
WE'RE THE ONLY TENANTS.
-NORTH
TESSIER-ASHPOOL
FUMP
WE ALSO OWN THE ENTIRE BUILDING.
RALLAX CORP.
UMBREL
FUMP

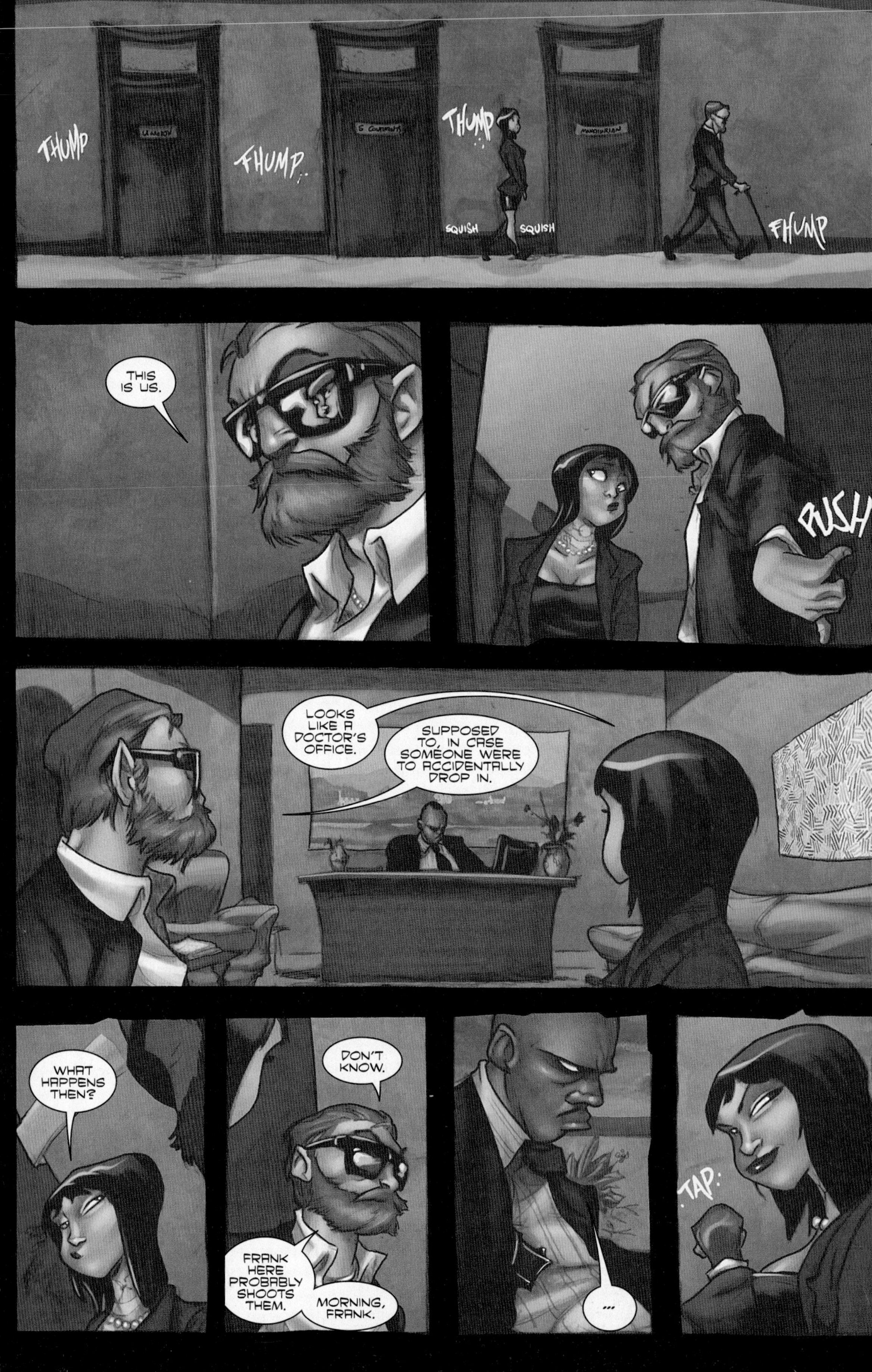
THUMP
FHUMP
THUMP
SQUISH
SQUISH
FHUMP
THIS IS US.
PUSH
LOOKS LIKE A DOCTOR'S OFFICE.
SUPPOSED TO, IN CASE SOMEONE WERE TO ACCIDENTALLY DROP IN.
WHAT HAPPENS THEN?
DON'T KNOW.
FRANK HERE PROBABLY SHOOTS THEM.
MORNING, FRANK.
...
TAP

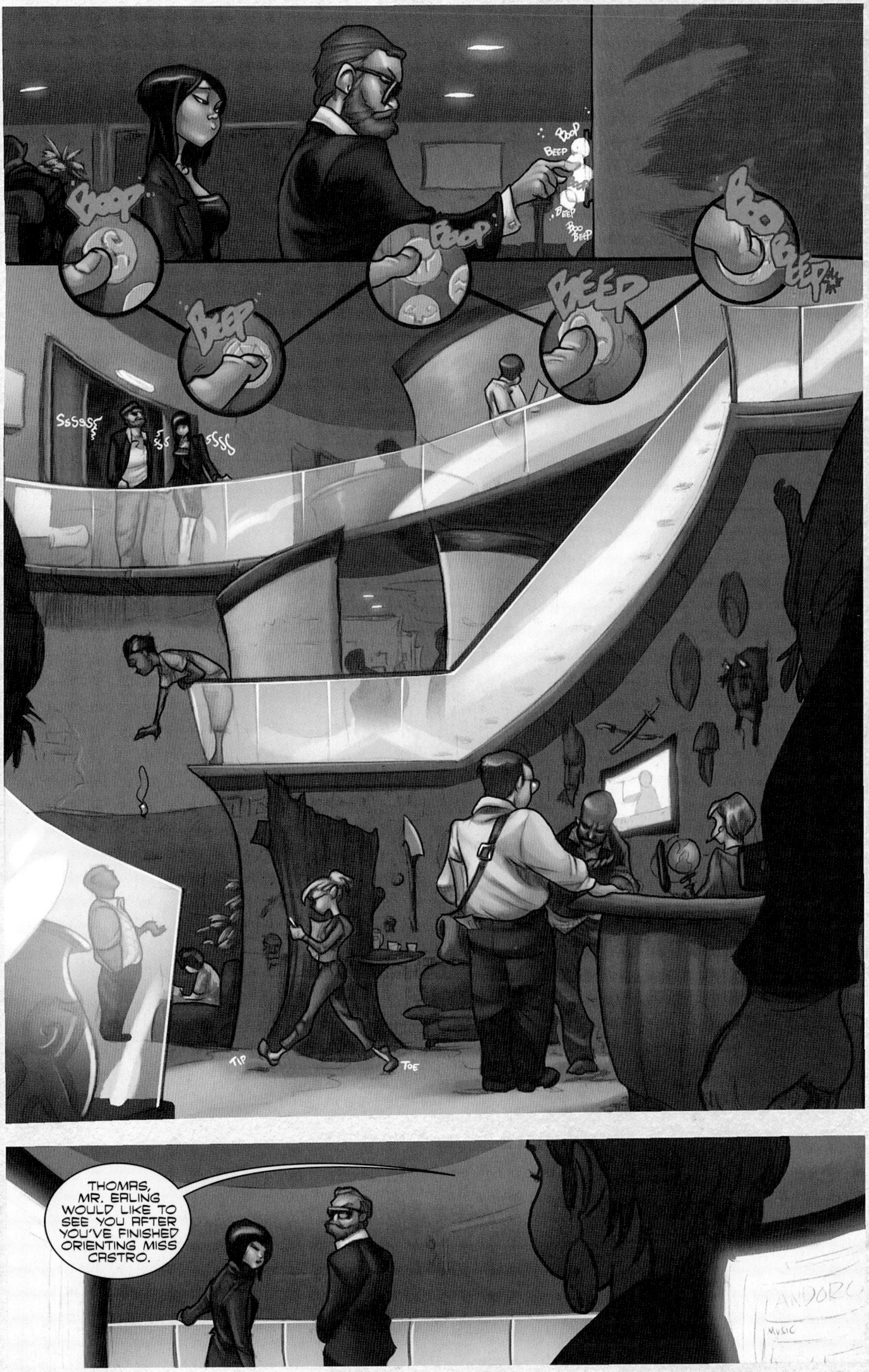
BOOP
BEEP
BEEP
BOO BEEP
BOOP
BEEP
BOOP
BEEP
BOO BEEP
SSSSS
SSSS
TIP
TOE
THOMAS, MR. EARLING WOULD LIKE TO SEE YOU AFTER YOU'VE FINISHED ORIENTING MISS CASTRO.
MUSIC

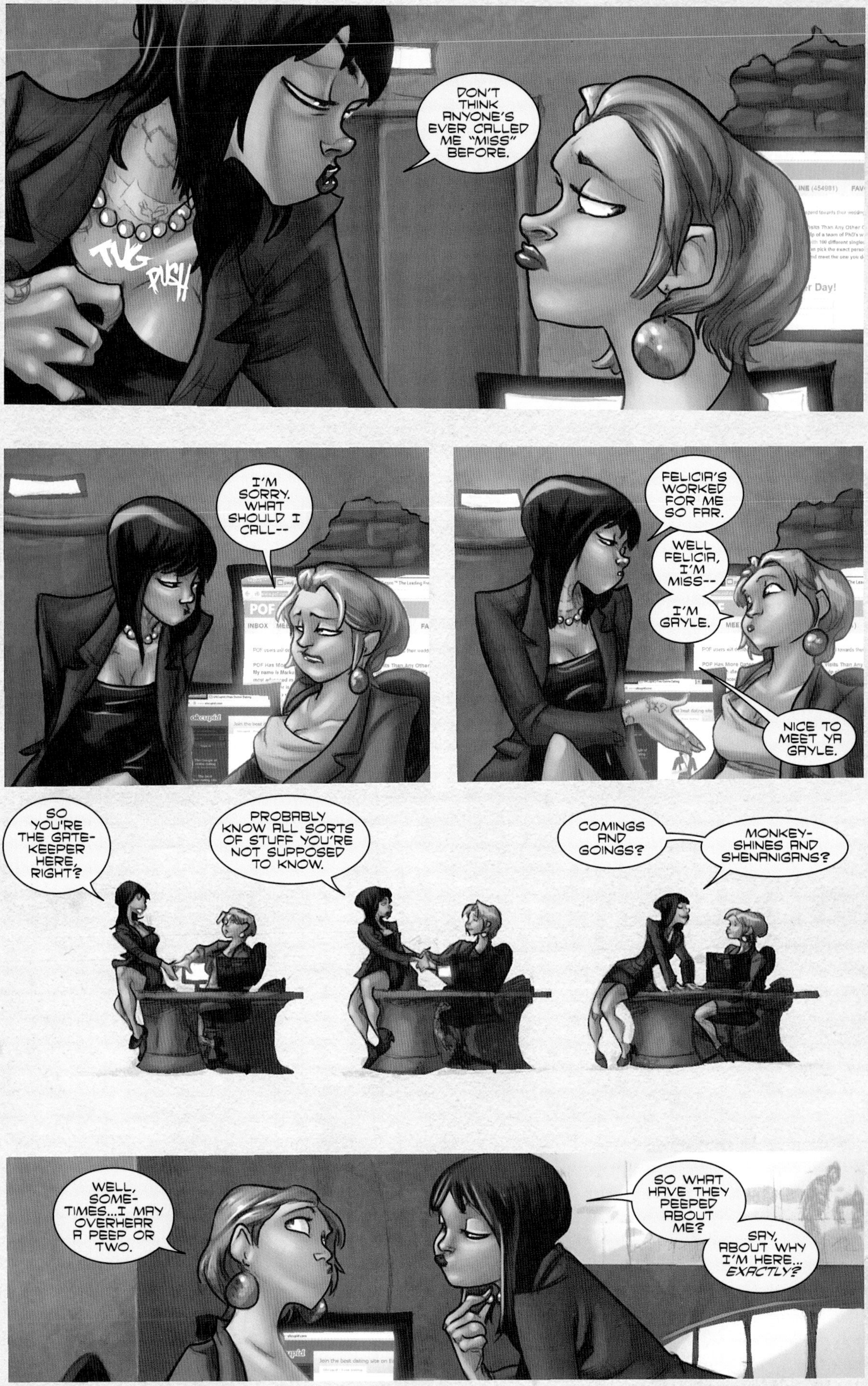
DON'T THINK ANYONE'S EVER CALLED ME "MISS" BEFORE.
TUG
PUSH
I'M SORRY. WHAT SHOULD I CALL--
FELICIA'S WORKED FOR ME SO FAR.
WELL FELICIA, I'M MISS--
I'M GAYLE.
NICE TO MEET YA GAYLE.
SO YOU'RE THE GATE-KEEPER HERE, RIGHT?
PROBABLY KNOW ALL SORTS OF STUFF YOU'RE NOT SUPPOSED TO KNOW.
COMINGS AND GOINGS?
MONKEY-SHINES AND SHENANIGANS?
WELL, SOME-TIMES...I MAY OVERHEAR A PEEP OR TWO.
SO WHAT HAVE THEY PEEPED ABOUT ME?
SAY, ABOUT WHY I'M HERE... *EXACTLY*?

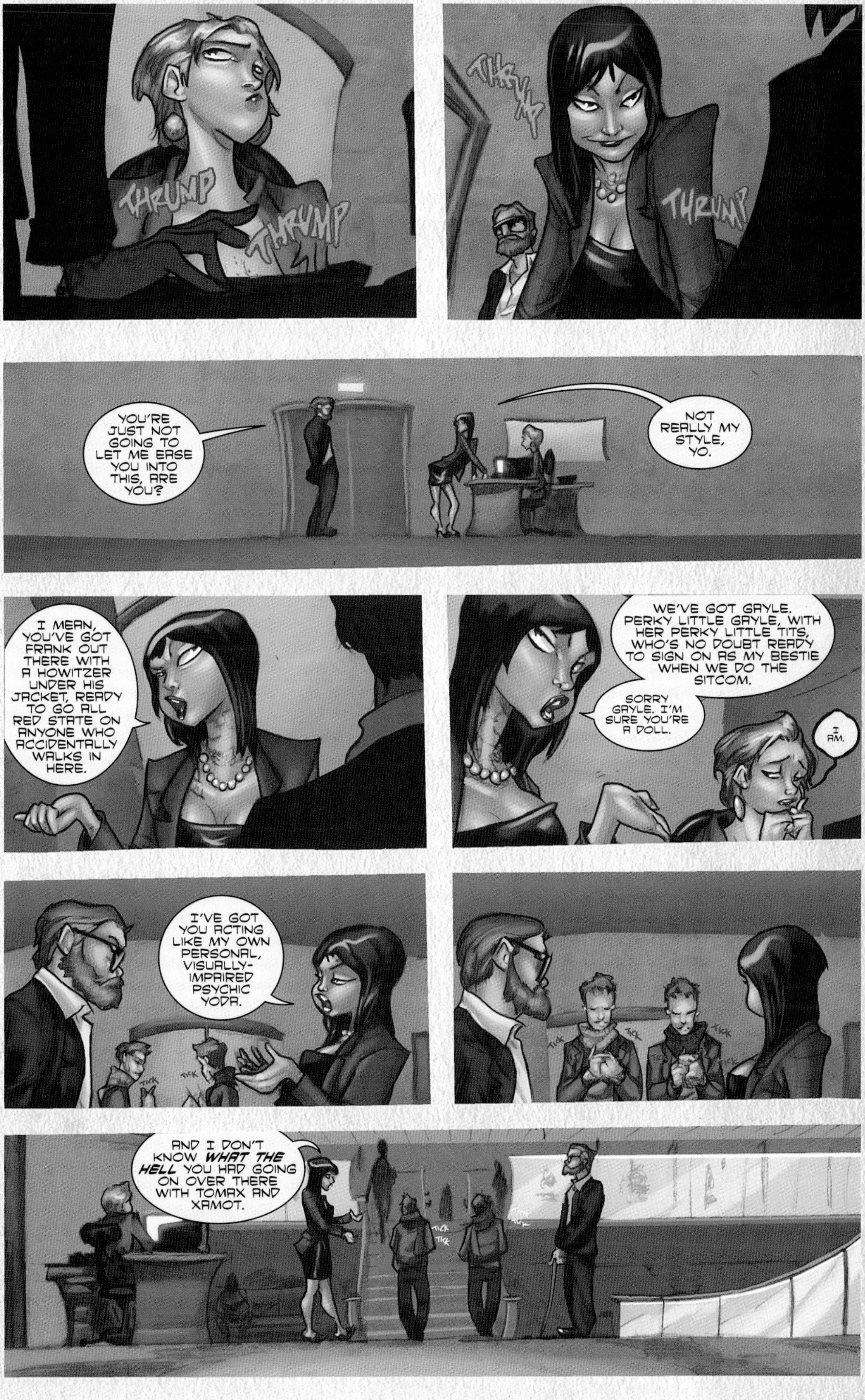
THRUMP
THRUMP
THRUMP
THRUMP
YOU'RE JUST NOT GOING TO LET ME EASE YOU INTO THIS, ARE YOU?
NOT REALLY MY STYLE, YO.
I MEAN, YOU'VE GOT FRANK OUT THERE WITH A HOWITZER UNDER HIS JACKET, READY TO GO ALL RED STATE ON ANYONE WHO ACCIDENTALLY WALKS IN HERE.
WE'VE GOT GAYLE. PERKY LITTLE GAYLE, WITH HER PERKY LITTLE TITS, WHO'S NO DOUBT READY TO SIGN ON AS MY BESTIE WHEN WE DO THE SITCOM.
SORRY GAYLE. I'M SURE YOU'RE A DOLL.
I AM.
I'VE GOT YOU ACTING LIKE MY OWN PERSONAL, VISUALLY-IMPAIRED PSYCHIC YODA.
TICK
TICK
TICK
TICK
TICK
TICK
AND I DON'T KNOW ***WHAT THE HELL*** YOU HAD GOING ON OVER THERE WITH TOMAX AND XAMOT.
TICK
TICK
TICK
TICK

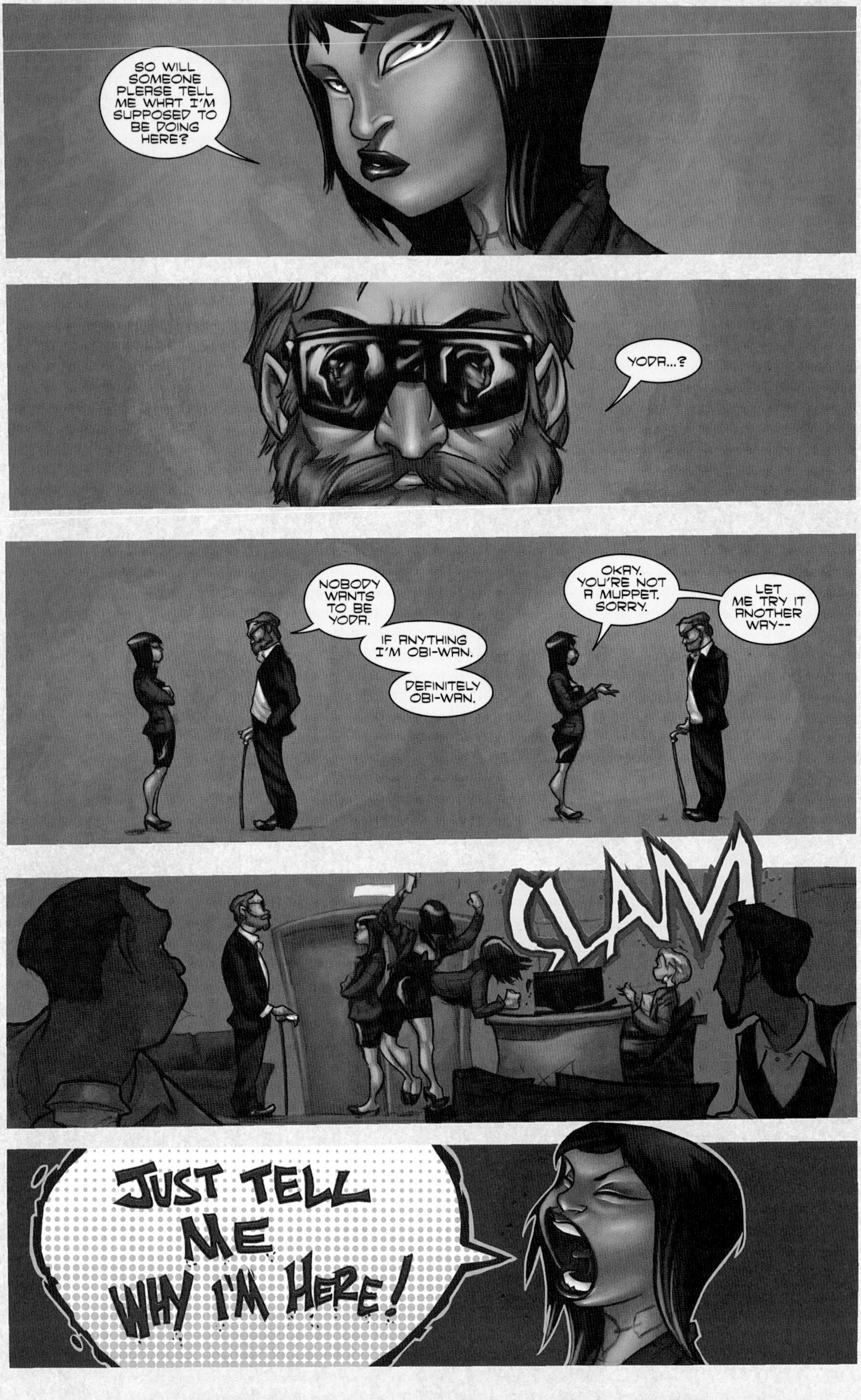
SO WILL SOMEONE PLEASE TELL ME WHAT I'M SUPPOSED TO BE DOING HERE?
YODA...?
NOBODY WANTS TO BE YODA.
IF ANYTHING I'M OBI-WAN.
DEFINITELY OBI-WAN.
OKAY. YOU'RE NOT A MUPPET. SORRY.
LET ME TRY IT ANOTHER WAY--
SLAM
JUST TELL ME WHY I'M HERE!

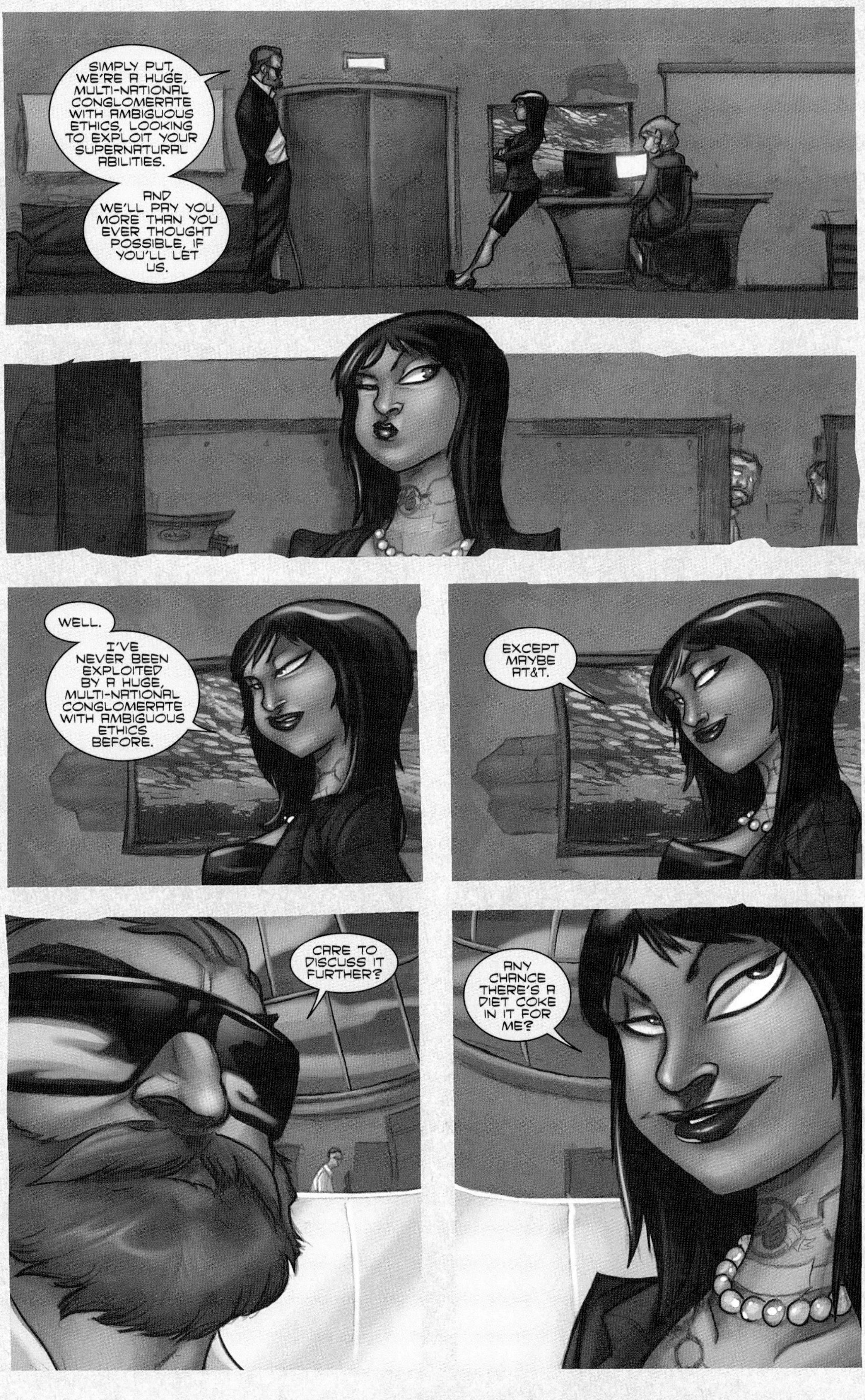
SIMPLY PUT, WE'RE A HUGE, MULTI-NATIONAL CONGLOMERATE WITH AMBIGUOUS ETHICS, LOOKING TO EXPLOIT YOUR SUPERNATURAL ABILITIES.
AND WE'LL PAY YOU MORE THAN YOU EVER THOUGHT POSSIBLE, IF YOU'LL LET US.
WELL.
I'VE NEVER BEEN EXPLOITED BY A HUGE, MULTI-NATIONAL CONGLOMERATE WITH AMBIGUOUS ETHICS BEFORE.
EXCEPT MAYBE AT&T.
CARE TO DISCUSS IT FURTHER?
ANY CHANCE THERE'S A DIET COKE IN IT FOR ME?

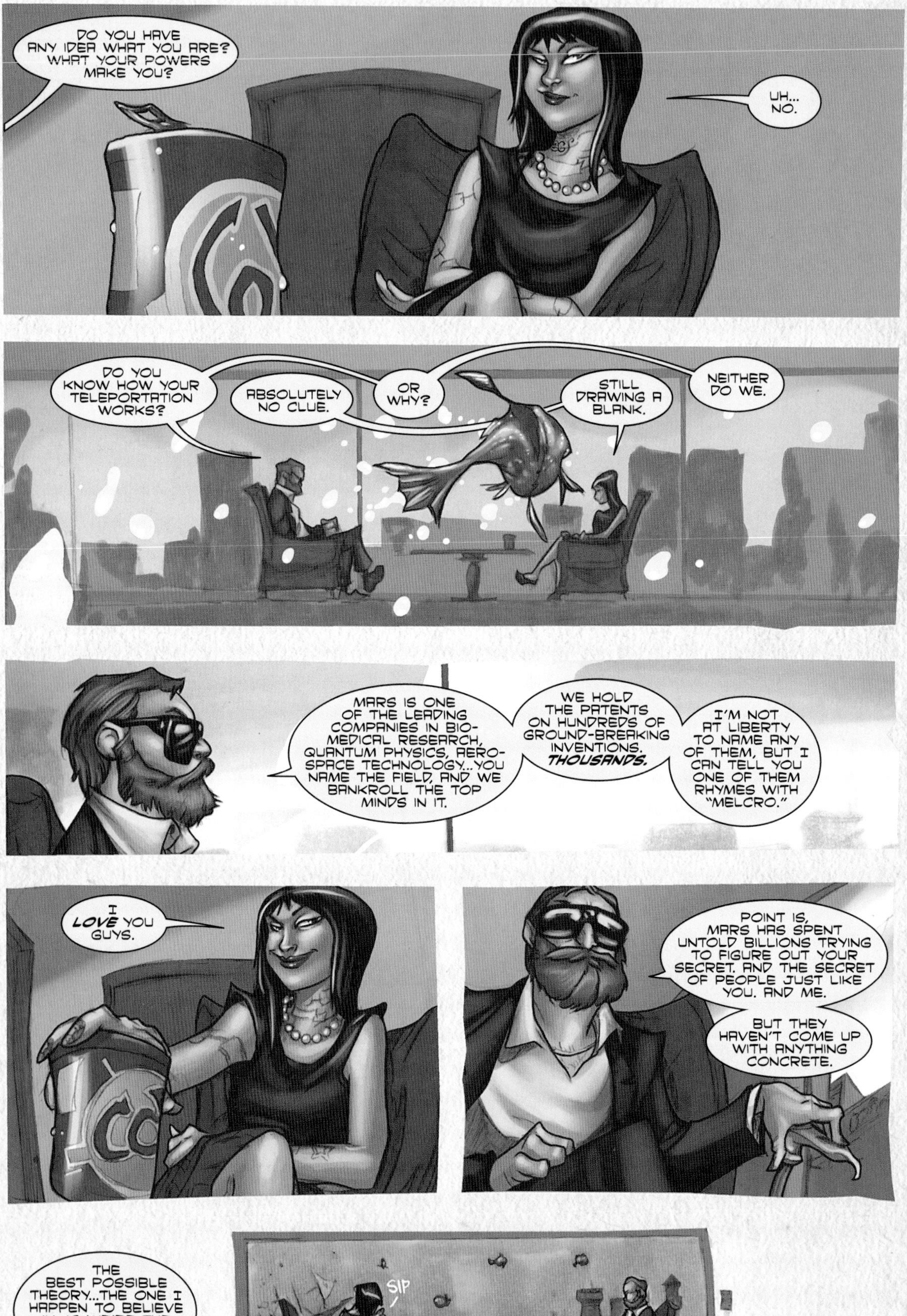
DO YOU HAVE ANY IDEA WHAT YOU ARE? WHAT YOUR POWERS MAKE YOU?
UH... NO.
DO YOU KNOW HOW YOUR TELEPORTATION WORKS?
ABSOLUTELY NO CLUE.
OR WHY?
STILL DRAWING A BLANK.
NEITHER DO WE.
MARS IS ONE OF THE LEADING COMPANIES IN BIO-MEDICAL RESEARCH, QUANTUM PHYSICS, AERO-SPACE TECHNOLOGY...YOU NAME THE FIELD, AND WE BANKROLL THE TOP MINDS IN IT.
WE HOLD THE PATENTS ON HUNDREDS OF GROUND-BREAKING INVENTIONS. THOUSANDS.
I'M NOT AT LIBERTY TO NAME ANY OF THEM, BUT I CAN TELL YOU ONE OF THEM RHYMES WITH "MELCRO."
I LOVE YOU GUYS.
POINT IS, MARS HAS SPENT UNTOLD BILLIONS TRYING TO FIGURE OUT YOUR SECRET. AND THE SECRET OF PEOPLE JUST LIKE YOU. AND ME.
BUT THEY HAVEN'T COME UP WITH ANYTHING CONCRETE.
THE BEST POSSIBLE THEORY...THE ONE I HAPPEN TO BELIEVE IN, IS WE'RE THE NEXT STAGE OF EVOLUTION.
SIP
ANTHROPOLOGISTS HAVE SEARCHED CENTURIES FOR THE FABLED "MISSING LINK."

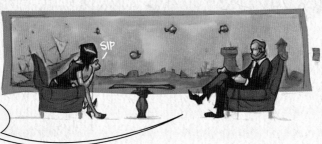

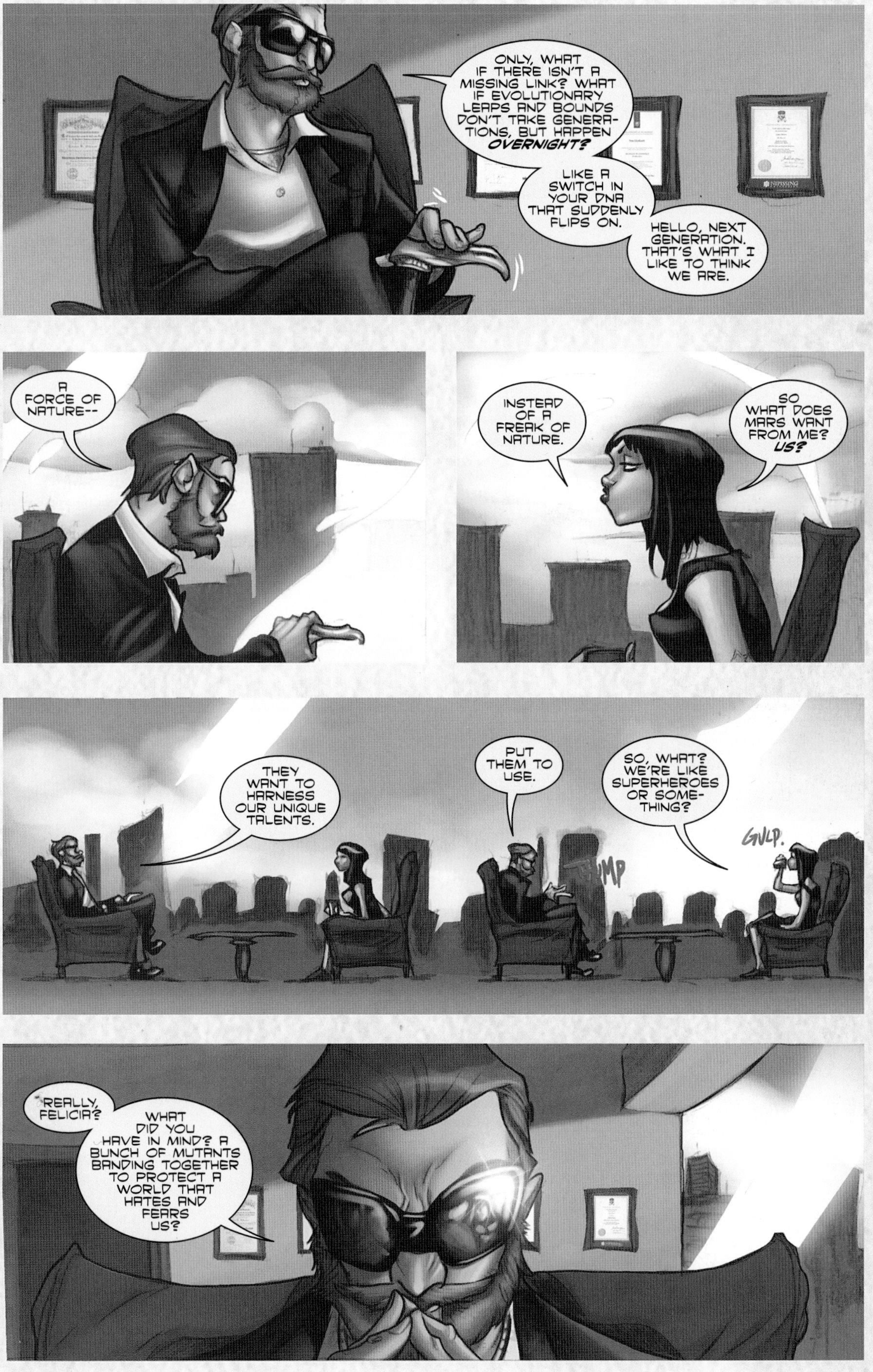
ONLY, WHAT IF THERE ISN'T A MISSING LINK? WHAT IF EVOLUTIONARY LEAPS AND BOUNDS DON'T TAKE GENERATIONS, BUT HAPPEN OVERNIGHT?
LIKE A SWITCH IN YOUR DNA THAT SUDDENLY FLIPS ON.
HELLO, NEXT GENERATION. THAT'S WHAT I LIKE TO THINK WE ARE.
A FORCE OF NATURE--
INSTEAD OF A FREAK OF NATURE.
SO WHAT DOES MARS WANT FROM ME? US?
THEY WANT TO HARNESS OUR UNIQUE TALENTS.
PUT THEM TO USE.
SO, WHAT? WE'RE LIKE SUPERHEROES OR SOMETHING?
GULP.
REALLY, FELICIA?
WHAT DID YOU HAVE IN MIND? A BUNCH OF MUTANTS BANDING TOGETHER TO PROTECT A WORLD THAT HATES AND FEARS US?

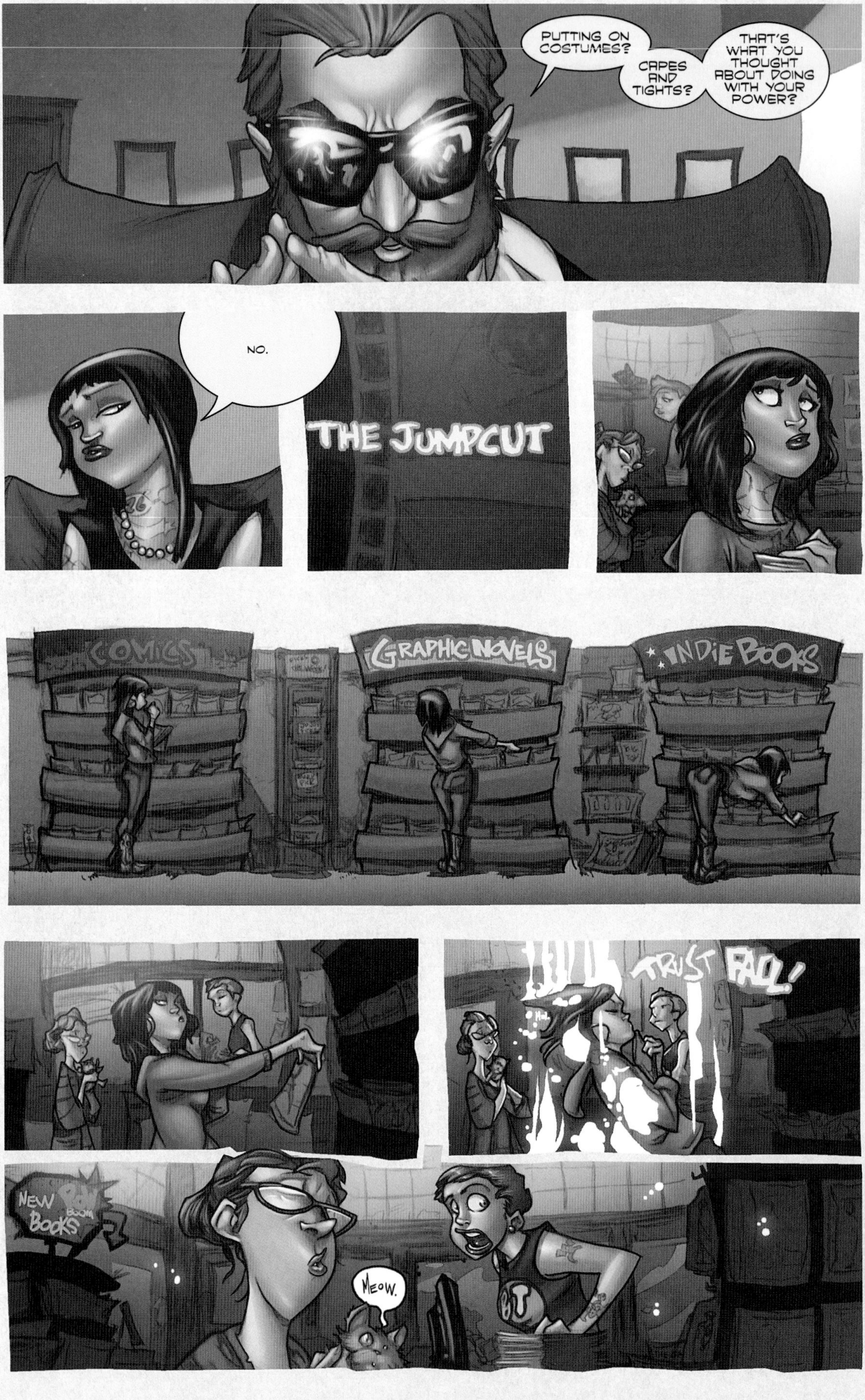
PUTTING ON COSTUMES?
CAPES AND TIGHTS?
THAT'S WHAT YOU THOUGHT ABOUT DOING WITH YOUR POWER?
NO.
THE JUMPCUT
COMICS
GRAPHIC NOVELS
INDIE BOOKS
TRUST FALL!
NEW BOOKS
MEOW.

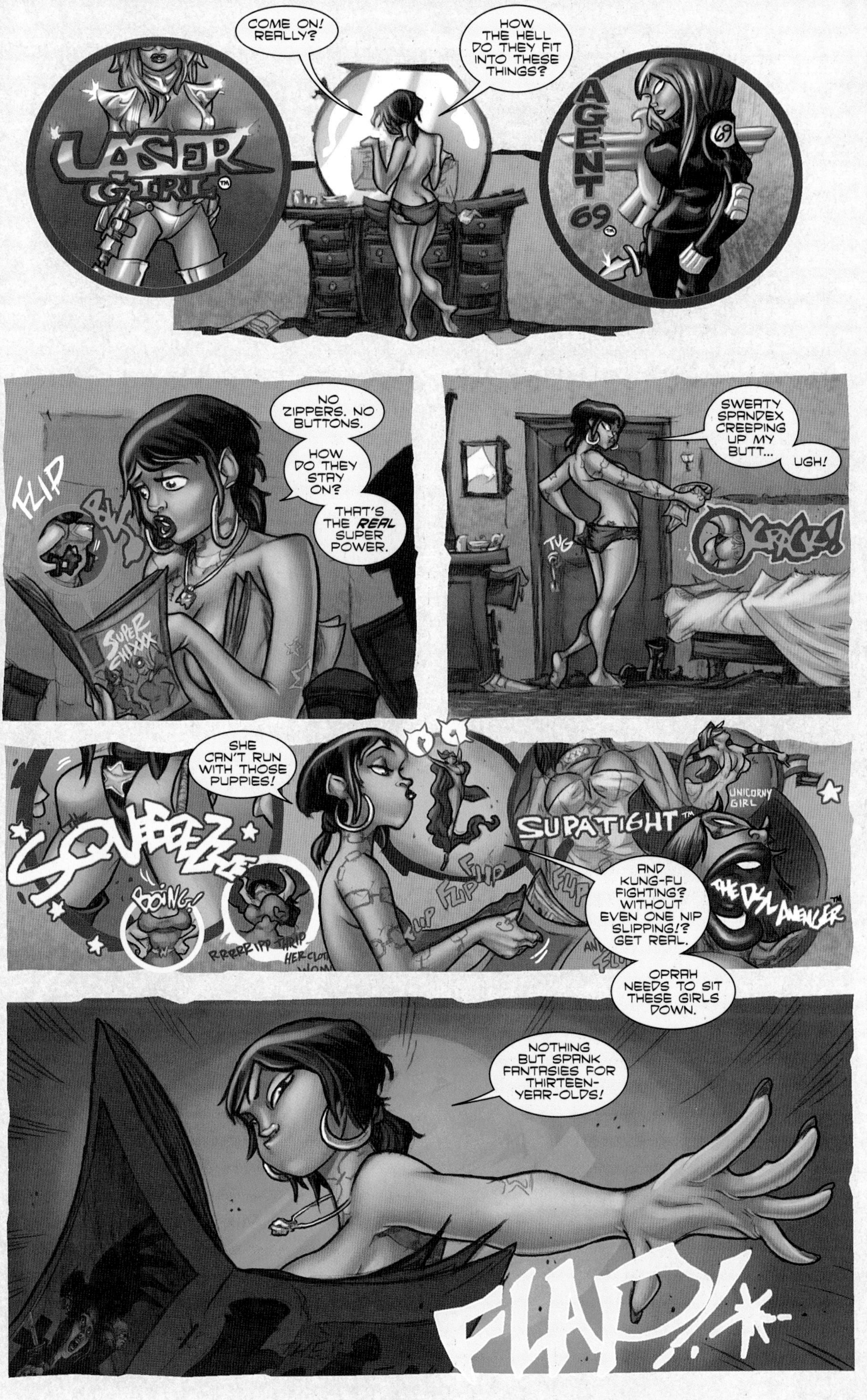
LASER GIRL™
COME ON! REALLY?
HOW THE HELL DO THEY FIT INTO THESE THINGS?
AGENT 69.™
FLIP
NO ZIPPERS. NO BUTTONS.
HOW DO THEY STAY ON?
THAT'S THE **REAL** SUPER POWER.
SUPER CHIXXX
SWEATY SPANDEX CREEPING UP MY BUTT...
UGH!
TUG
SHE CAN'T RUN WITH THOSE PUPPIES!
SQUEEEZE
BOING!
SUPATIGHT™
UNICORNY GIRL
AND KUNG-FU FIGHTING? WITHOUT EVEN ONE NIP SLIPPING!? GET REAL.
THE DSL AVENGER™
OPRAH NEEDS TO SIT THESE GIRLS DOWN.
NOTHING BUT SPANK FANTASIES FOR THIRTEEN-YEAR-OLDS!
FLAP!

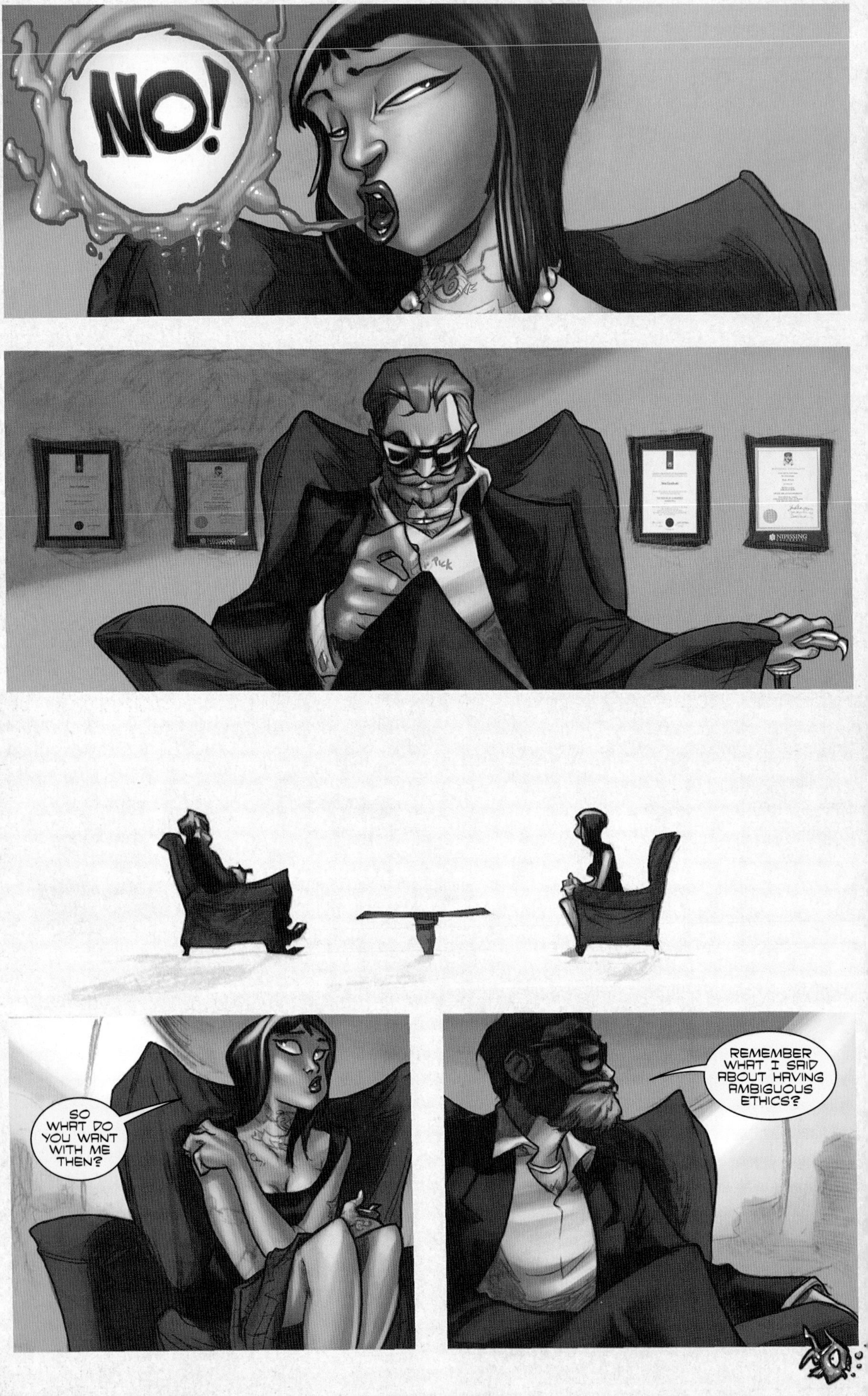
NO!
SO WHAT DO YOU WANT WITH ME THEN?
REMEMBER WHAT I SAID ABOUT HAVING AMBIGUOUS ETHICS?

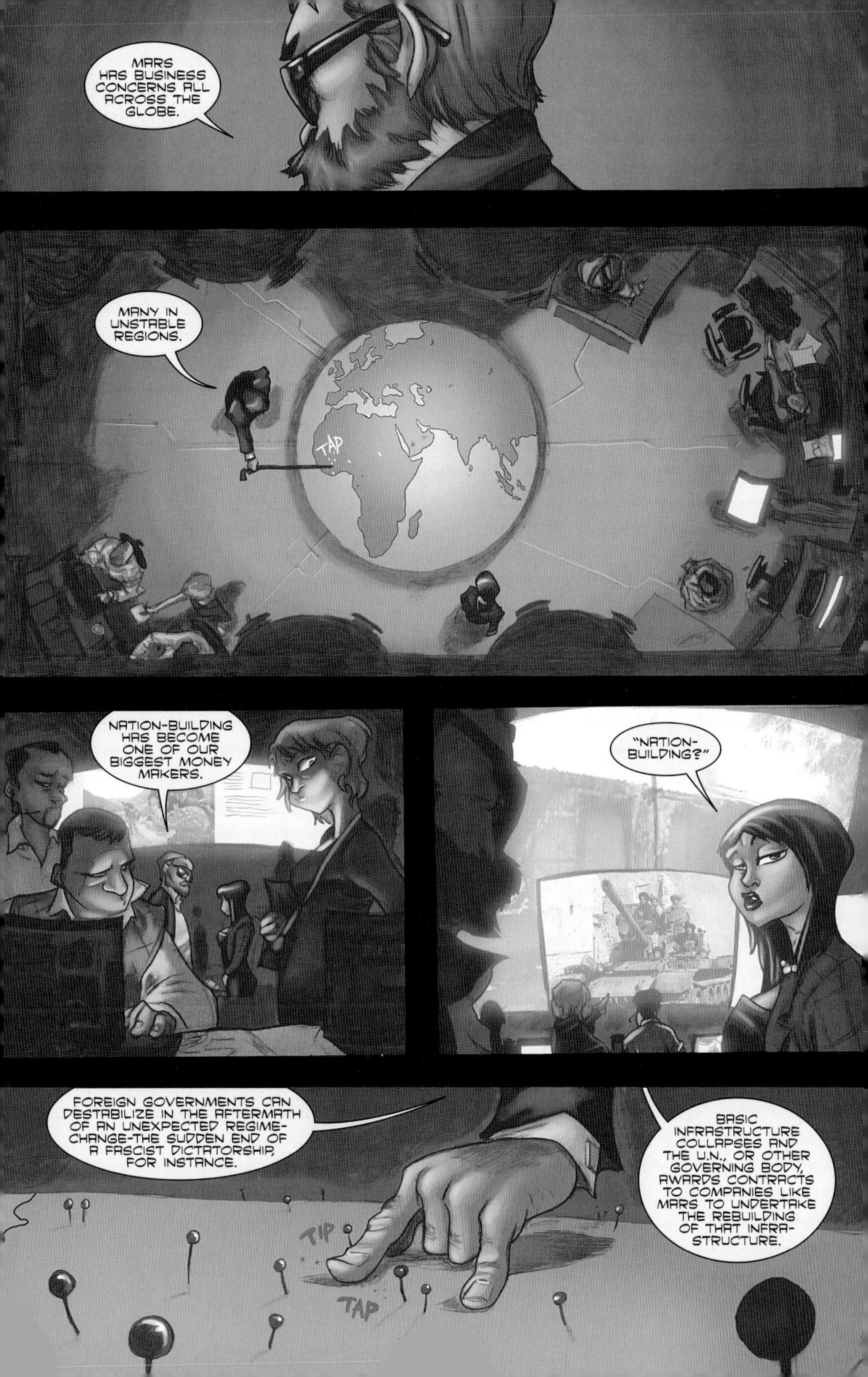
MARS HAS BUSINESS CONCERNS ALL ACROSS THE GLOBE.
MANY IN UNSTABLE REGIONS.
TAP
NATION-BUILDING HAS BECOME ONE OF OUR BIGGEST MONEY MAKERS.
"NATION-BUILDING?"
FOREIGN GOVERNMENTS CAN DESTABILIZE IN THE AFTERMATH OF AN UNEXPECTED REGIME-CHANGE-THE SUDDEN END OF A FASCIST DICTATORSHIP, FOR INSTANCE.
BASIC INFRASTRUCTURE COLLAPSES AND THE U.N., OR OTHER GOVERNING BODY, AWARDS CONTRACTS TO COMPANIES LIKE MARS TO UNDERTAKE THE REBUILDING OF THAT INFRA-STRUCTURE.
TIP
TAP

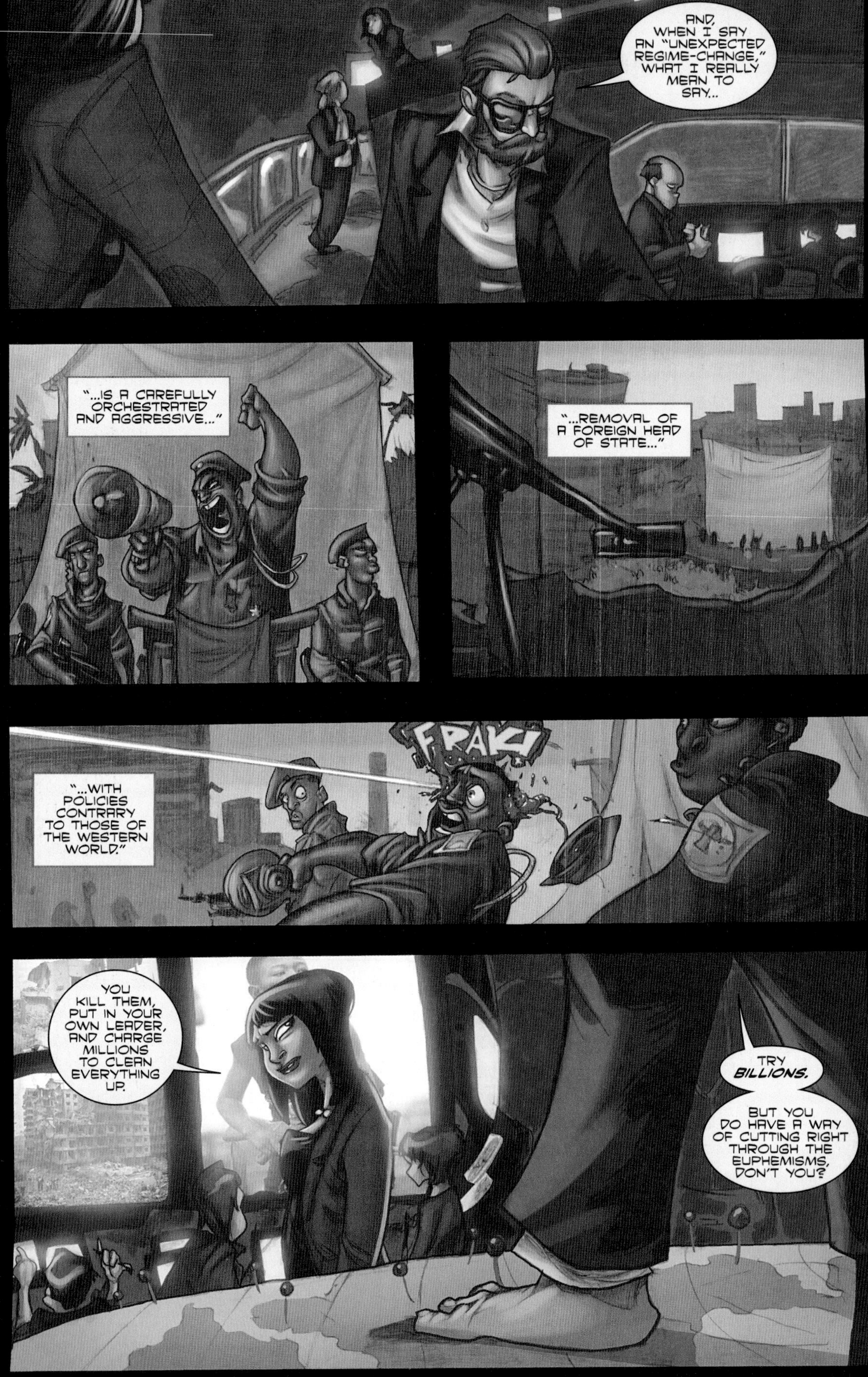
AND, WHEN I SAY AN "UNEXPECTED REGIME-CHANGE," WHAT I REALLY MEAN TO SAY...
"...IS A CAREFULLY ORCHESTRATED AND AGGRESSIVE..."
"...REMOVAL OF A FOREIGN HEAD OF STATE..."
"...WITH POLICIES CONTRARY TO THOSE OF THE WESTERN WORLD."
FRAK!
YOU KILL THEM, PUT IN YOUR OWN LEADER, AND CHARGE MILLIONS TO CLEAN EVERYTHING UP.
TRY *BILLIONS.*
BUT YOU DO HAVE A WAY OF CUTTING RIGHT THROUGH THE EUPHEMISMS, DON'T YOU?

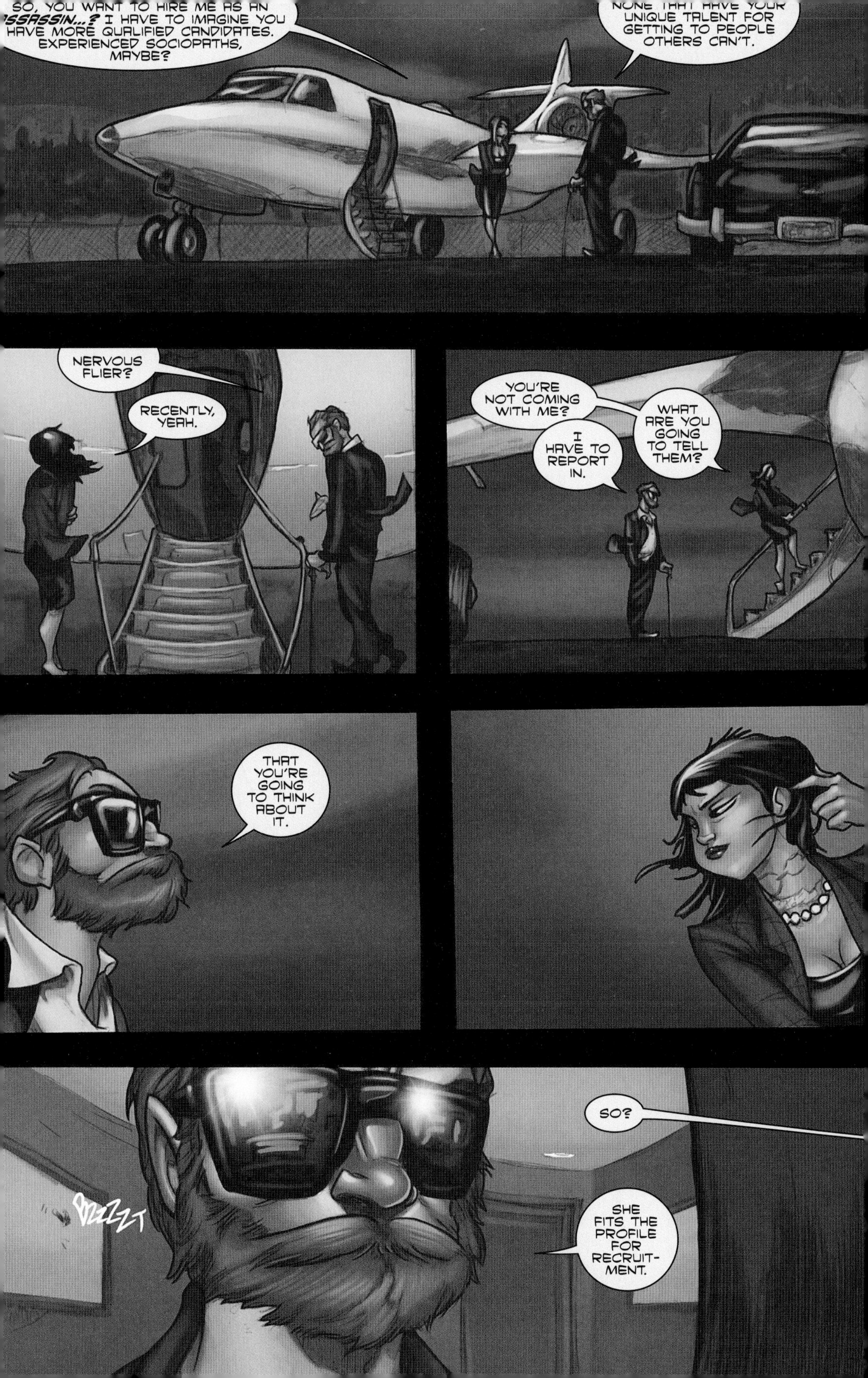
SO, YOU WANT TO HIRE ME AS AN SSASSIN...? I HAVE TO IMAGINE YOU HAVE MORE QUALIFIED CANDIDATES. EXPERIENCED SOCIOPATHS, MAYBE?
NONE THAT HAVE YOUR UNIQUE TALENT FOR GETTING TO PEOPLE OTHERS CAN'T.
NERVOUS FLIER?
RECENTLY, YEAH.
YOU'RE NOT COMING WITH ME?
I HAVE TO REPORT IN.
WHAT ARE YOU GOING TO TELL THEM?
THAT YOU'RE GOING TO THINK ABOUT IT.
BZZZZT
SO?
SHE FITS THE PROFILE FOR RECRUIT-MENT.

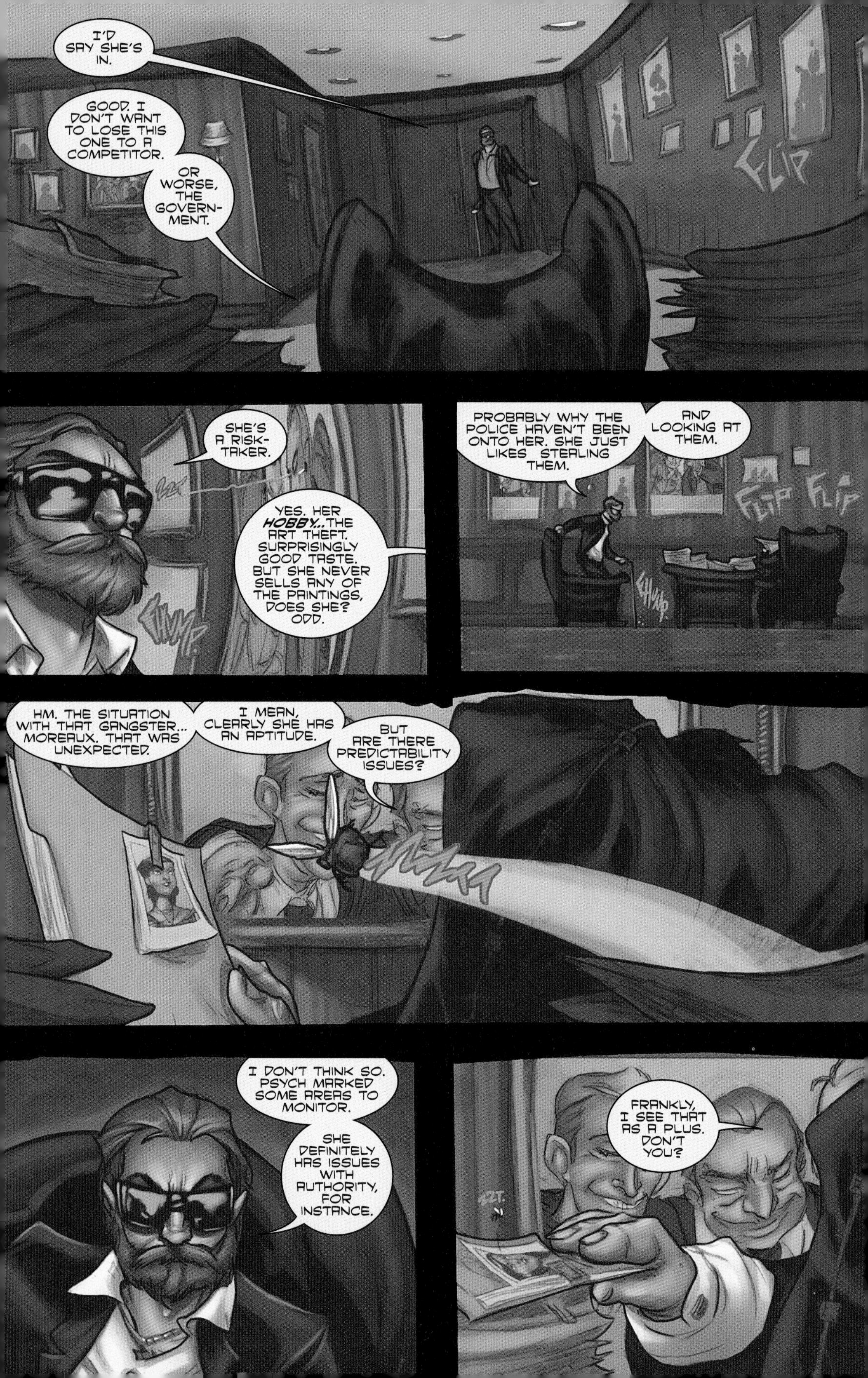
I'D SAY SHE'S IN.
GOOD. I DON'T WANT TO LOSE THIS ONE TO A COMPETITOR.
OR WORSE, THE GOVERNMENT.
FLIP
SHE'S A RISK-TAKER.
ZZT
YES. HER *HOBBY*... THE ART THEFT. SURPRISINGLY GOOD TASTE. BUT SHE NEVER SELLS ANY OF THE PAINTINGS, DOES SHE? ODD.
THUMP
PROBABLY WHY THE POLICE HAVEN'T BEEN ONTO HER. SHE JUST LIKES STEALING THEM.
AND LOOKING AT THEM.
FLIP FLIP
THUMP
HM. THE SITUATION WITH THAT GANGSTER... MOREAUX. THAT WAS UNEXPECTED.
I MEAN, CLEARLY SHE HAS AN APTITUDE.
BUT ARE THERE PREDICTABILITY ISSUES?
I DON'T THINK SO. PSYCH MARKED SOME AREAS TO MONITOR.
SHE DEFINITELY HAS ISSUES WITH AUTHORITY, FOR INSTANCE.
FRANKLY, I SEE THAT AS A PLUS. DON'T YOU?
ZZT.

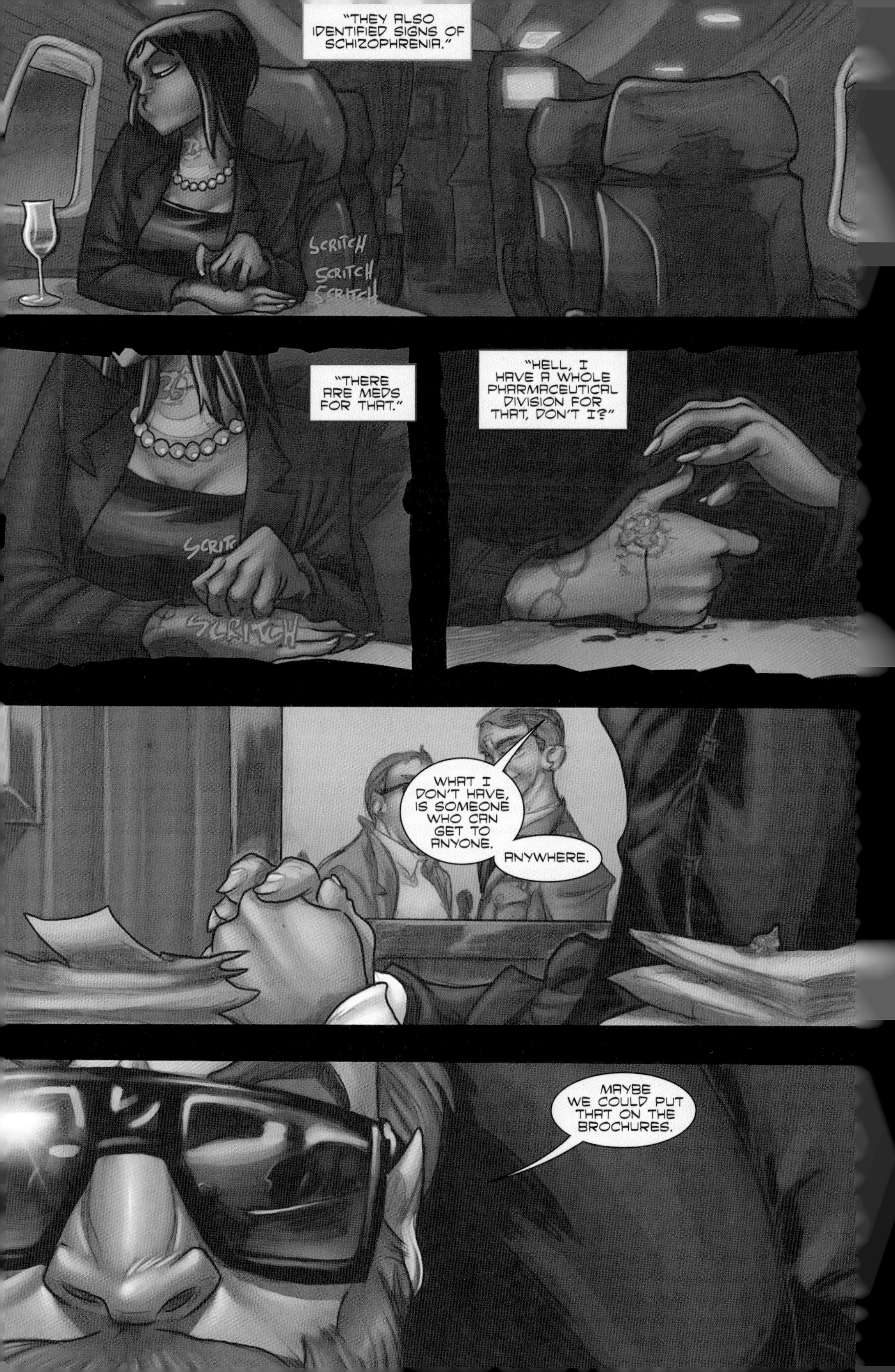
"THEY ALSO IDENTIFIED SIGNS OF SCHIZOPHRENIA."
SCRITCH
SCRITCH
SCRITCH
"THERE ARE MEDS FOR THAT."
SCRITC
SCRITCH
"HELL, I HAVE A WHOLE PHARMACEUTICAL DIVISION FOR THAT, DON'T I?"
WHAT I DON'T HAVE, IS SOMEONE WHO CAN GET TO ANYONE.
ANYWHERE.
MAYBE WE COULD PUT THAT ON THE BROCHURES.

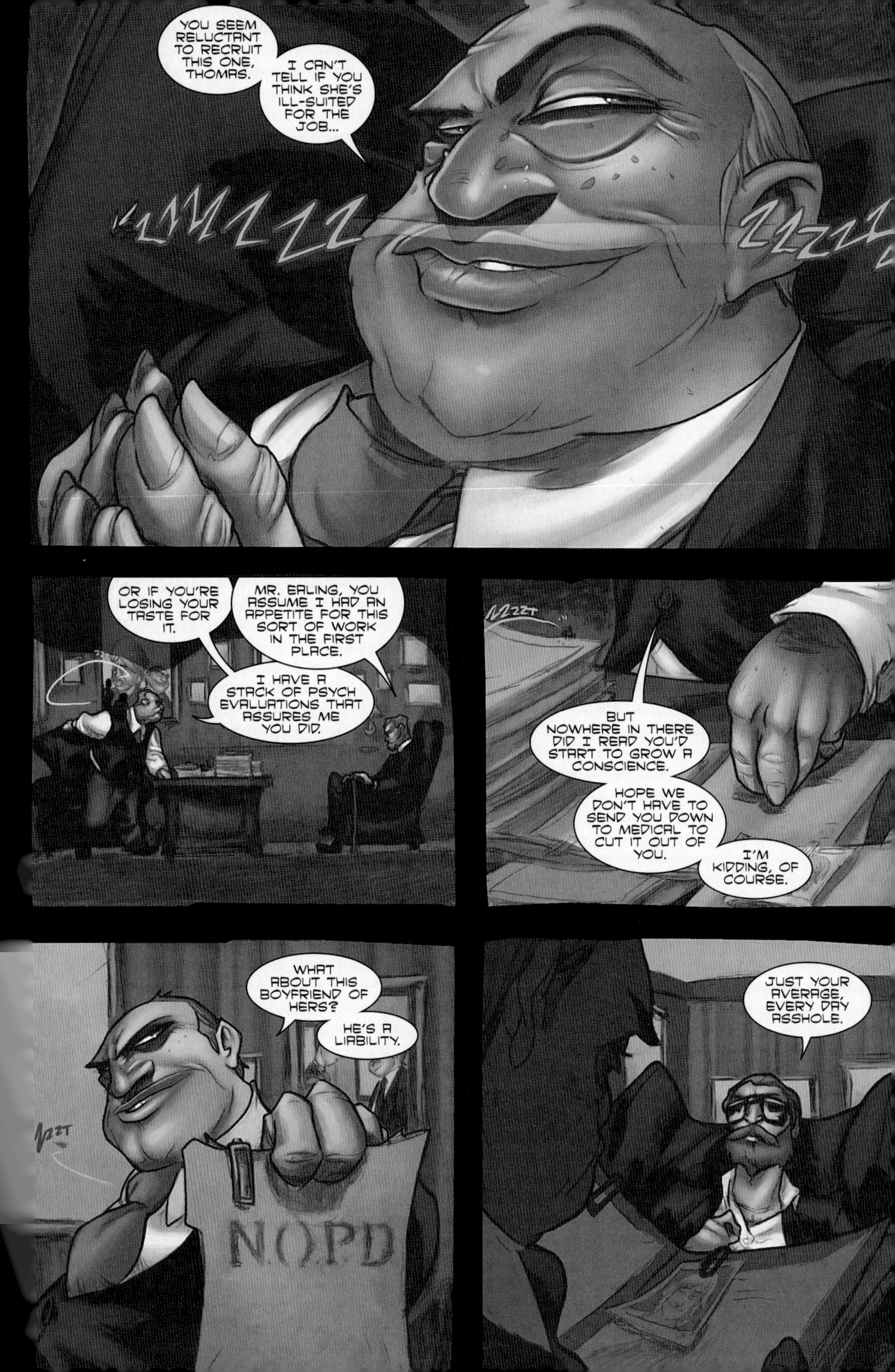
YOU SEEM RELUCTANT TO RECRUIT THIS ONE, THOMAS.
I CAN'T TELL IF YOU THINK SHE'S ILL-SUITED FOR THE JOB...
OR IF YOU'RE LOSING YOUR TASTE FOR IT.
MR. EARLING, YOU ASSUME I HAD AN APPETITE FOR THIS SORT OF WORK IN THE FIRST PLACE.
I HAVE A STACK OF PSYCH EVALUATIONS THAT ASSURES ME YOU DID.
BUT NOWHERE IN THERE DID I READ YOU'D START TO GROW A CONSCIENCE.
HOPE WE DON'T HAVE TO SEND YOU DOWN TO MEDICAL TO CUT IT OUT OF YOU.
I'M KIDDING, OF COURSE.
WHAT ABOUT THIS BOYFRIEND OF HERS?
HE'S A LIABILITY.
N.O.P.D
JUST YOUR AVERAGE, EVERY DAY ASSHOLE.

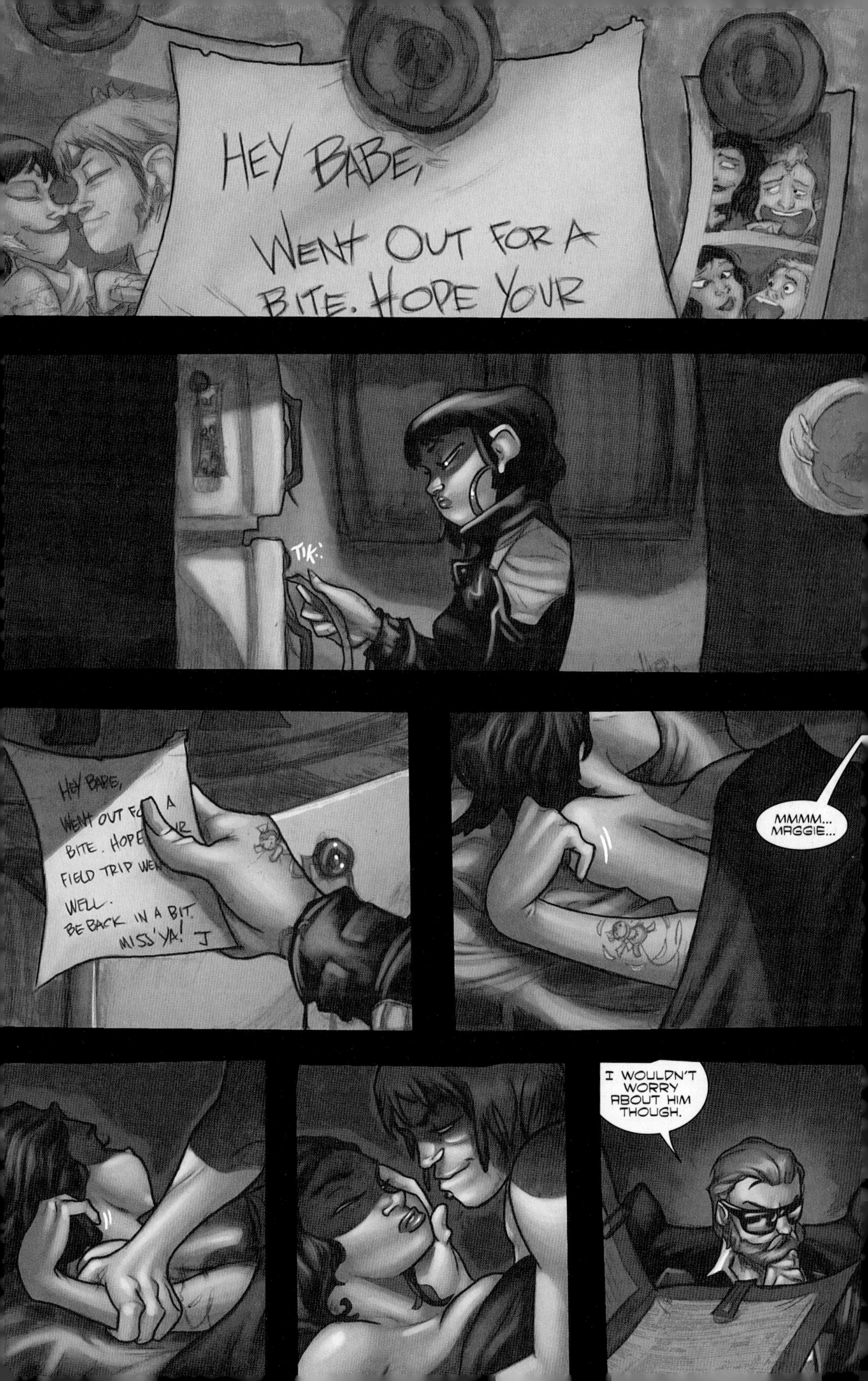
HEY BABE,
WENT OUT FOR A
BITE. HOPE YOUR
TIK:
HEY BABE,
WENT OUT FO A
BITE. HOPE R
FIELD TRIP WE
WELL.
BE BACK IN A BIT.
MISS'YA! J
MMMM... MAGGIE...
I WOULDN'T WORRY ABOUT HIM THOUGH.

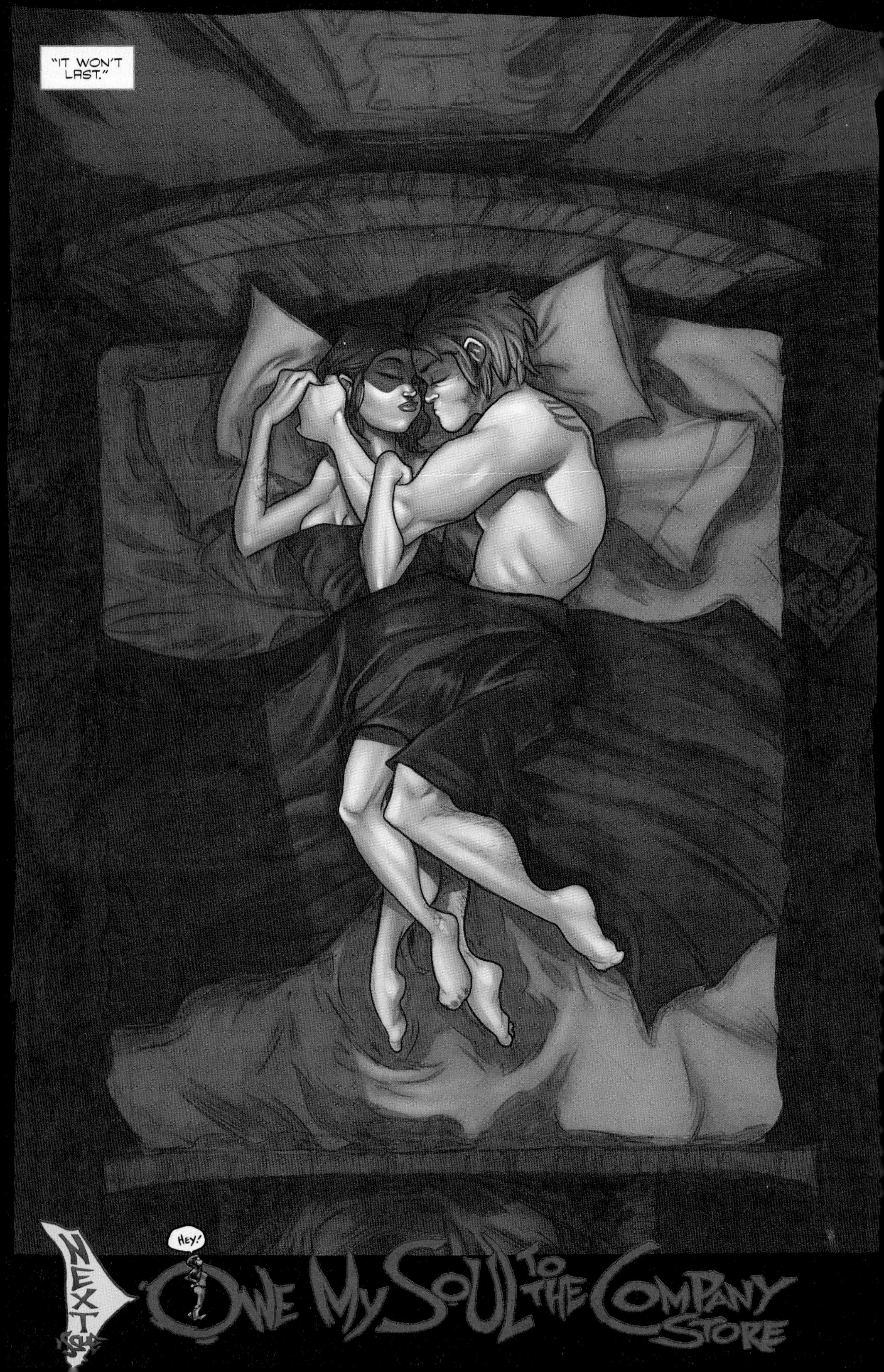
"IT WON'T LAST."
HEY!
NEXT ISSUE
OWE MY SOUL TO THE COMPANY STORE

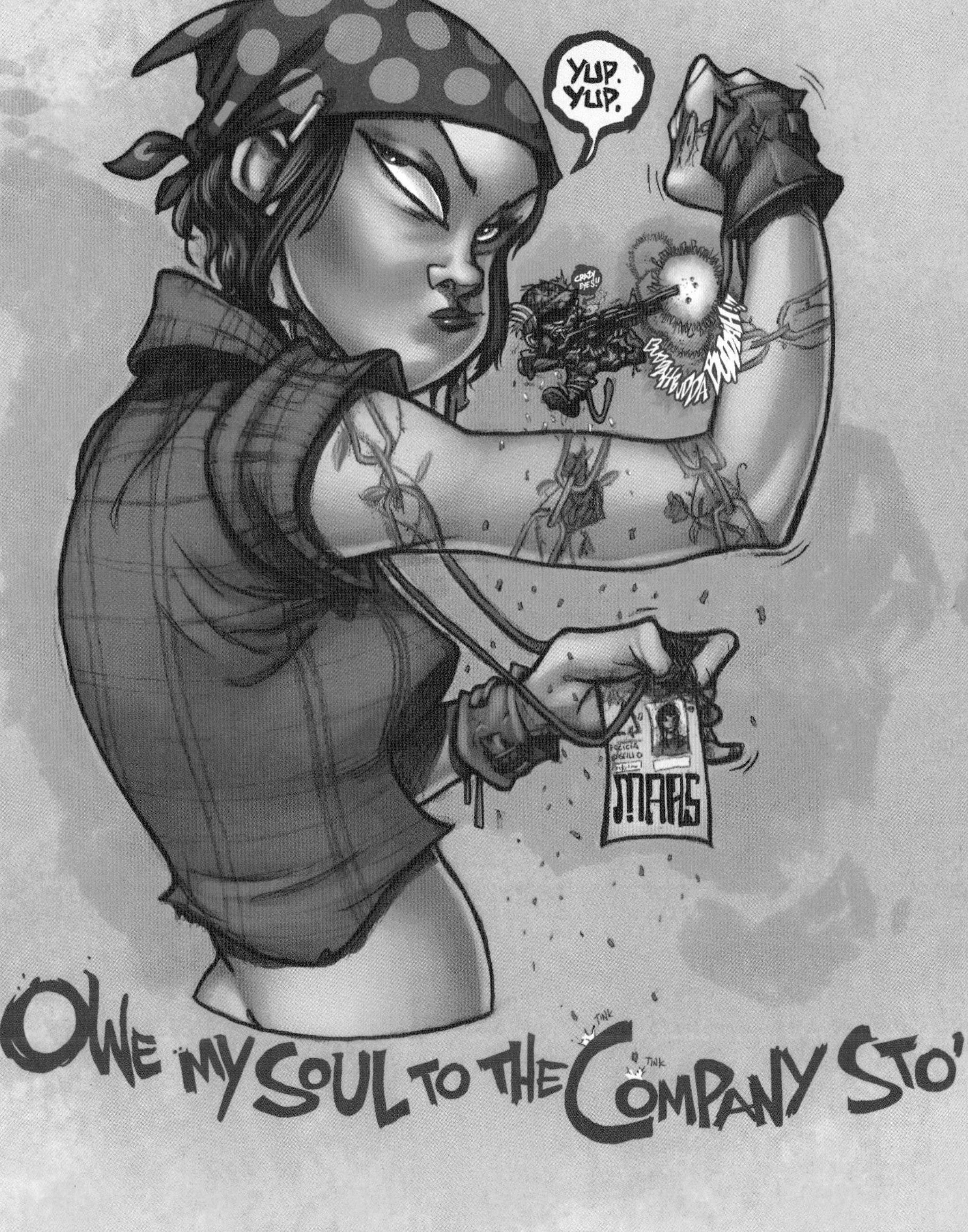
YUP. YUP.
CRAZY EYES!!
J!MARS
OWE MY SOUL TO THE COMPANY STO'
TINK
TINK

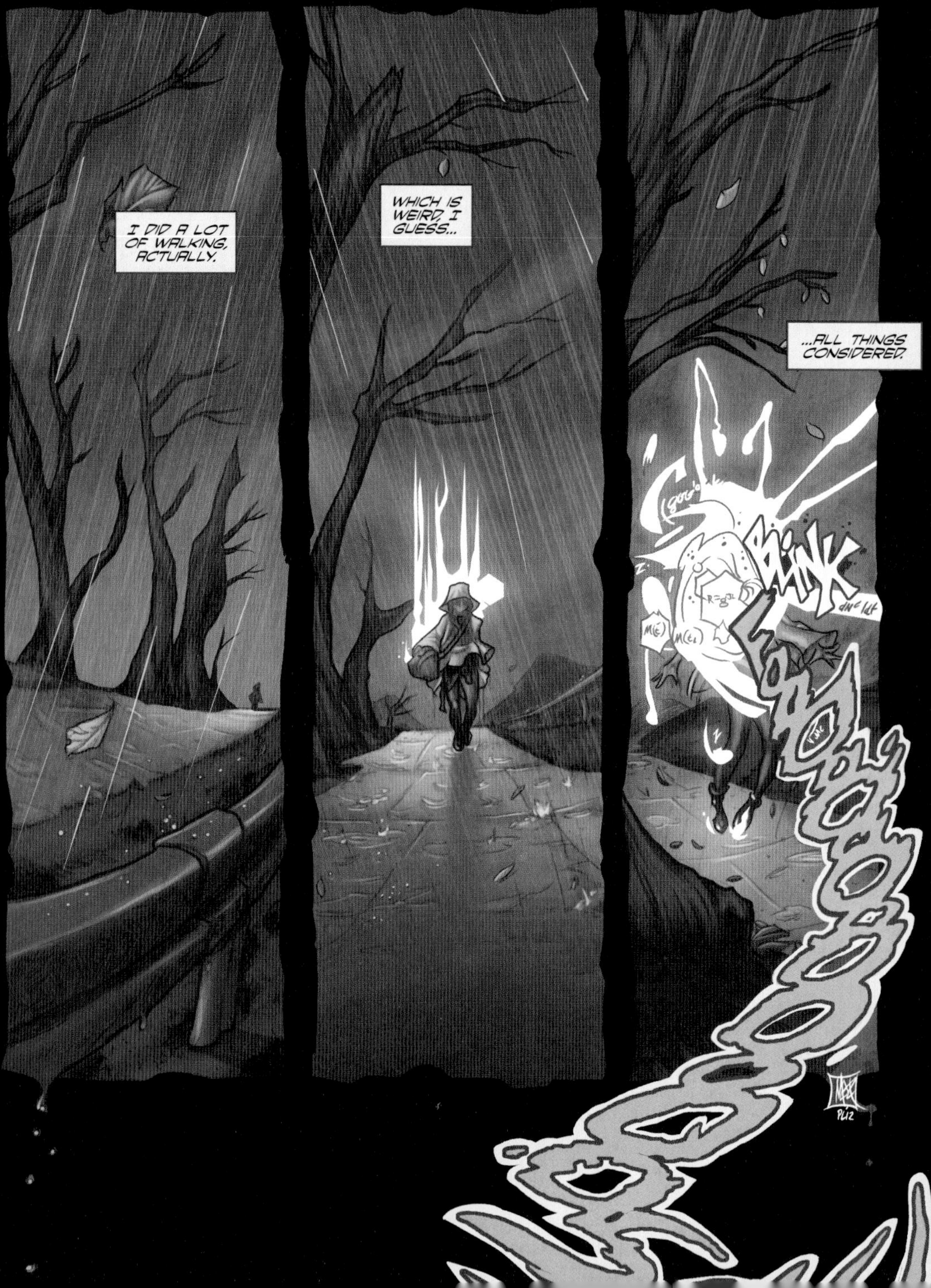
I DID A LOT OF WALKING, ACTUALLY.
WHICH IS WEIRD, I GUESS...
...ALL THINGS CONSIDERED.
BLINK

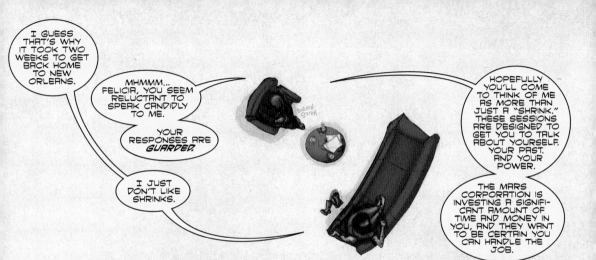

I GUESS THAT'S WHY IT TOOK TWO WEEKS TO GET BACK HOME TO NEW ORLEANS.

MHMMM... FELICIA, YOU SEEM RELUCTANT TO SPEAK CANDIDLY TO ME.

YOUR RESPONSES ARE *GUARDED.*

I JUST DON'T LIKE SHRINKS.

HOPEFULLY YOU'LL COME TO THINK OF ME AS MORE THAN JUST A "SHRINK." THESE SESSIONS ARE DESIGNED TO GET YOU TO TALK ABOUT YOURSELF. YOUR PAST. AND YOUR POWER.

THE MARS CORPORATION IS INVESTING A SIGNIFICANT AMOUNT OF TIME AND MONEY IN YOU, AND THEY WANT TO BE CERTAIN YOU CAN HANDLE THE JOB.

THERE'S NOTHING I CAN'T HANDLE.

TAP

IT WAS A MOMENT OF HIGH STRESS WHEN YOU FIRST DISCOVERED YOUR TALENT?

"YOU COULD SAY THAT."

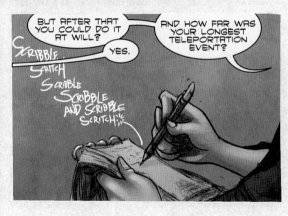

BUT AFTER THAT YOU COULD DO IT AT WILL?

YES.

AND HOW FAR WAS YOUR LONGEST TELEPORTATION EVENT?

SCRIBBLE
SCRITCH
Scribble
Scribble
AND SCRIBBLE
SCRITCH

I DON'T KNOW. A FEW MILES. MAYBE A LITTLE MORE.

BASICALLY IF I CAN SEE IT, I CAN BLINK TO IT.

UNTIL RECENTLY, ANYWAY.

SCRIBBLE
SCRITCH
SCRITCH
FLIP

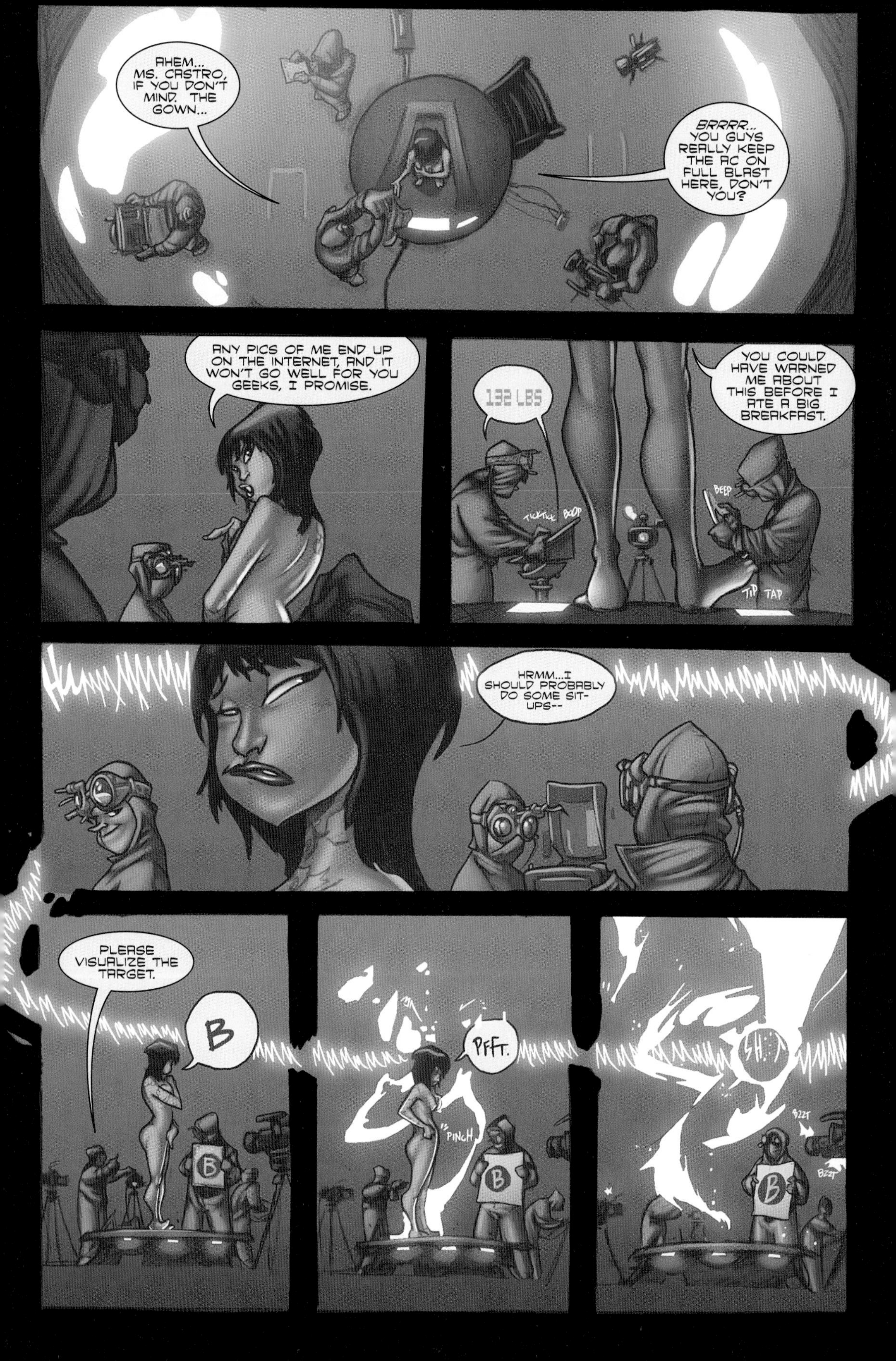
AHEM... MS. CASTRO, IF YOU DON'T MIND. THE GOWN...
BRRRR... YOU GUYS REALLY KEEP THE AC ON FULL BLAST HERE, DON'T YOU?
ANY PICS OF ME END UP ON THE INTERNET, AND IT WON'T GO WELL FOR YOU GEEKS, I PROMISE.
132 LBS
YOU COULD HAVE WARNED ME ABOUT THIS BEFORE I ATE A BIG BREAKFAST.
TICKTICK
BOOP
BEEP
TIP TAP
HRMM...I SHOULD PROBABLY DO SOME SIT-UPS--
PLEASE VISUALIZE THE TARGET.
B
PFFT.
PINCH
SH!T
BZZT
BZZT

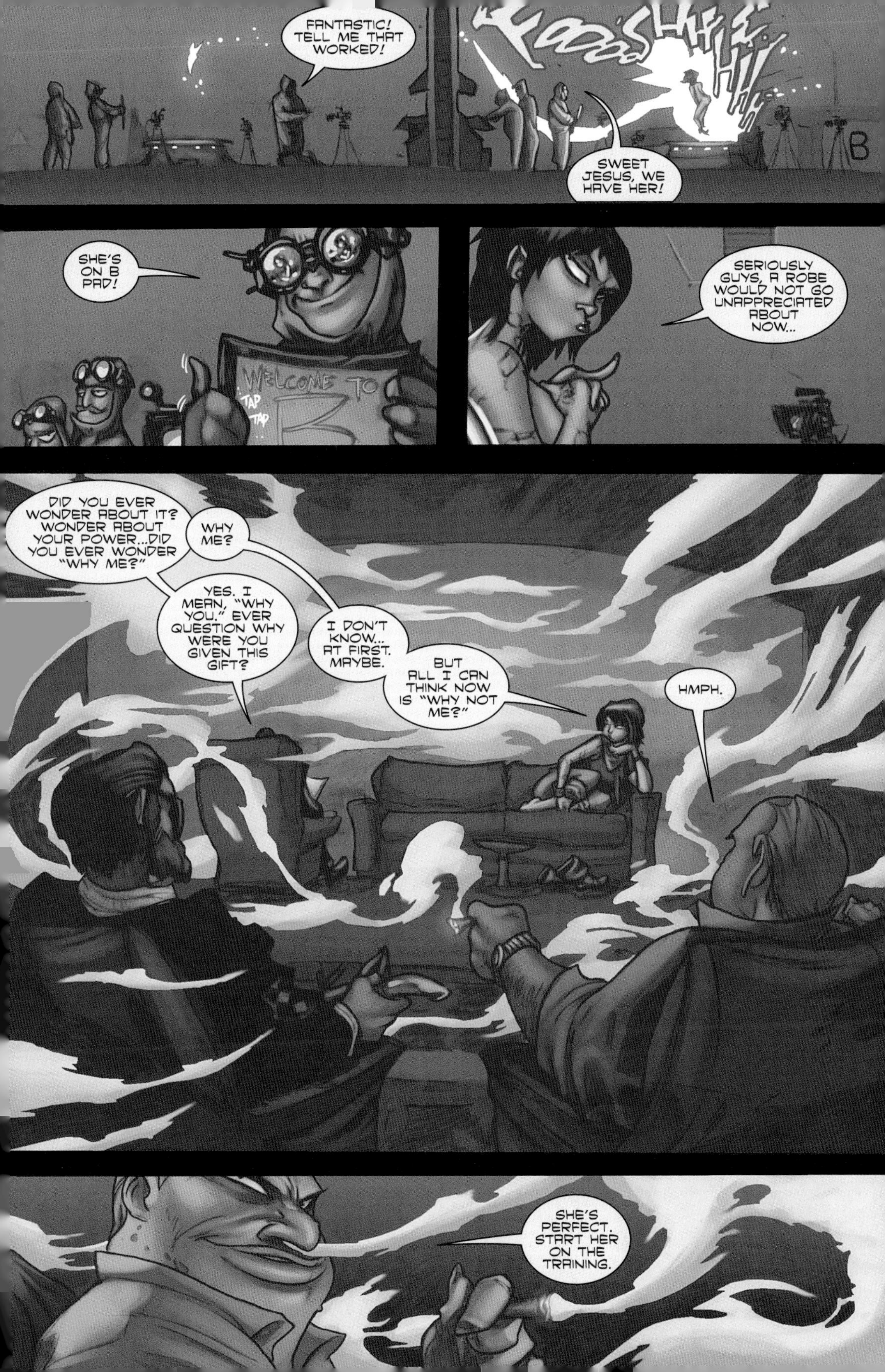
FANTASTIC! TELL ME THAT WORKED!
SWEET JESUS, WE HAVE HER!
B
SHE'S ON B PAD!
WELCOME TO B
TAP TAP
SERIOUSLY GUYS, A ROBE WOULD NOT GO UNAPPRECIATED ABOUT NOW...
DID YOU EVER WONDER ABOUT IT? WONDER ABOUT YOUR POWER...DID YOU EVER WONDER "WHY ME?"
WHY ME?
YES. I MEAN, "WHY YOU." EVER QUESTION WHY WERE YOU GIVEN THIS GIFT?
I DON'T KNOW... AT FIRST. MAYBE.
BUT ALL I CAN THINK NOW IS "WHY NOT ME?"
HMPH.
SHE'S PERFECT. START HER ON THE TRAINING.

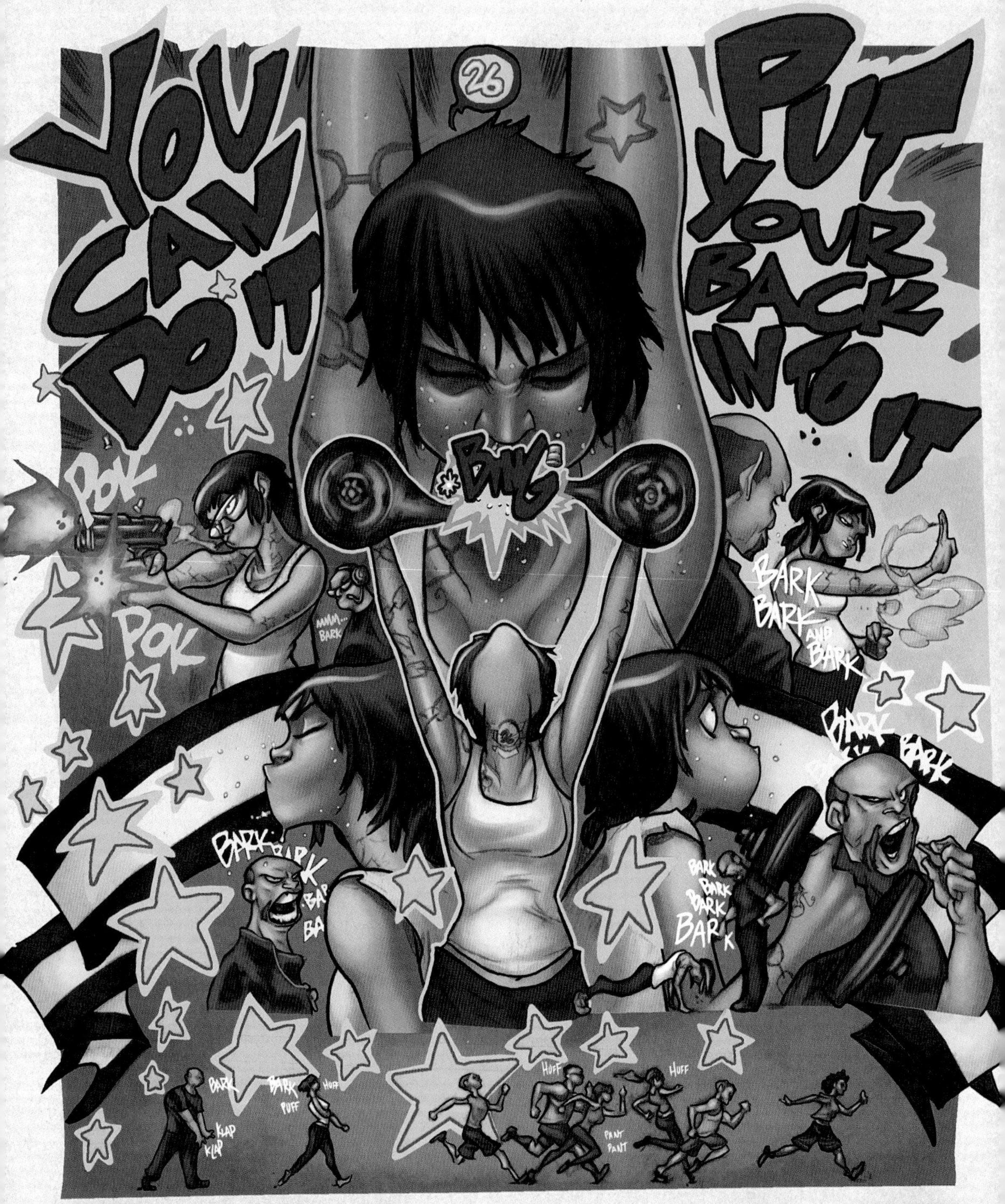
YOU CAN DO IT
26
PUT YOUR BACK INTO IT
POK
BANG
POK
MMM... BARK
BARK BARK AND BARK
BARK BARK
BARK BARK BAP BA
BARK BARK BARK BAR K
BARK
BARK PUFF
HUFF
KLAP KLAP
HUFF
HUFF
PANT PANT

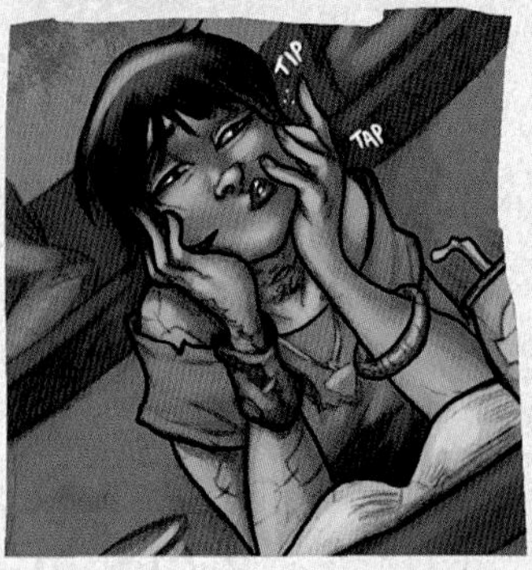
TIP
TAP

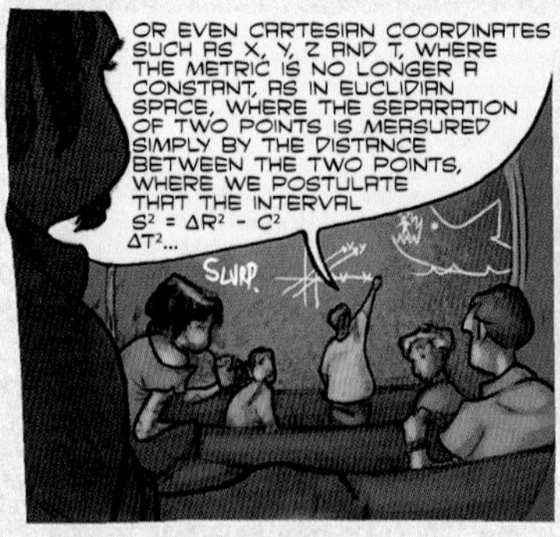
OR EVEN CARTESIAN COORDINATES SUCH AS X, Y, Z AND T, WHERE THE METRIC IS NO LONGER A CONSTANT, AS IN EUCLIDIAN SPACE, WHERE THE SEPARATION OF TWO POINTS IS MEASURED SIMPLY BY THE DISTANCE BETWEEN THE TWO POINTS, WHERE WE POSTULATE THAT THE INTERVAL $S^2 = \Delta R^2 - C^2 \Delta T^2$...
SLURP

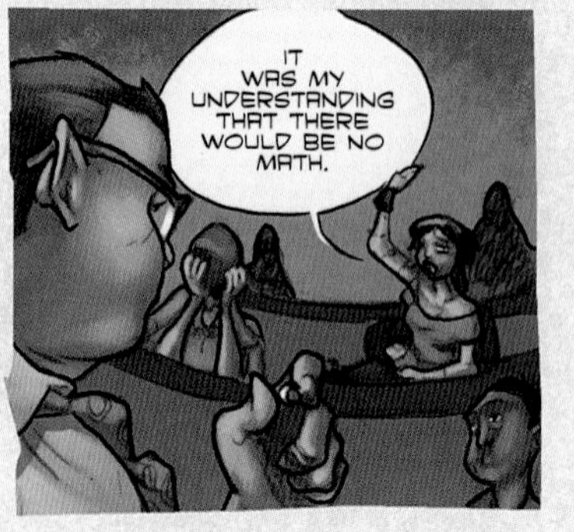
IT WAS MY UNDERSTANDING THAT THERE WOULD BE NO MATH.

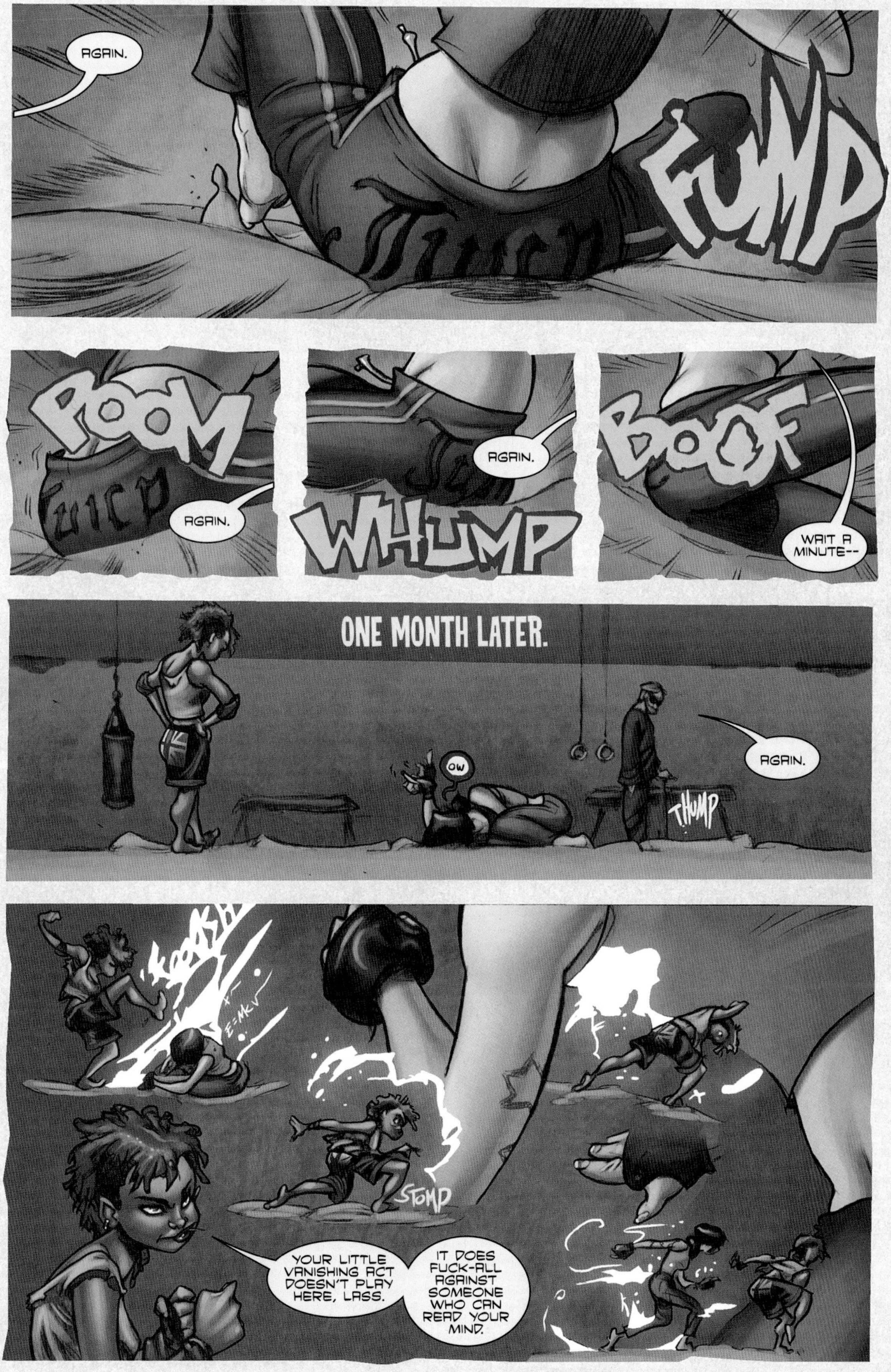
AGAIN.
FUMP
POOM
AGAIN.
AGAIN.
WHUMP
BOOF
WAIT A MINUTE--
ONE MONTH LATER.
OW
AGAIN.
THUMP
STOMP
YOUR LITTLE VANISHING ACT DOESN'T PLAY HERE, LASS.
IT DOES FUCK-ALL AGAINST SOMEONE WHO CAN READ YOUR MIND.

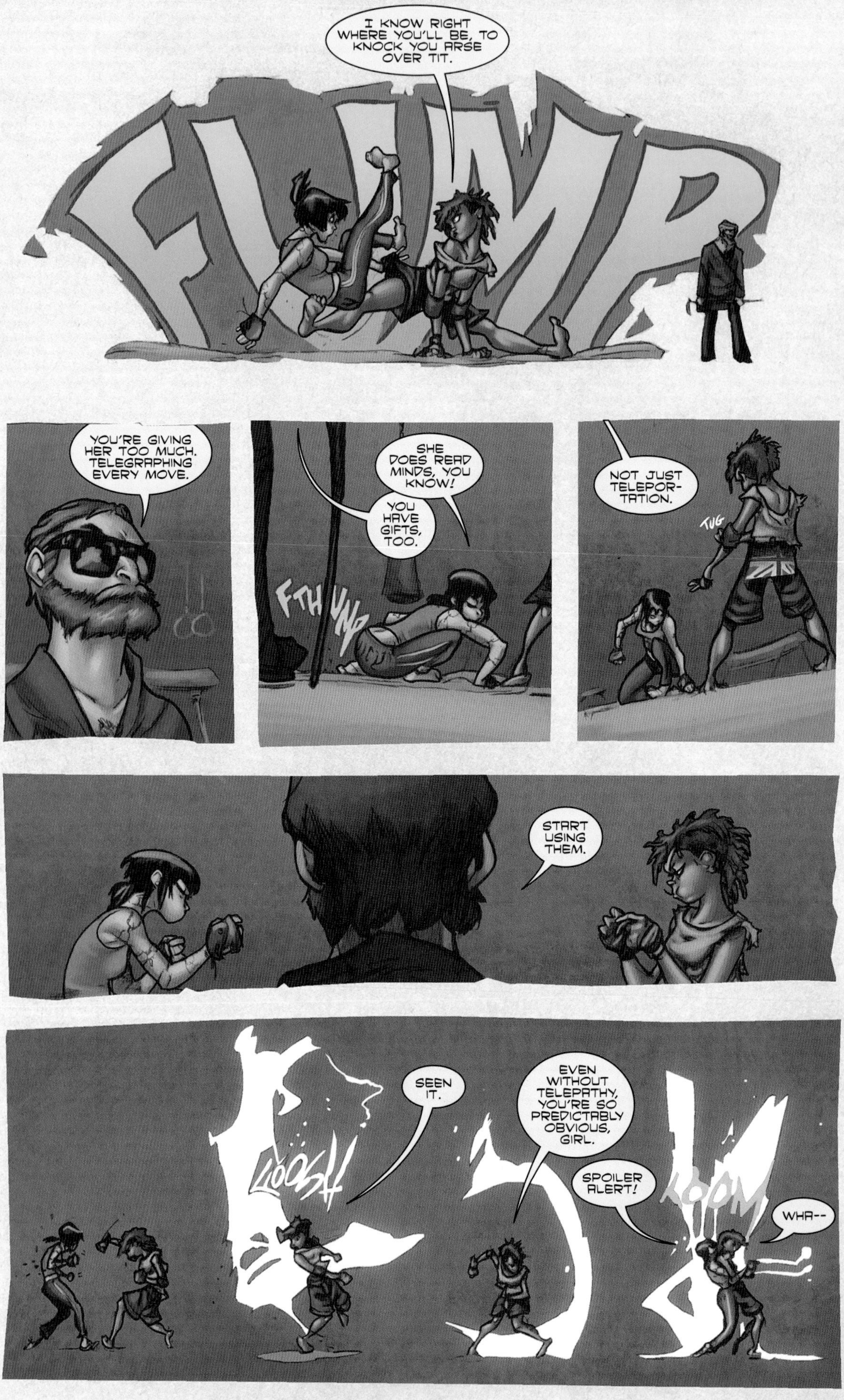
I KNOW RIGHT WHERE YOU'LL BE, TO KNOCK YOU ARSE OVER TIT.
FLUMP
YOU'RE GIVING HER TOO MUCH. TELEGRAPHING EVERY MOVE.
SHE DOES READ MINDS, YOU KNOW!
YOU HAVE GIFTS, TOO.
FTHUMP
NOT JUST TELEPORTATION.
TUG
START USING THEM.
SEEN IT.
WOOSH
EVEN WITHOUT TELEPATHY, YOU'RE SO PREDICTABLY OBVIOUS, GIRL.
SPOILER ALERT!
WHA--

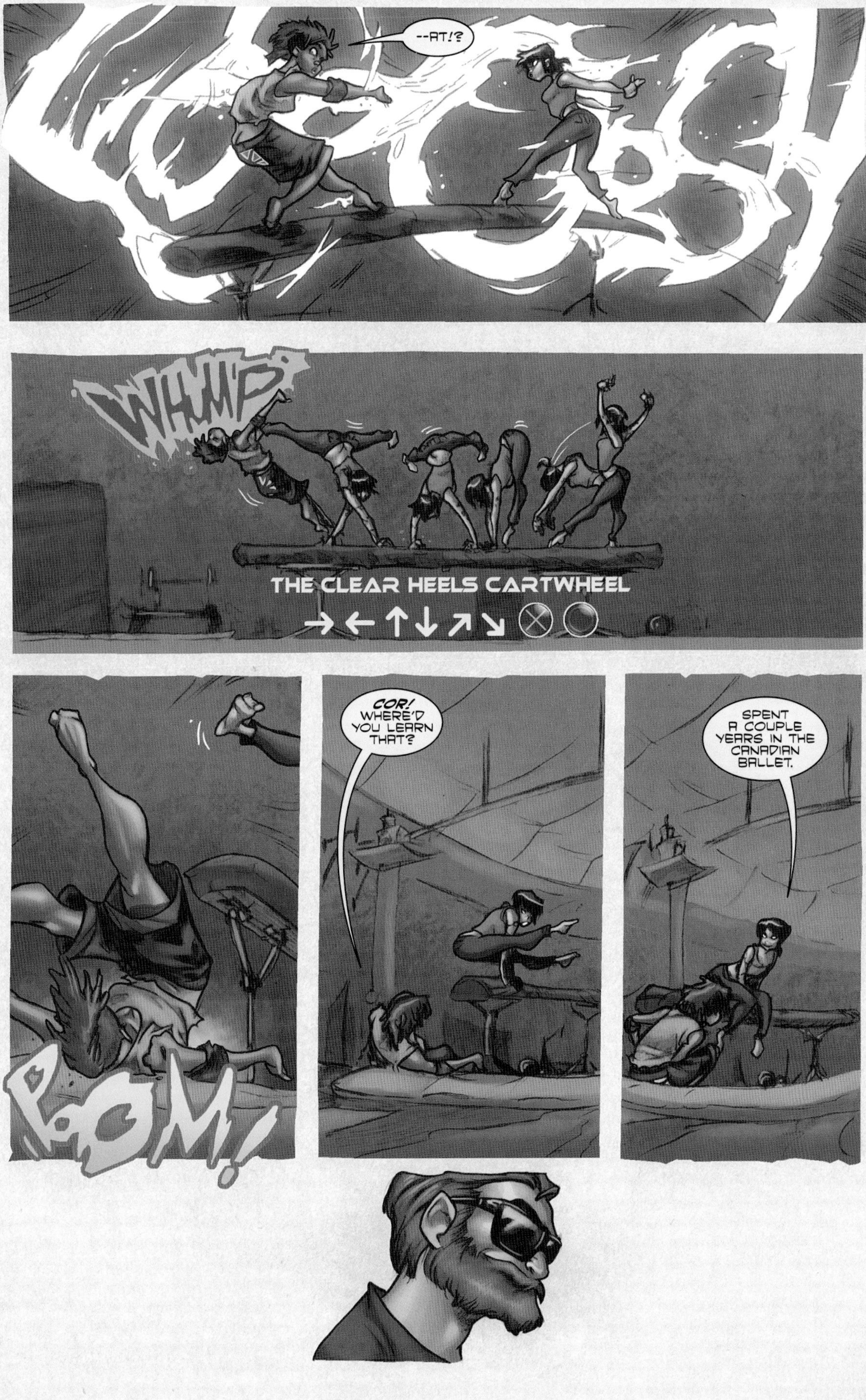
--AT!?
WHUMP
THE CLEAR HEELS CARTWHEEL
→ ← ↑ ↓ ↗ ↘
BOOM!
COR! WHERE'D YOU LEARN THAT?
SPENT A COUPLE YEARS IN THE CANADIAN BALLET.

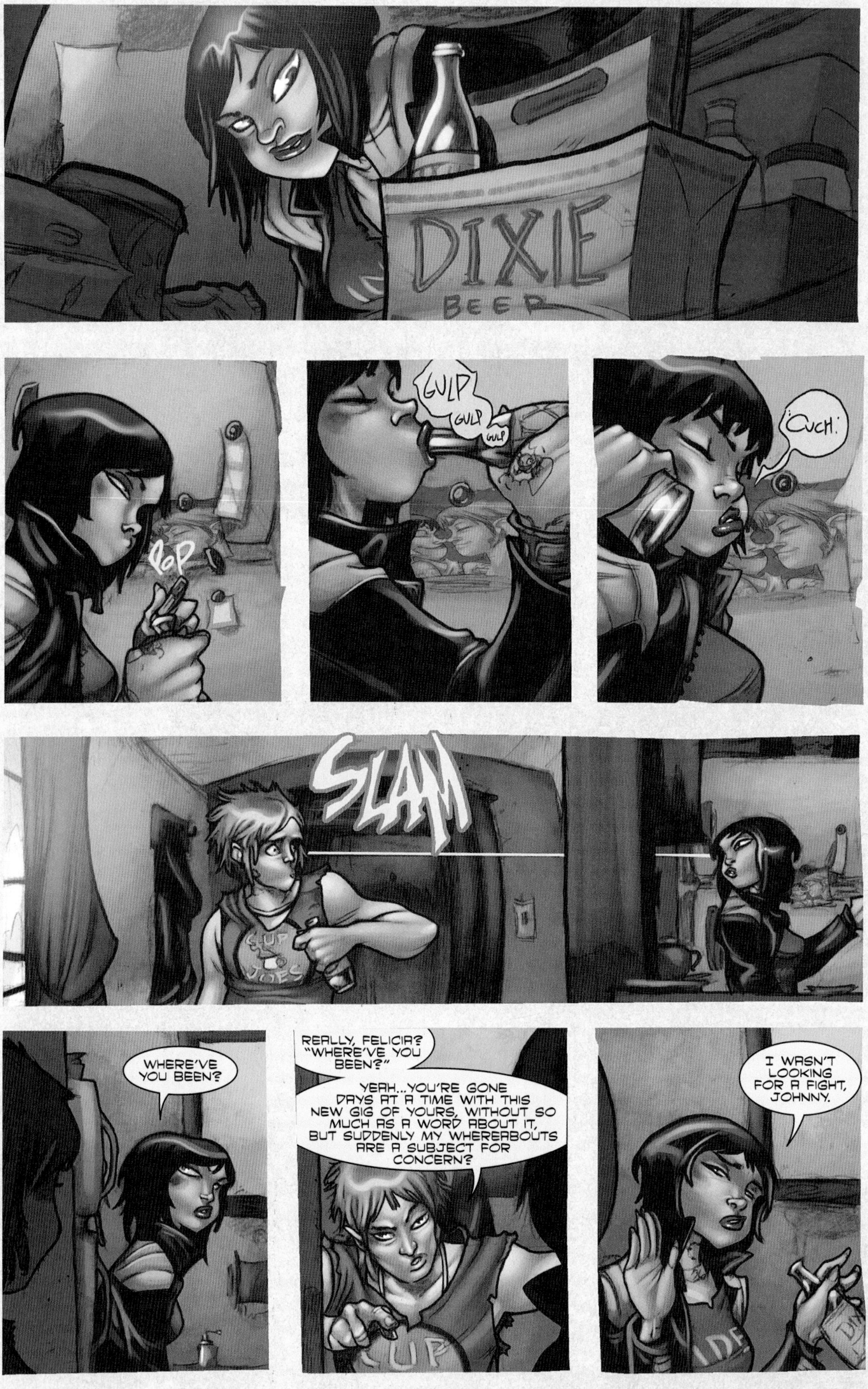
DIXIE
BEER
POP
GULP
GULP
GULP
¡OUCH!
SLAM
CUP JOE'S
WHERE'VE YOU BEEN?
REALLY, FELICIA? "WHERE'VE YOU BEEN?"
YEAH...YOU'RE GONE DAYS AT A TIME WITH THIS NEW GIG OF YOURS, WITHOUT SO MUCH AS A WORD ABOUT IT, BUT SUDDENLY MY WHEREABOUTS ARE A SUBJECT FOR CONCERN?
I WASN'T LOOKING FOR A FIGHT, JOHNNY.

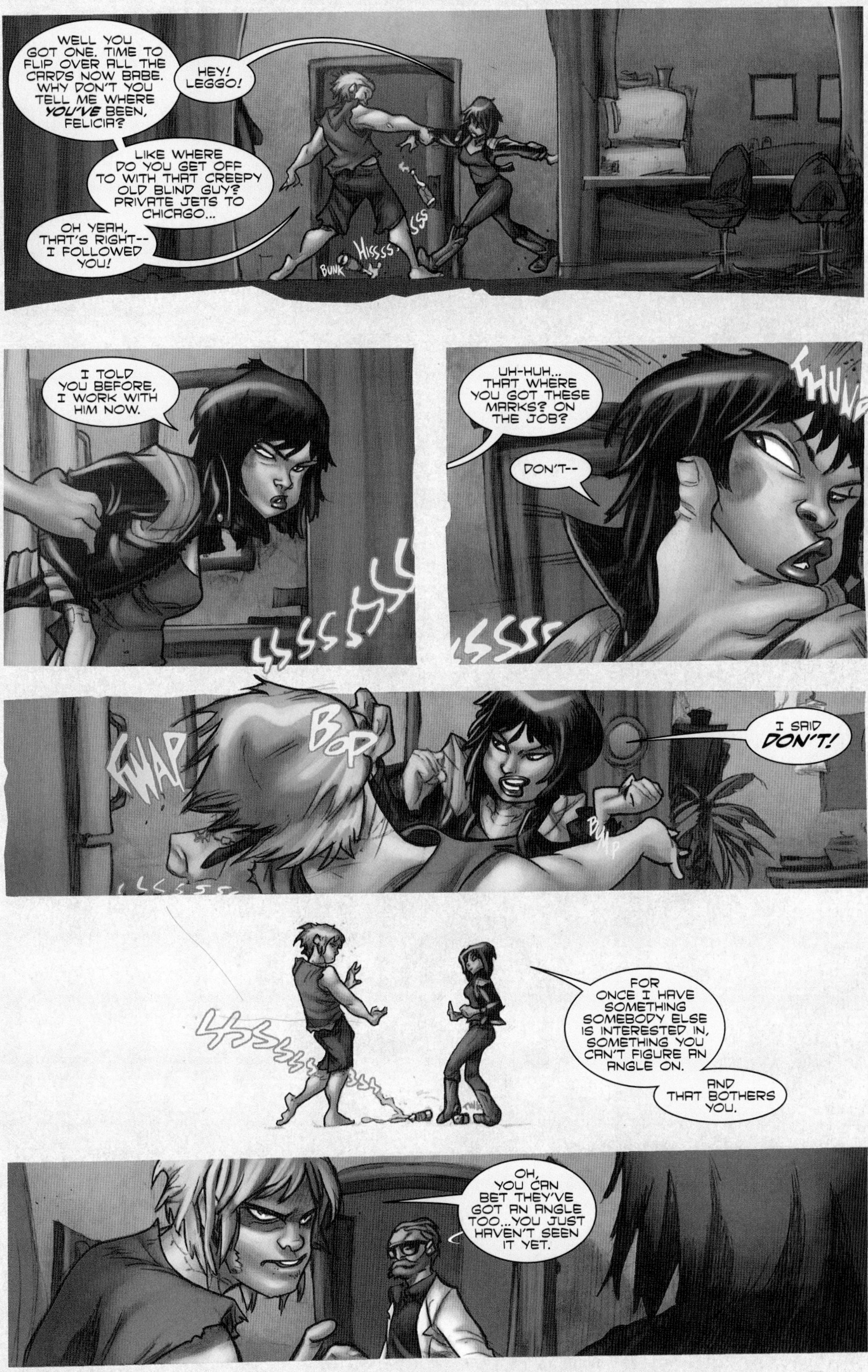
WELL YOU GOT ONE. TIME TO FLIP OVER ALL THE CARDS NOW BABE. WHY DON'T YOU TELL ME WHERE ***YOU'VE*** BEEN, FELICIA?
HEY! LEGGO!
LIKE WHERE DO YOU GET OFF TO WITH THAT CREEPY OLD BLIND GUY? PRIVATE JETS TO CHICAGO...
OH YEAH, THAT'S RIGHT-- I FOLLOWED YOU!
SSS
HISSSS
BUNK
I TOLD YOU BEFORE, I WORK WITH HIM NOW.
SSSSSSS
UH-HUH... THAT WHERE YOU GOT THESE MARKS? ON THE JOB?
DON'T--
THUNG
SSSSS
FWAP
BOP
I SAID ***DON'T!***
BUMP
SSSSSSS
FOR ONCE I HAVE SOMETHING SOMEBODY ELSE IS INTERESTED IN, SOMETHING YOU CAN'T FIGURE AN ANGLE ON.
AND THAT BOTHERS YOU.
OH, YOU CAN BET THEY'VE GOT AN ANGLE TOO...YOU JUST HAVEN'T SEEN IT YET.

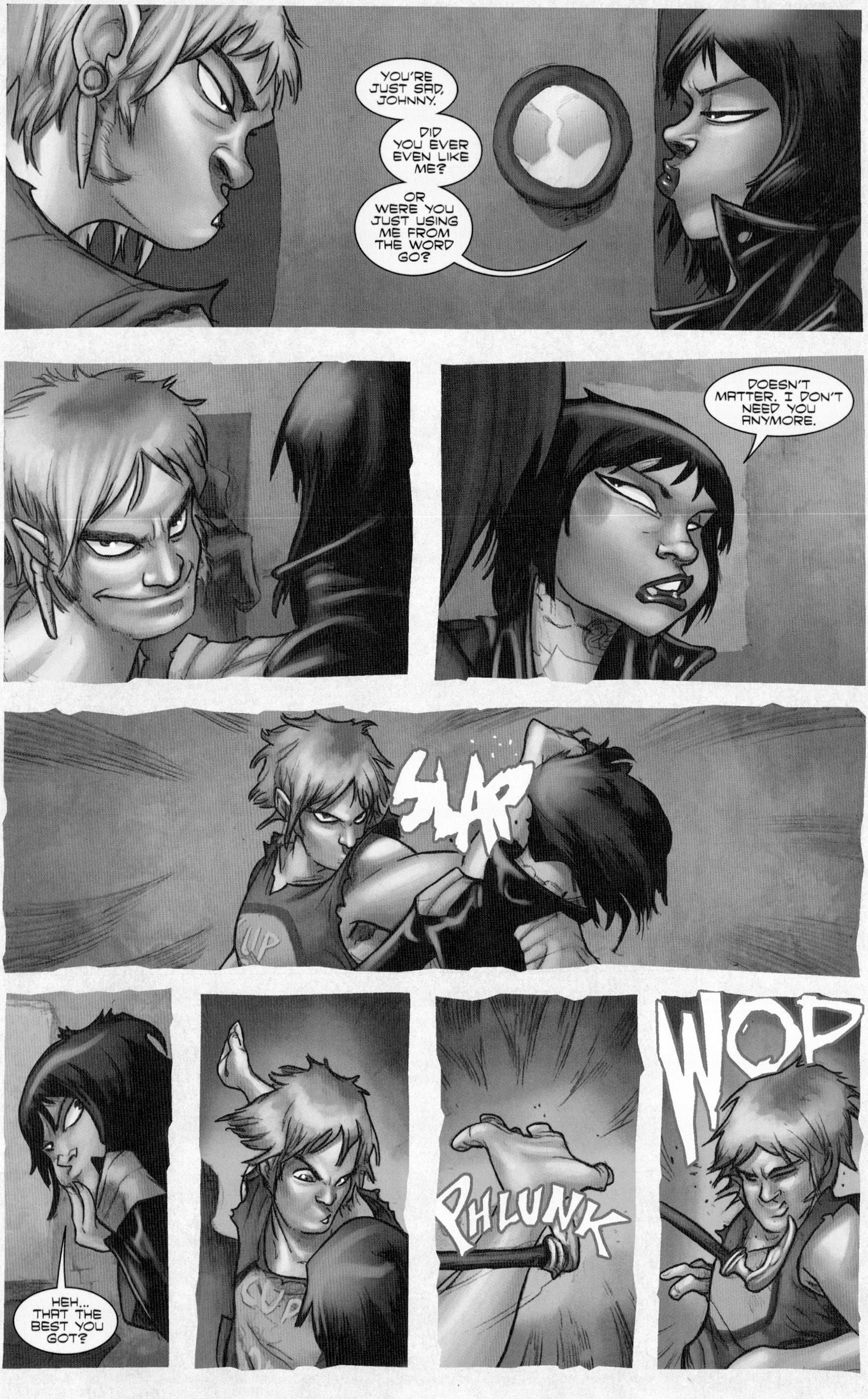
YOU'RE JUST SAD, JOHNNY.
DID YOU EVER EVEN LIKE ME?
OR WERE YOU JUST USING ME FROM THE WORD GO?
DOESN'T MATTER. I DON'T NEED YOU ANYMORE.
SLAP
HEH... THAT THE BEST YOU GOT?
PHLUNK
WOP

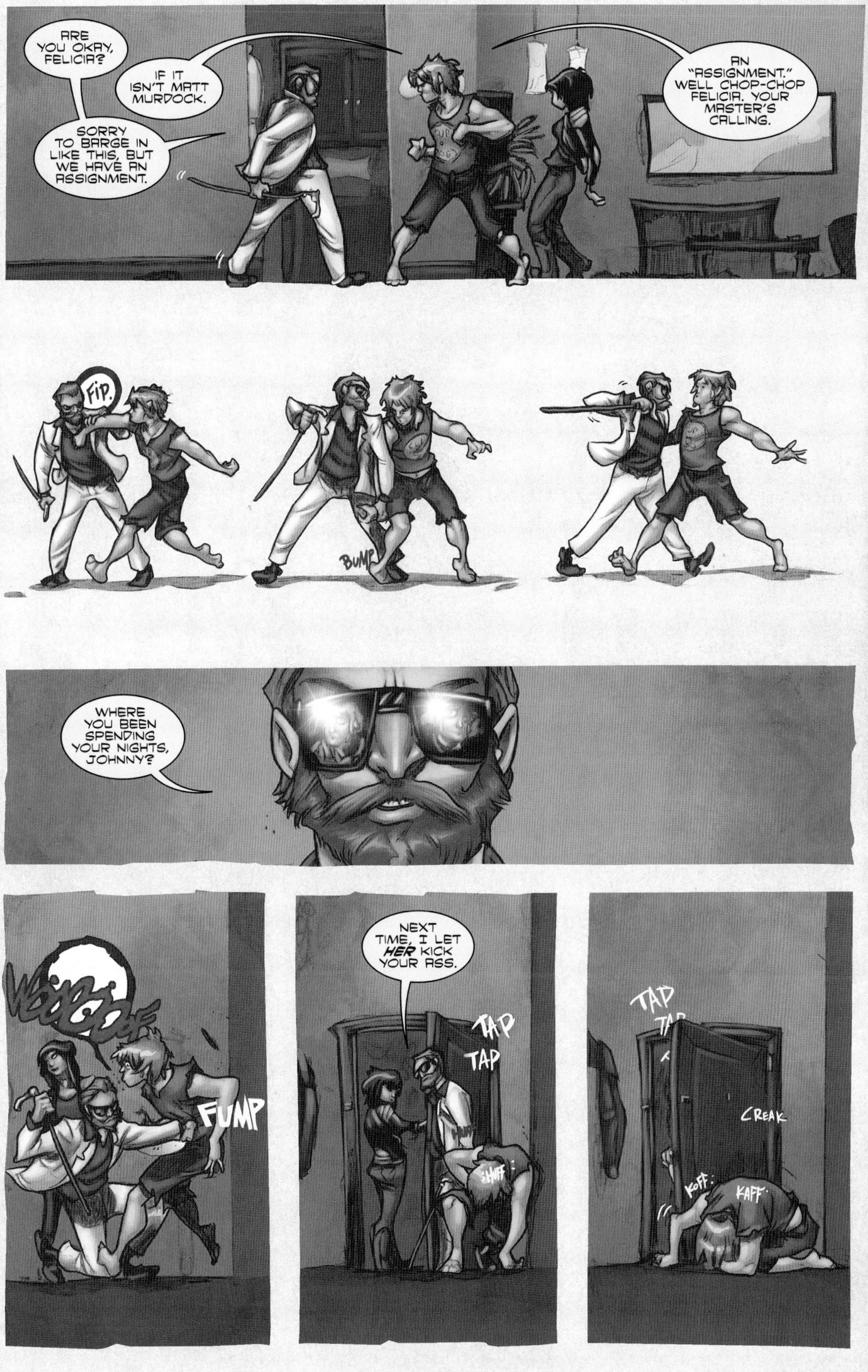
ARE YOU OKAY, FELICIA?
SORRY TO BARGE IN LIKE THIS, BUT WE HAVE AN ASSIGNMENT.
IF IT ISN'T MATT MURDOCK.
AN "ASSIGNMENT." WELL CHOP-CHOP FELICIA. YOUR MASTER'S CALLING.
FIP.
BUMP
WHERE YOU BEEN SPENDING YOUR NIGHTS, JOHNNY?
FUMP
NEXT TIME, I LET *HER* KICK YOUR ASS.
TAP
TAP
HUFF
TAP
CREAK
KOFF
KAFF

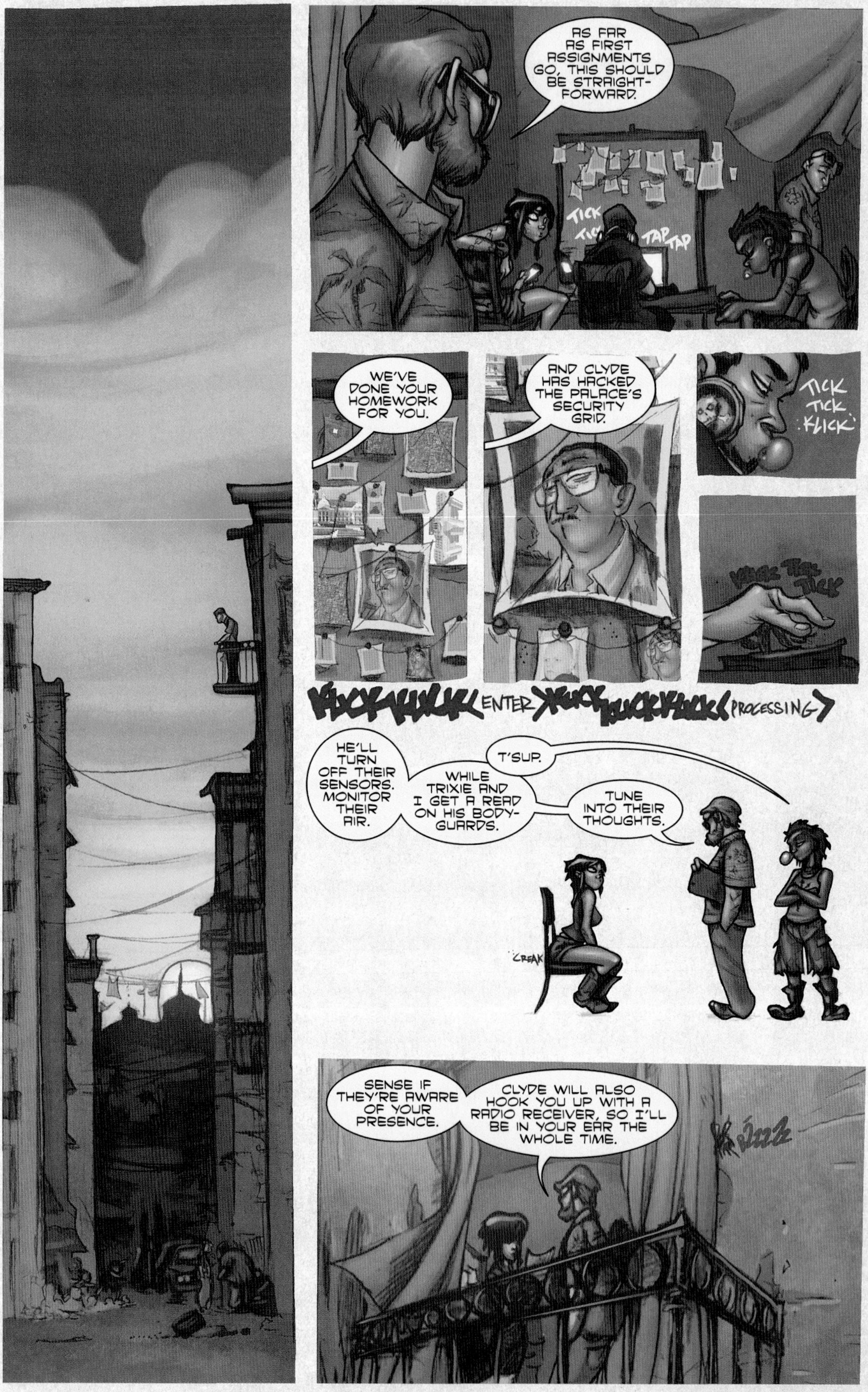
AS FAR AS FIRST ASSIGNMENTS GO, THIS SHOULD BE STRAIGHT-FORWARD.
TICK TICK
TAP TAP
WE'VE DONE YOUR HOMEWORK FOR YOU.
AND CLYDE HAS HACKED THE PALACE'S SECURITY GRID.
TICK TICK KLICK
ENTER
PROCESSING
HE'LL TURN OFF THEIR SENSORS. MONITOR THEIR AIR.
T'SUP.
WHILE TRIXIE AND I GET A READ ON HIS BODY-GUARDS.
TUNE INTO THEIR THOUGHTS.
CREAK
SENSE IF THEY'RE AWARE OF YOUR PRESENCE.
CLYDE WILL ALSO HOOK YOU UP WITH A RADIO RECEIVER, SO I'LL BE IN YOUR EAR THE WHOLE TIME.

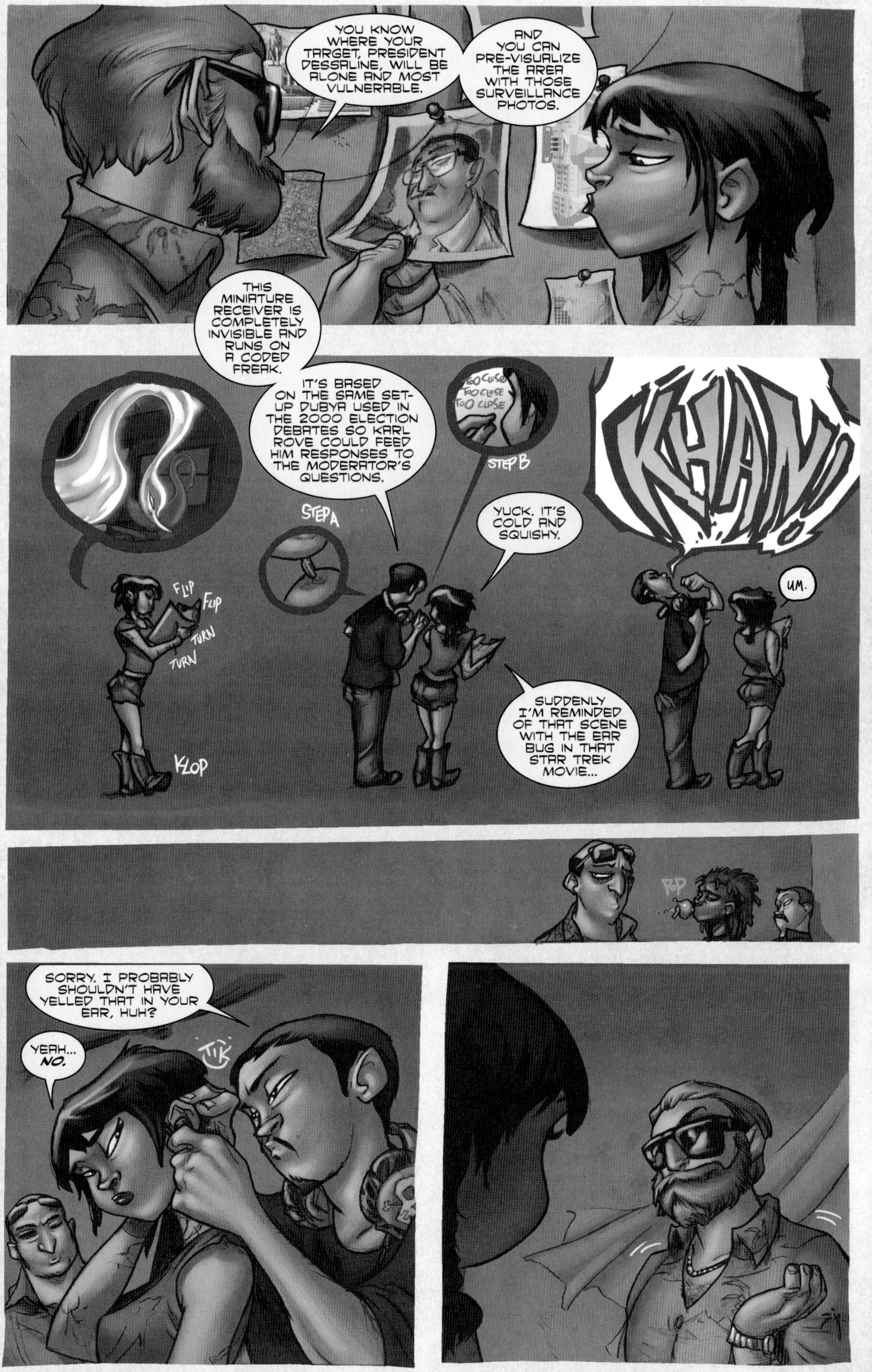
YOU KNOW WHERE YOUR TARGET, PRESIDENT DESSALINE, WILL BE ALONE AND MOST VULNERABLE.
AND YOU CAN PRE-VISUALIZE THE AREA WITH THOSE SURVEILLANCE PHOTOS.
THIS MINIATURE RECEIVER IS COMPLETELY INVISIBLE AND RUNS ON A CODED FREAK.
FLIP
FLIP
TURN
TURN
KLOP
IT'S BASED ON THE SAME SET-UP DUBYA USED IN THE 2000 ELECTION DEBATES SO KARL ROVE COULD FEED HIM RESPONSES TO THE MODERATOR'S QUESTIONS.
STEP A
TOO CLOSE TOO CLOSE TOO CLOSE
STEP B
YUCK. IT'S COLD AND SQUISHY.
SUDDENLY I'M REMINDED OF THAT SCENE WITH THE EAR BUG IN THAT STAR TREK MOVIE...
KHAN!
UM.
POP
SORRY. I PROBABLY SHOULDN'T HAVE YELLED THAT IN YOUR EAR, HUH?
YEAH... **NO.**
TIK

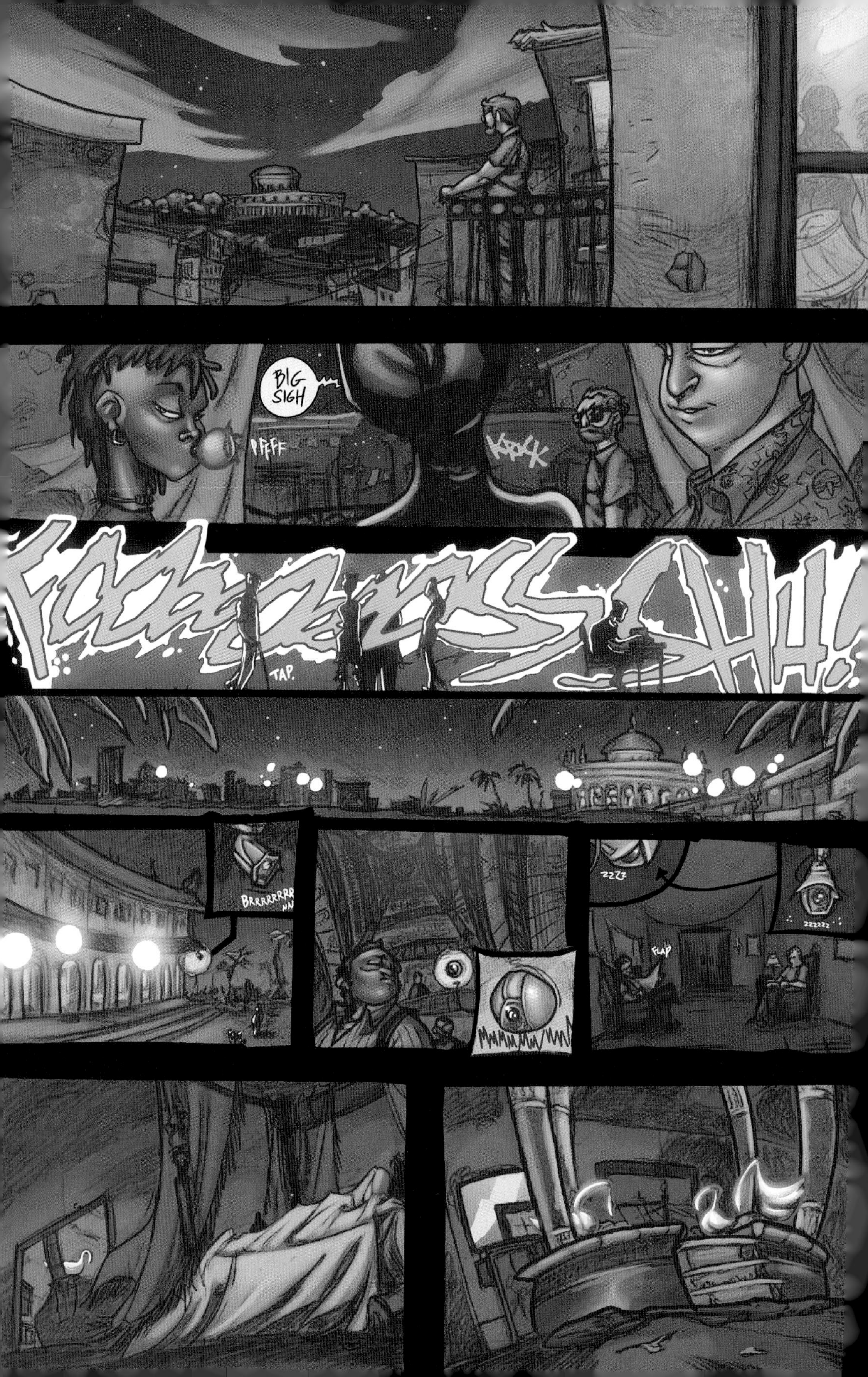
BIG SIGH
PFFFF
TAP.
BRRRRRRRNN
zzzz
zzzzzz
FLAP

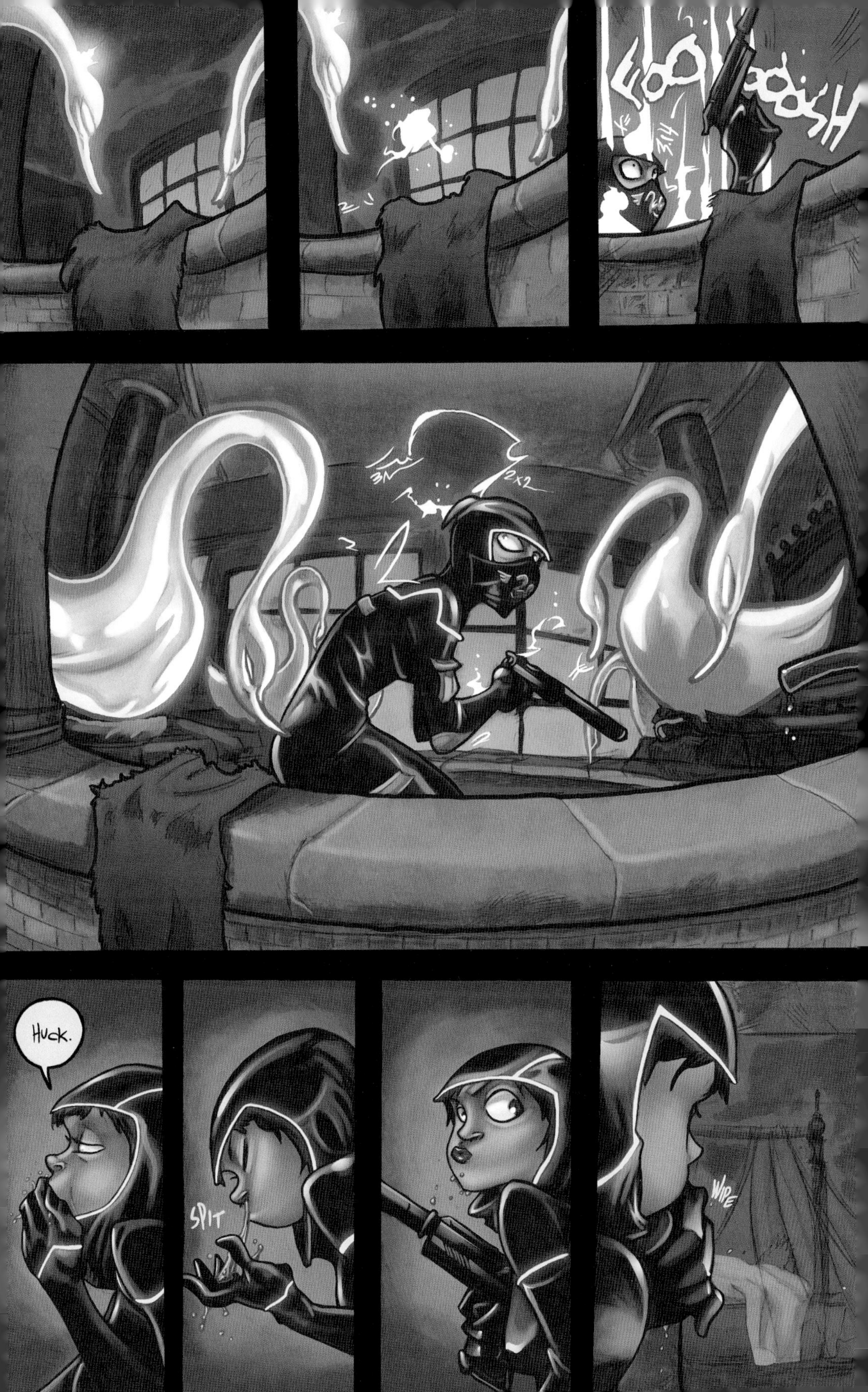
HUCK.
SPIT
WIPE

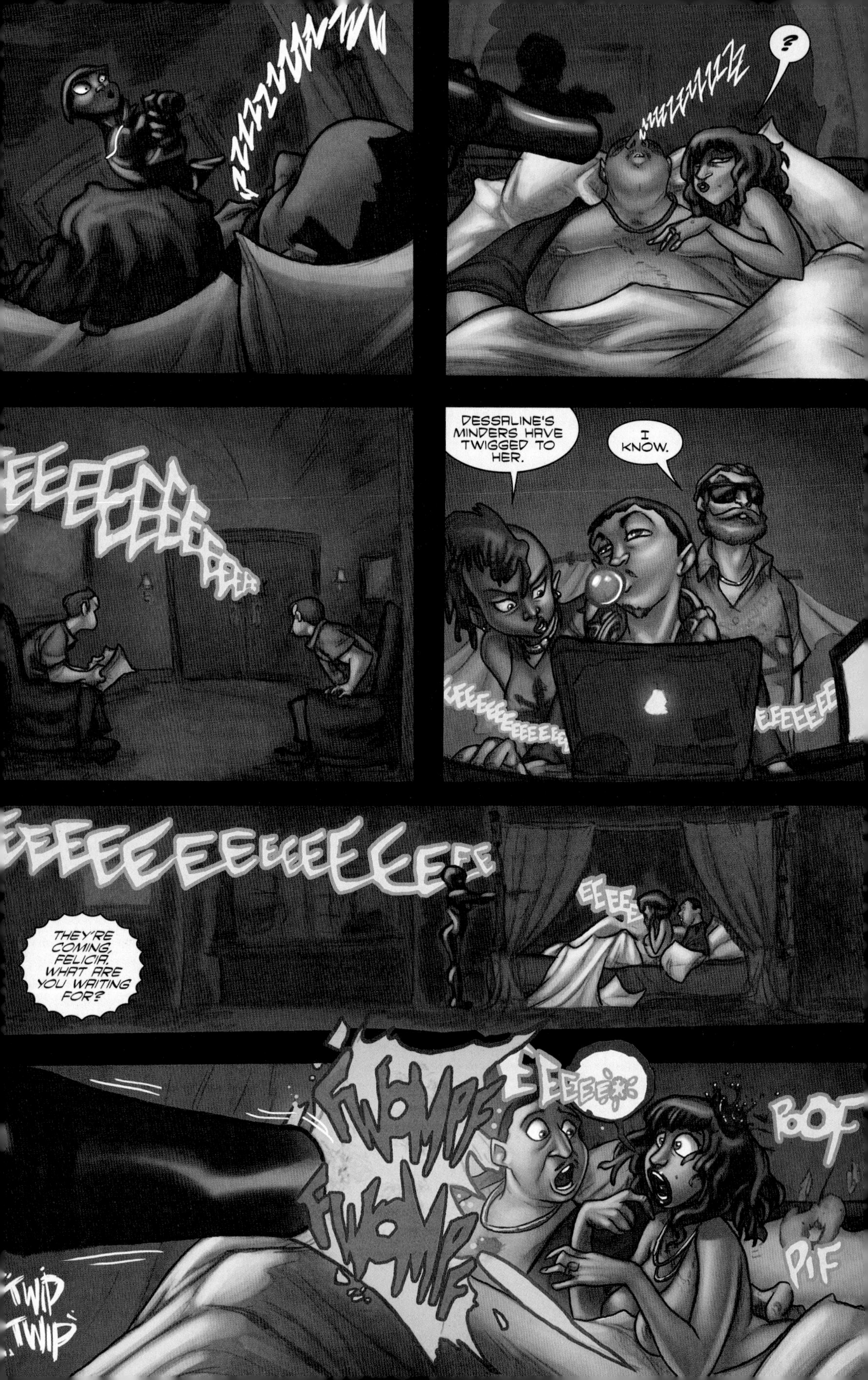
ZZZZZZZZZZZZZZZZ
ZZZZZZZZZZZZZZZZ
?
DESSALINE'S MINDERS HAVE TWIGGED TO HER.
I KNOW.
THEY'RE COMING, FELICIA, WHAT ARE YOU WAITING FOR?
FWOMPF
FWOMPF
POOF
PIF
TWIP
TWIP

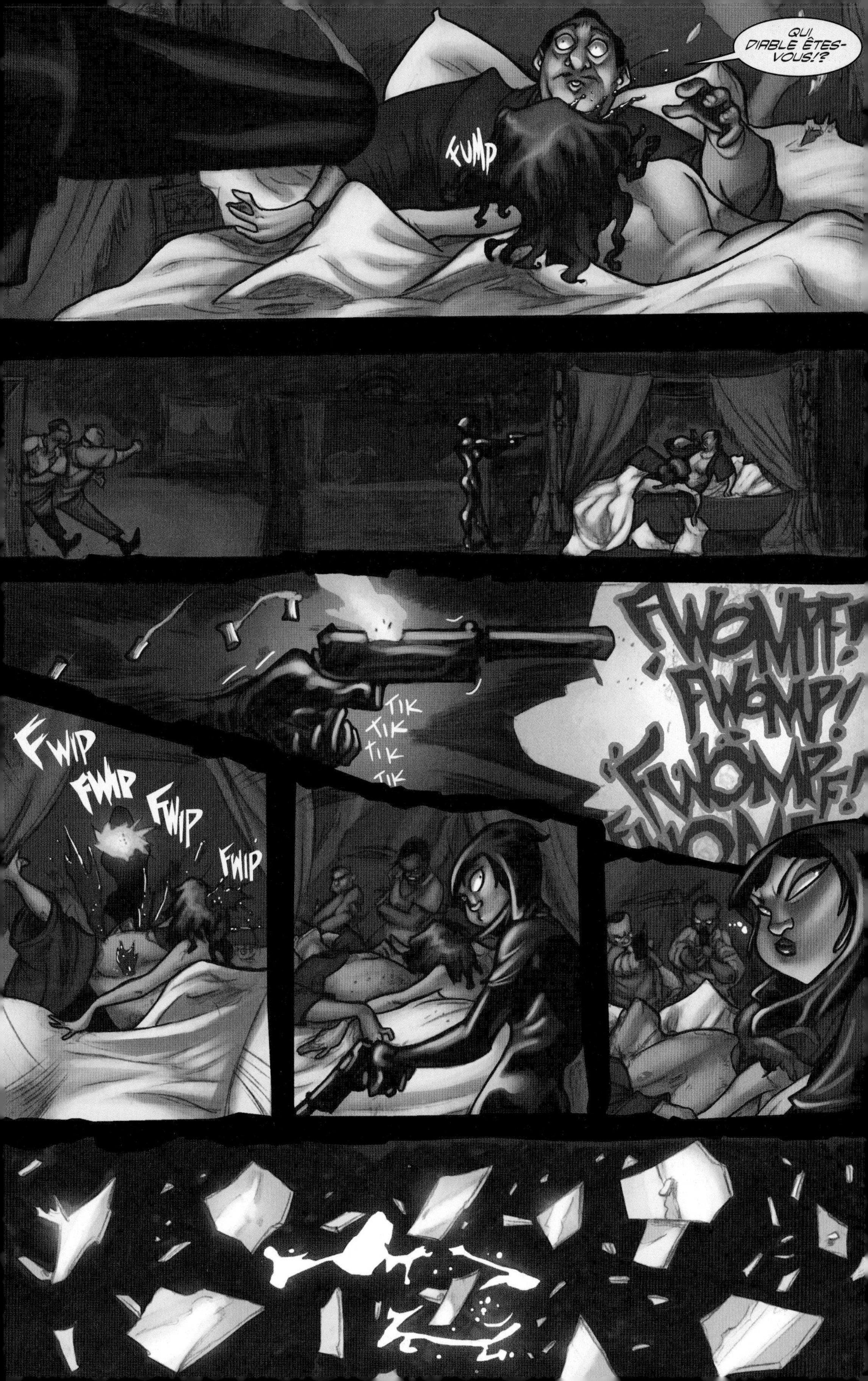
QUI DIABLE ÊTES-VOUS!?
FUMP
TIK
TIK
TIK
TIK
FWOMP!
FWOMP!
FWOMP!
FWIP
FWIP
FWIP
FWIP

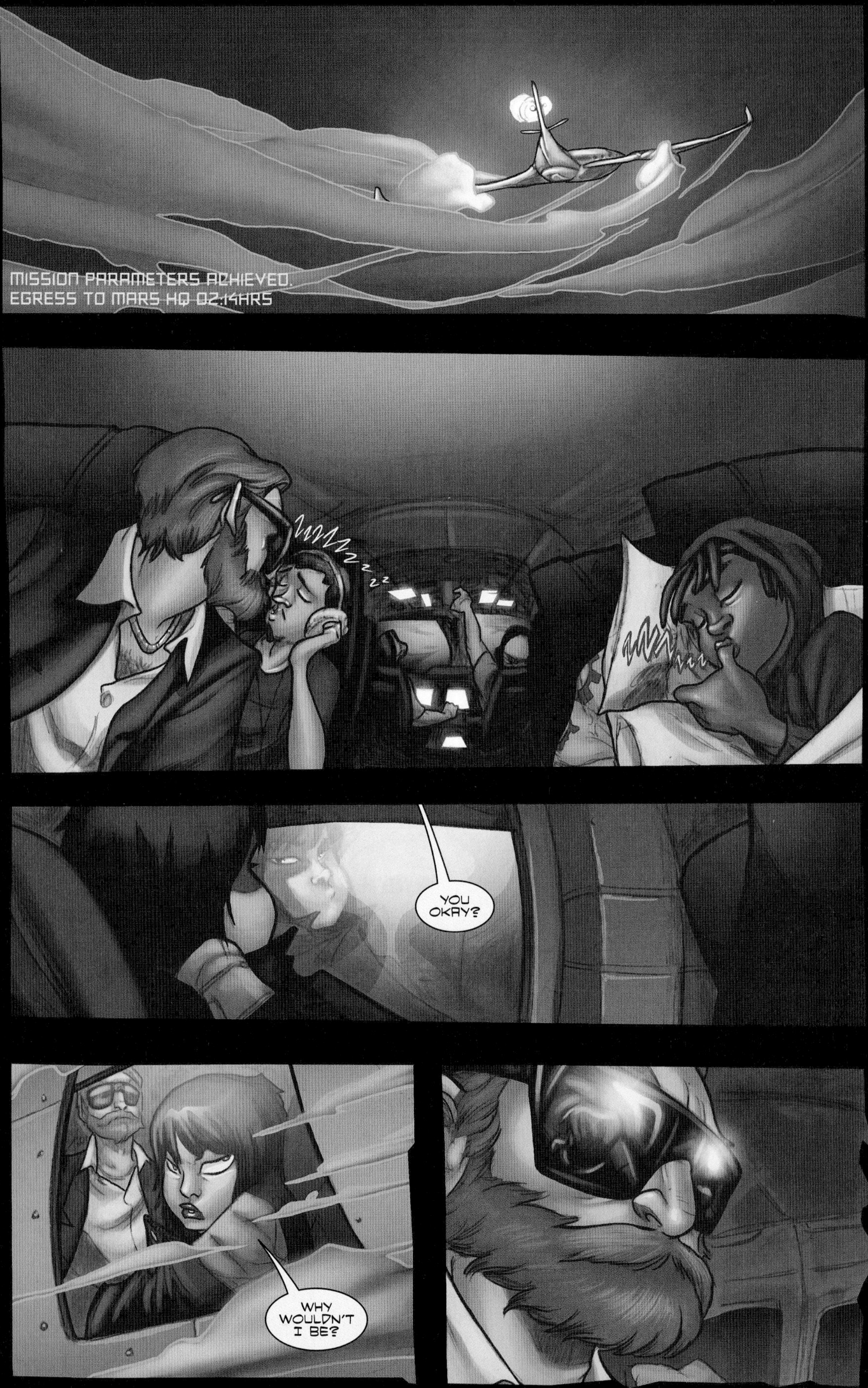
MISSION PARAMETERS ACHIEVED.
EGRESS TO MARS HQ 02:14HRS
ZZZZZ
ZZZ
YOU OKAY?
WHY WOULDN'T I BE?

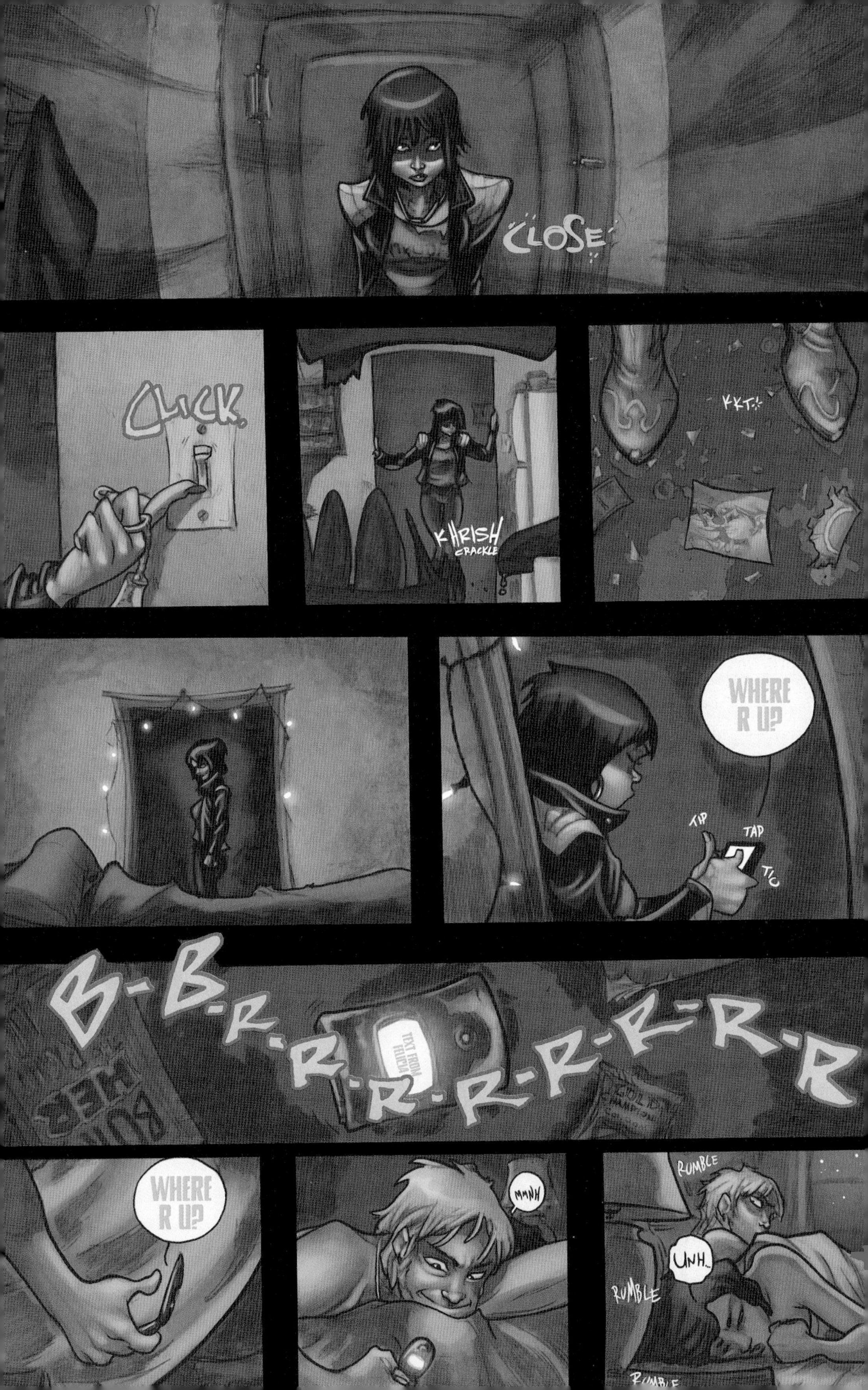
CLOSE
CLICK.
KHRISH
CRACKLE
KKT
WHERE R U?
TIP
TAP
TIC
B-B-R-R-R-R-R-R-R-R-R-R-R
TEXT FROM FELICIA
WHERE R U?
MMNH
RUMBLE
UNH...
RUMBLE

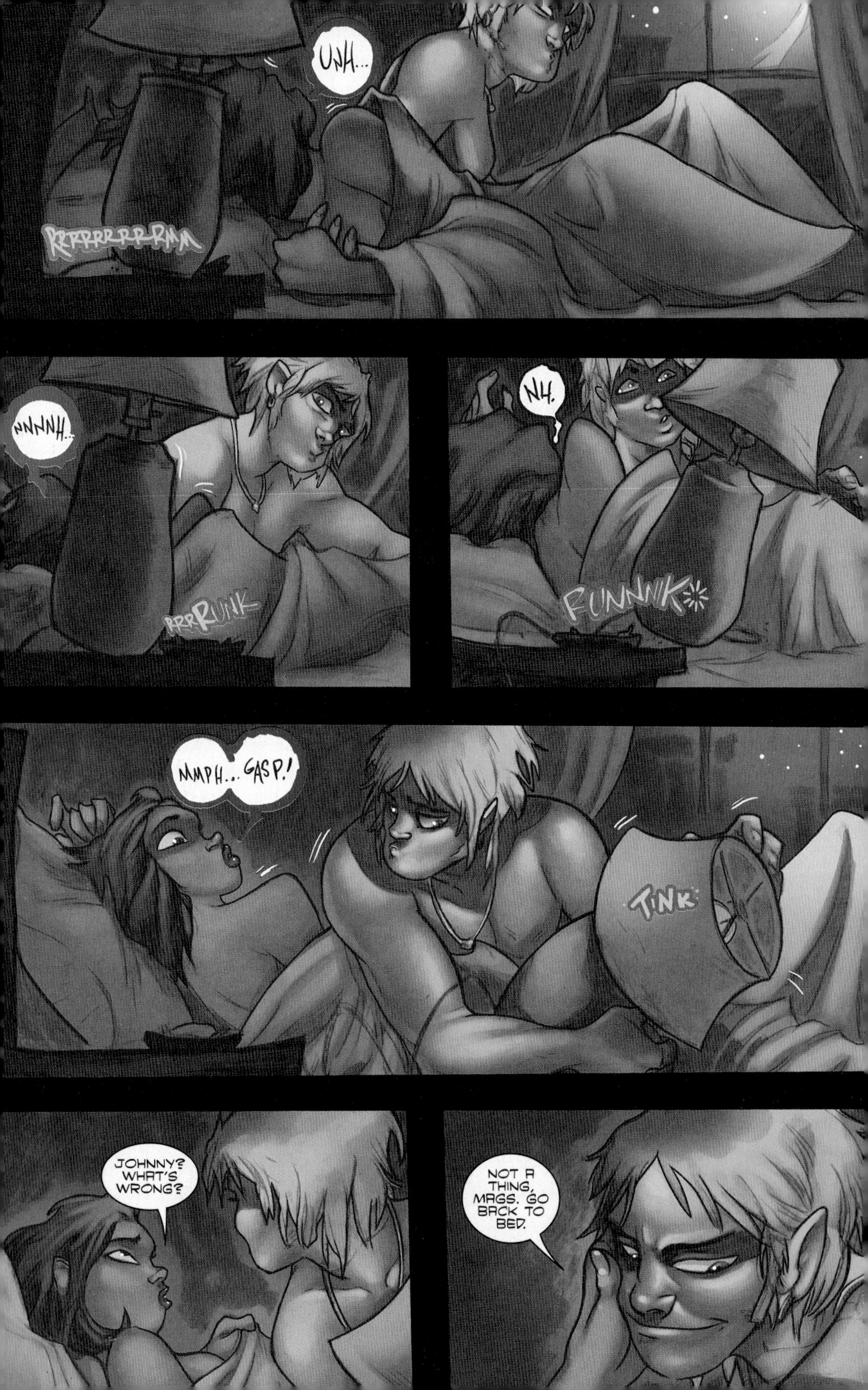
UNH...
RRRRRRRRRMM
NNNNH...
RRRRUNK
NH.
FUNNNK
MMPH... GASP!
TINK
JOHNNY? WHAT'S WRONG?
NOT A THING, MAGS. GO BACK TO BED.

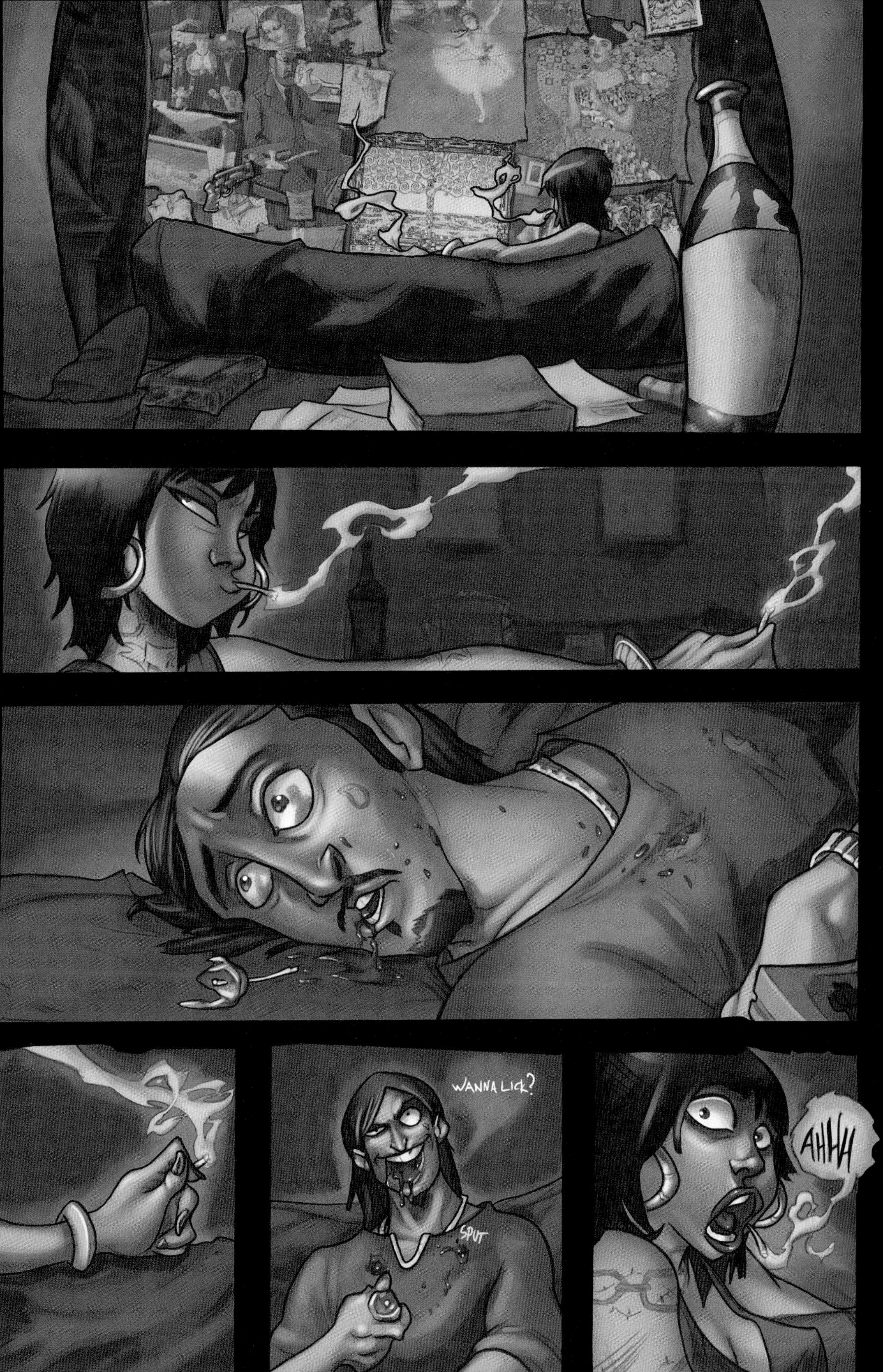
WANNA LICK?
SPUT
AHHH

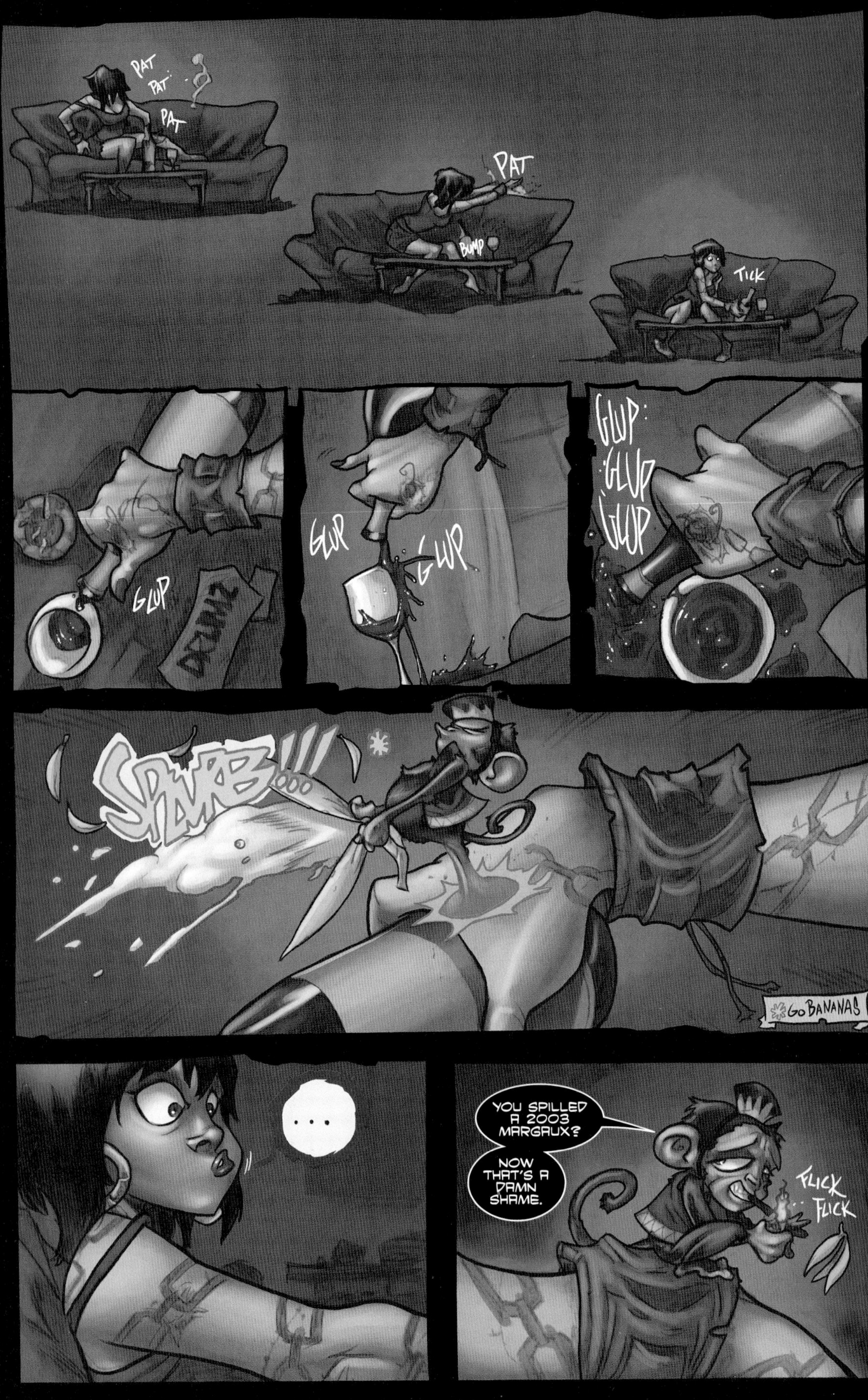
PAT
PAT
PAT
PAT
BUMP
TICK
GLUP
GLUP
GLUP
GLUP
GLUP
GLUP
GO BANANAS
. . .
YOU SPILLED A 2003 MARGAUX?
NOW THAT'S A DAMN SHAME.
FLICK
FLICK

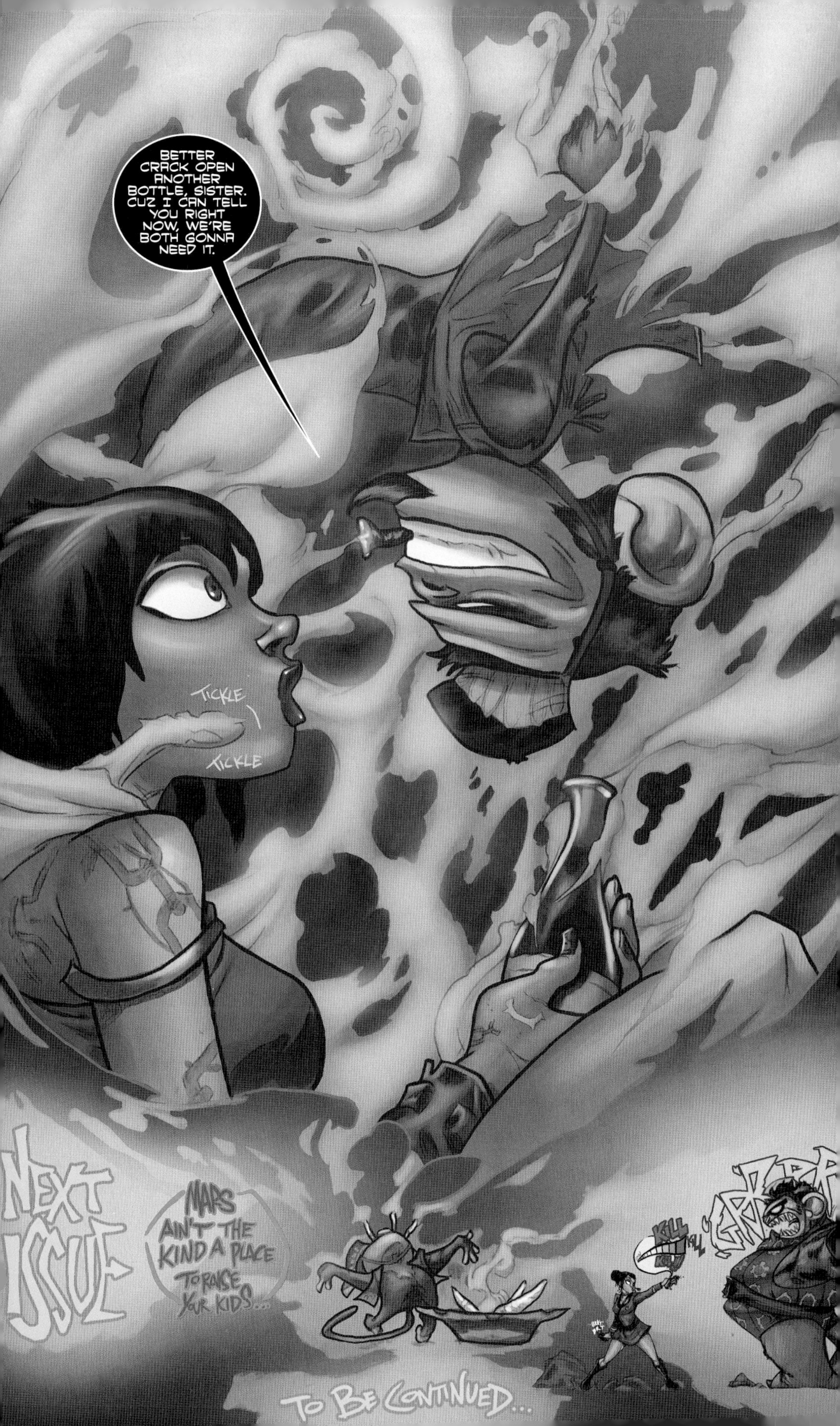
BETTER CRACK OPEN ANOTHER BOTTLE, SISTER. CUZ I CAN TELL YOU RIGHT NOW, WE'RE BOTH GONNA NEED IT.
TICKLE
TICKLE
NEXT ISSUE
MARS AIN'T THE KIND A PLACE TO RAISE YOUR KIDS...
KILL
KILL
GRRR
TO BE CONTINUED...

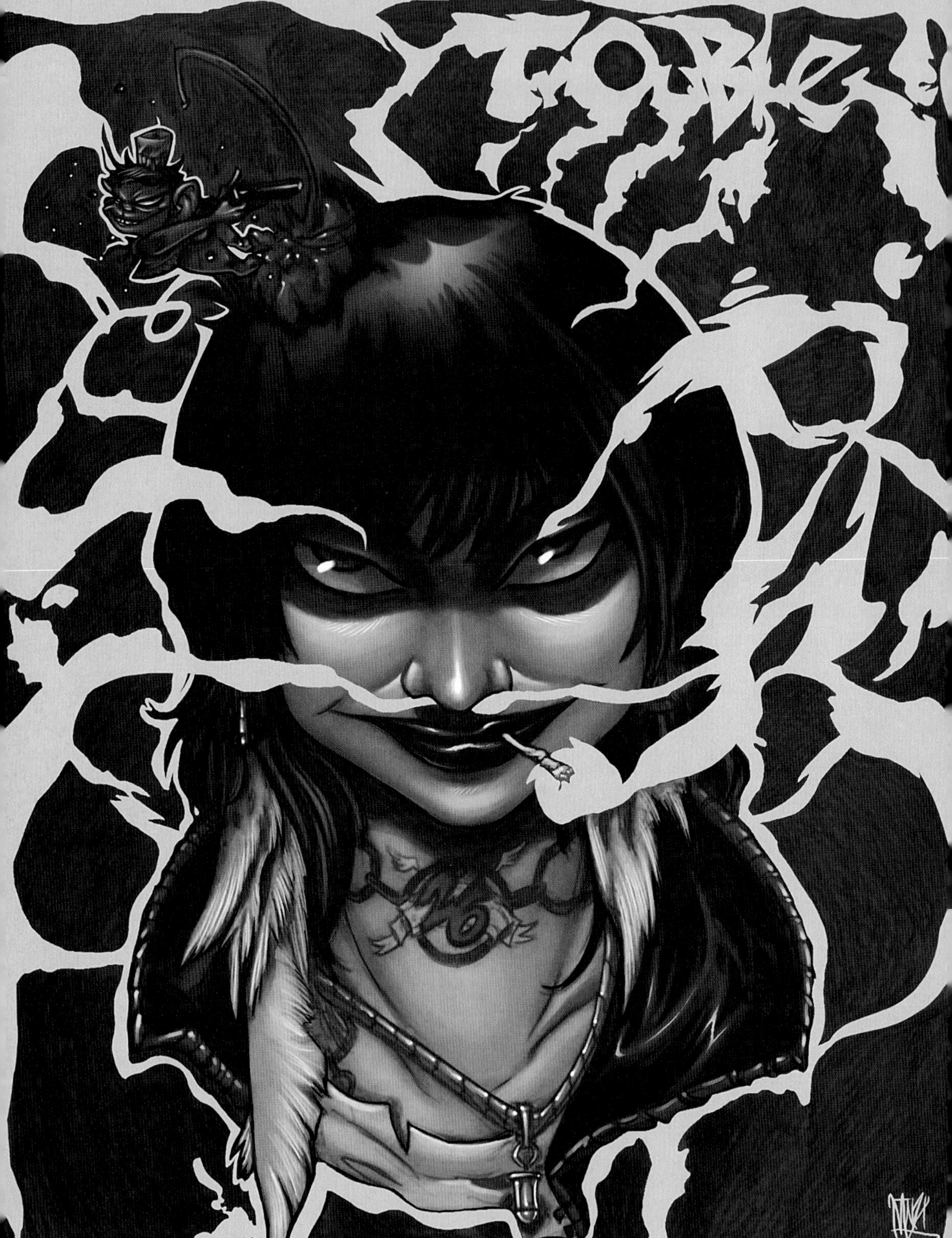

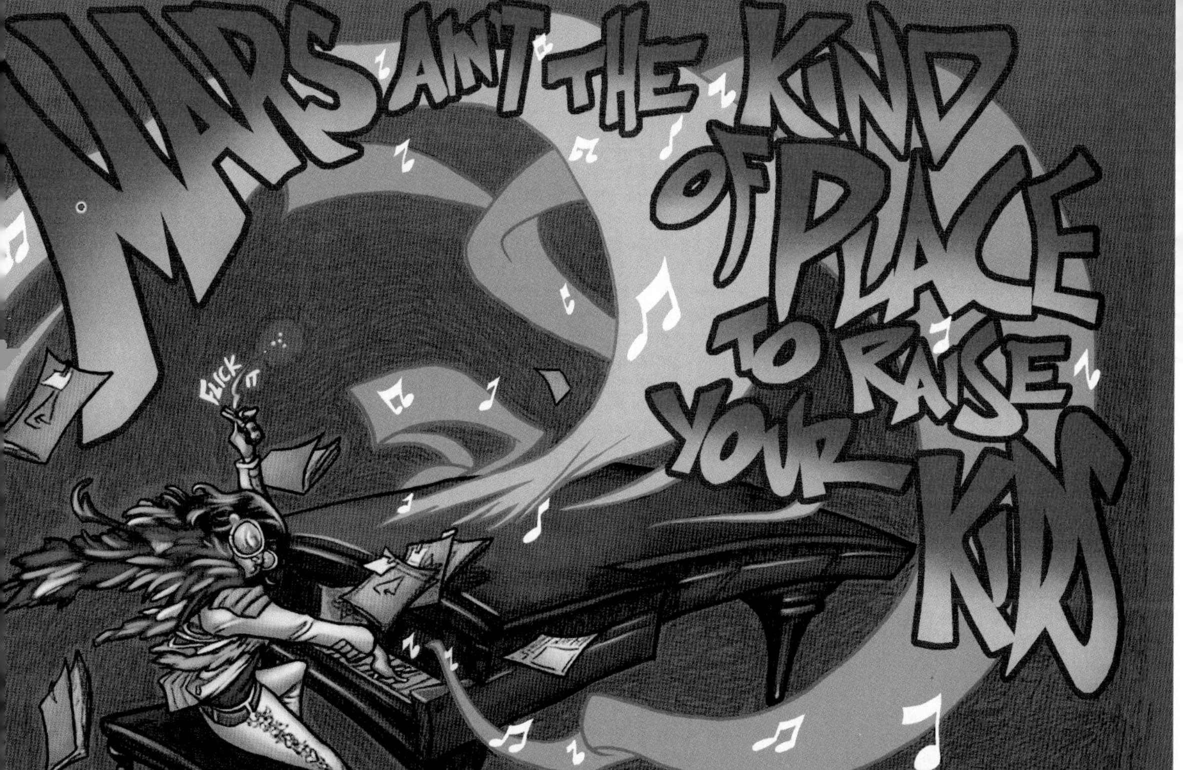
MARS AIN'T THE KIND OF PLACE TO RAISE YOUR KIDS
FLICK
2013 PL'13

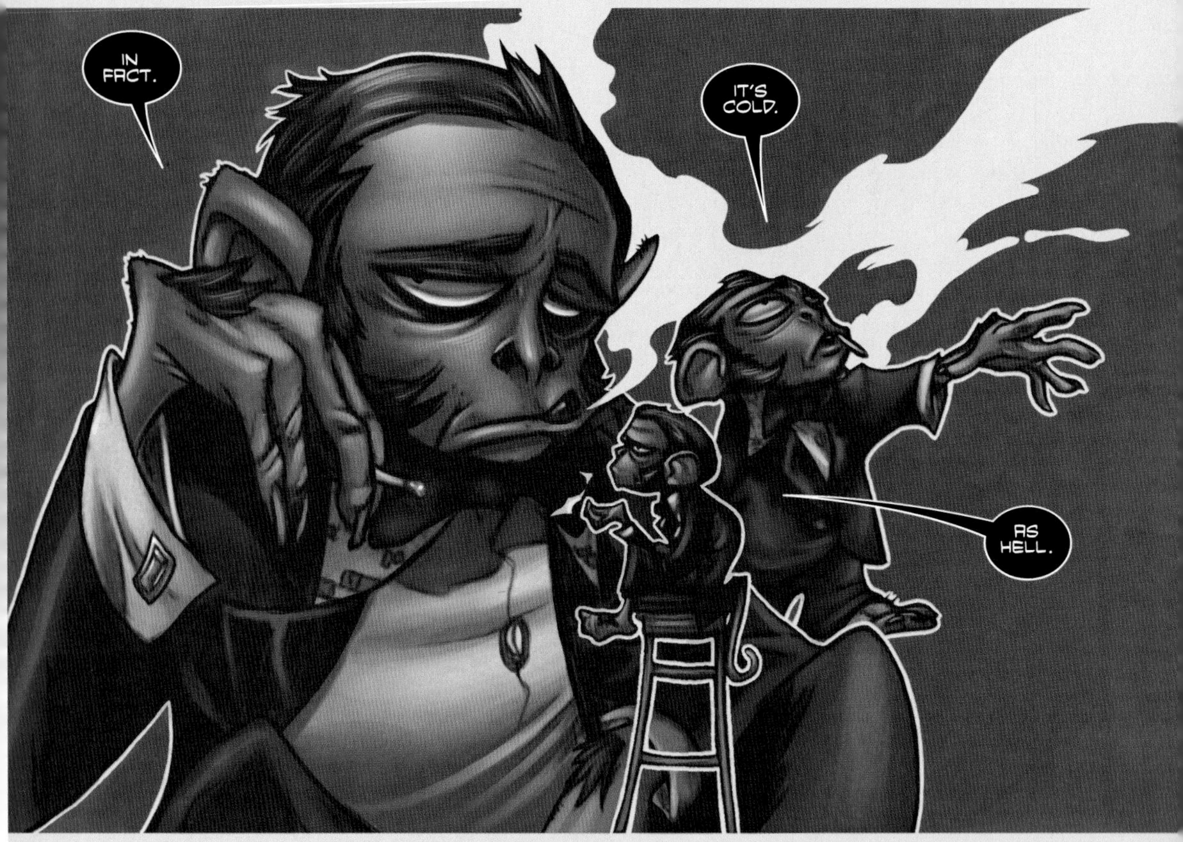
IN FACT.
IT'S COLD.
AS HELL.

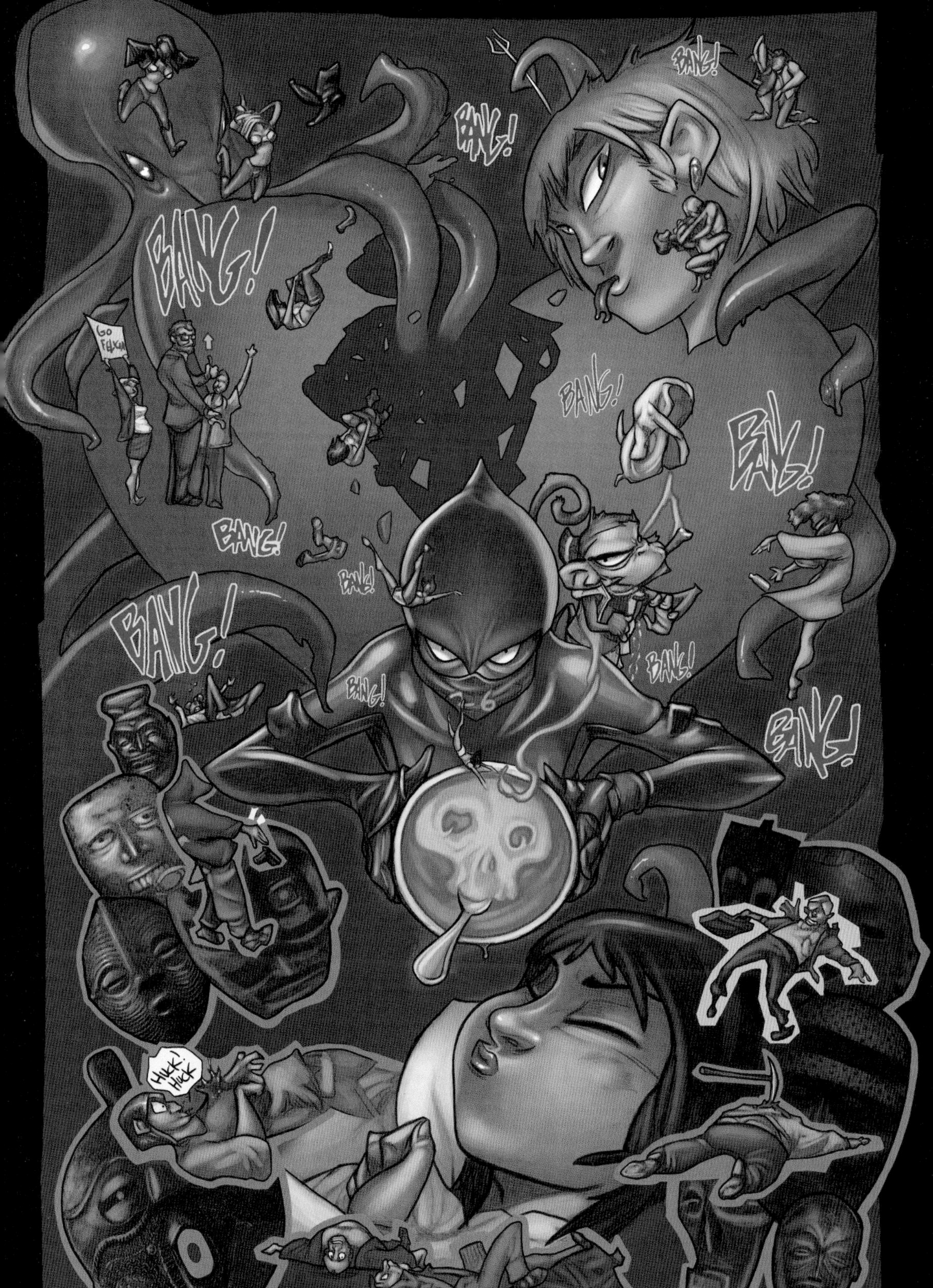
BANG!
BANG!
BANG!
GO
BANG!
BANG!
BANG!
BANG!
BANG!
BANG!
BANG!
BANG!
HUCK! HUCK

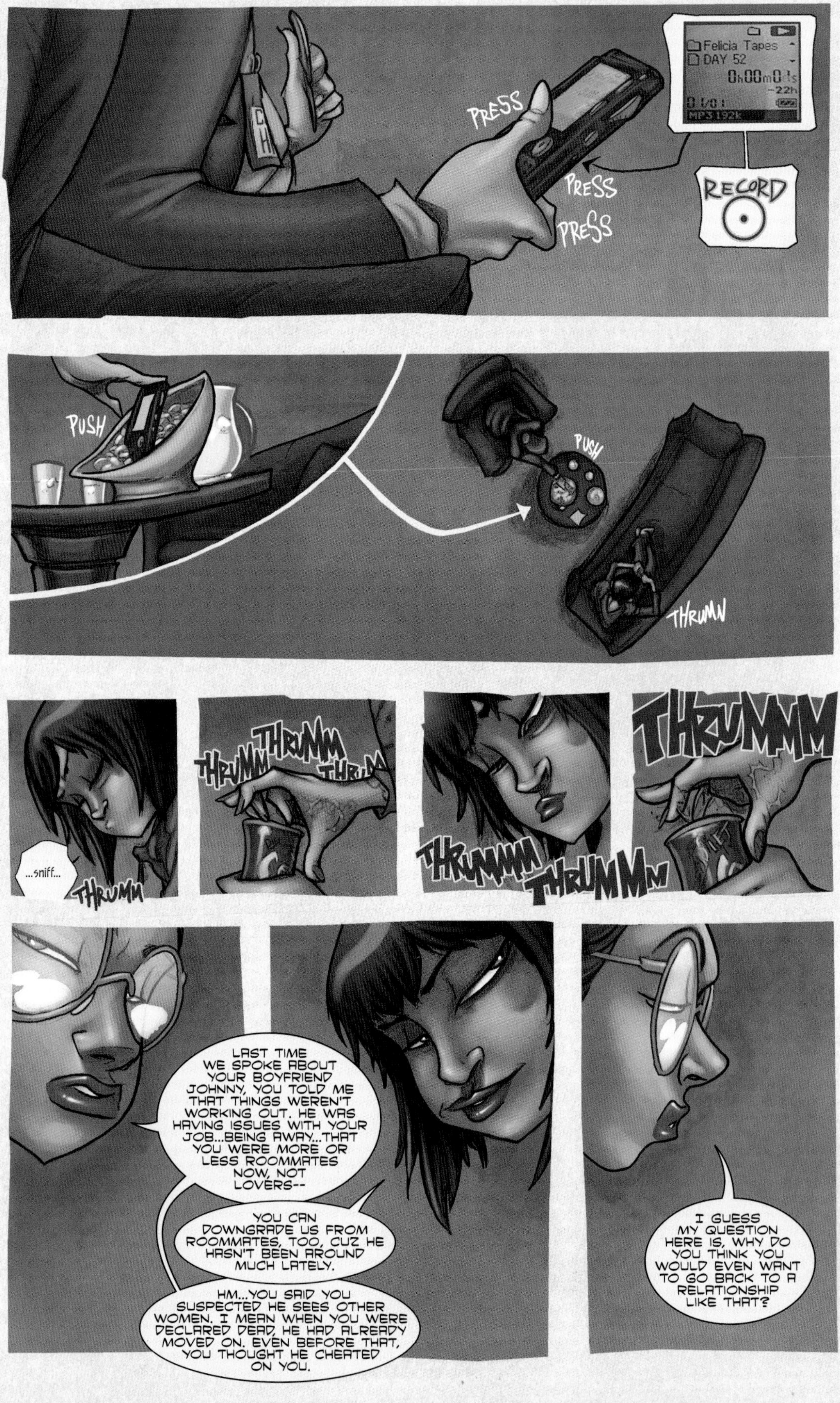

Felicia Tapes
DAY 52
0h00m01s
-22h
MP3 192k
PRESS
PRESS
PRESS
RECORD
PUSH
PUSH
THRUMN
...sniff...
THRUMM
THRUMM
THRUMM
THRUM
THRUMMM
THRUMMMM
THRUMMMM
LAST TIME WE SPOKE ABOUT YOUR BOYFRIEND JOHNNY, YOU TOLD ME THAT THINGS WEREN'T WORKING OUT. HE WAS HAVING ISSUES WITH YOUR JOB...BEING AWAY...THAT YOU WERE MORE OR LESS ROOMMATES NOW, NOT LOVERS--
YOU CAN DOWNGRADE US FROM ROOMMATES, TOO, CUZ HE HASN'T BEEN AROUND MUCH LATELY.
HM...YOU SAID YOU SUSPECTED HE SEES OTHER WOMEN. I MEAN WHEN YOU WERE DECLARED DEAD, HE HAD ALREADY MOVED ON. EVEN BEFORE THAT, YOU THOUGHT HE CHEATED ON YOU.
I GUESS MY QUESTION HERE IS, WHY DO YOU THINK YOU WOULD EVEN WANT TO GO BACK TO A RELATIONSHIP LIKE THAT?

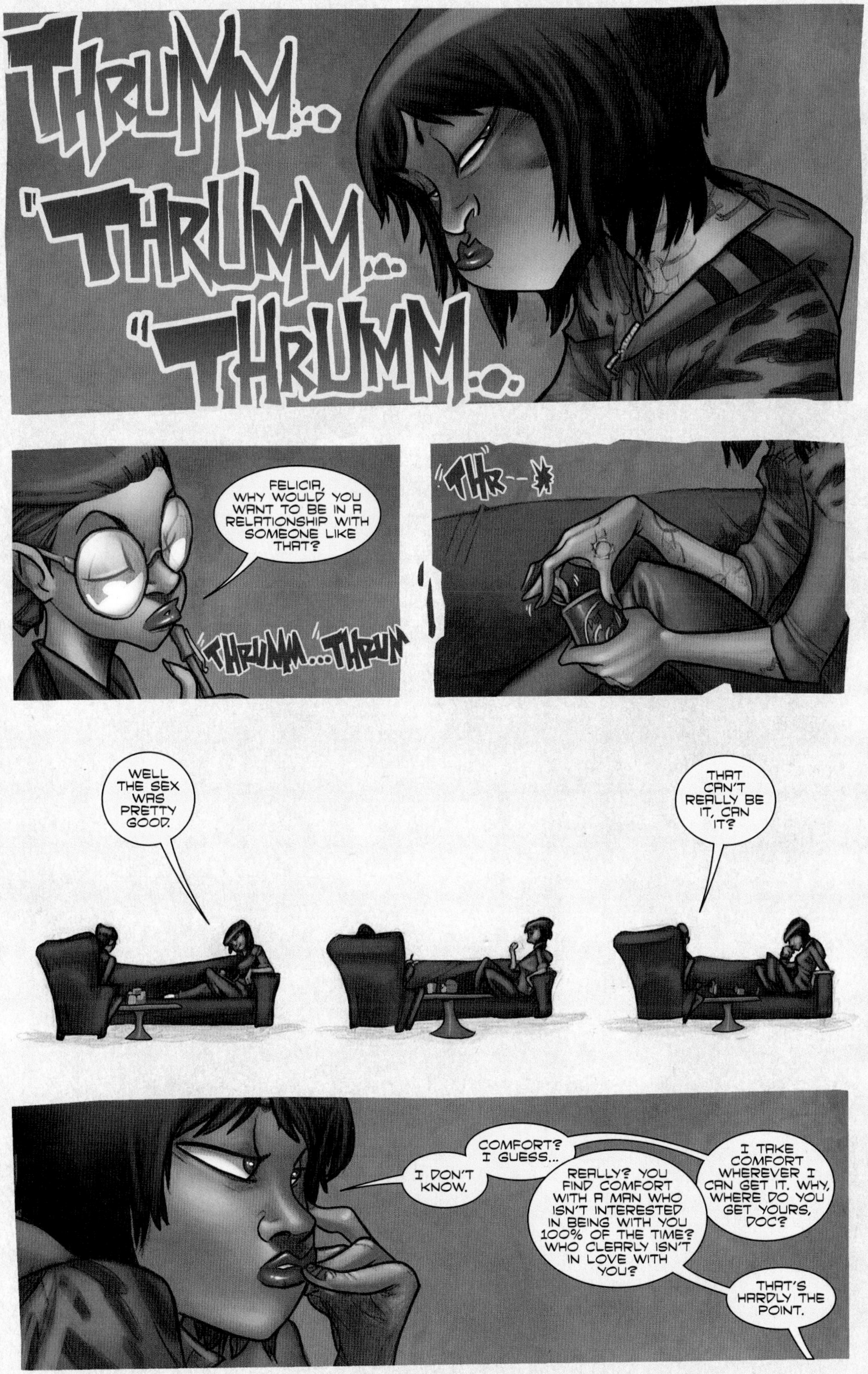
THRUMM...
THRUMM...
THRUMM...
FELICIA, WHY WOULD YOU WANT TO BE IN A RELATIONSHIP WITH SOMEONE LIKE THAT?
THRUMM...THRUM
THR--
WELL THE SEX WAS PRETTY GOOD.
THAT CAN'T REALLY BE IT, CAN IT?
I DON'T KNOW.
COMFORT? I GUESS...
REALLY? YOU FIND COMFORT WITH A MAN WHO ISN'T INTERESTED IN BEING WITH YOU 100% OF THE TIME? WHO CLEARLY ISN'T IN LOVE WITH YOU?
I TAKE COMFORT WHEREVER I CAN GET IT. WHY, WHERE DO YOU GET YOURS, DOC?
THAT'S HARDLY THE POINT.

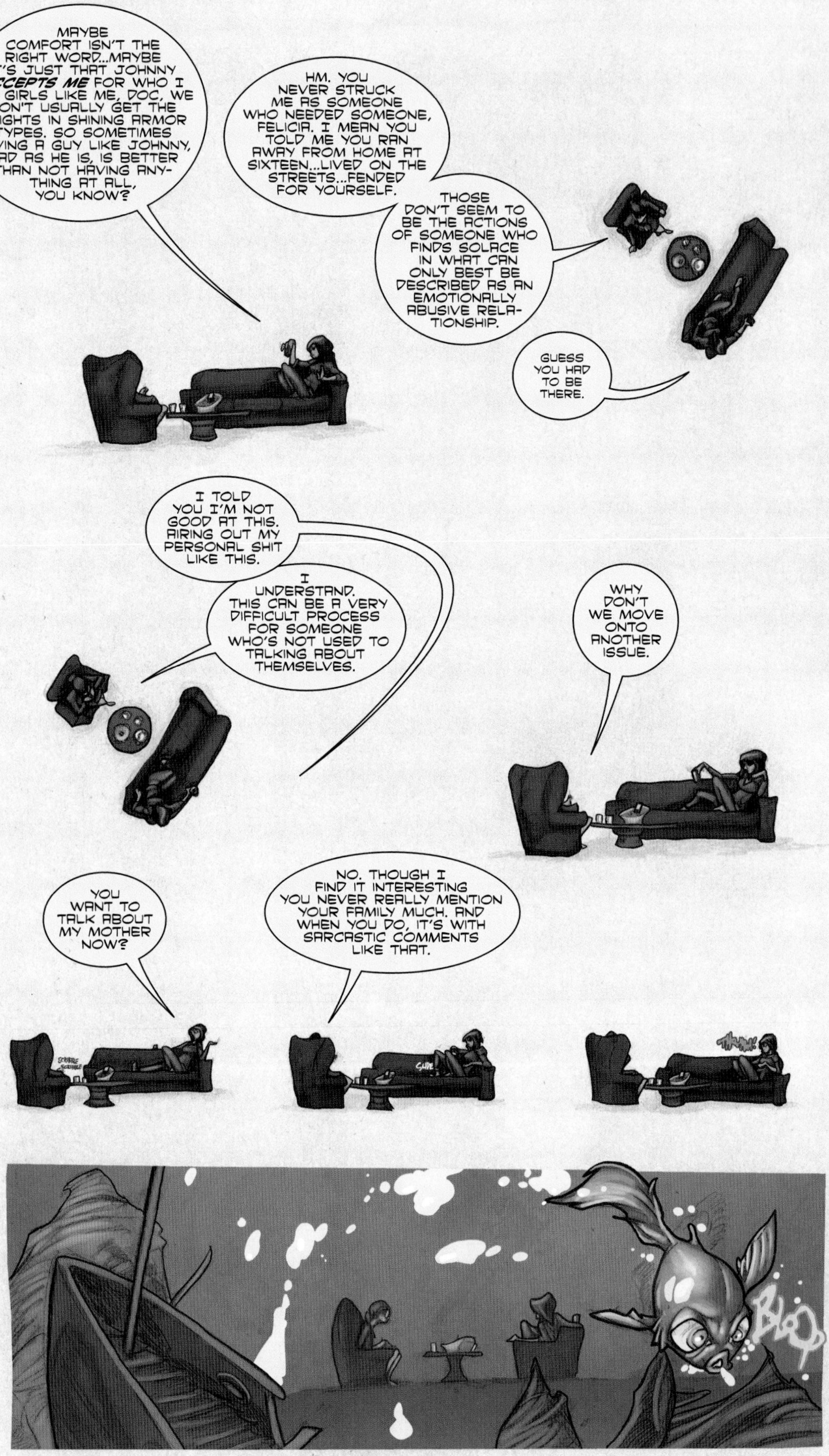
MAYBE COMFORT ISN'T THE RIGHT WORD...MAYBE IT'S JUST THAT JOHNNY ACCEPTS ME FOR WHO I AM. GIRLS LIKE ME, DOC, WE DON'T USUALLY GET THE KNIGHTS IN SHINING ARMOR TYPES. SO SOMETIMES HAVING A GUY LIKE JOHNNY, BAD AS HE IS, IS BETTER THAN NOT HAVING ANYTHING AT ALL, YOU KNOW?
HM. YOU NEVER STRUCK ME AS SOMEONE WHO NEEDED SOMEONE, FELICIA. I MEAN YOU TOLD ME YOU RAN AWAY FROM HOME AT SIXTEEN...LIVED ON THE STREETS...FENDED FOR YOURSELF.
THOSE DON'T SEEM TO BE THE ACTIONS OF SOMEONE WHO FINDS SOLACE IN WHAT CAN ONLY BEST BE DESCRIBED AS AN EMOTIONALLY ABUSIVE RELATIONSHIP.
GUESS YOU HAD TO BE THERE.
I TOLD YOU I'M NOT GOOD AT THIS. AIRING OUT MY PERSONAL SHIT LIKE THIS.
I UNDERSTAND. THIS CAN BE A VERY DIFFICULT PROCESS FOR SOMEONE WHO'S NOT USED TO TALKING ABOUT THEMSELVES.
WHY DON'T WE MOVE ONTO ANOTHER ISSUE.
YOU WANT TO TALK ABOUT MY MOTHER NOW?
SCRIBBLE SCRIBBLE
NO. THOUGH I FIND IT INTERESTING YOU NEVER REALLY MENTION YOUR FAMILY MUCH. AND WHEN YOU DO, IT'S WITH SARCASTIC COMMENTS LIKE THAT.

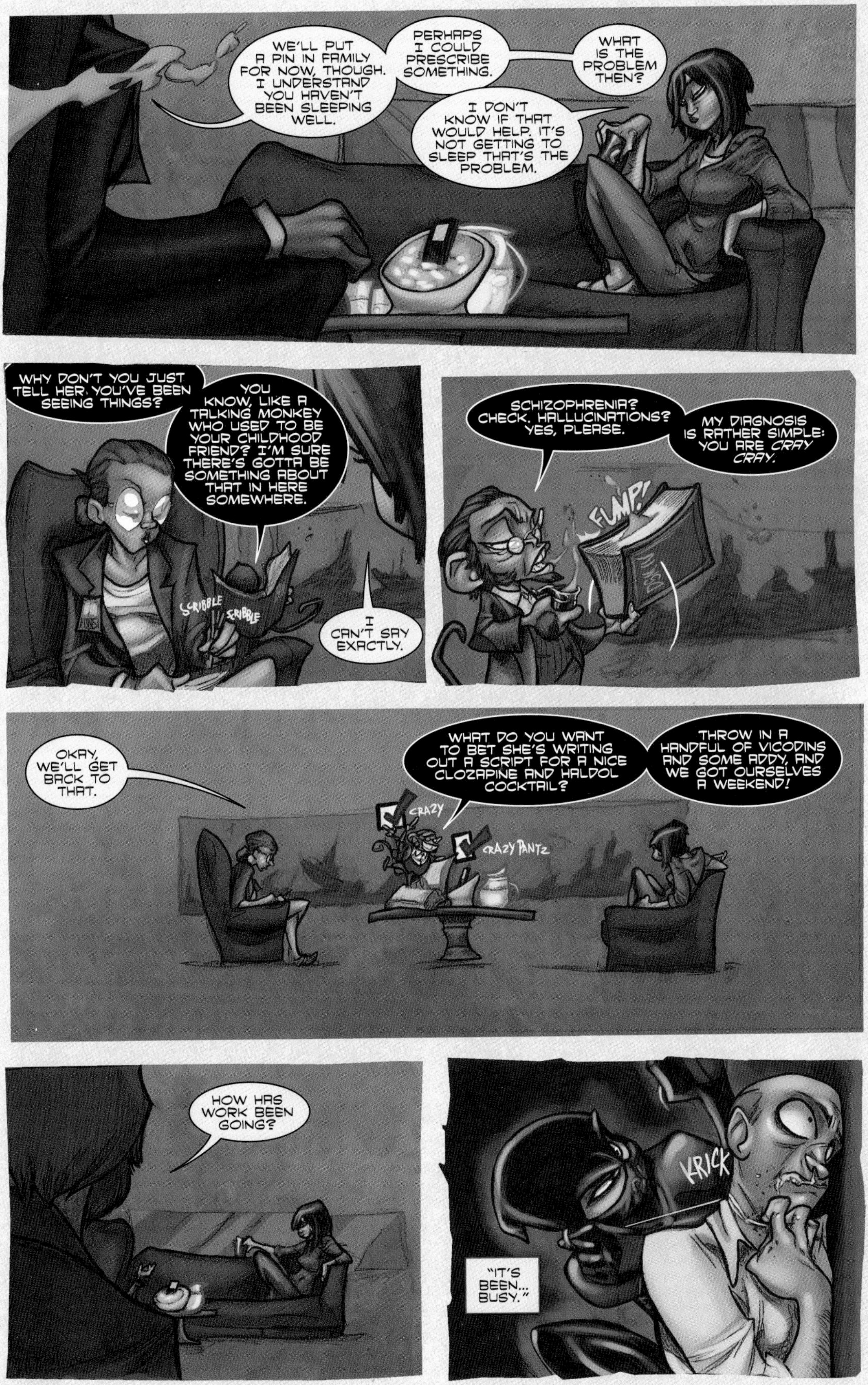
WE'LL PUT A PIN IN FAMILY FOR NOW, THOUGH. I UNDERSTAND YOU HAVEN'T BEEN SLEEPING WELL.
PERHAPS I COULD PRESCRIBE SOMETHING.
WHAT IS THE PROBLEM THEN?
I DON'T KNOW IF THAT WOULD HELP. IT'S NOT GETTING TO SLEEP THAT'S THE PROBLEM.
WHY DON'T YOU JUST TELL HER YOU'VE BEEN SEEING THINGS?
YOU KNOW, LIKE A TALKING MONKEY WHO USED TO BE YOUR CHILDHOOD FRIEND? I'M SURE THERE'S GOTTA BE SOMETHING ABOUT THAT IN HERE SOMEWHERE.
SCRIBBLE
SCRIBBLE
I CAN'T SAY EXACTLY.
SCHIZOPHRENIA? CHECK. HALLUCINATIONS? YES, PLEASE.
MY DIAGNOSIS IS RATHER SIMPLE: YOU ARE *CRAY CRAY*.
FUMP!
OKAY, WE'LL GET BACK TO THAT.
WHAT DO YOU WANT TO BET SHE'S WRITING OUT A SCRIPT FOR A NICE CLOZAPINE AND HALDOL COCKTAIL?
THROW IN A HANDFUL OF VICODINS AND SOME ADDY, AND WE GOT OURSELVES A WEEKEND!
CRAZY
CRAZY PANTZ
HOW HAS WORK BEEN GOING?
KRICK
"IT'S BEEN... BUSY."

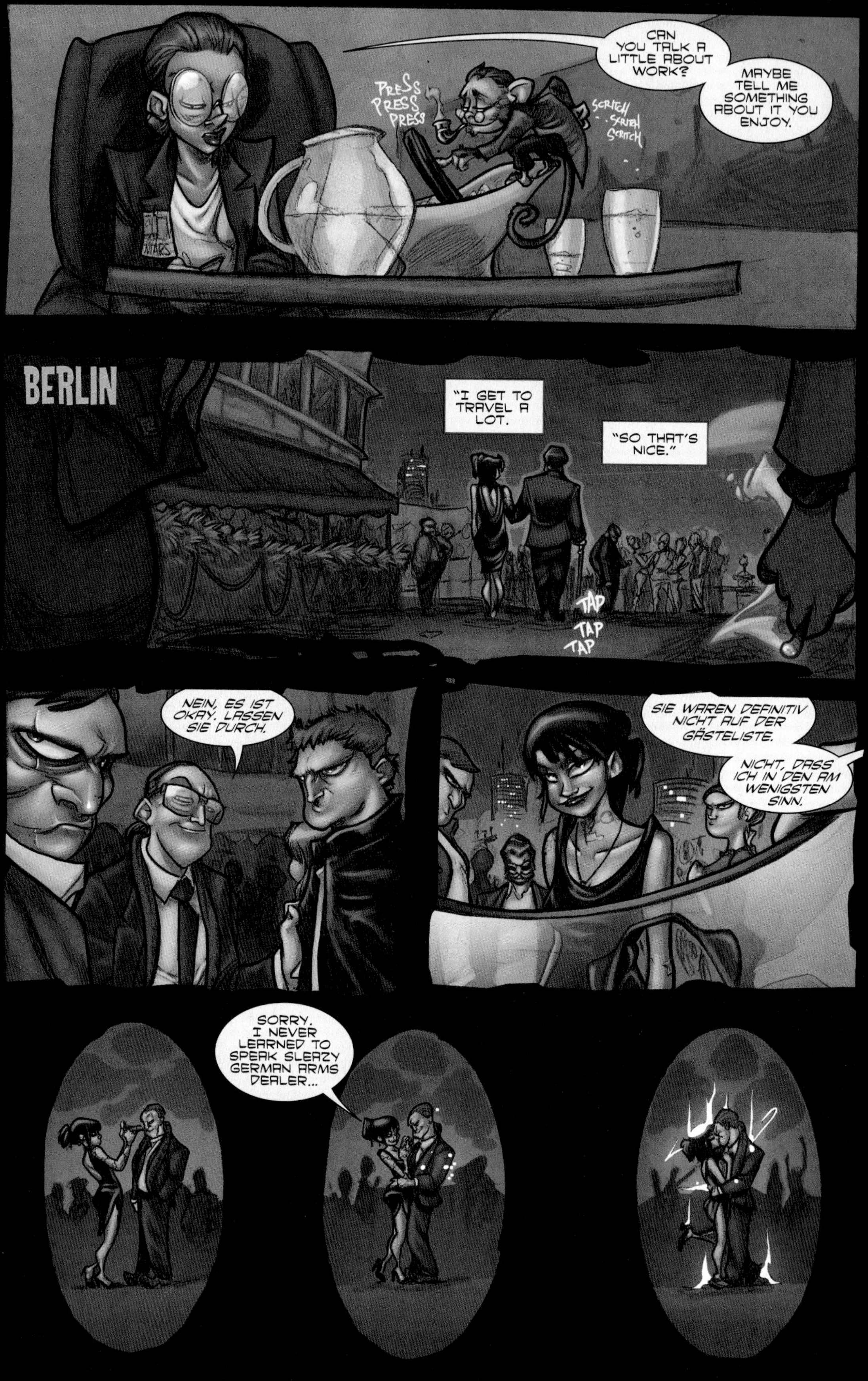
PRESS PRESS PRESS
CAN YOU TALK A LITTLE ABOUT WORK?
SCRITCH SCRITCH SCRITCH
MAYBE TELL ME SOMETHING ABOUT IT YOU ENJOY.
BERLIN
"I GET TO TRAVEL A LOT.
"SO THAT'S NICE."
TAP TAP TAP
NEIN, ES IST OKAY. LASSEN SIE DURCH.
SIE WAREN DEFINITIV NICHT AUF DER GÄSTELISTE.
NICHT, DASS ICH IN DEN AM WENIGSTEN SINN.
SORRY. I NEVER LEARNED TO SPEAK SLEAZY GERMAN ARMS DEALER...

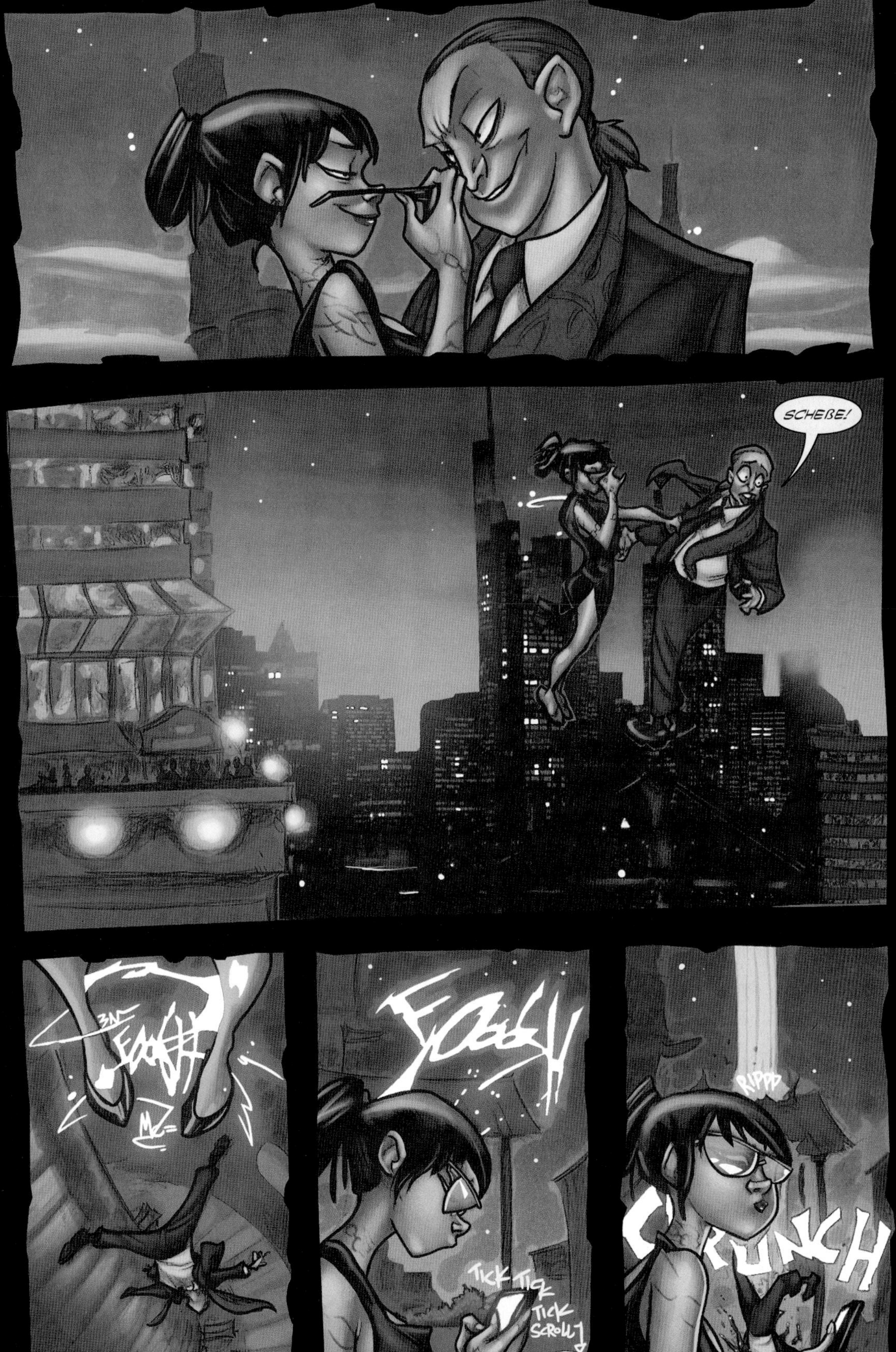
SCHEßE!
TICK TICK TICK SCROLL
SEND
RIPPP
CRUNCH

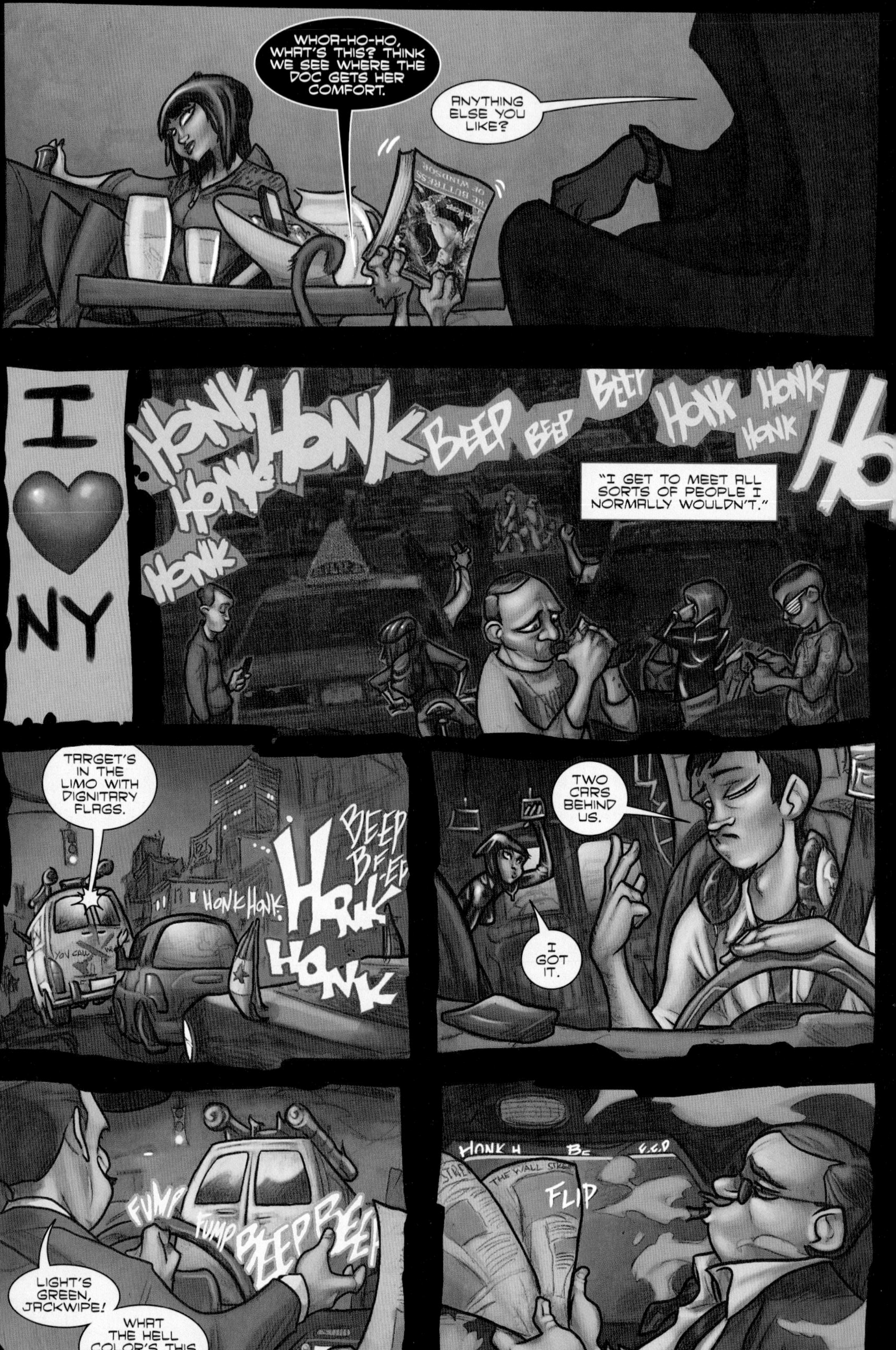
WHOR-HO-HO, WHAT'S THIS? THINK WE SEE WHERE THE DOC GETS HER COMFORT.
ANYTHING ELSE YOU LIKE?
I ♥ NY
HONK HONK HONK HONK HONK BEEP BEEP BEEP HONK HONK HONK
"I GET TO MEET ALL SORTS OF PEOPLE I NORMALLY WOULDN'T."
TARGET'S IN THE LIMO WITH DIGNITARY FLAGS.
HONK HONK
BEEP BEEP HONK HONK
TWO CARS BEHIND US.
I GOT IT.
FUMP FUMP BEEP BEEP
LIGHT'S GREEN, JACKWIPE!
WHAT THE HELL COLOR'S THIS GUY WRITING FOR?
FLIP

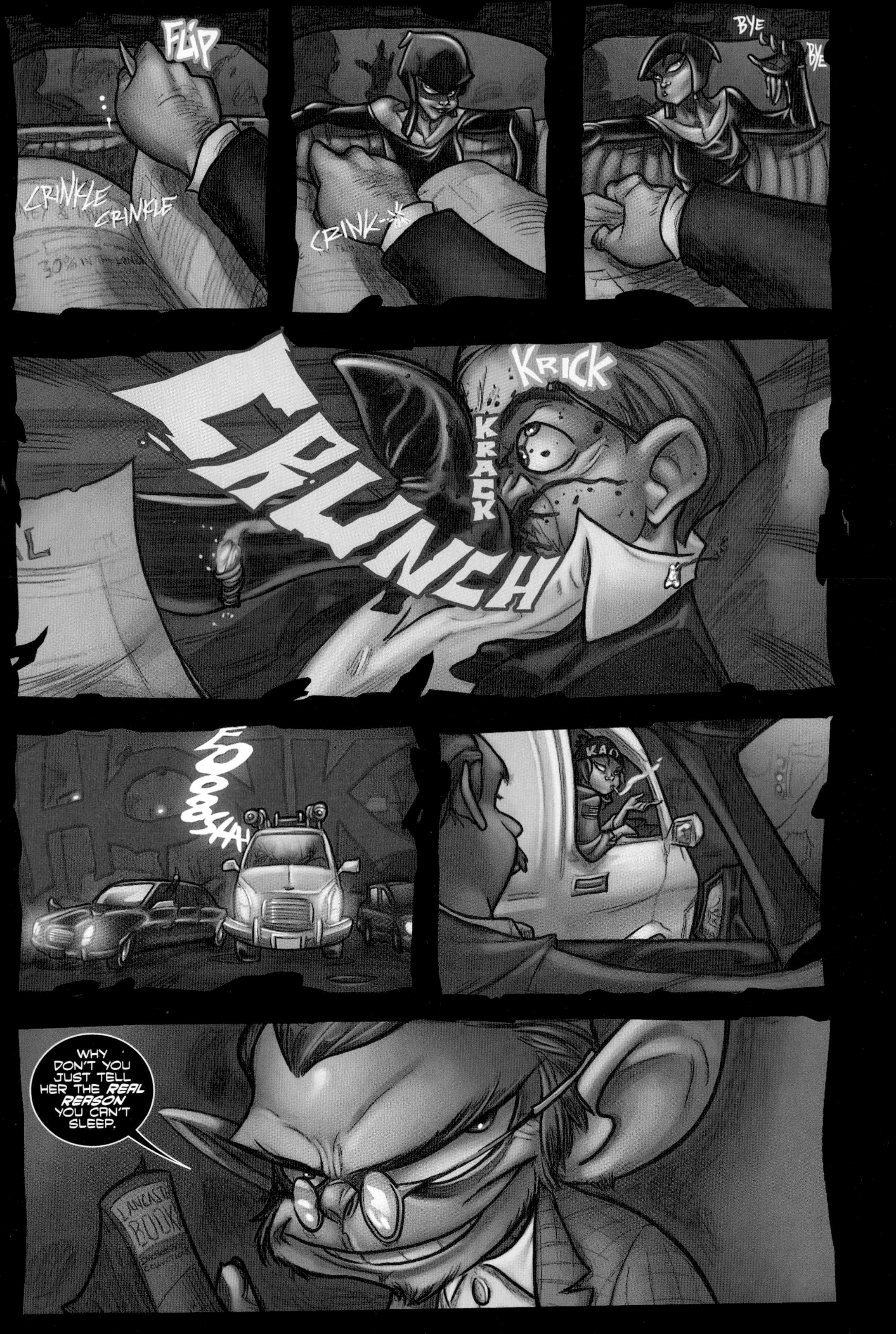
FLIP
CRINKLE CRINKLE
CRINK-
BYE
BYE
CRUNCH
KRICK
KRACK
WHY DON'T YOU JUST TELL HER THE *REAL REASON* YOU CAN'T SLEEP.

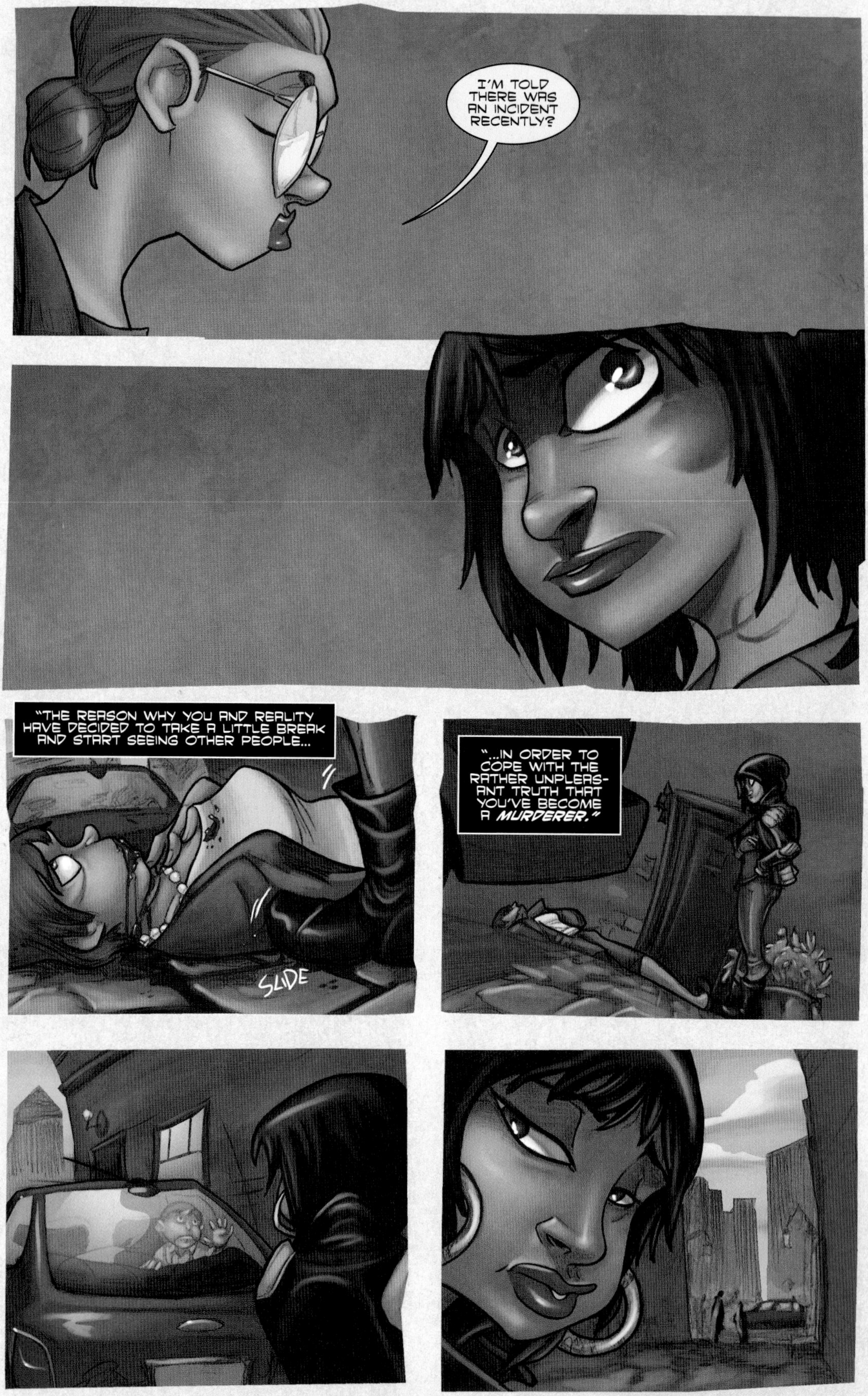
I'M TOLD THERE WAS AN INCIDENT RECENTLY?
"THE REASON WHY YOU AND REALITY HAVE DECIDED TO TAKE A LITTLE BREAK AND START SEEING OTHER PEOPLE...
SLIDE
"...IN ORDER TO COPE WITH THE RATHER UNPLEAS-ANT TRUTH THAT YOU'VE BECOME A *MURDERER.*"

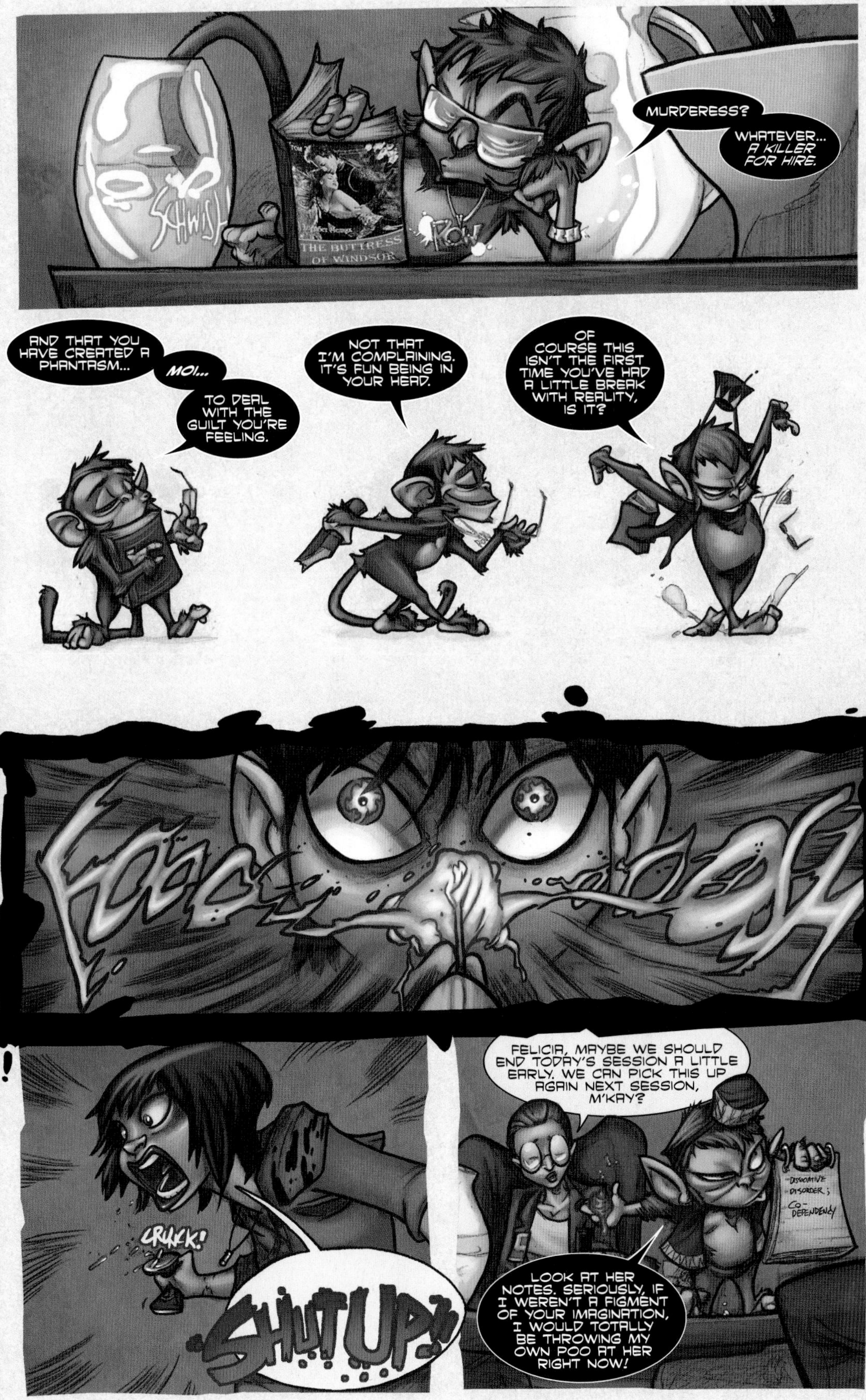

MURDERESS?
WHATEVER... A KILLER FOR HIRE.
SCHWISH
THE BUTTRESS OF WINDSOR
AND THAT YOU HAVE CREATED A PHANTASM...
MOI...
TO DEAL WITH THE GUILT YOU'RE FEELING.
NOT THAT I'M COMPLAINING. IT'S FUN BEING IN YOUR HEAD.
OF COURSE THIS ISN'T THE FIRST TIME YOU'VE HAD A LITTLE BREAK WITH REALITY, IS IT?
CRUNCK!
SHUT UP!!
FELICIA, MAYBE WE SHOULD END TODAY'S SESSION A LITTLE EARLY. WE CAN PICK THIS UP AGAIN NEXT SESSION, M'KAY?
-DISSOCIATIVE DISORDER;
CO-DEPENDENCY
LOOK AT HER NOTES. SERIOUSLY, IF I WEREN'T A FIGMENT OF YOUR IMAGINATION, I WOULD TOTALLY BE THROWING MY OWN POO AT HER RIGHT NOW!

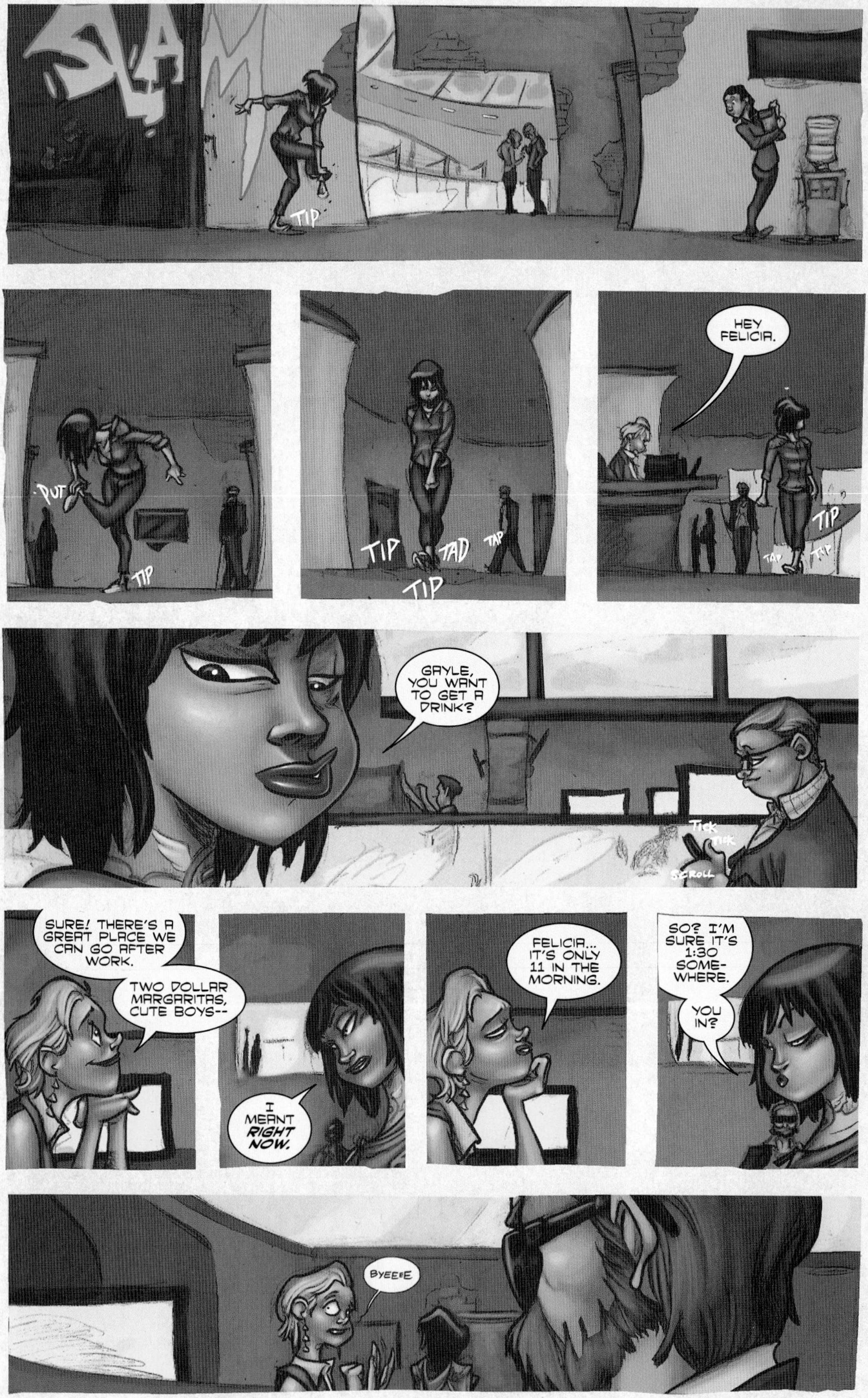
SLAM
TIP
PUT
TIP
TIP
TAD
TAP
TIP
HEY FELICIA.
TIP
TAP
TIP
GAYLE, YOU WANT TO GET A DRINK?
TICK
TICK
SCROLL
SURE! THERE'S A GREAT PLACE WE CAN GO AFTER WORK.
TWO DOLLAR MARGARITAS, CUTE BOYS--
I MEANT *RIGHT NOW.*
FELICIA... IT'S ONLY 11 IN THE MORNING.
SO? I'M SURE IT'S 1:30 SOME-WHERE.
YOU IN?
BYEEEE

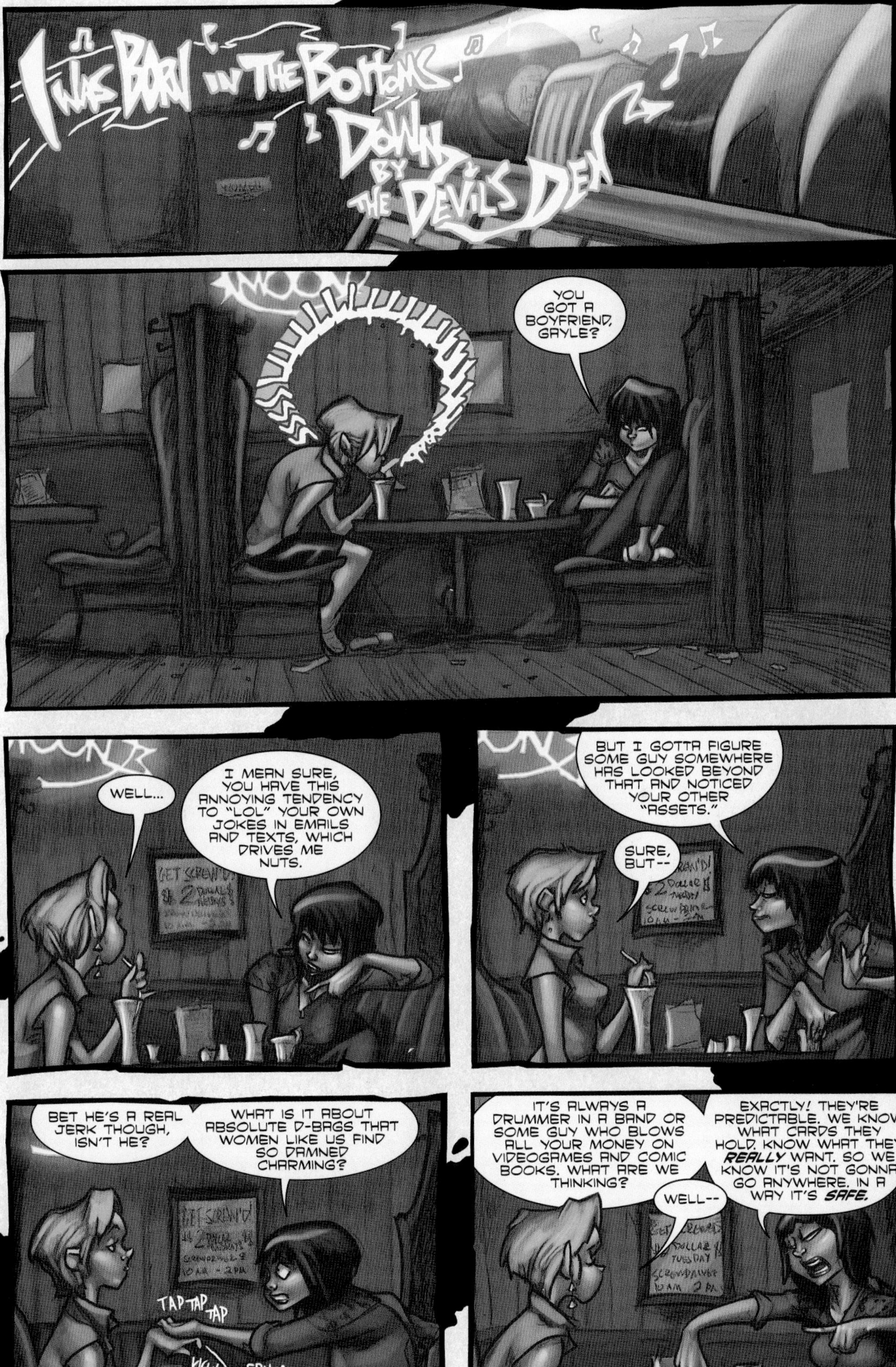

I WAS BORN IN THE BOTTOMS
DOWN BY THE DEVIL'S DEN
YOU GOT A BOYFRIEND, GAYLE?
WELL...
I MEAN SURE, YOU HAVE THIS ANNOYING TENDENCY TO "LOL" YOUR OWN JOKES IN EMAILS AND TEXTS, WHICH DRIVES ME NUTS.
BUT I GOTTA FIGURE SOME GUY SOMEWHERE HAS LOOKED BEYOND THAT AND NOTICED YOUR OTHER "ASSETS."
SURE, BUT--
BET HE'S A REAL JERK THOUGH, ISN'T HE?
WHAT IS IT ABOUT ABSOLUTE D-BAGS THAT WOMEN LIKE US FIND SO DAMNED CHARMING?
TAP TAP TAP
KICK'D
SPILLS
IT'S ALWAYS A DRUMMER IN A BAND OR SOME GUY WHO BLOWS ALL YOUR MONEY ON VIDEOGAMES AND COMIC BOOKS. WHAT ARE WE THINKING?
WELL--
EXACTLY! THEY'RE PREDICTABLE. WE KNOW WHAT CARDS THEY HOLD. KNOW WHAT THEY *REALLY* WANT. SO WE KNOW IT'S NOT GONNA GO ANYWHERE. IN A WAY IT'S *SAFE.*

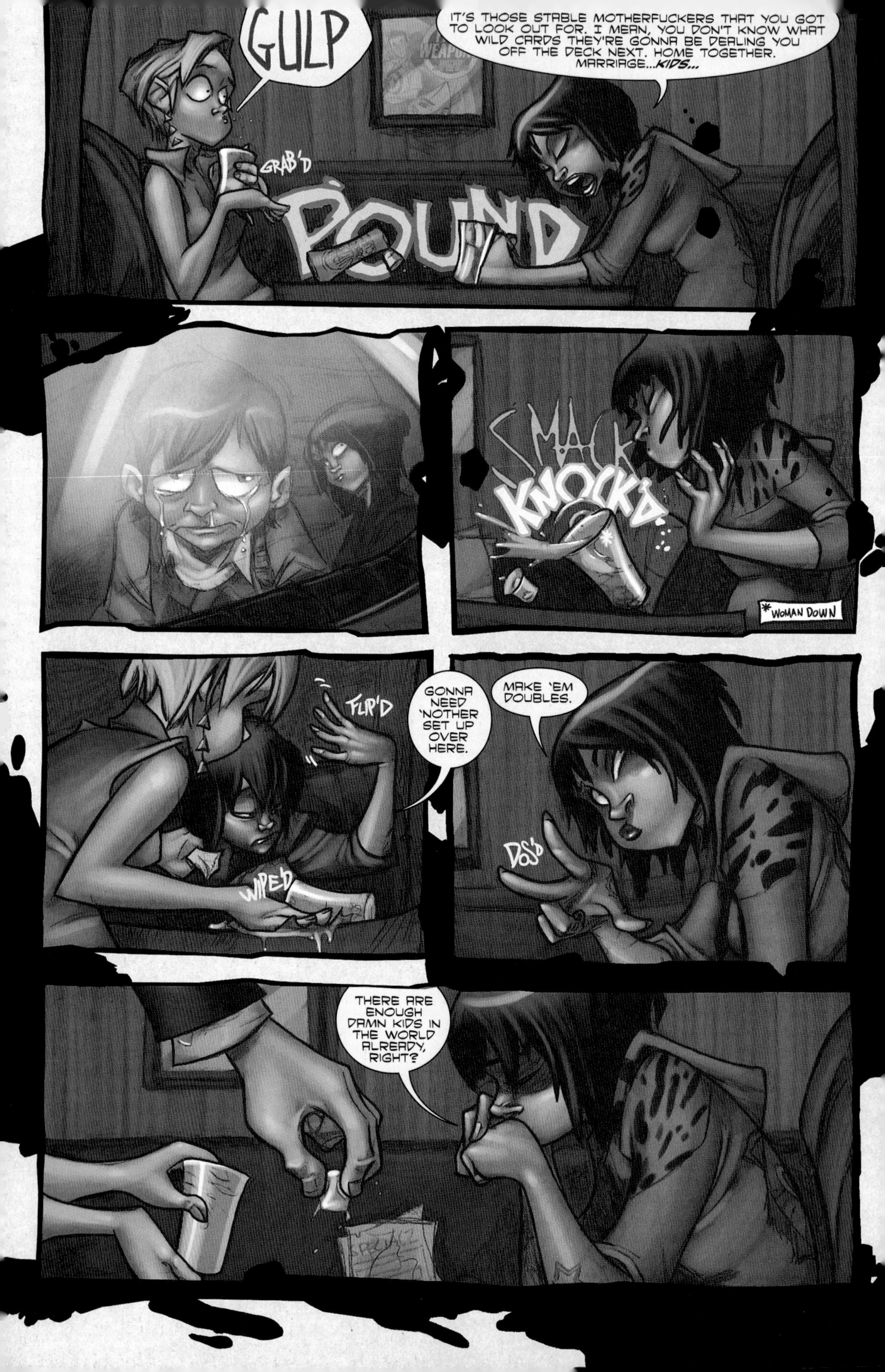
GULP
IT'S THOSE STABLE MOTHERFUCKERS THAT YOU GOT TO LOOK OUT FOR. I MEAN, YOU DON'T KNOW WHAT WILD CARDS THEY'RE GONNA BE DEALING YOU OFF THE DECK NEXT. HOME TOGETHER. MARRIAGE...KIDS...
GRAB'D
POUND
SMACK
KNOCK'D
*WOMAN DOWN
FLIP'D
WIPE'D
GONNA NEED 'NOTHER SET UP OVER HERE.
MAKE 'EM DOUBLES.
DOS'D
THERE ARE ENOUGH DAMN KIDS IN THE WORLD ALREADY, RIGHT?

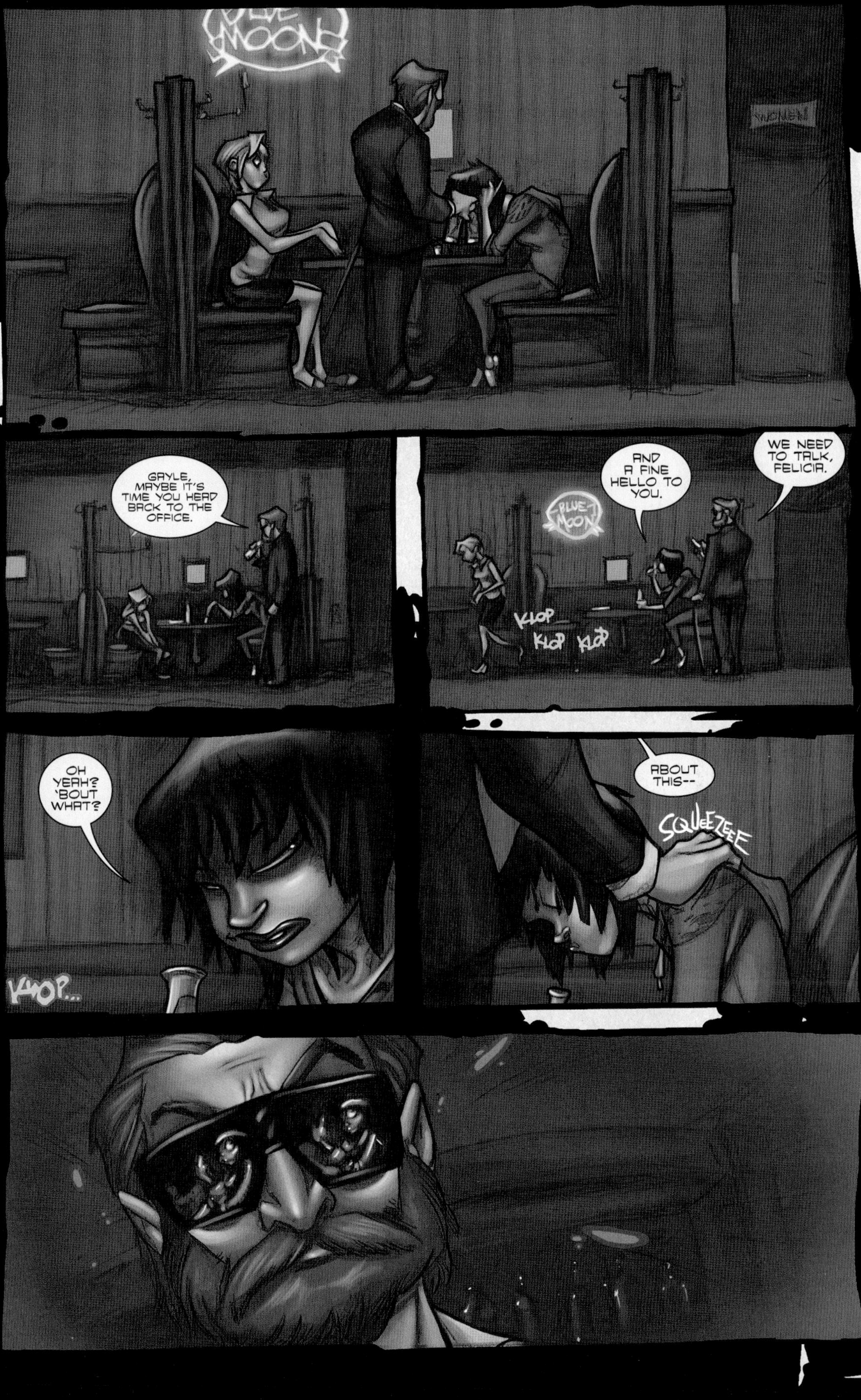
WOMEN
GAYLE, MAYBE IT'S TIME YOU HEAD BACK TO THE OFFICE.
BLUE MOON
AND A FINE HELLO TO YOU.
WE NEED TO TALK, FELICIA.
KLOP
KLOP KLOP
OH YEAH? 'BOUT WHAT?
KLOP...
ABOUT THIS--
SQUEEZEEE

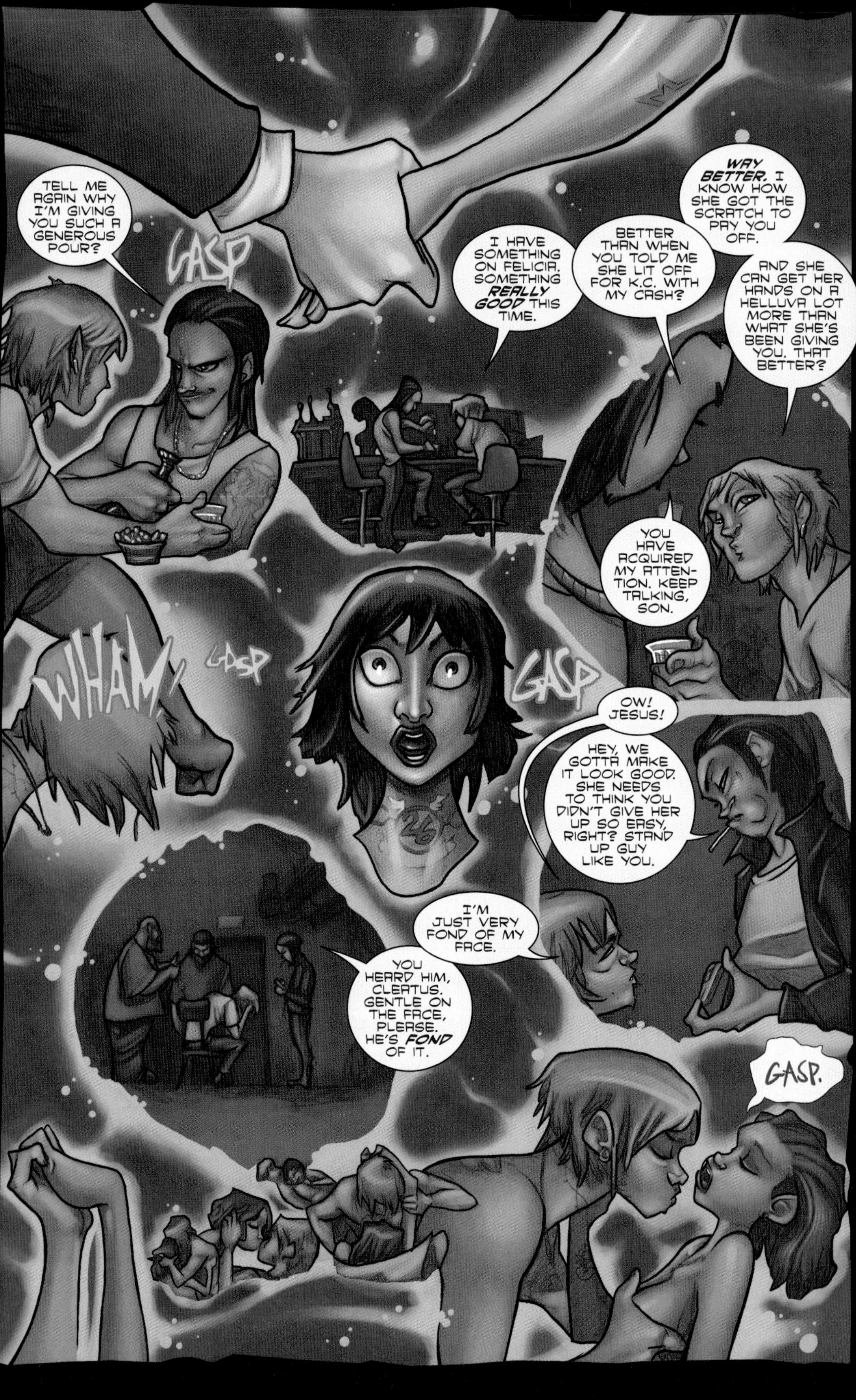

TELL ME AGAIN WHY I'M GIVING YOU SUCH A GENEROUS POUR?
GASP
I HAVE SOMETHING ON FELICIA. SOMETHING REALLY GOOD THIS TIME.
BETTER THAN WHEN YOU TOLD ME SHE LIT OFF FOR K.C. WITH MY CASH?
WAY BETTER. I KNOW HOW SHE GOT THE SCRATCH TO PAY YOU OFF.
AND SHE CAN GET HER HANDS ON A HELLUVA LOT MORE THAN WHAT SHE'S BEEN GIVING YOU. THAT BETTER?
YOU HAVE ACQUIRED MY ATTEN-TION. KEEP TALKING, SON.
WHAM!
GASP
GASP
OW! JESUS!
HEY, WE GOTTA MAKE IT LOOK GOOD. SHE NEEDS TO THINK YOU DIDN'T GIVE HER UP SO EASY, RIGHT? STAND UP GUY LIKE YOU.
I'M JUST VERY FOND OF MY FACE.
YOU HEARD HIM, CLEATUS. GENTLE ON THE FACE, PLEASE. HE'S FOND OF IT.
GASP.

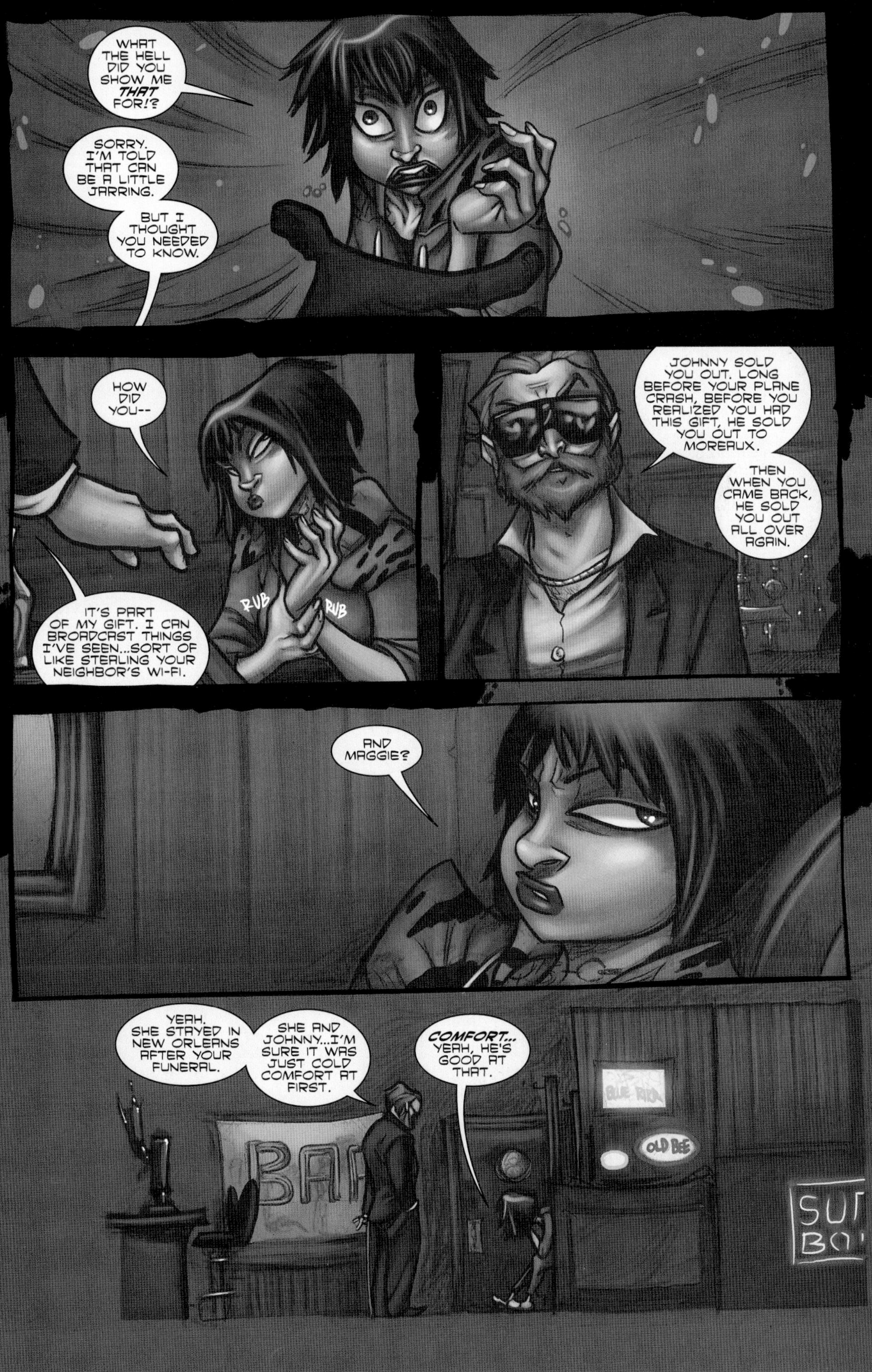
WHAT THE HELL DID YOU SHOW ME THAT FOR!?
SORRY. I'M TOLD THAT CAN BE A LITTLE JARRING.
BUT I THOUGHT YOU NEEDED TO KNOW.
HOW DID YOU--
IT'S PART OF MY GIFT. I CAN BROADCAST THINGS I'VE SEEN...SORT OF LIKE STEALING YOUR NEIGHBOR'S WI-FI.
RUB
RUB
JOHNNY SOLD YOU OUT. LONG BEFORE YOUR PLANE CRASH, BEFORE YOU REALIZED YOU HAD THIS GIFT, HE SOLD YOU OUT TO MOREAUX.
THEN WHEN YOU CAME BACK, HE SOLD YOU OUT ALL OVER AGAIN.
AND MAGGIE?
YEAH. SHE STAYED IN NEW ORLEANS AFTER YOUR FUNERAL.
SHE AND JOHNNY...I'M SURE IT WAS JUST COLD COMFORT AT FIRST.
COMFORT... YEAH, HE'S GOOD AT THAT.
OLD BEE
SU
BO

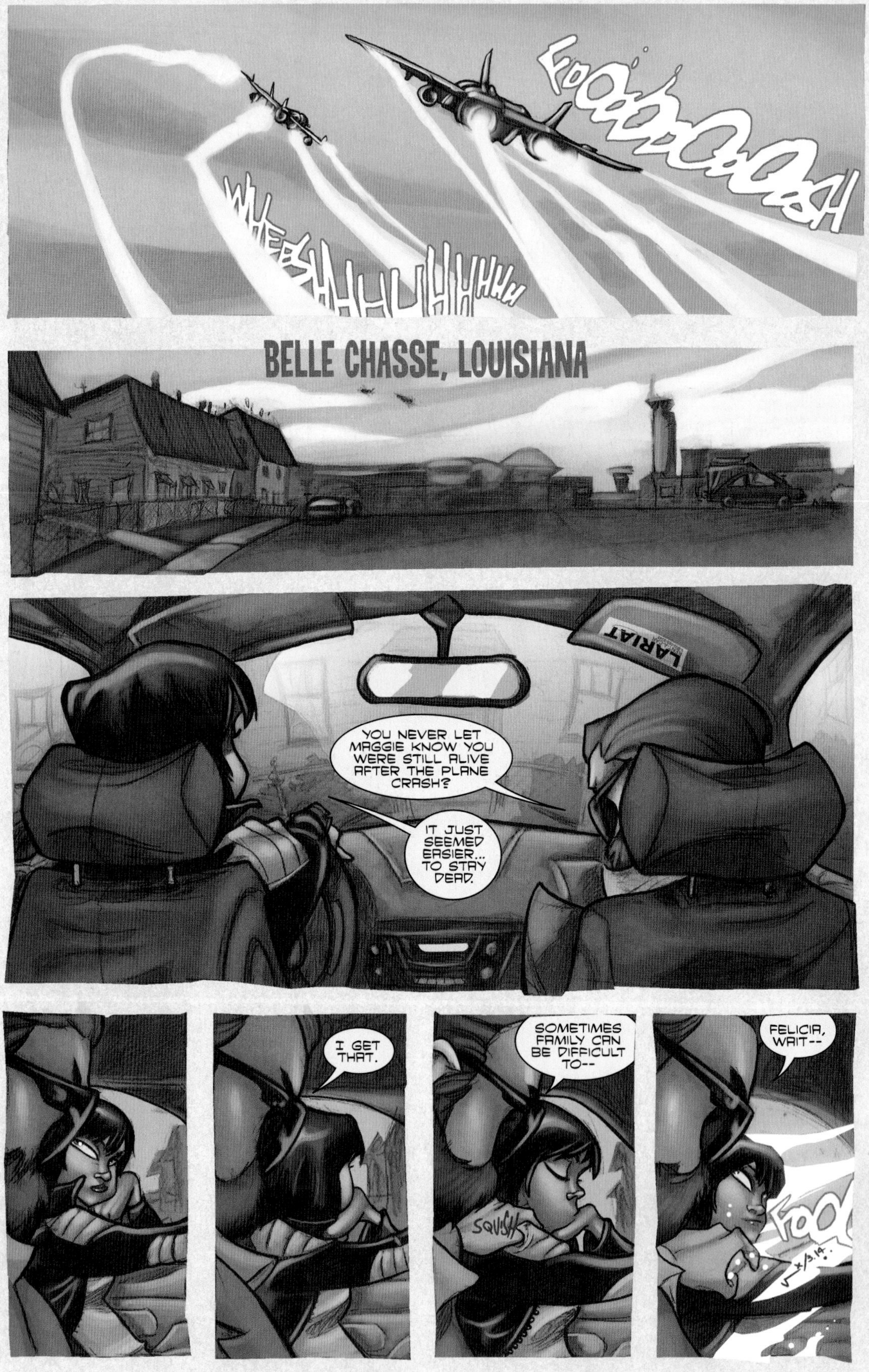
FOOOOOOOSH
WHEESHHHHHHHHH
BELLE CHASSE, LOUISIANA
LARIAT
YOU NEVER LET MAGGIE KNOW YOU WERE STILL ALIVE AFTER THE PLANE CRASH?
IT JUST SEEMED EASIER... TO STAY DEAD.
I GET THAT.
SOMETIMES FAMILY CAN BE DIFFICULT TO--
SQUISH
FELICIA, WAIT--
FOO

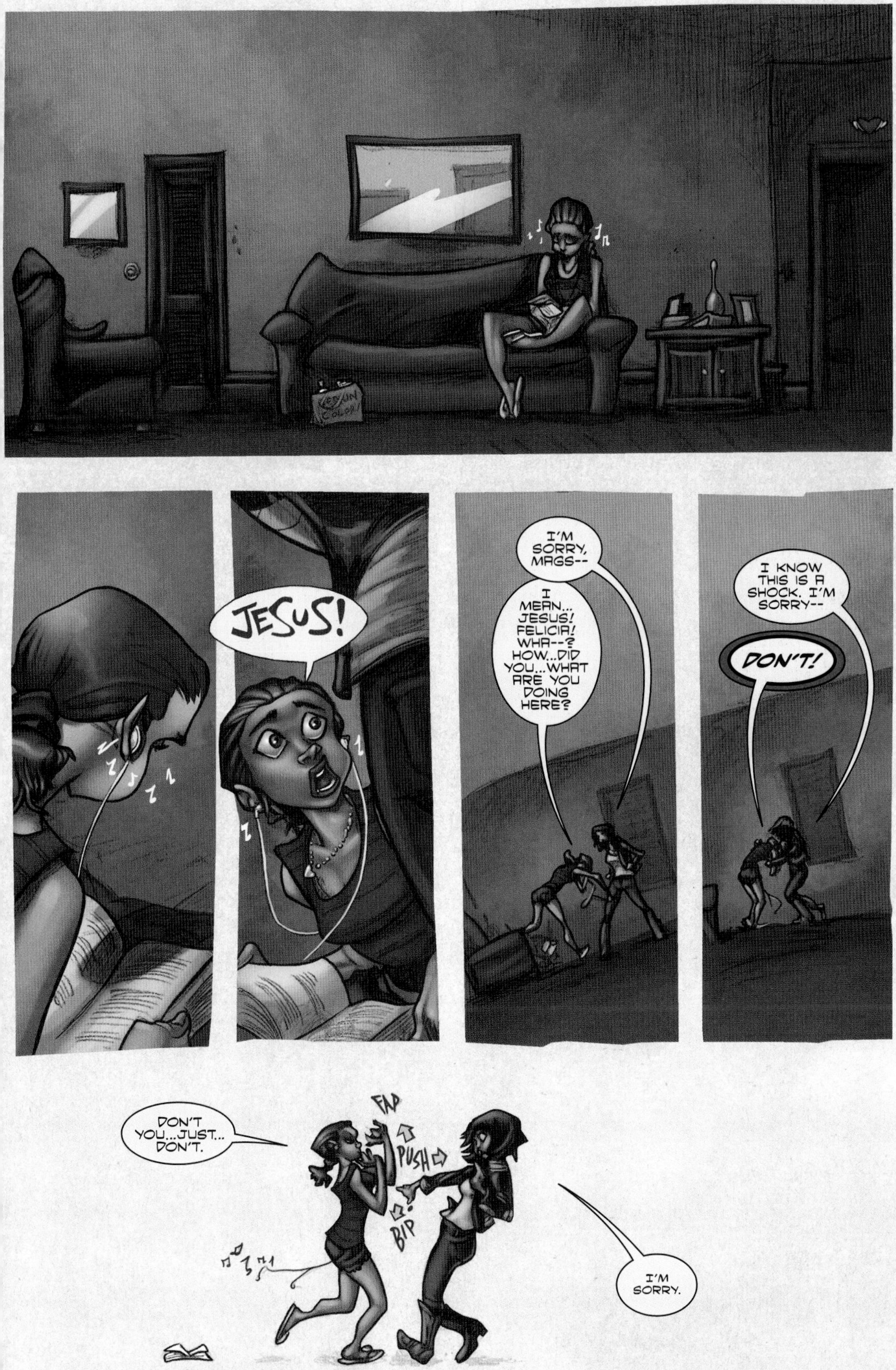
JESUS!
I'M SORRY, MAGS--
I MEAN... JESUS! FELICIA! WHA--? HOW...DID YOU...WHAT ARE YOU DOING HERE?
I KNOW THIS IS A SHOCK. I'M SORRY--
DON'T!
DON'T YOU...JUST... DON'T.
FAP
PUSH
BIP
I'M SORRY.

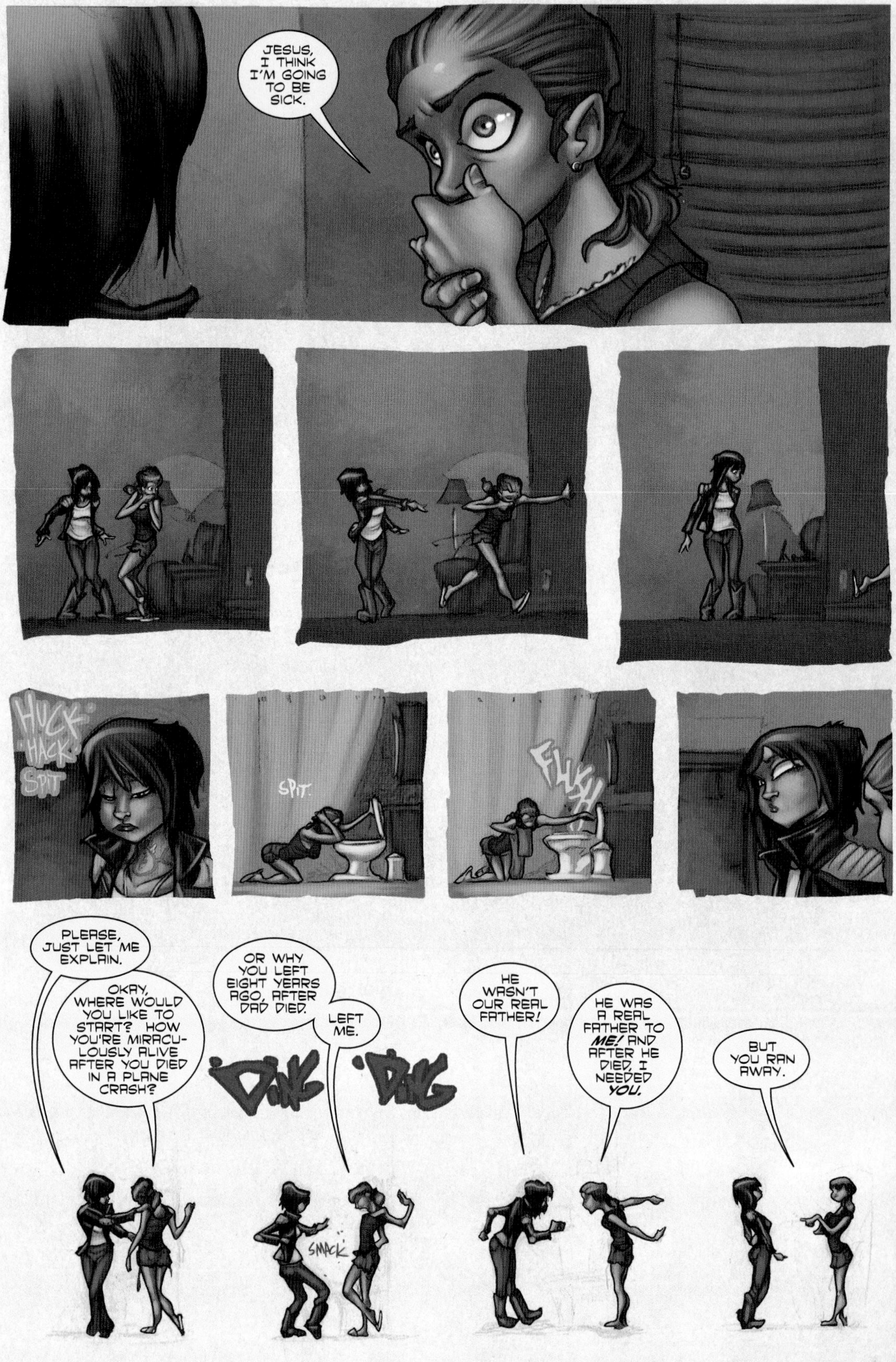

JESUS, I THINK I'M GOING TO BE SICK.
HUCK HACK SPIT
SPIT.
FLUSH
PLEASE, JUST LET ME EXPLAIN.
OKAY, WHERE WOULD YOU LIKE TO START? HOW YOU'RE MIRACULOUSLY ALIVE AFTER YOU DIED IN A PLANE CRASH?
OR WHY YOU LEFT EIGHT YEARS AGO, AFTER DAD DIED.
LEFT ME.
DING DONG
SMACK
HE WASN'T OUR REAL FATHER!
HE WAS A REAL FATHER TO ME! AND AFTER HE DIED, I NEEDED YOU.
BUT YOU RAN AWAY.

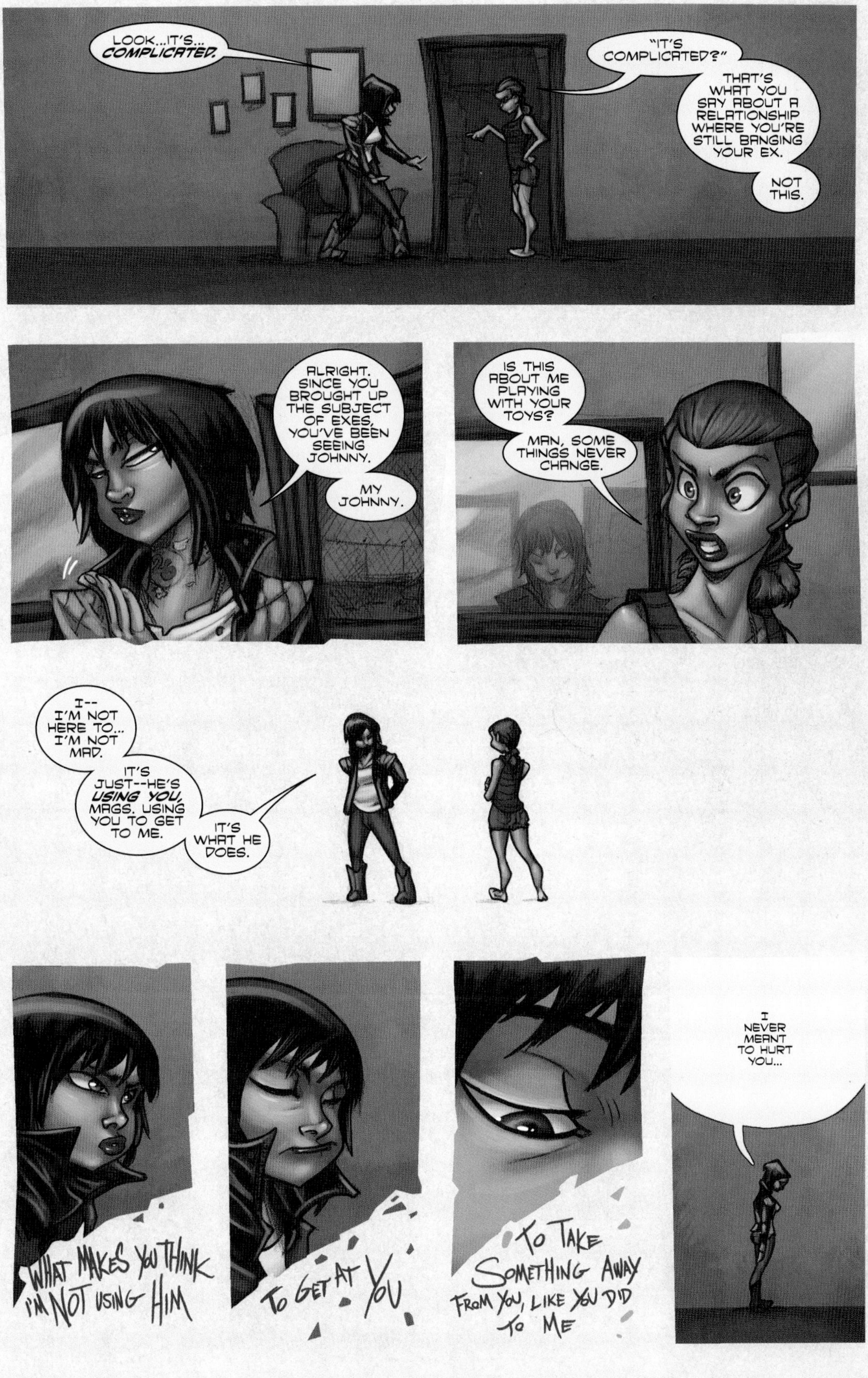
LOOK...IT'S... *COMPLICATED.*
"IT'S COMPLICATED?"
THAT'S WHAT YOU SAY ABOUT A RELATIONSHIP WHERE YOU'RE STILL BANGING YOUR EX.
NOT THIS.
ALRIGHT. SINCE YOU BROUGHT UP THE SUBJECT OF EXES, YOU'VE BEEN SEEING JOHNNY.
MY JOHNNY.
IS THIS ABOUT ME PLAYING WITH YOUR TOYS?
MAN, SOME THINGS NEVER CHANGE.
I-- I'M NOT HERE TO... I'M NOT MAD.
IT'S JUST--HE'S *USING YOU,* MAGS. USING YOU TO GET TO ME.
IT'S WHAT HE DOES.
WHAT MAKES YOU THINK I'M NOT USING HIM
TO GET AT YOU
TO TAKE SOMETHING AWAY FROM YOU, LIKE YOU DID TO ME
I NEVER MEANT TO HURT YOU...

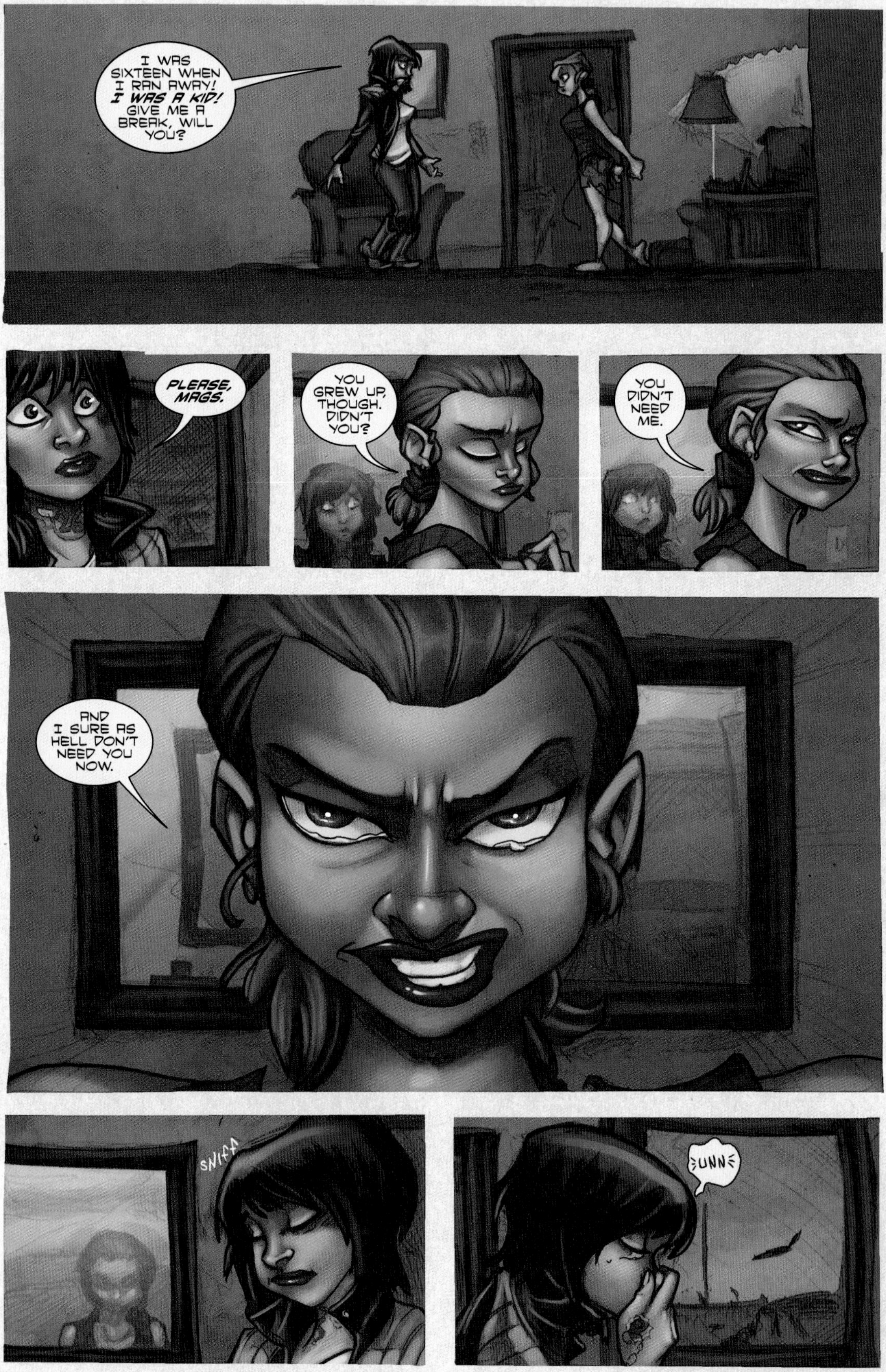
I WAS SIXTEEN WHEN I RAN AWAY! I WAS A KID! GIVE ME A BREAK, WILL YOU?
PLEASE, MAGS.
YOU GREW UP, THOUGH. DIDN'T YOU?
YOU DIDN'T NEED ME.
AND I SURE AS HELL DON'T NEED YOU NOW.
SNIFF
UNN

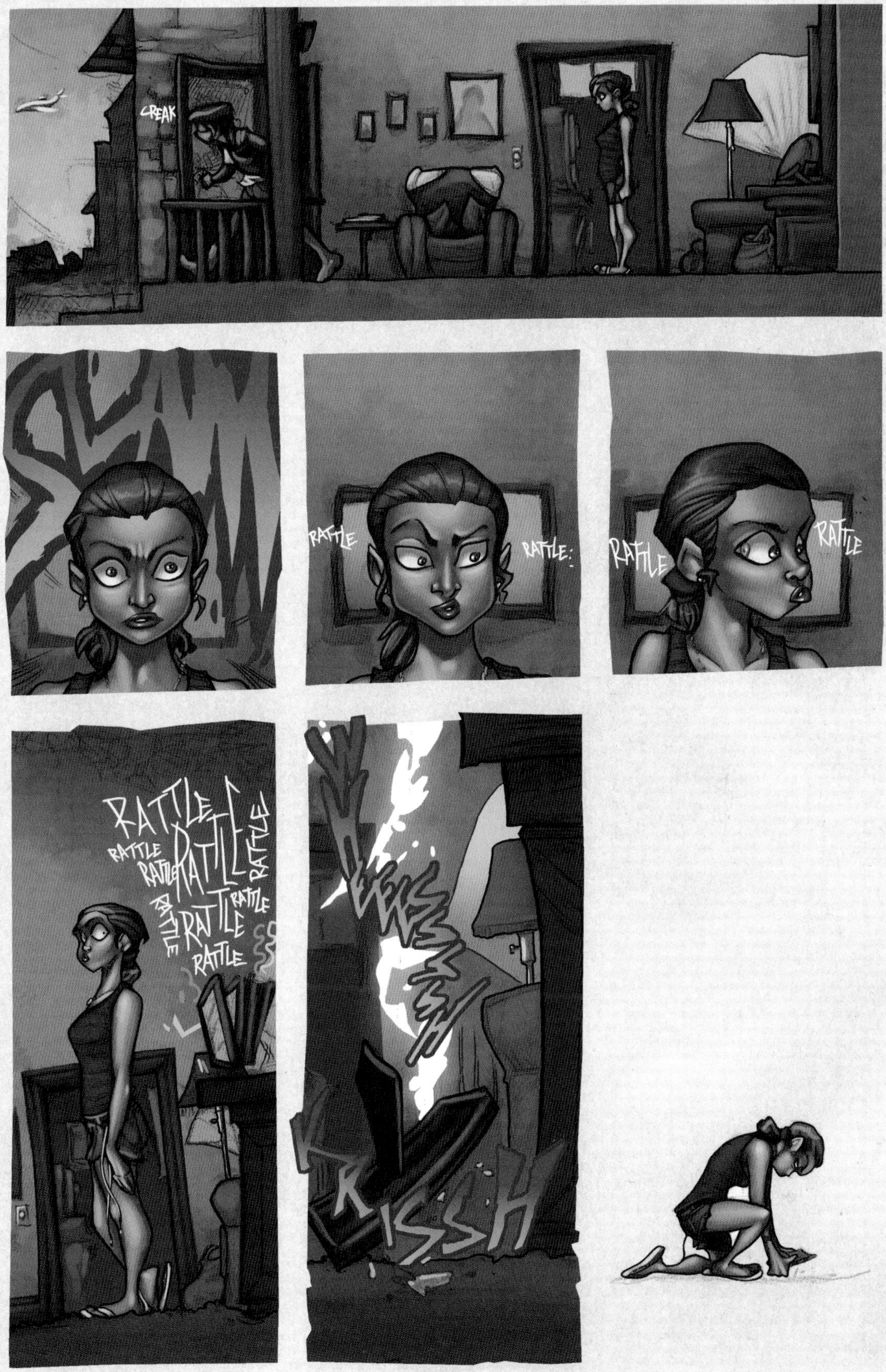
CREAK
RATTLE
RATTLE
RATTLE
RATTLE
RATTLE RATTLE RATTLE RATTLE RATTLE RATTLE RATTLE RATTLE RATTLE RATTLE RATTLE
KRISSH

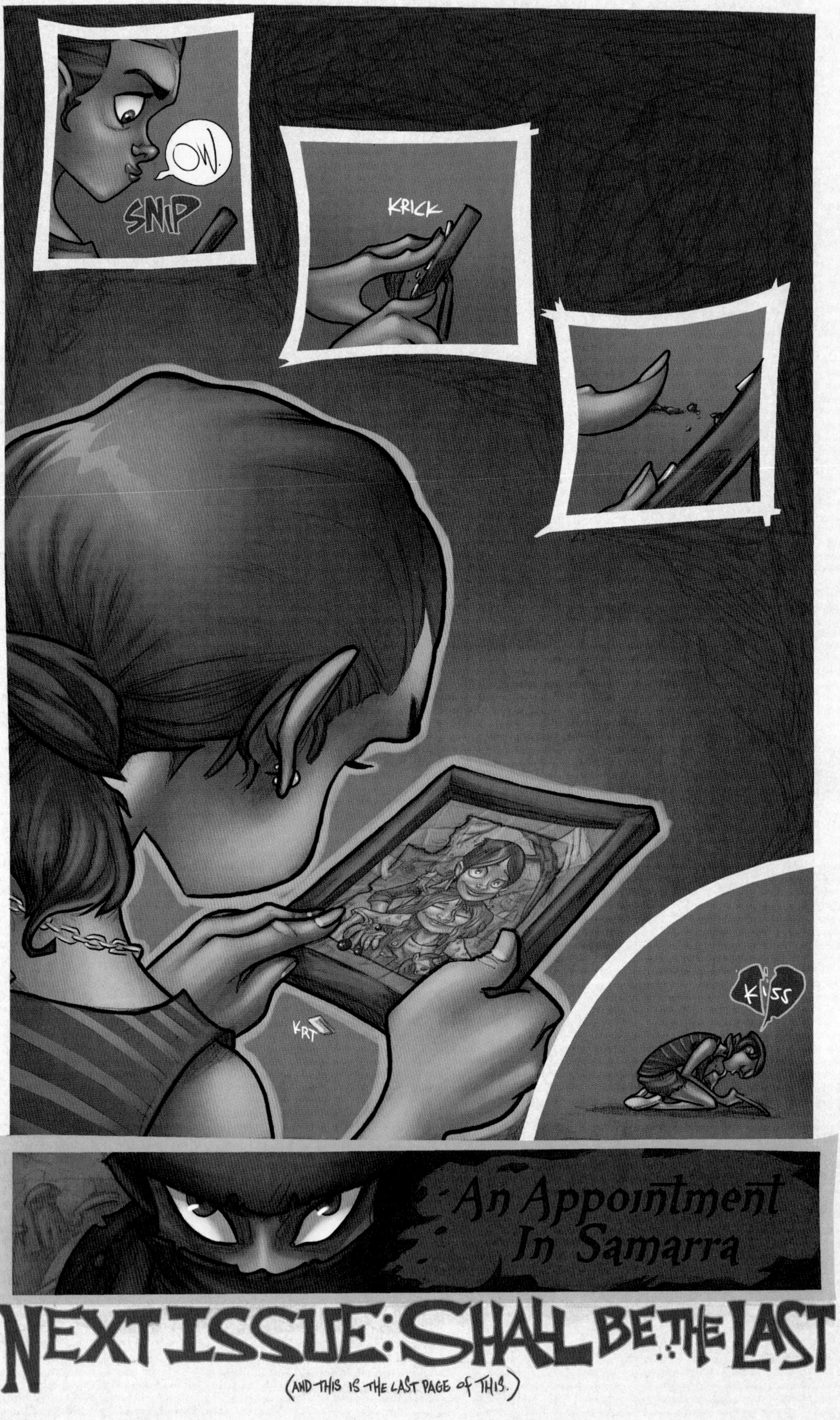
OW.
SNIP
KRICK
KRT
KISS
An Appointment In Samarra
NEXT ISSUE: SHALL BE THE LAST
(AND THIS IS THE LAST PAGE OF THIS.)

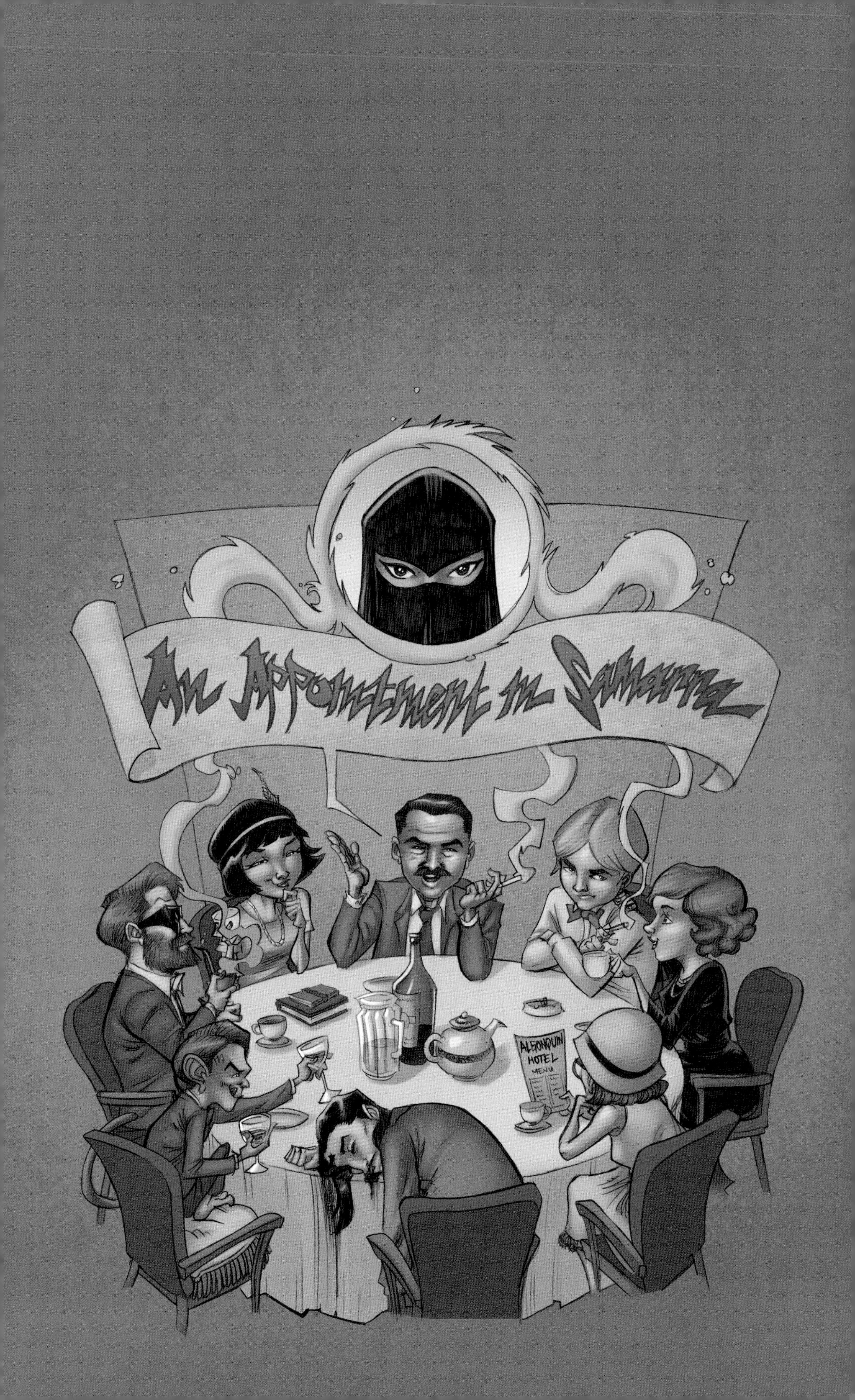
An Appointment in Samarra
ALGONQUIN
HOTEL
MENU

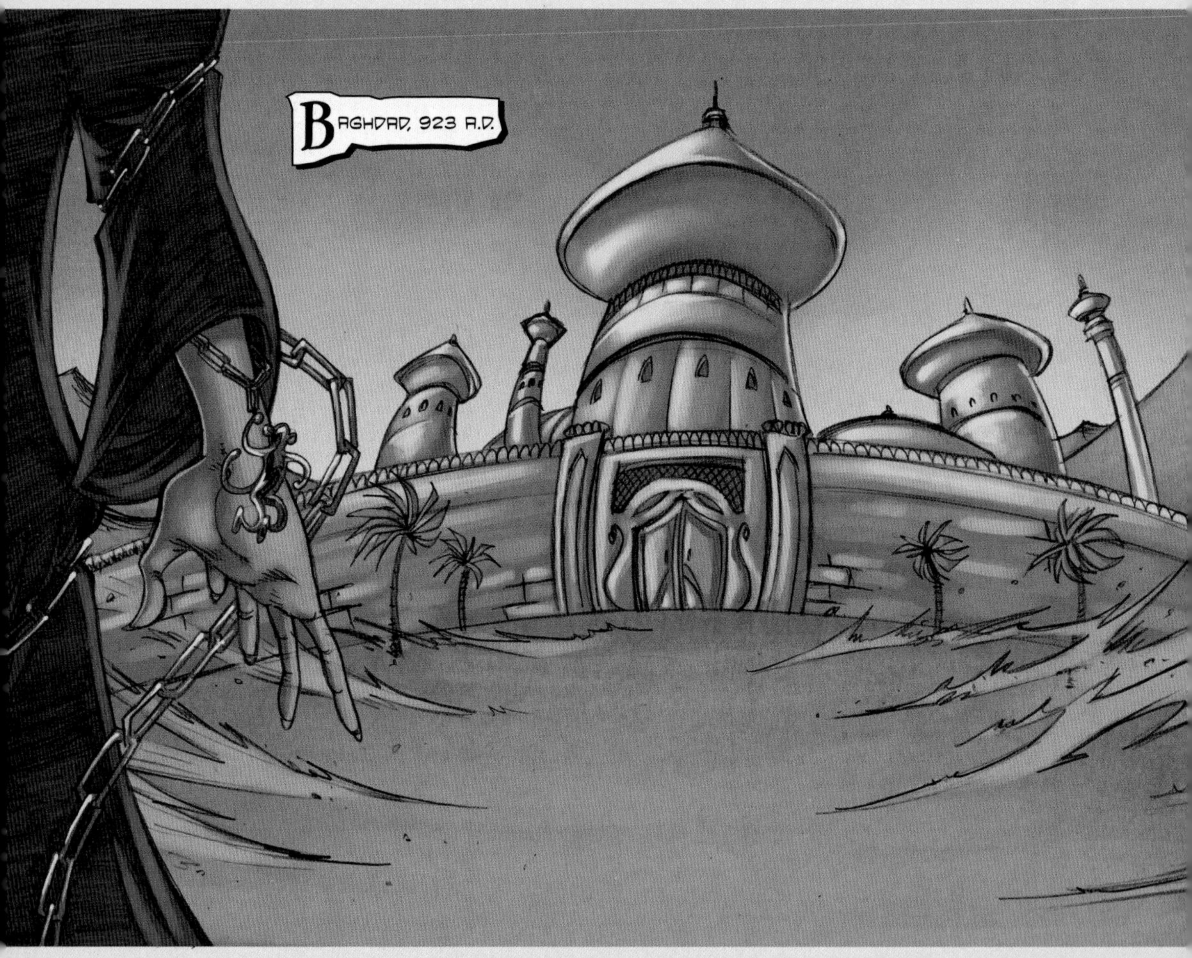
BAGHDAD, 923 A.D.

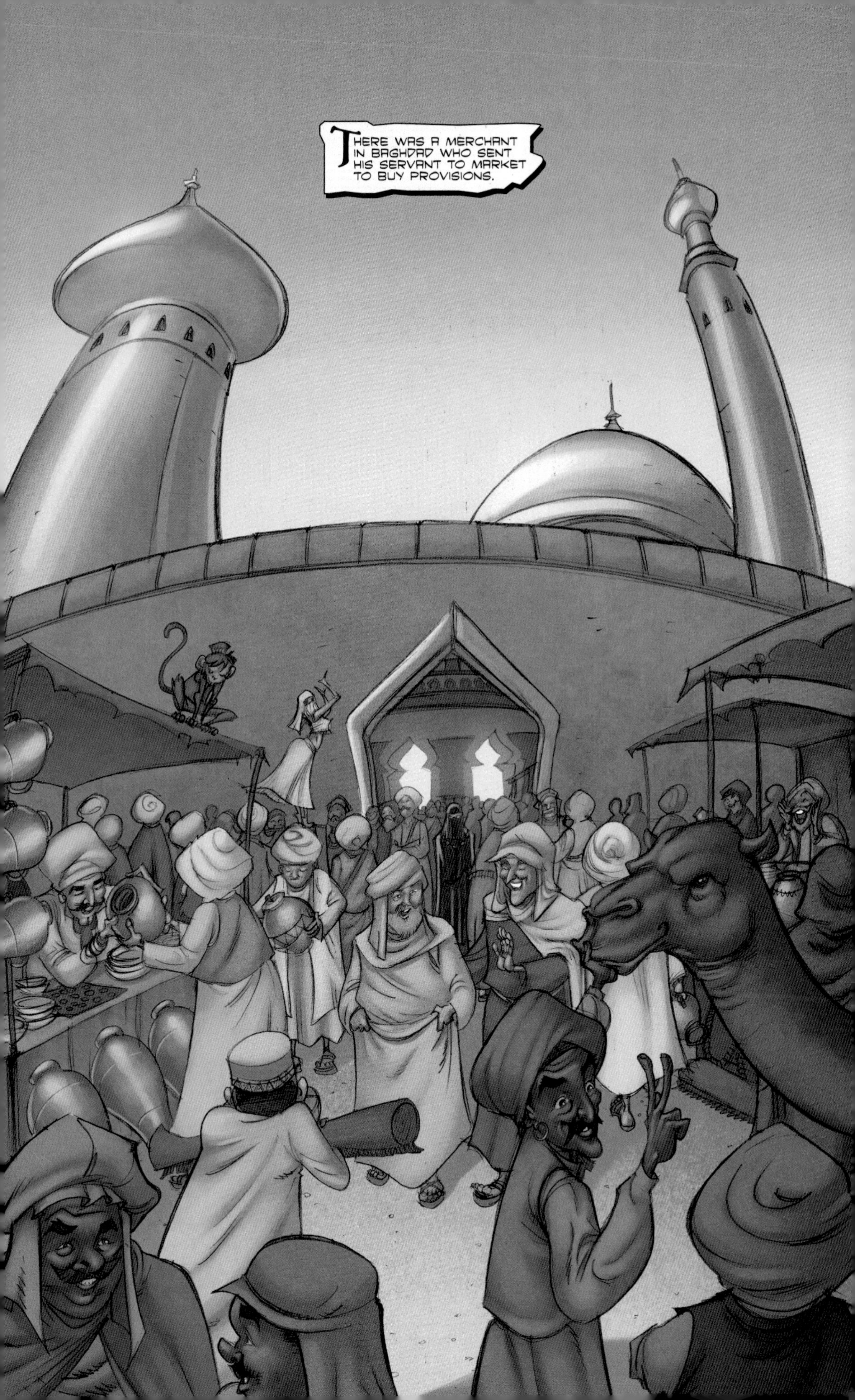
THERE WAS A MERCHANT IN BAGHDAD WHO SENT HIS SERVANT TO MARKET TO BUY PROVISIONS.

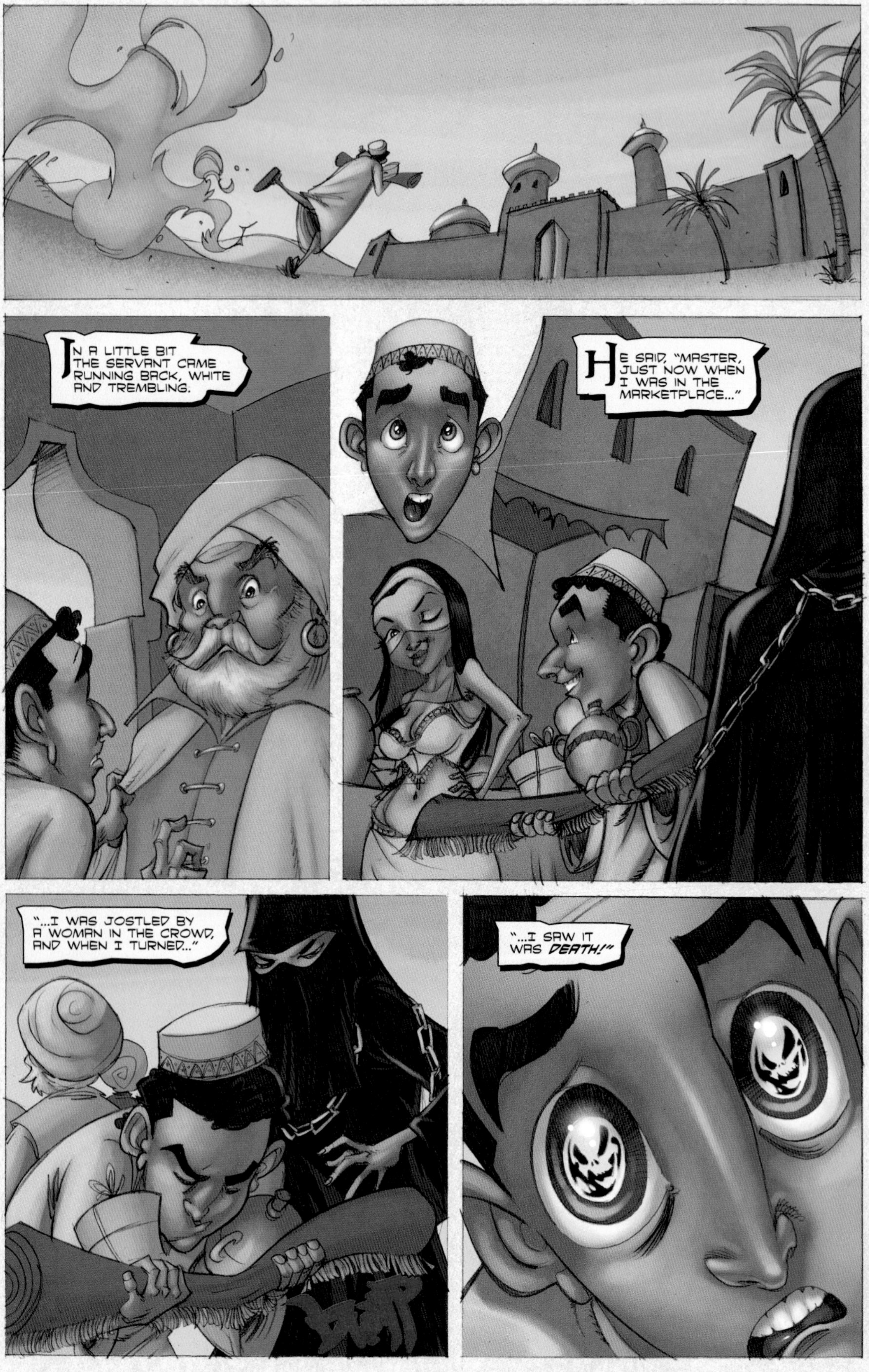
In a little bit the servant came running back, white and trembling.
He said, "Master, just now when I was in the marketplace..."
"...I was jostled by a woman in the crowd, and when I turned..."
"...I saw it was *death!*"

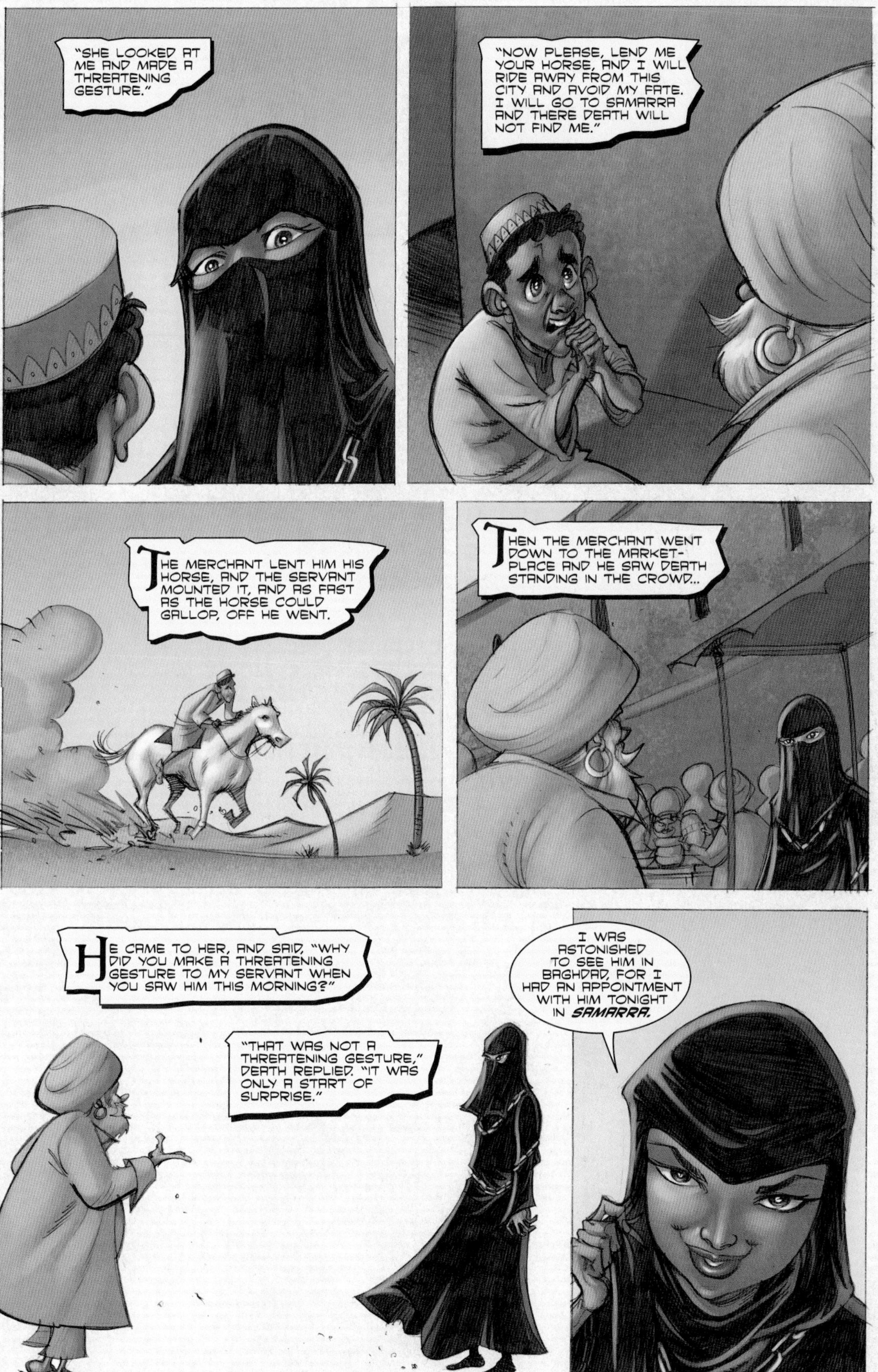
"SHE LOOKED AT ME AND MADE A THREATENING GESTURE."
"NOW PLEASE, LEND ME YOUR HORSE, AND I WILL RIDE AWAY FROM THIS CITY AND AVOID MY FATE. I WILL GO TO SAMARRA AND THERE DEATH WILL NOT FIND ME."
THE MERCHANT LENT HIM HIS HORSE, AND THE SERVANT MOUNTED IT, AND AS FAST AS THE HORSE COULD GALLOP, OFF HE WENT.
THEN THE MERCHANT WENT DOWN TO THE MARKET-PLACE AND HE SAW DEATH STANDING IN THE CROWD...
HE CAME TO HER, AND SAID, "WHY DID YOU MAKE A THREATENING GESTURE TO MY SERVANT WHEN YOU SAW HIM THIS MORNING?"
"THAT WAS NOT A THREATENING GESTURE," DEATH REPLIED. "IT WAS ONLY A START OF SURPRISE."
I WAS ASTONISHED TO SEE HIM IN BAGHDAD, FOR I HAD AN APPOINTMENT WITH HIM TONIGHT IN SAMARRA.

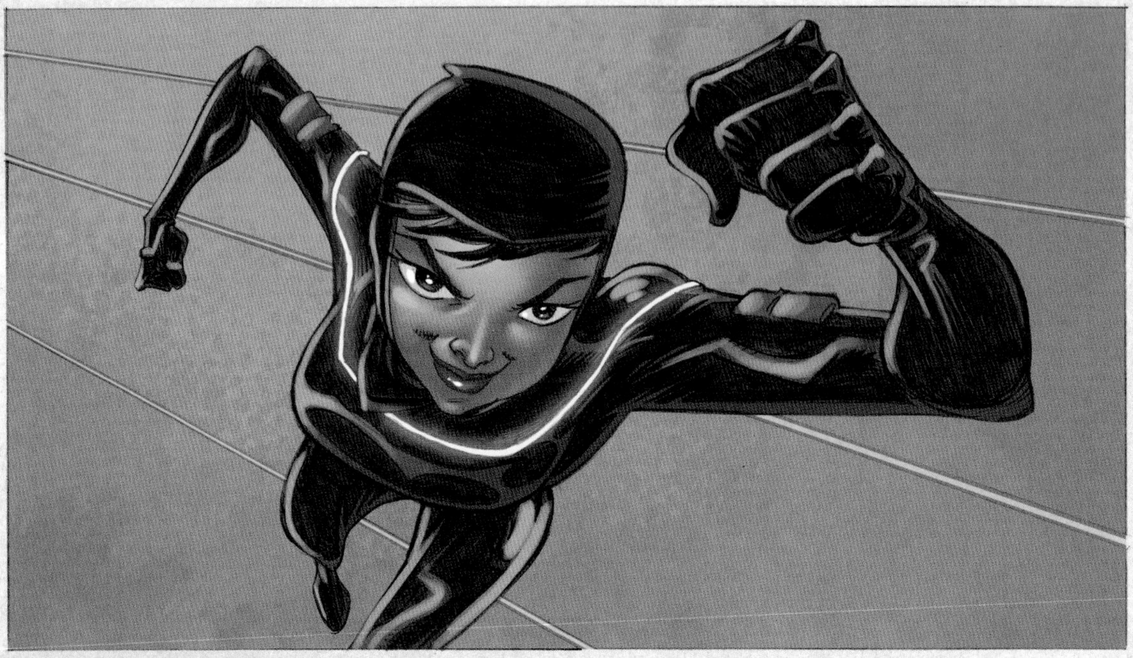

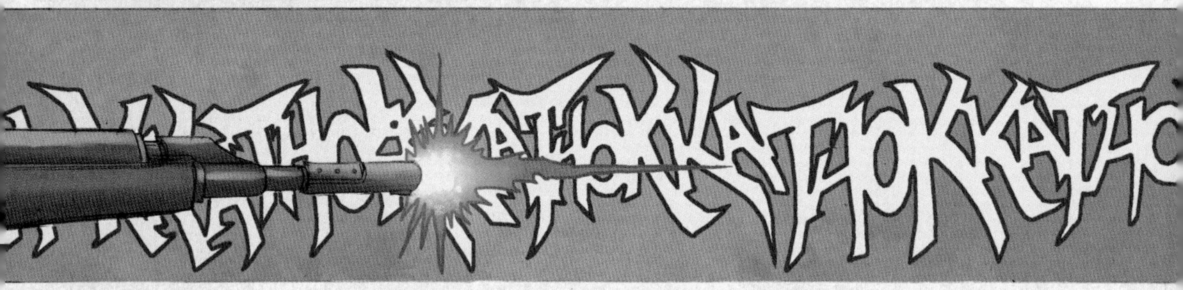
KATHOKKATHOKKATHO

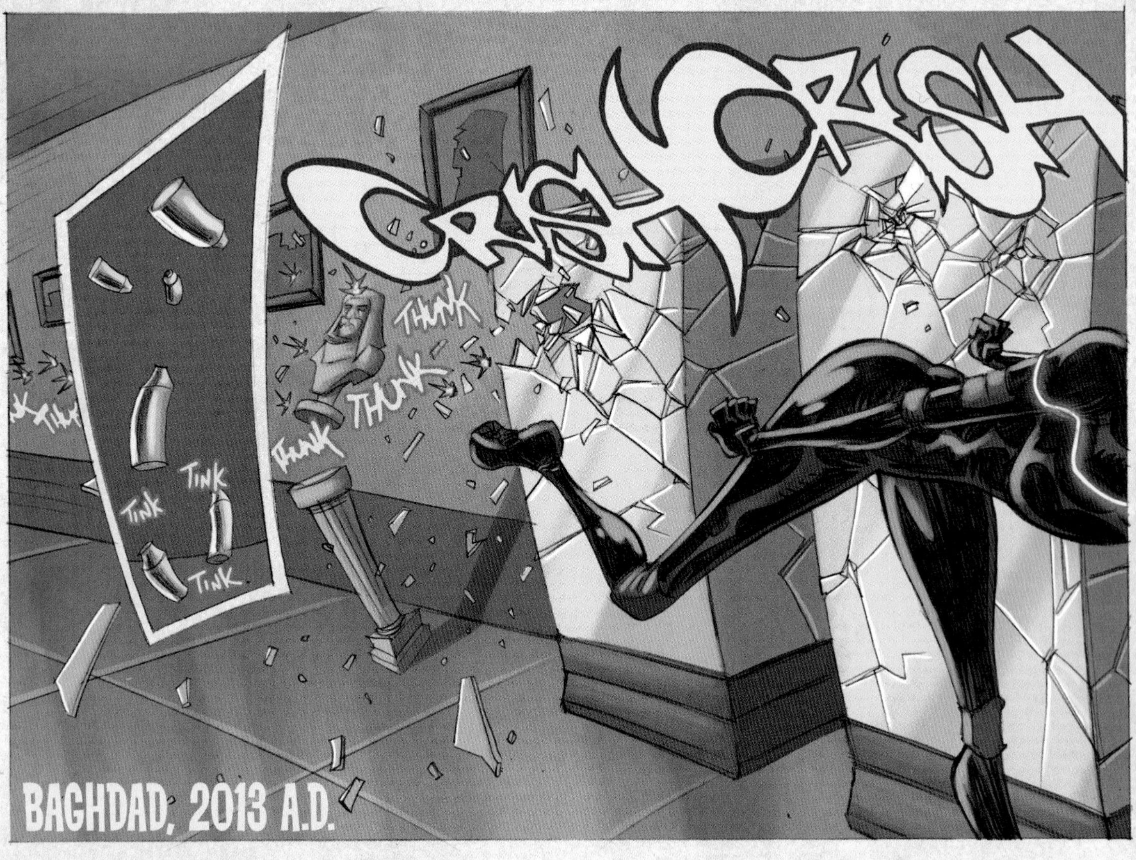
CRISH
CRISH
THUNK
THUNK
THUNK
TINK
TINK
TINK

BAGHDAD, 2013 A.D.

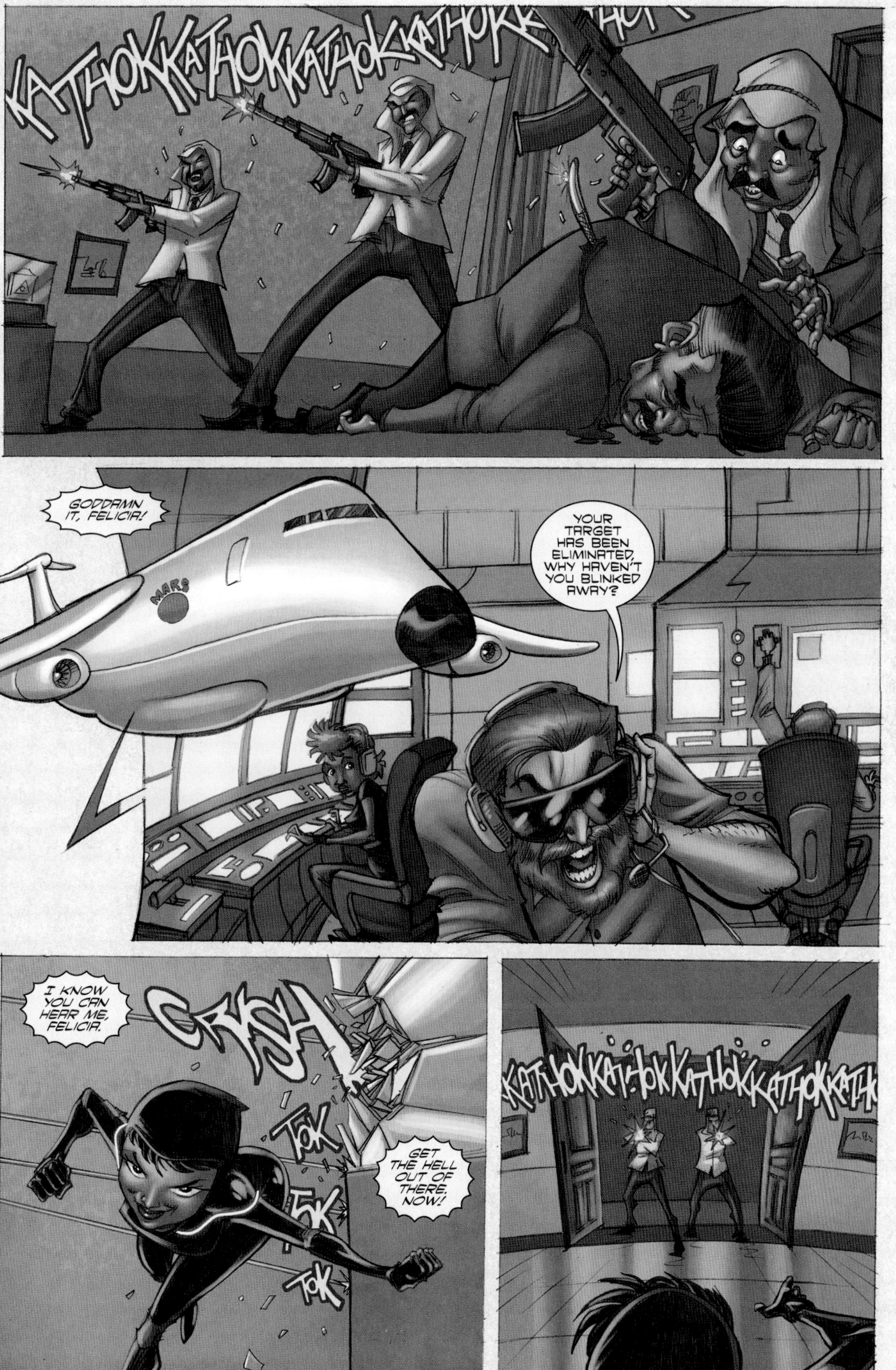
KATHOKKATHOKKATHOKKATHOKK
GODDAMN IT, FELICIA!
MARS
YOUR TARGET HAS BEEN ELIMINATED, WHY HAVEN'T YOU BLINKED AWAY?
I KNOW YOU CAN HEAR ME, FELICIA.
CRASH
TOK
TOK
TOK
GET THE HELL OUT OF THERE. NOW!
KATHOKKATHOKKATHOKKATHOKKATHO

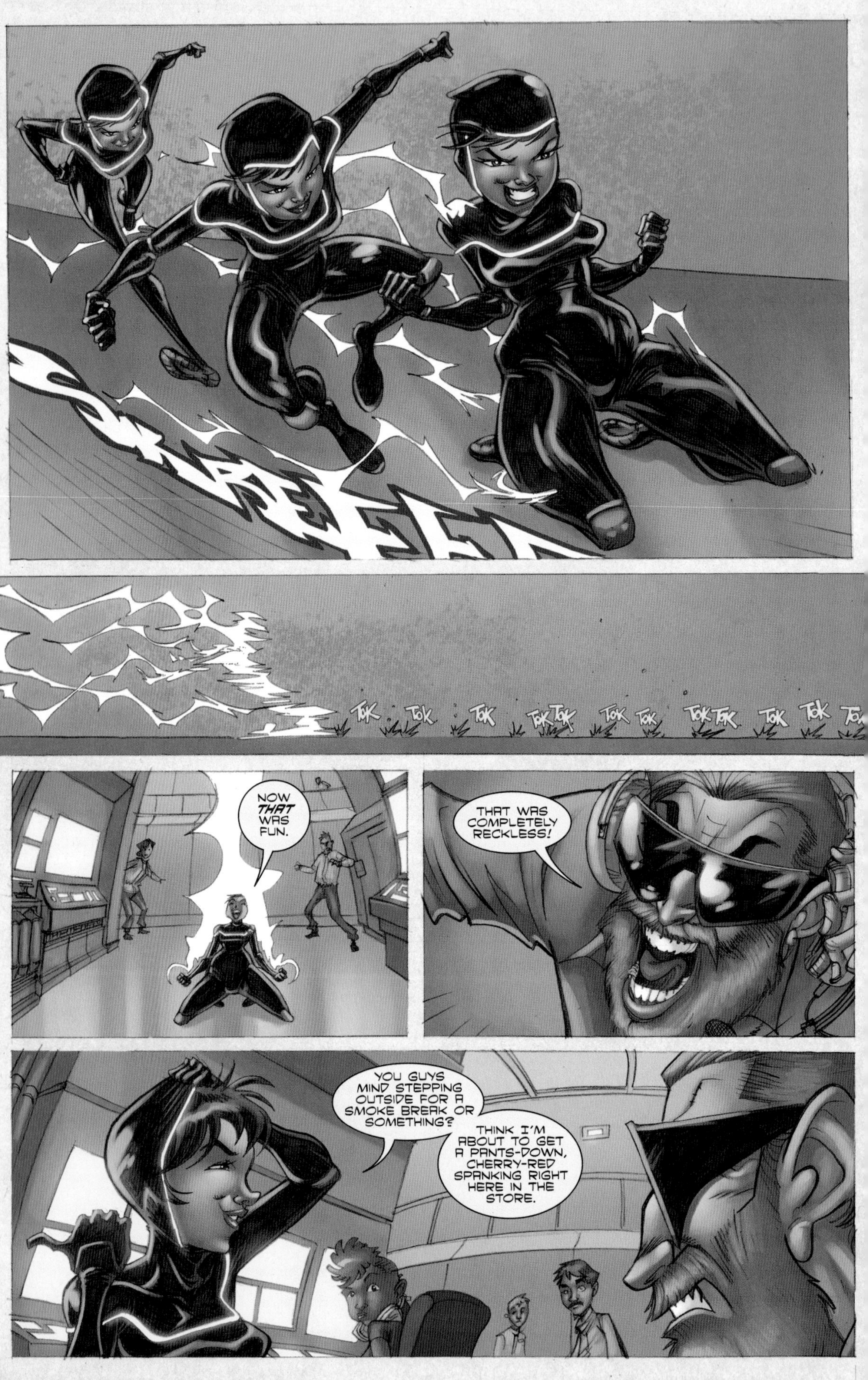
TOK TOK TOK TOK TOK TOK TOK TOK TOK TOK TOK TOK
NOW *THAT* WAS FUN.
THAT WAS COMPLETELY RECKLESS!
YOU GUYS MIND STEPPING OUTSIDE FOR A SMOKE BREAK OR SOMETHING?
THINK I'M ABOUT TO GET A PANTS-DOWN, CHERRY-RED SPANKING RIGHT HERE IN THE STORE.

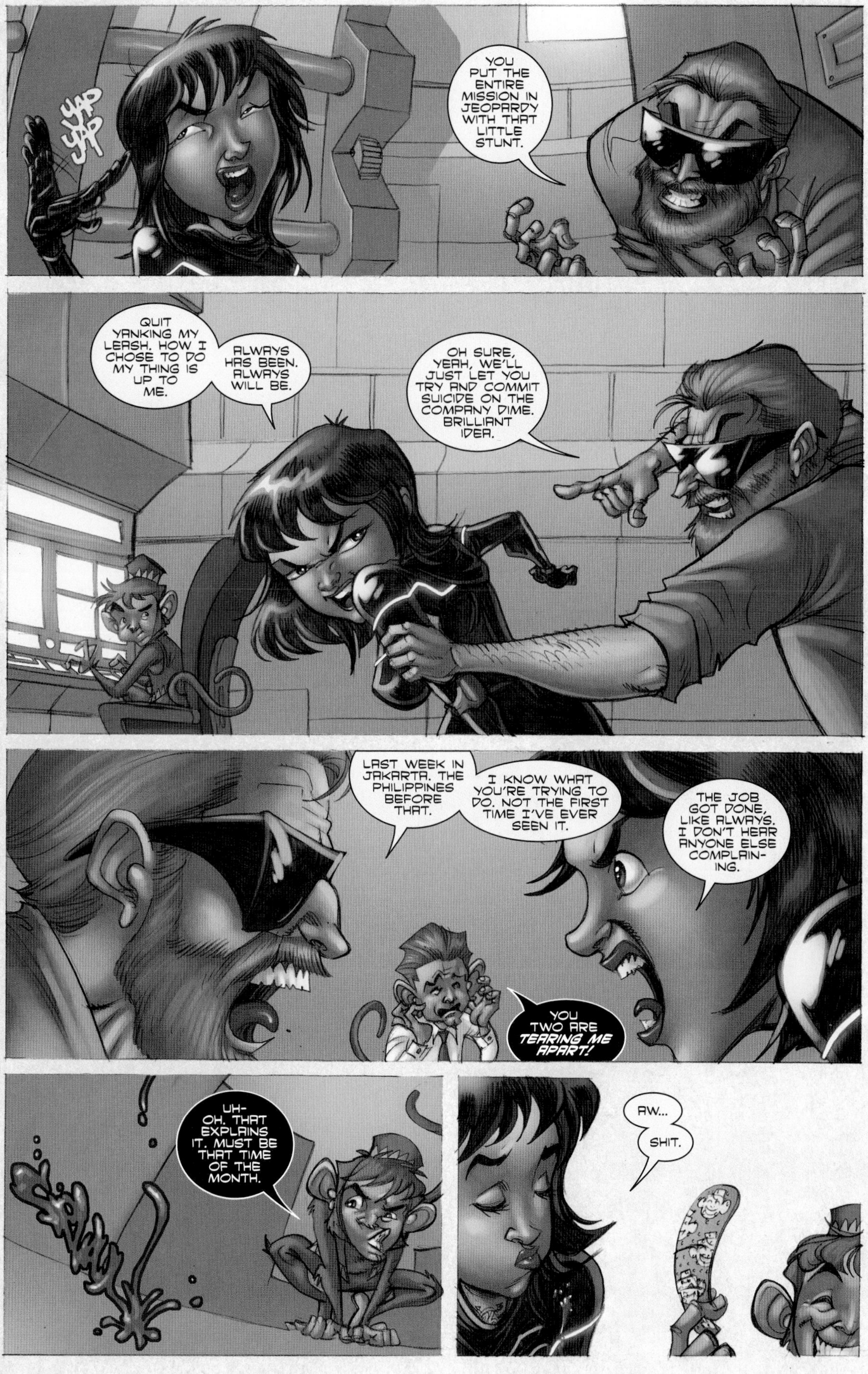

YAP YAP
YOU PUT THE ENTIRE MISSION IN JEOPARDY WITH THAT LITTLE STUNT.
QUIT YANKING MY LEASH. HOW I CHOSE TO DO MY THING IS UP TO ME.
ALWAYS HAS BEEN. ALWAYS WILL BE.
OH SURE, YEAH, WE'LL JUST LET YOU TRY AND COMMIT SUICIDE ON THE COMPANY DIME. BRILLIANT IDEA.
LAST WEEK IN JAKARTA. THE PHILIPPINES BEFORE THAT.
I KNOW WHAT YOU'RE TRYING TO DO. NOT THE FIRST TIME I'VE EVER SEEN IT.
THE JOB GOT DONE, LIKE ALWAYS. I DON'T HEAR ANYONE ELSE COMPLAINING.
YOU TWO ARE TEARING ME APART!
UH-OH. THAT EXPLAINS IT. MUST BE THAT TIME OF THE MONTH.
AW...
SHIT.

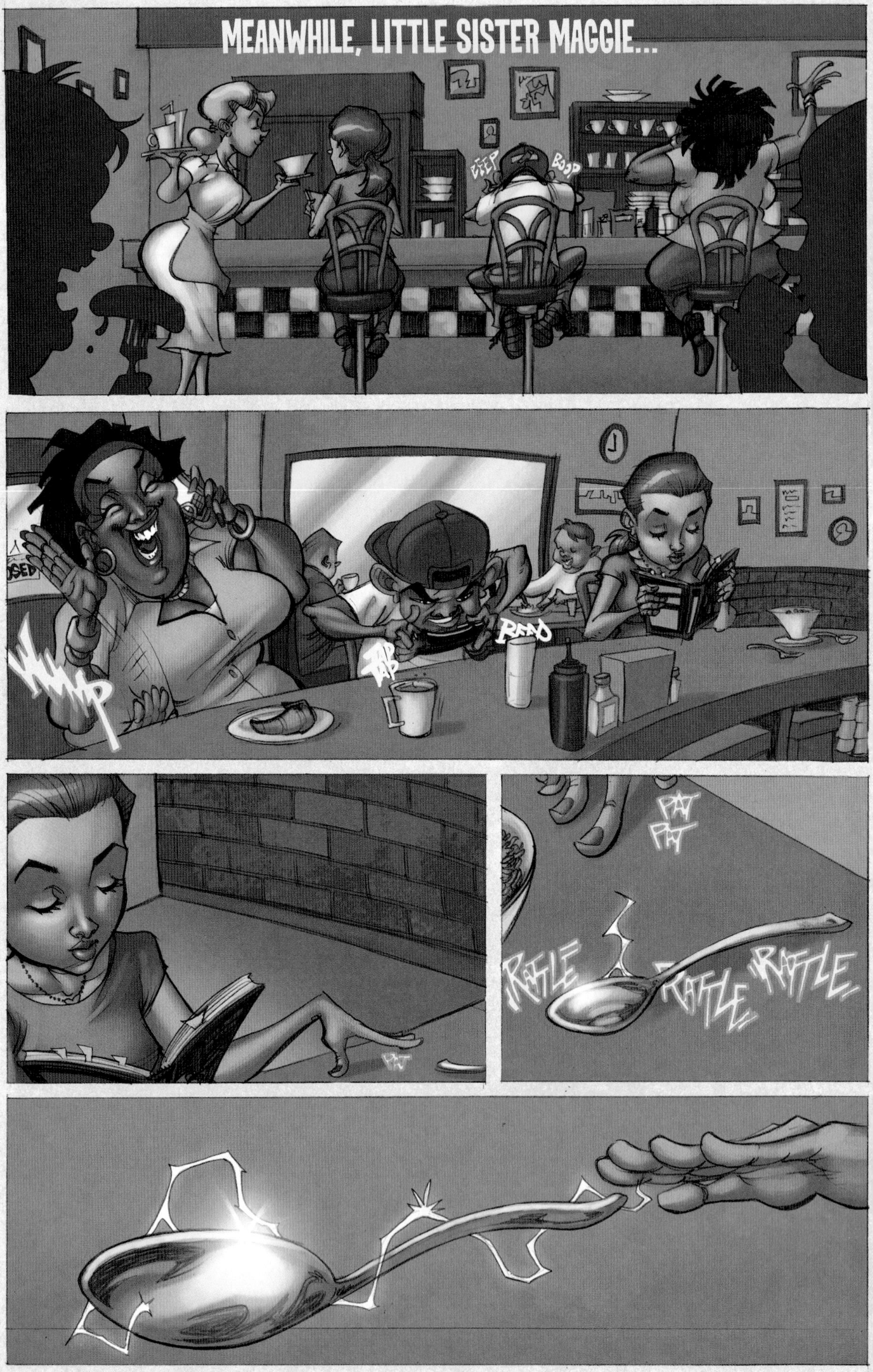
MEANWHILE, LITTLE SISTER MAGGIE...
BEEP
BOOP
TAP TAP
PAT
PAT PAT
RATTLE
RATTLE
RATTLE

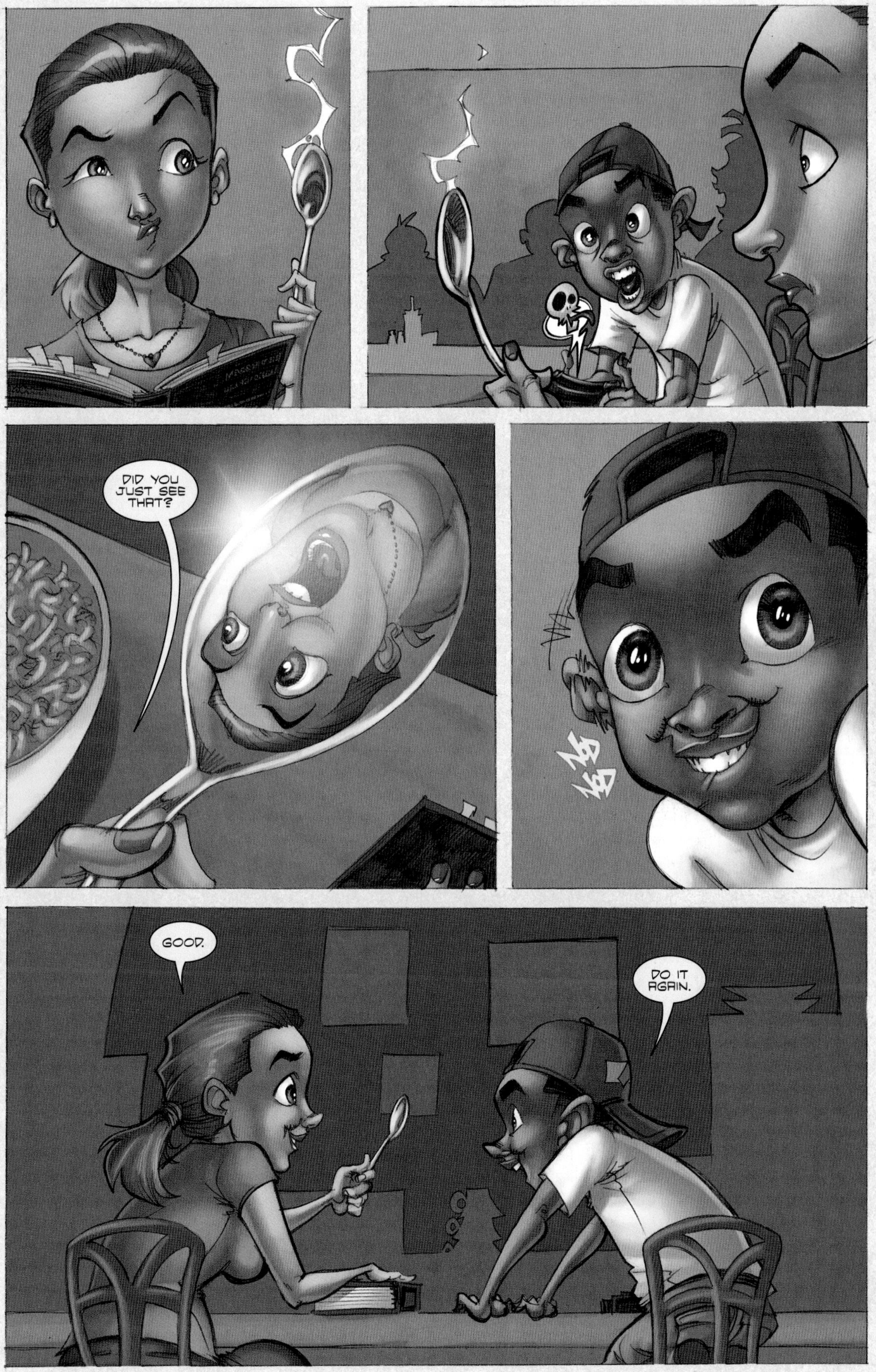
DID YOU JUST SEE THAT?
NOD NOD
GOOD.
DO IT AGAIN.

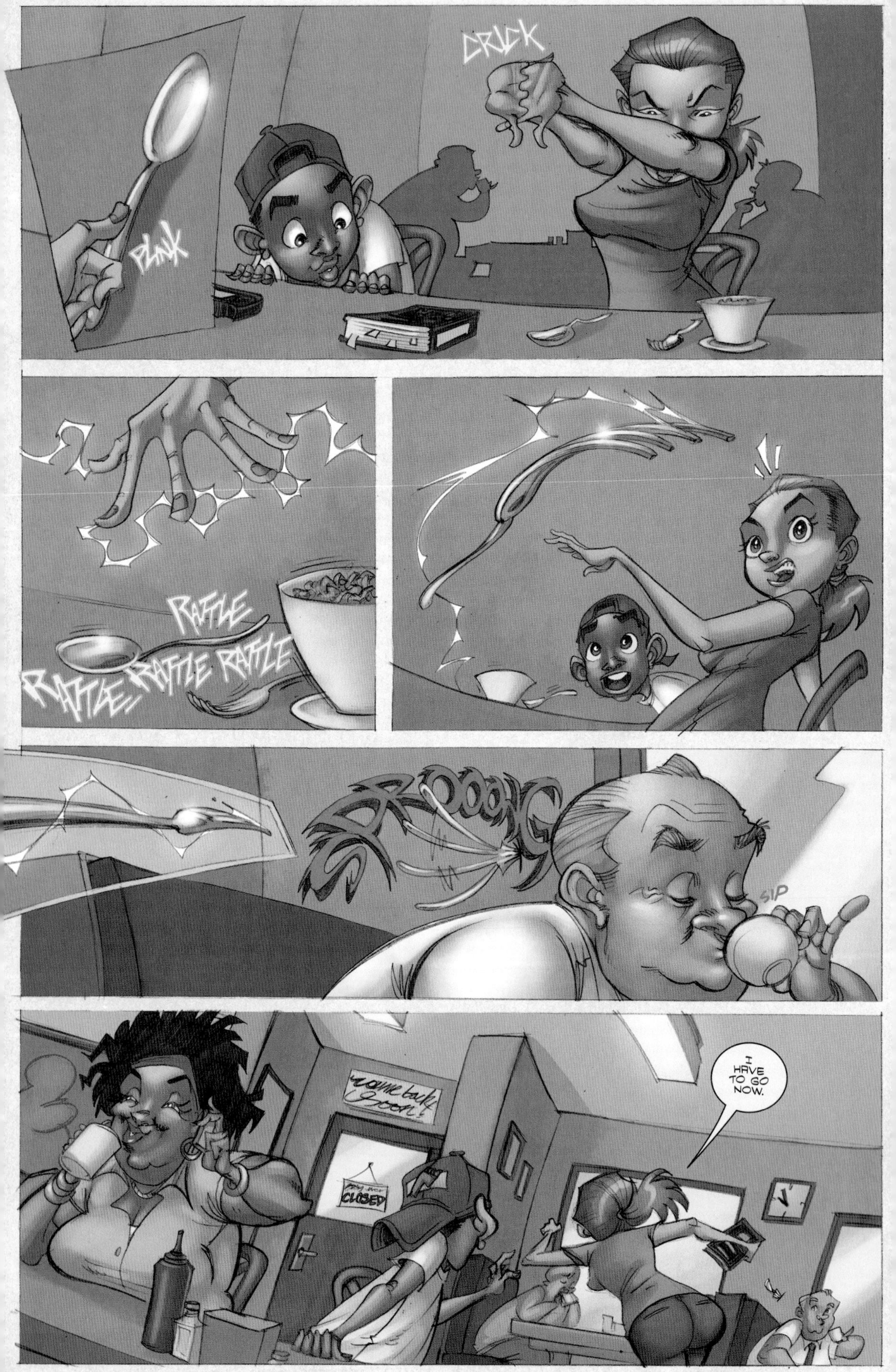
PLINK
CRICK
RATTLE
RATTLE RATTLE RATTLE
SIP
Come back Soon!
CLOSED
I HAVE TO GO NOW.

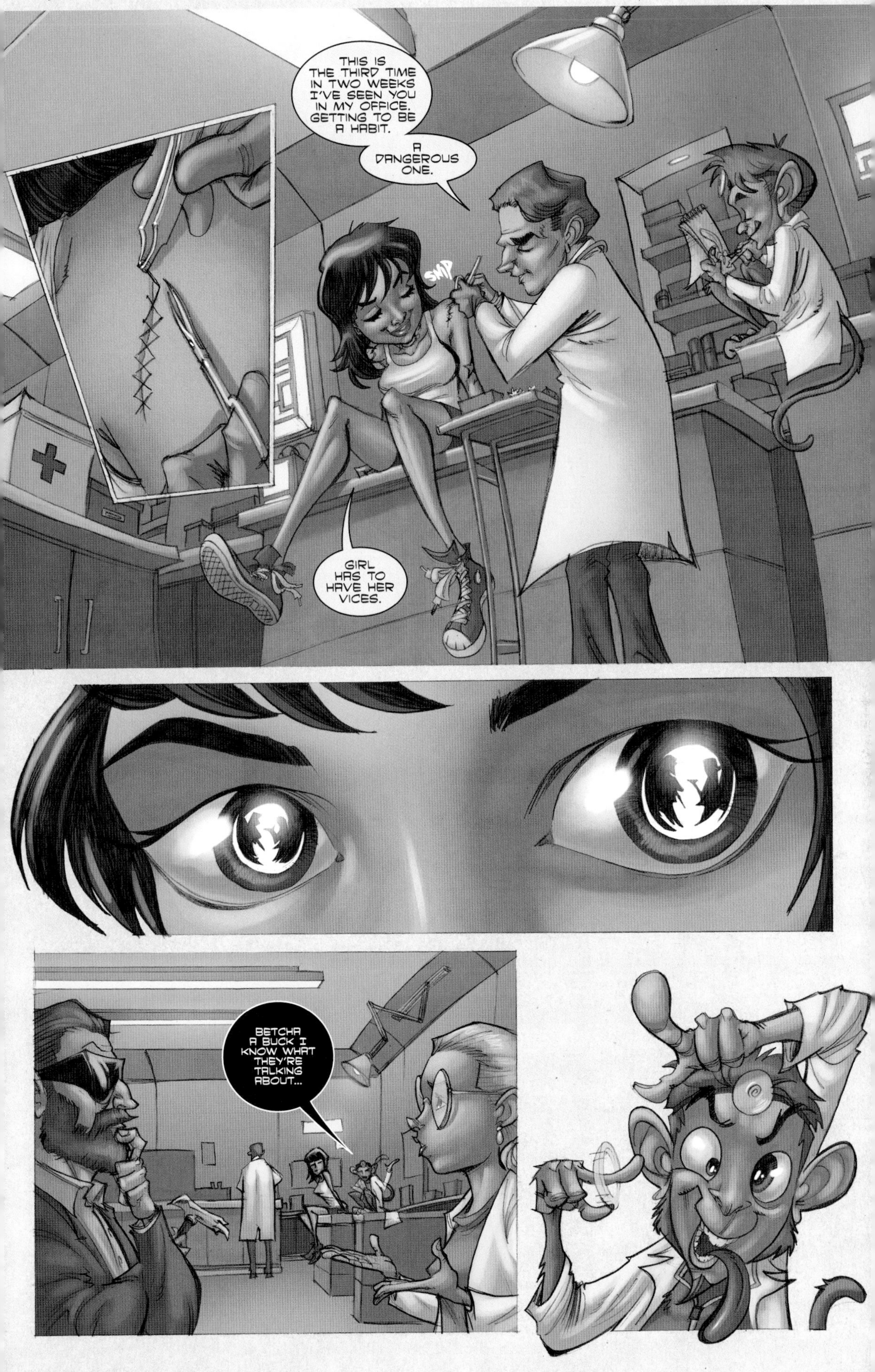
THIS IS THE THIRD TIME IN TWO WEEKS I'VE SEEN YOU IN MY OFFICE. GETTING TO BE A HABIT.
A DANGEROUS ONE.
SMP
GIRL HAS TO HAVE HER VICES.
BETCHA A BUCK I KNOW WHAT THEY'RE TALKING ABOUT...

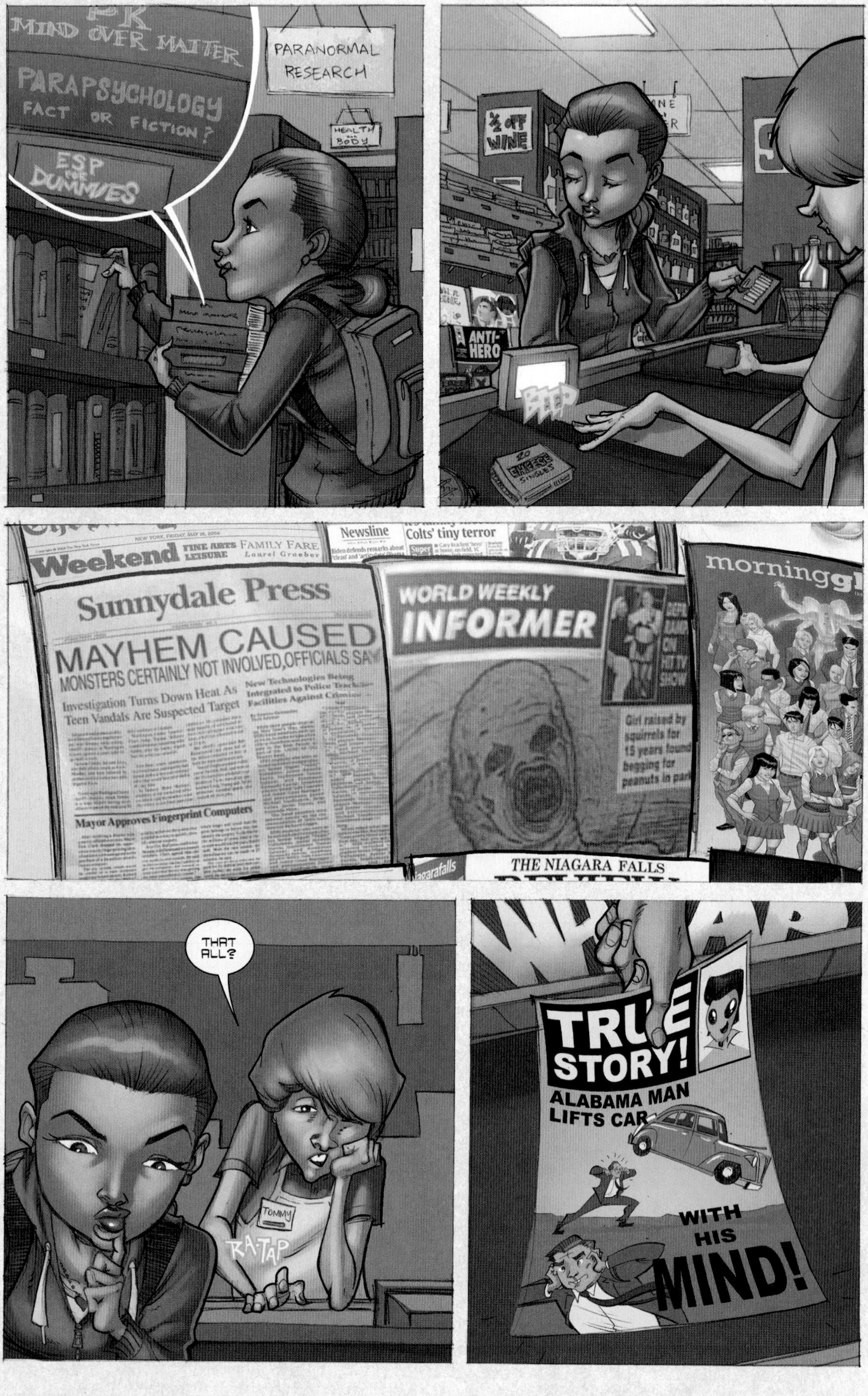

MIND OVER MATTER
PARAPSYCHOLOGY FACT OR FICTION?
ESP FOR DUMMIES
PARANORMAL RESEARCH
HEALTH and BODY
1/2 OFF WINE
ANTI-HERO
BEEP
20 CHEESE SINGLES
Weekend
FINE ARTS LEISURE
FAMILY FARE
Newsline
Colts' tiny terror
Sunnydale Press
MAYHEM CAUSED
MONSTERS CERTAINLY NOT INVOLVED,OFFICIALS SA
Investigation Turns Down Heat As Teen Vandals Are Suspected Target
Mayor Approves Fingerprint Computers
WORLD WEEKLY INFORMER
Girl raised by squirrels for 15 years found begging for peanuts in par
THE NIAGARA FALLS
THAT ALL?
TOMMY
RA-TAP
TRUE STORY!
ALABAMA MAN LIFTS CAR
WITH HIS MIND!

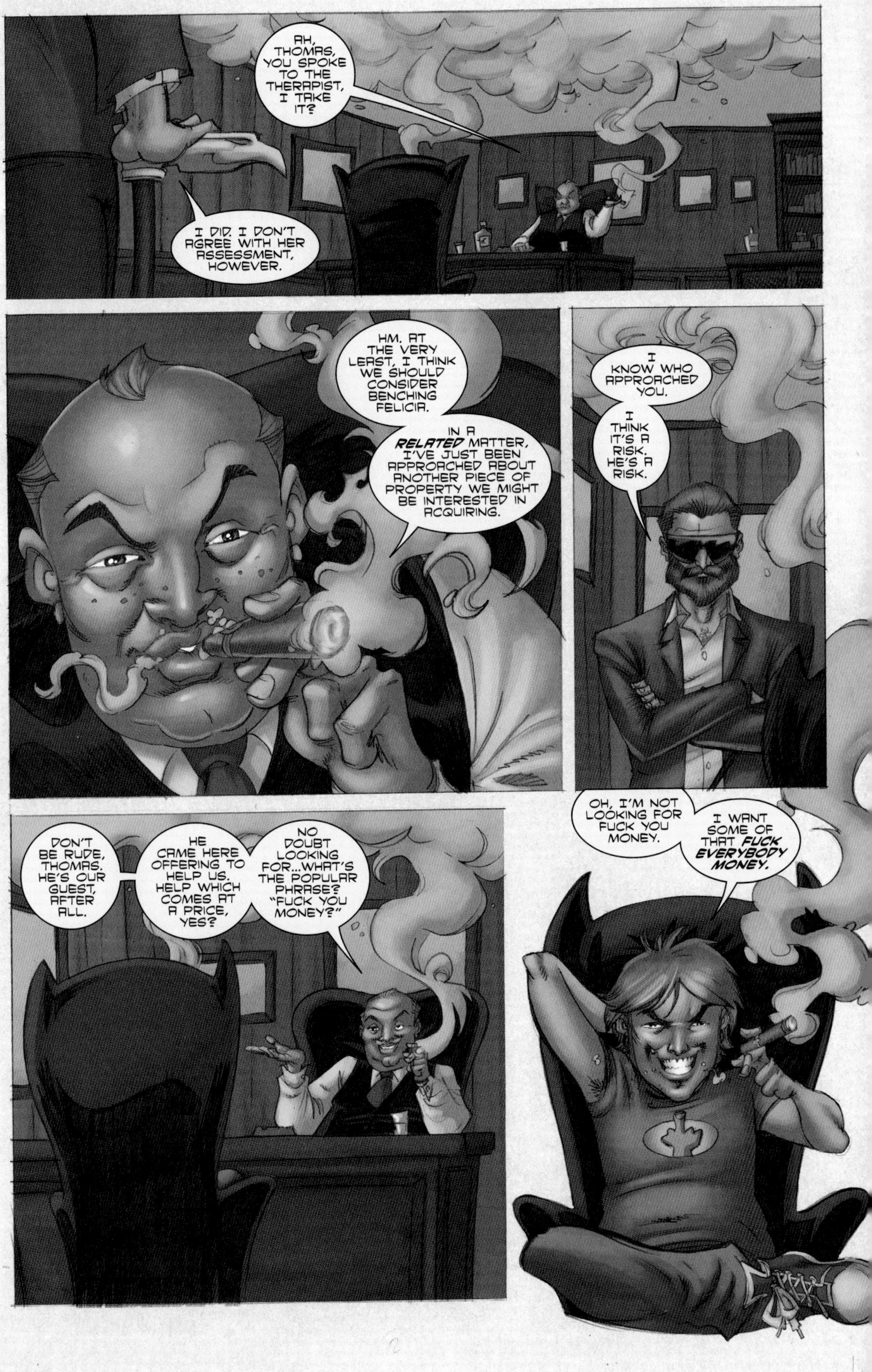
AH, THOMAS, YOU SPOKE TO THE THERAPIST, I TAKE IT?
I DID. I DON'T AGREE WITH HER ASSESSMENT, HOWEVER.
HM. AT THE VERY LEAST, I THINK WE SHOULD CONSIDER BENCHING FELICIA.
IN A *RELATED* MATTER, I'VE JUST BEEN APPROACHED ABOUT ANOTHER PIECE OF PROPERTY WE MIGHT BE INTERESTED IN ACQUIRING.
I KNOW WHO APPROACHED YOU.
I THINK IT'S A RISK. HE'S A RISK.
DON'T BE RUDE, THOMAS. HE'S OUR GUEST, AFTER ALL.
HE CAME HERE OFFERING TO HELP US. HELP WHICH COMES AT A PRICE, YES?
NO DOUBT LOOKING FOR...WHAT'S THE POPULAR PHRASE? "FUCK YOU MONEY?"
OH, I'M NOT LOOKING FOR FUCK YOU MONEY.
I WANT SOME OF THAT *FUCK EVERYBODY MONEY.*

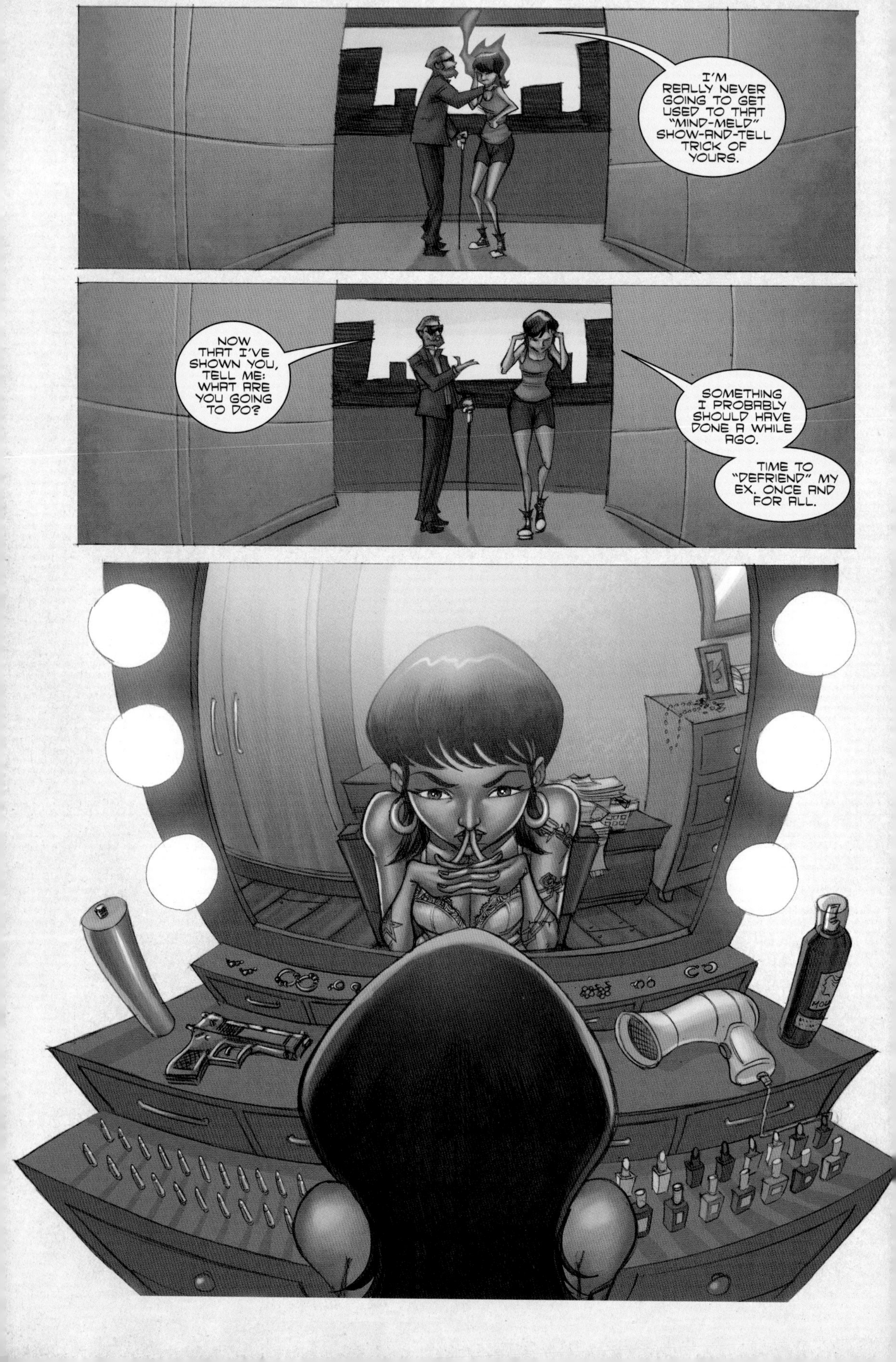
I'M REALLY NEVER GOING TO GET USED TO THAT "MIND-MELD" SHOW-AND-TELL TRICK OF YOURS.
NOW THAT I'VE SHOWN YOU, TELL ME: WHAT ARE YOU GOING TO DO?
SOMETHING I PROBABLY SHOULD HAVE DONE A WHILE AGO.
TIME TO "DEFRIEND" MY EX. ONCE AND FOR ALL.

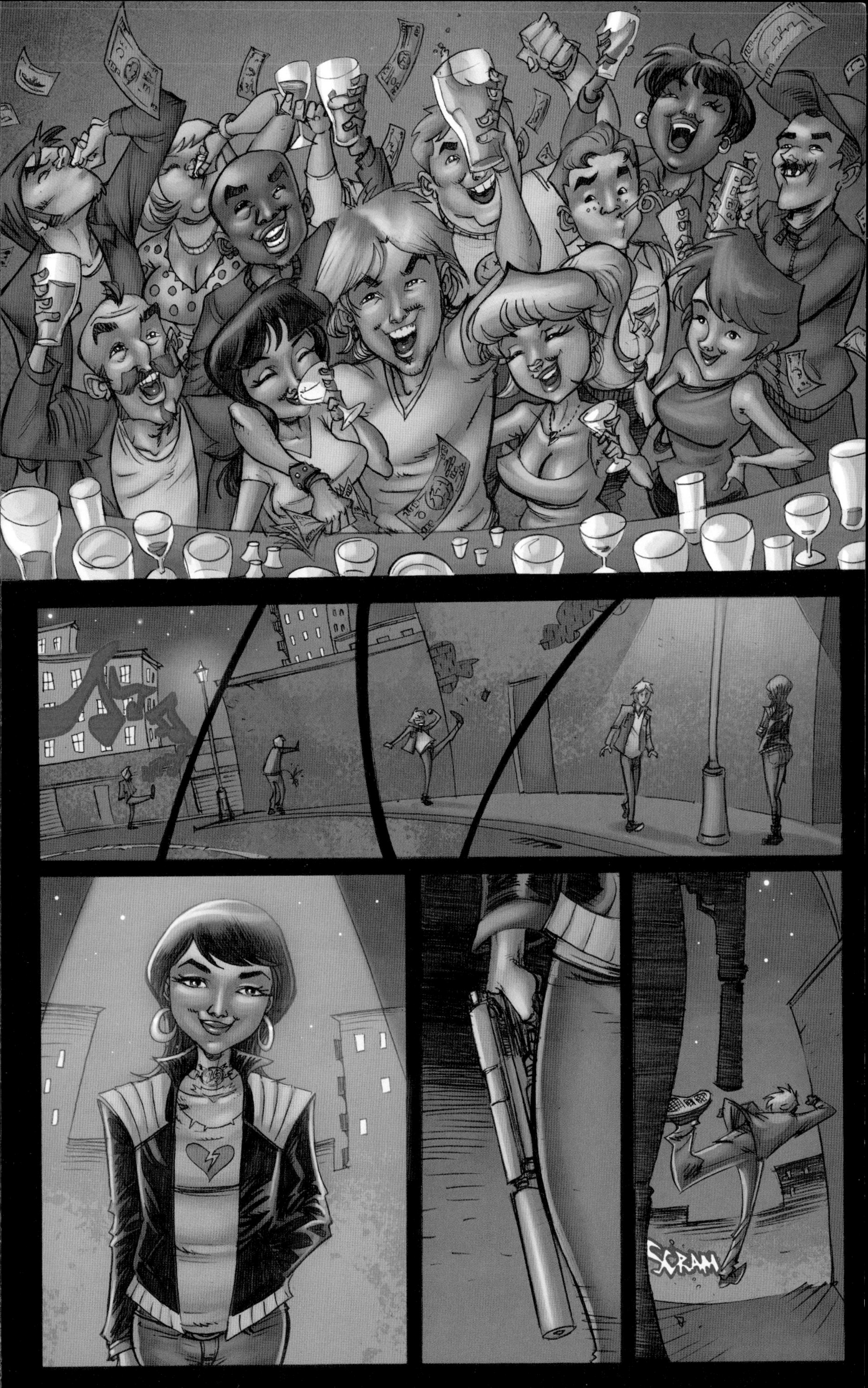
SCRAM

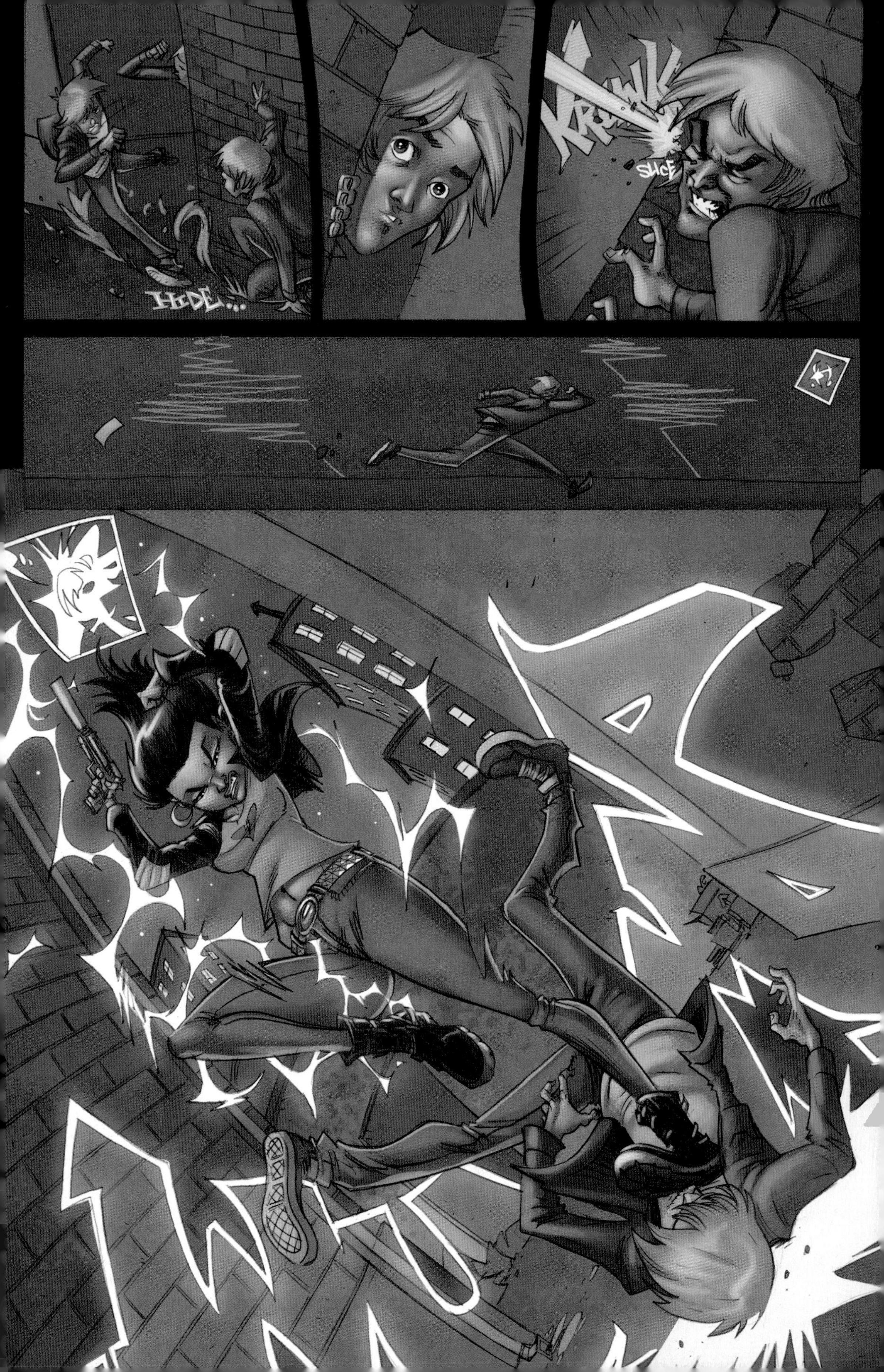
HIDE...
SLICE

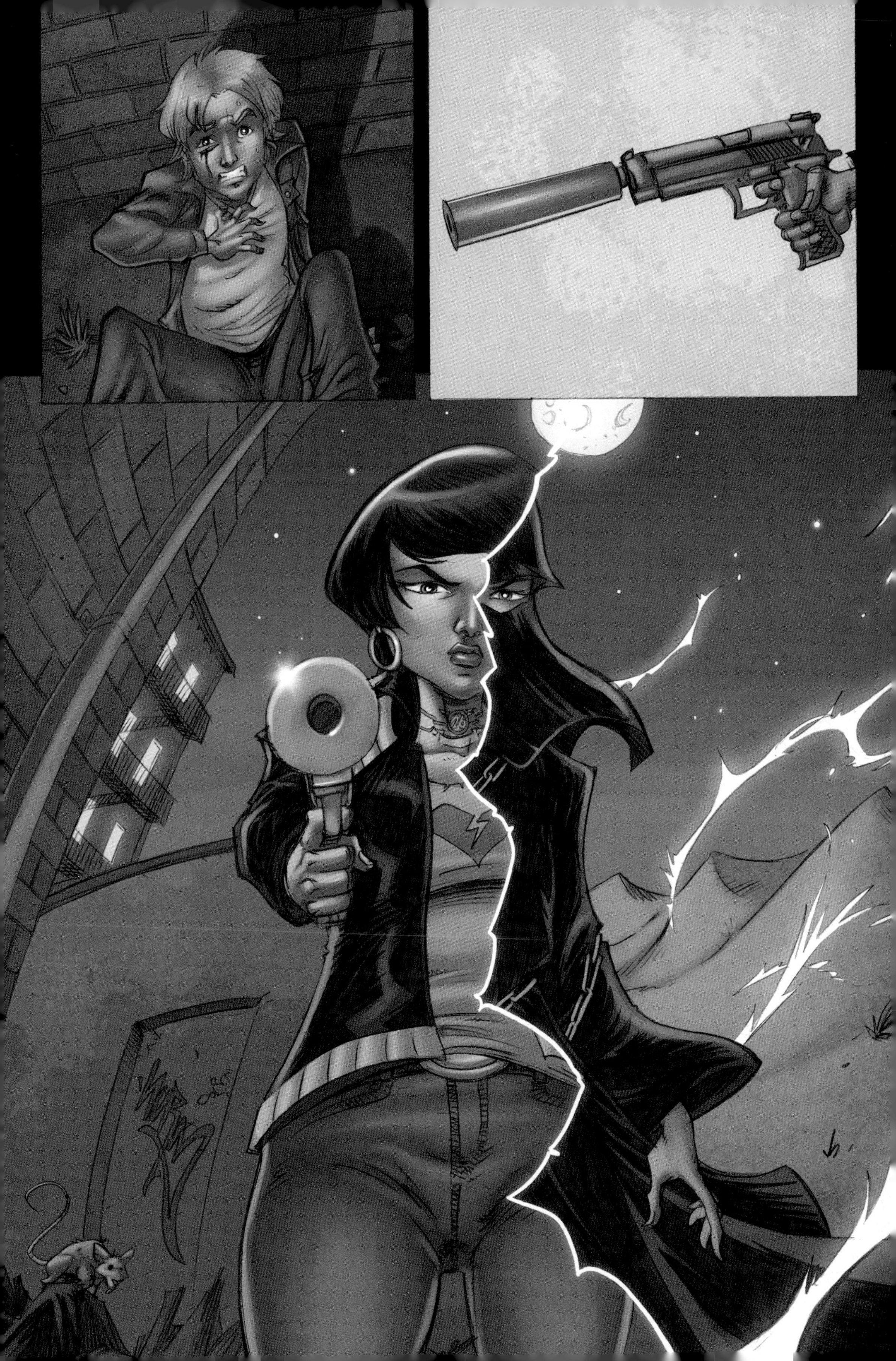

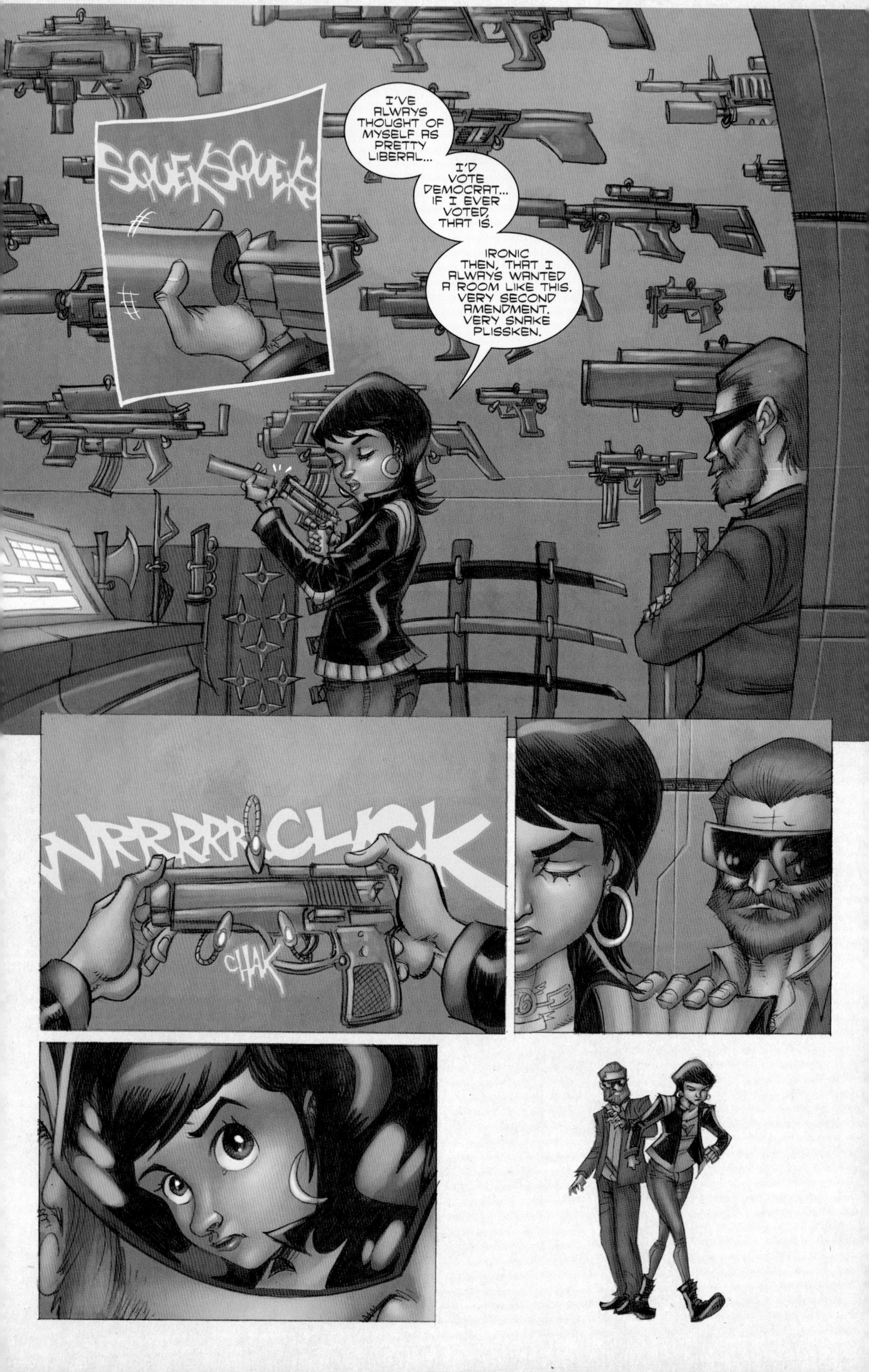
SQUEKSQUEKS
I'VE ALWAYS THOUGHT OF MYSELF AS PRETTY LIBERAL...
I'D VOTE DEMOCRAT... IF I EVER VOTED, THAT IS.
IRONIC THEN, THAT I ALWAYS WANTED A ROOM LIKE THIS. VERY SECOND AMENDMENT. VERY SNAKE PLISSKEN.
WRRRRRCLICK
CHAK

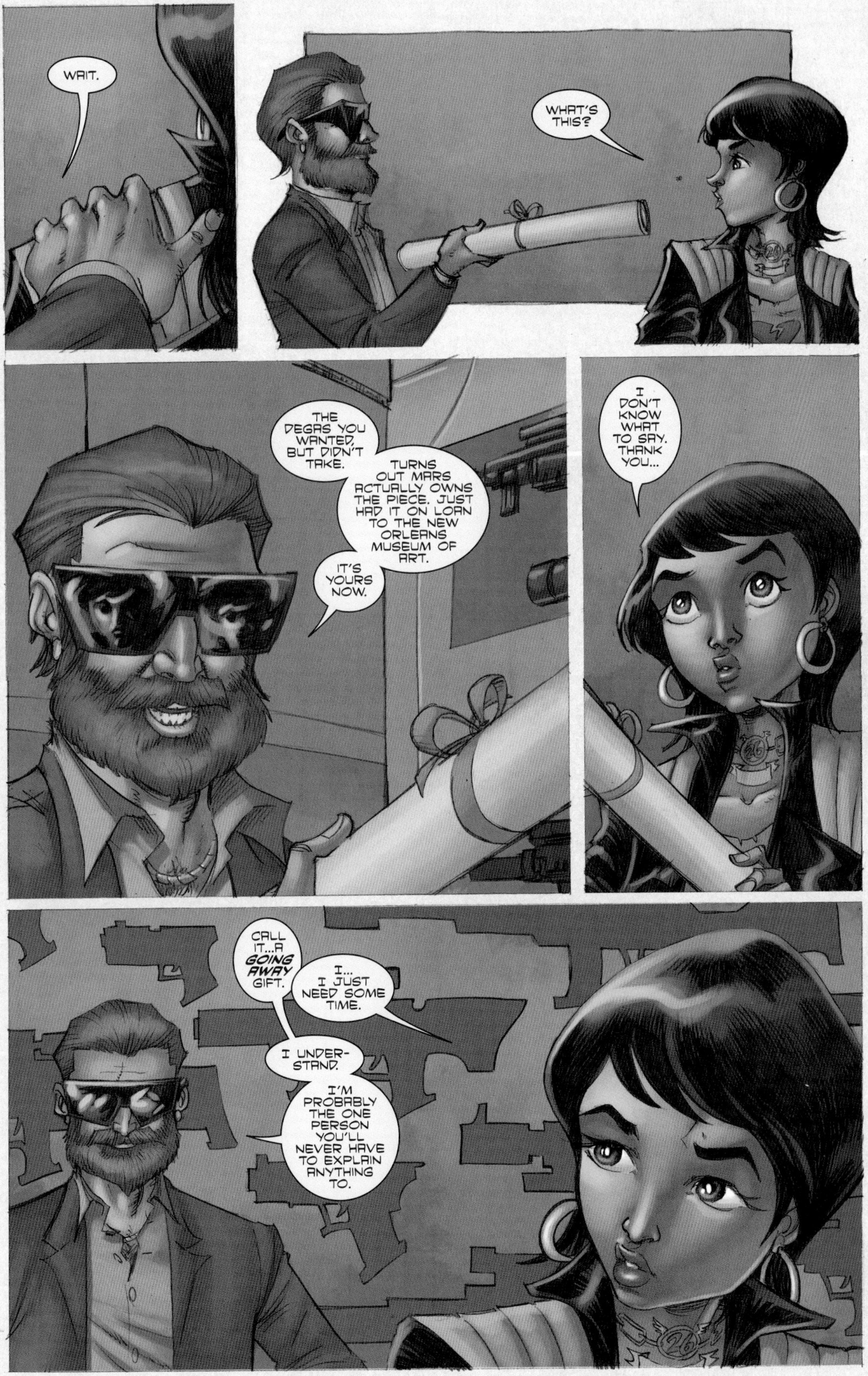
WAIT.
WHAT'S THIS?
THE DEGAS YOU WANTED, BUT DIDN'T TAKE.
TURNS OUT MARS ACTUALLY OWNS THE PIECE. JUST HAD IT ON LOAN TO THE NEW ORLEANS MUSEUM OF ART.
IT'S YOURS NOW.
I DON'T KNOW WHAT TO SAY. THANK YOU...
CALL IT...A ***GOING AWAY*** GIFT.
I... I JUST NEED SOME TIME.
I UNDER-STAND.
I'M PROBABLY THE ONE PERSON YOU'LL NEVER HAVE TO EXPLAIN ANYTHING TO.

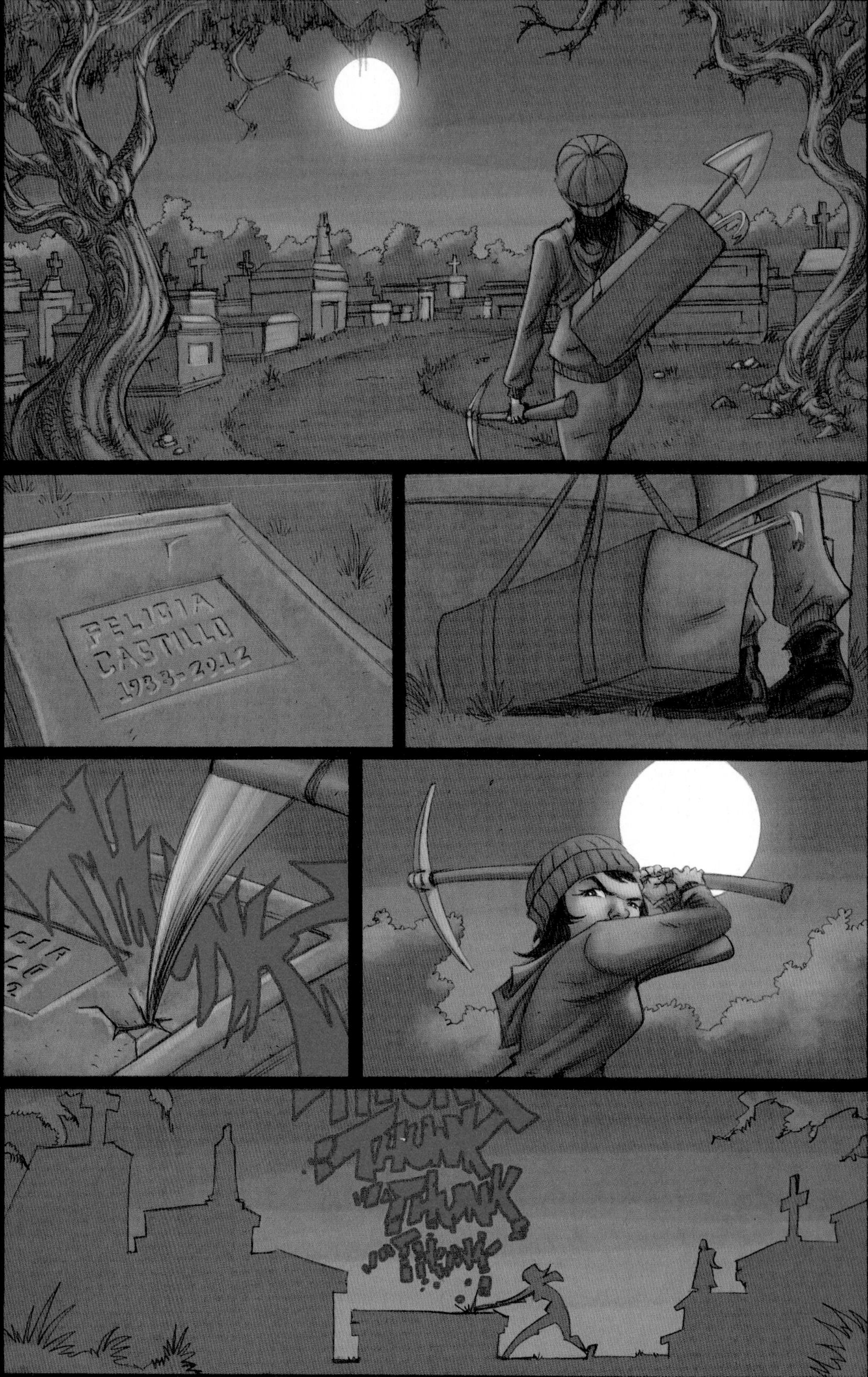
FELICIA
CASTILLO
1933-2012
THUNK
THUNK

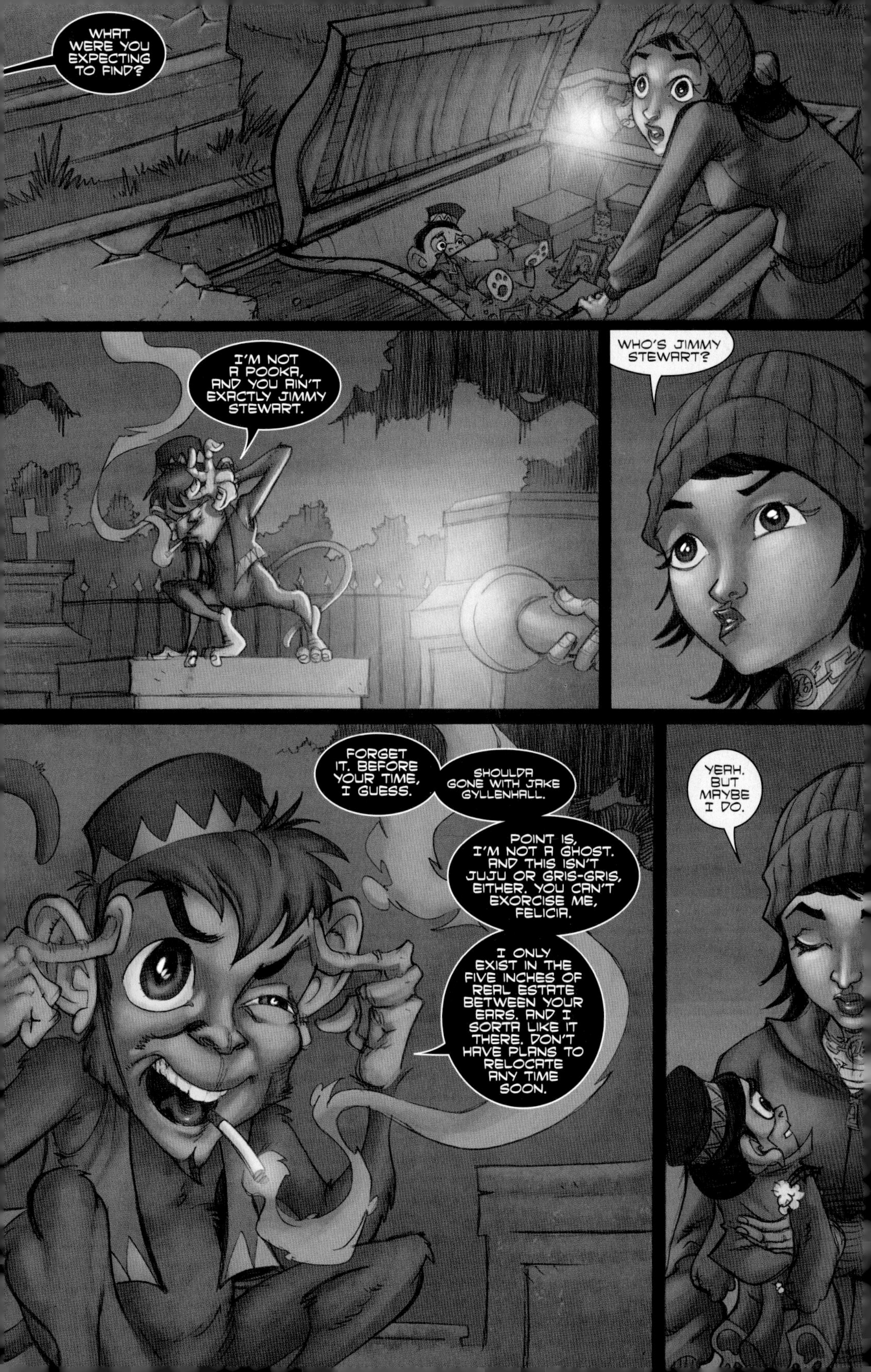
WHAT WERE YOU EXPECTING TO FIND?
I'M NOT A POOKA, AND YOU AIN'T EXACTLY JIMMY STEWART.
WHO'S JIMMY STEWART?
FORGET IT. BEFORE YOUR TIME, I GUESS.
SHOULDA GONE WITH JAKE GYLLENHALL.
POINT IS, I'M NOT A GHOST. AND THIS ISN'T JUJU OR GRIS-GRIS, EITHER. YOU CAN'T EXORCISE ME, FELICIA.
I ONLY EXIST IN THE FIVE INCHES OF REAL ESTATE BETWEEN YOUR EARS. AND I SORTA LIKE IT THERE. DON'T HAVE PLANS TO RELOCATE ANY TIME SOON.
YEAH. BUT MAYBE I DO.

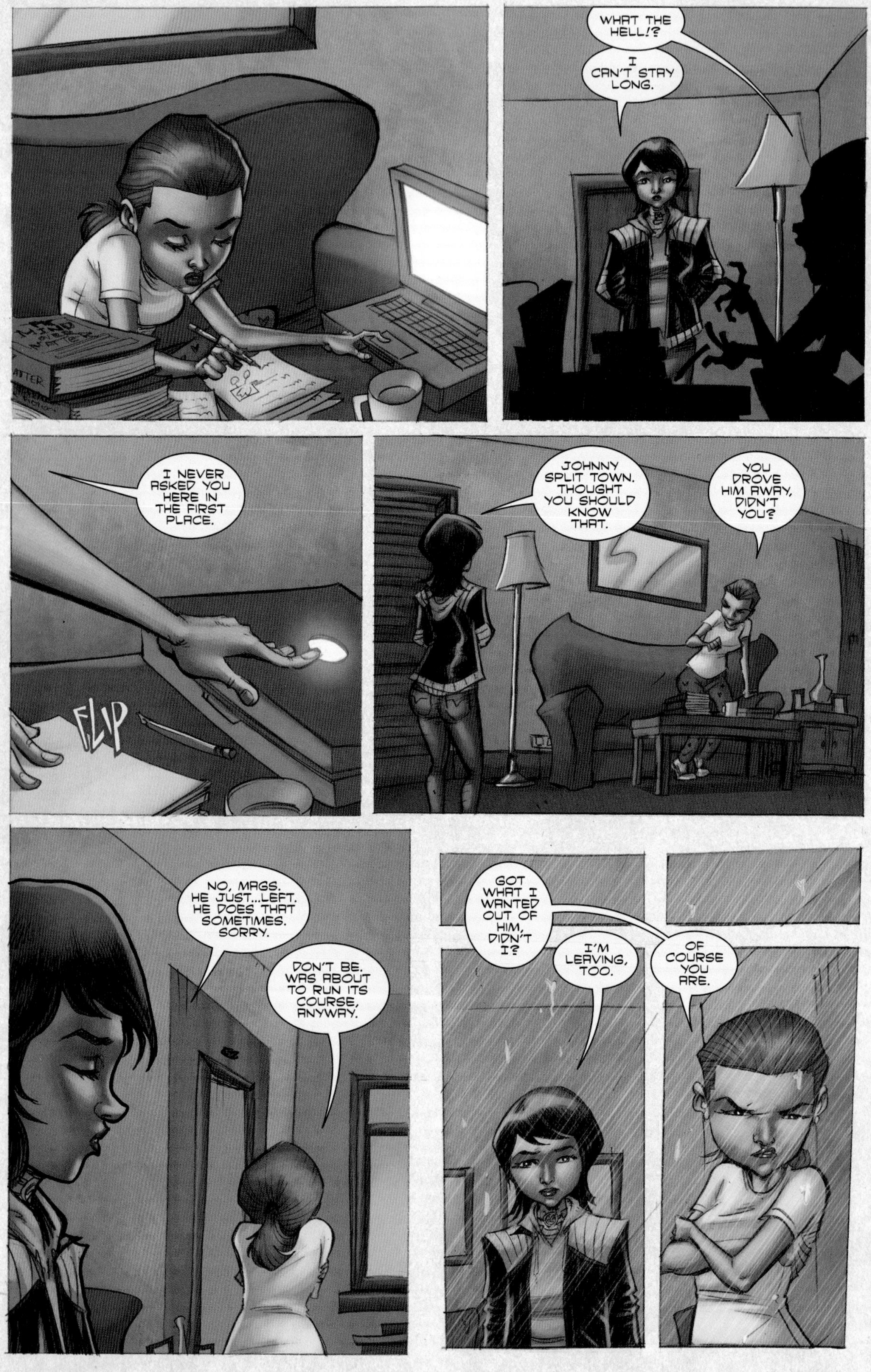
WHAT THE HELL!?
I CAN'T STAY LONG.
I NEVER ASKED YOU HERE IN THE FIRST PLACE.
FLIP
JOHNNY SPLIT TOWN. THOUGHT YOU SHOULD KNOW THAT.
YOU DROVE HIM AWAY, DIDN'T YOU?
NO, MAGS. HE JUST...LEFT. HE DOES THAT SOMETIMES. SORRY.
DON'T BE. WAS ABOUT TO RUN ITS COURSE, ANYWAY.
GOT WHAT I WANTED OUT OF HIM, DIDN'T I?
I'M LEAVING, TOO.
OF COURSE YOU ARE.

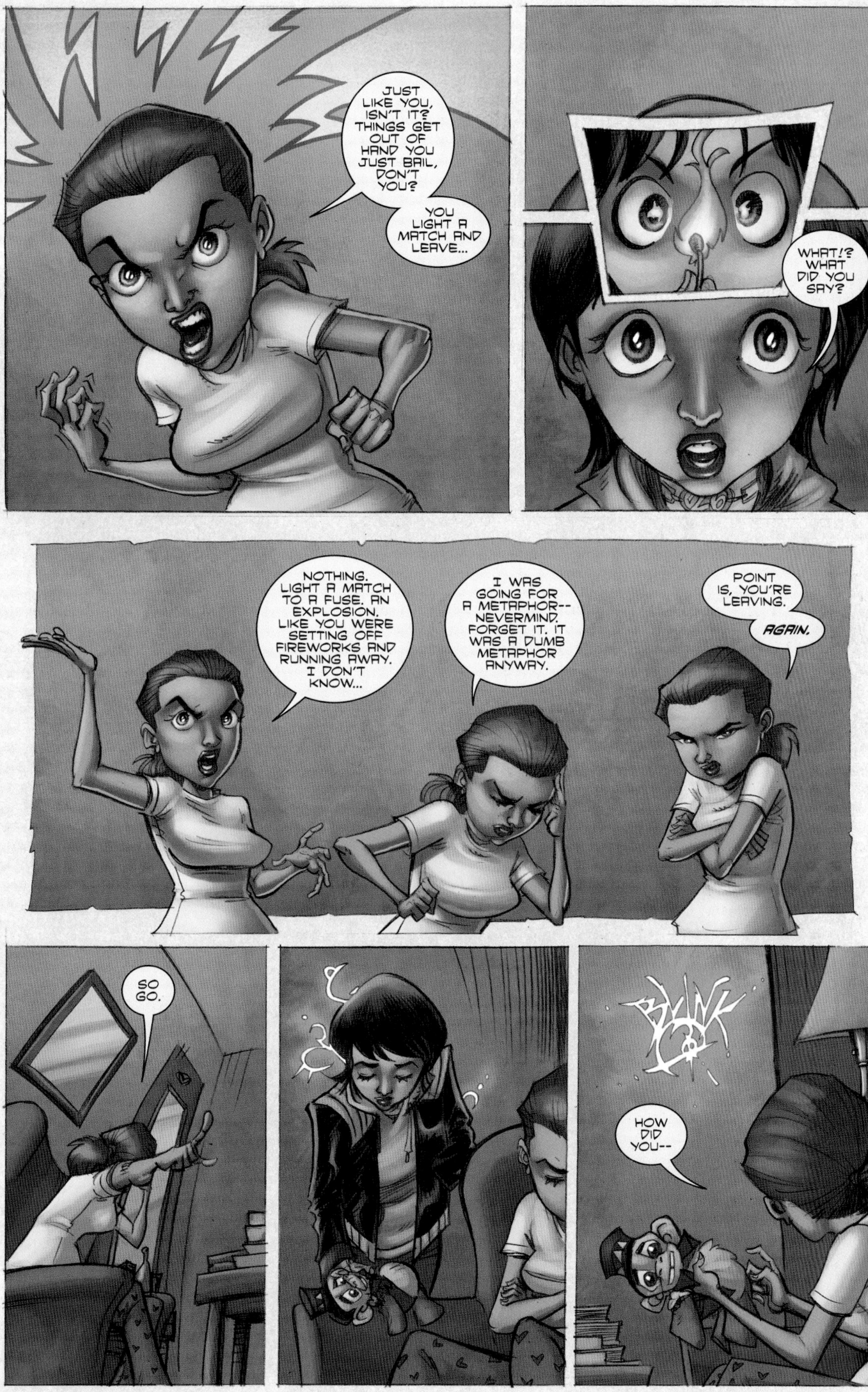
JUST LIKE YOU, ISN'T IT? THINGS GET OUT OF HAND YOU JUST BAIL, DON'T YOU?
YOU LIGHT A MATCH AND LEAVE...
WHAT!? WHAT DID YOU SAY?
NOTHING. LIGHT A MATCH TO A FUSE. AN EXPLOSION. LIKE YOU WERE SETTING OFF FIREWORKS AND RUNNING AWAY. I DON'T KNOW...
I WAS GOING FOR A METAPHOR-- NEVERMIND. FORGET IT. IT WAS A DUMB METAPHOR ANYWAY.
POINT IS, YOU'RE LEAVING.
AGAIN.
SO GO.
BLINK
HOW DID YOU--

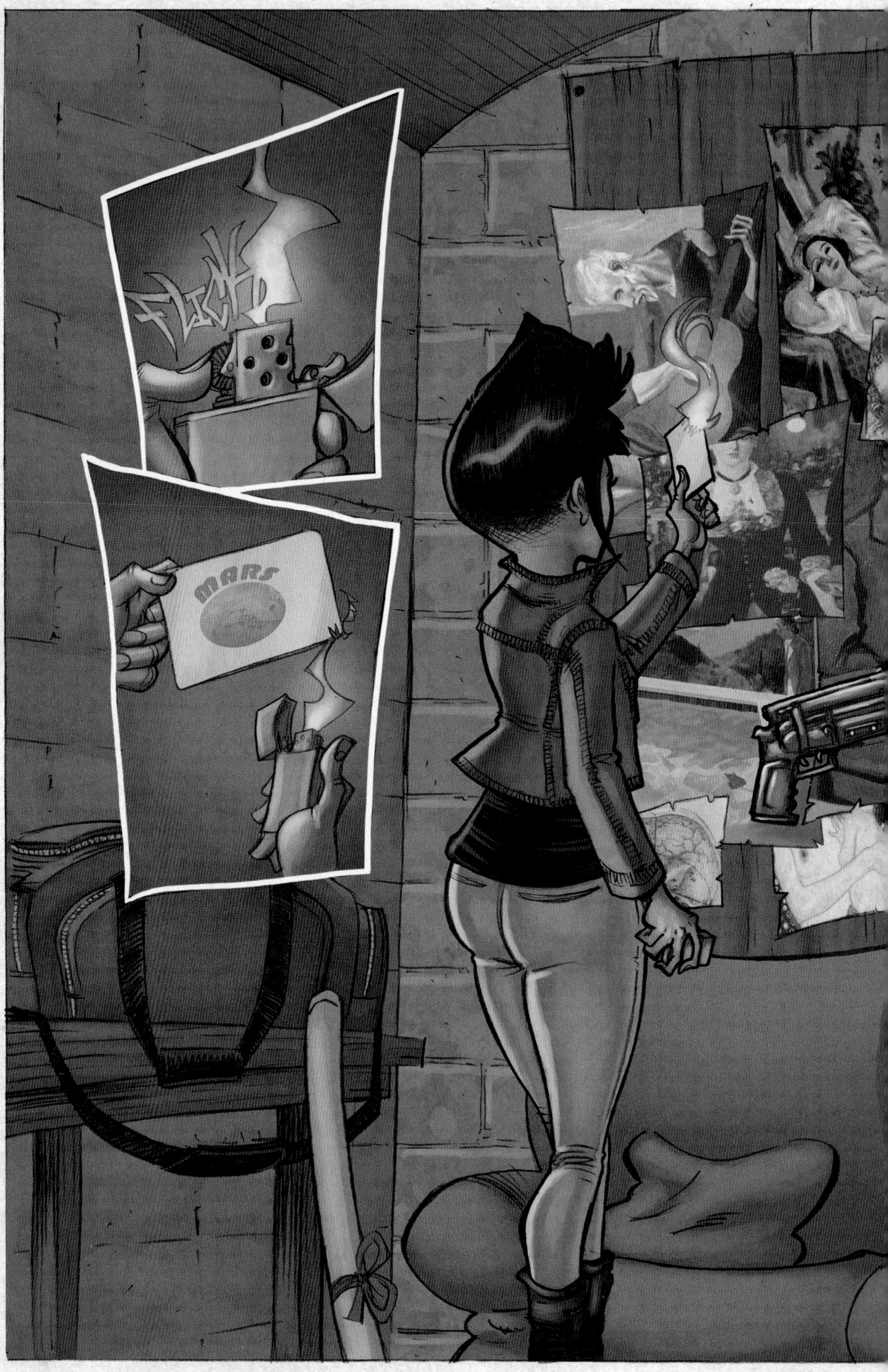
FLICK
MARS

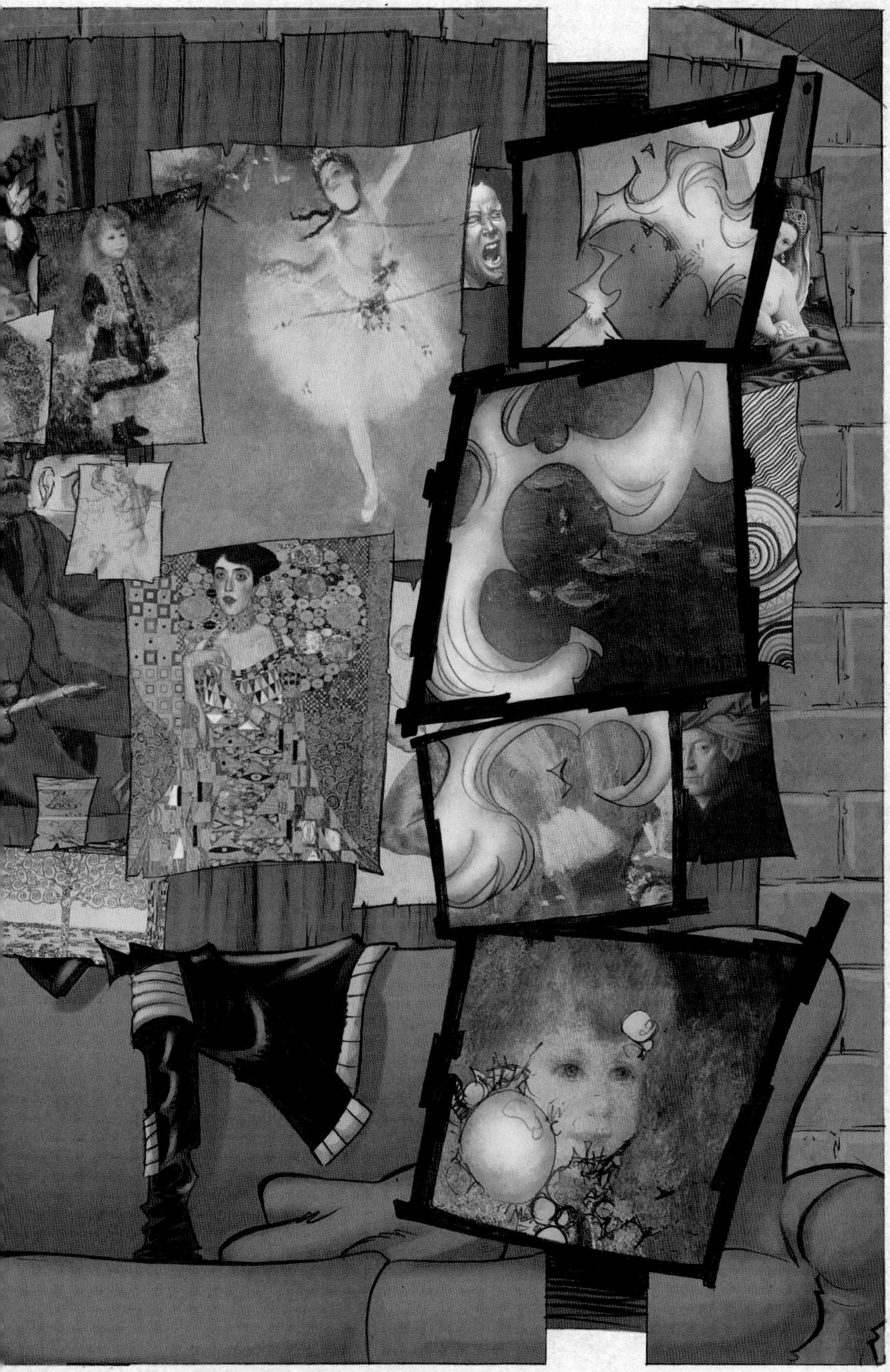

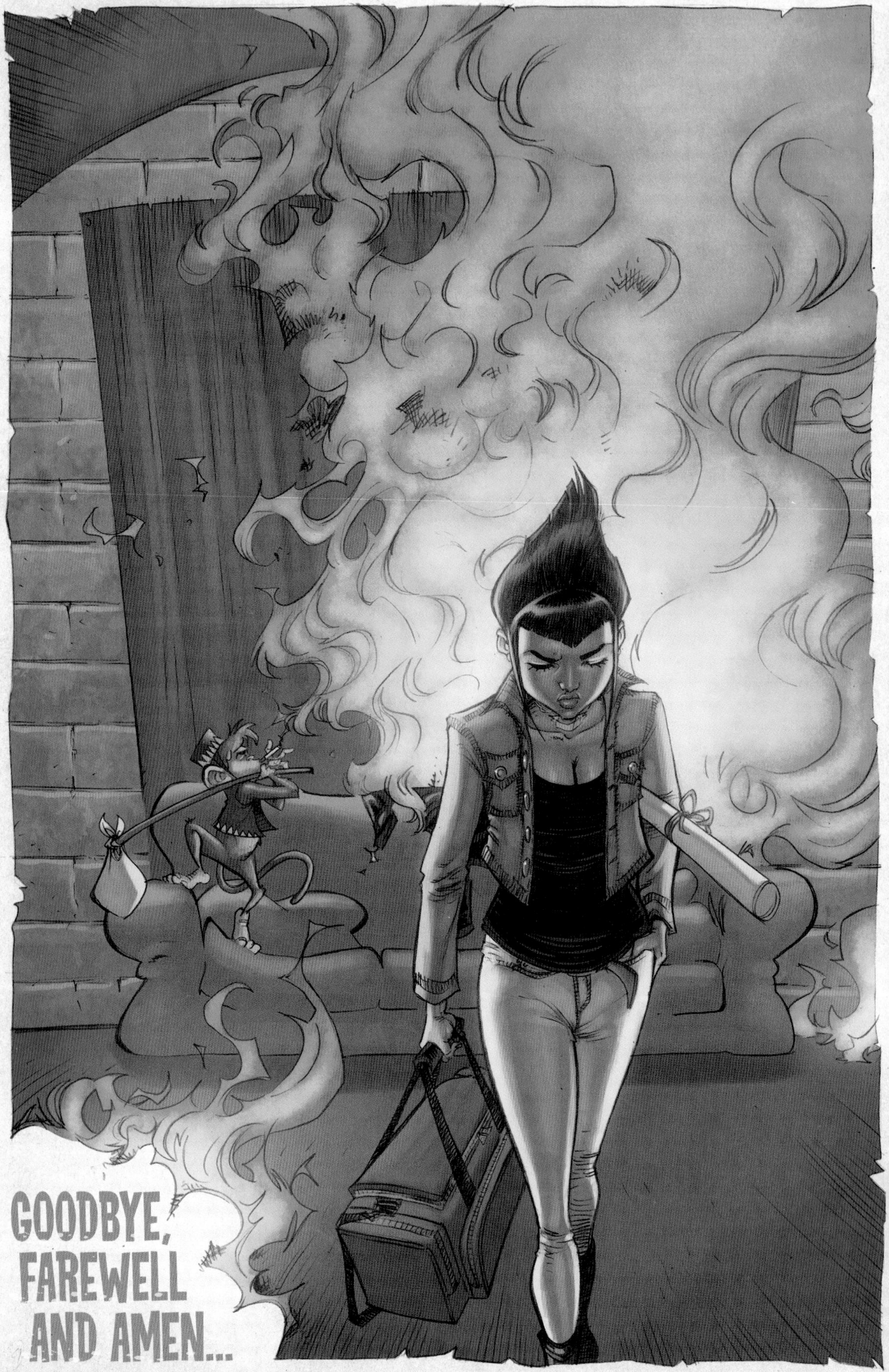
GOODBYE, FAREWELL AND AMEN...

I LOVE TROUBLE PEN PALZ

We asked our fans (all two of you) to write in and ask questions for our characters.

I'm gonna hate myself for writing this; I don't write into the "letters/comments" of comic books. Feels mad cliché. But Felicia is a doll, straight up. The kind of woman any guy should try to get to know, but most avoid for whatever reason.

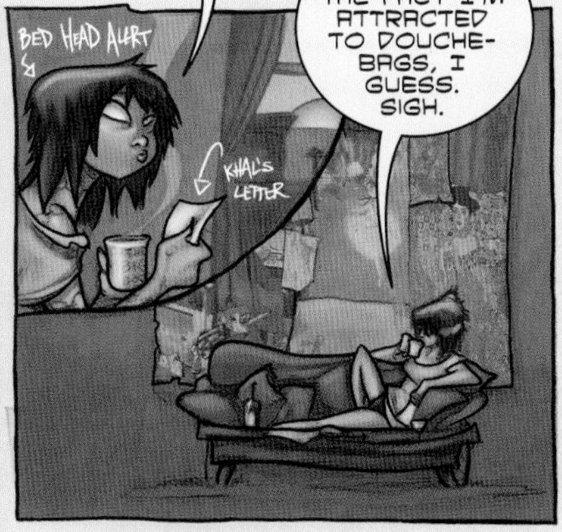
AW, KHAL... WHY COULDN'T I HAVE MET A NICE GUY LIKE YOU, FIRST, INSTEAD OF JOHNNY? SEEMS LIKE MY PROBLEM WITH GUYS IS TIMING.
BED HEAD ALERT
KHAL'S LETTER
WELL, TIMING, AND THE FACT I'M ATTRACTED TO DOUCHE-BAGS, I GUESS. SIGH.

I wonder, did Felicia have a code name while she was with Mars?

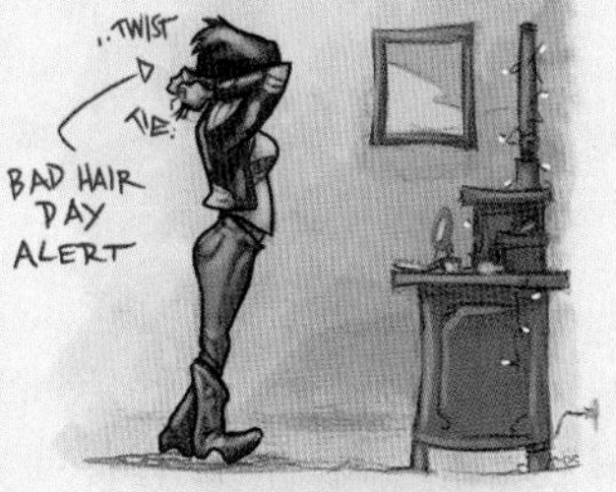
I LIKED TO GO BY "AGENT 26." AT LEAST, THAT'S WHAT I WROTE ON MY LUNCH WHEN I PUT IT IN THE BREAK ROOM FRIDGE, ESPECIALLY AFTER SOMEBODY JACKED MY ACTIVIA.
..TWIST
TIE
BAD HAIR DAY ALERT

Thanks for placing this story into the world. You've got a fan for life.
Sincerely, Khal,
Hamilton, NJ

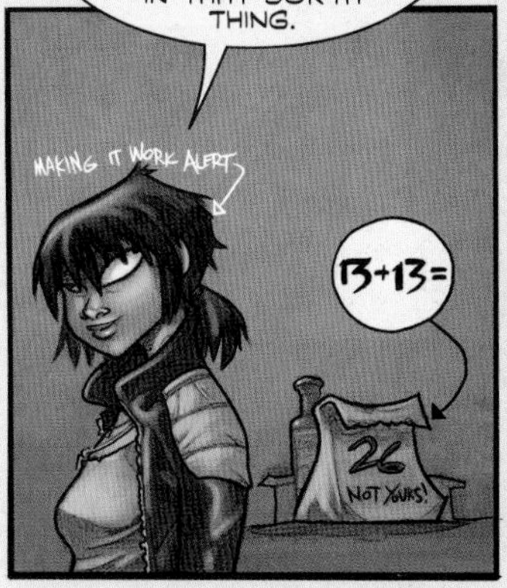
CASE YOU'RE WONDERING, 26 IS BAD LUCK 13 TIMES TWO--TURN IT AROUND FOR A LITTLE GOOD LUCK--IF YOU BELIEVE IN THAT SORTA THING.
MAKING IT WORK ALERT
13+13=
26
NOT YOURS!

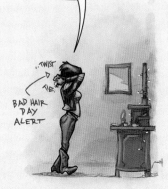

Hello I Love Trouble team. My questions are for Thomas: Felicia went through a traumatic event to trigger her power. Did something similar happen to you to trigger yours? And did you ever briefly think about spandex?

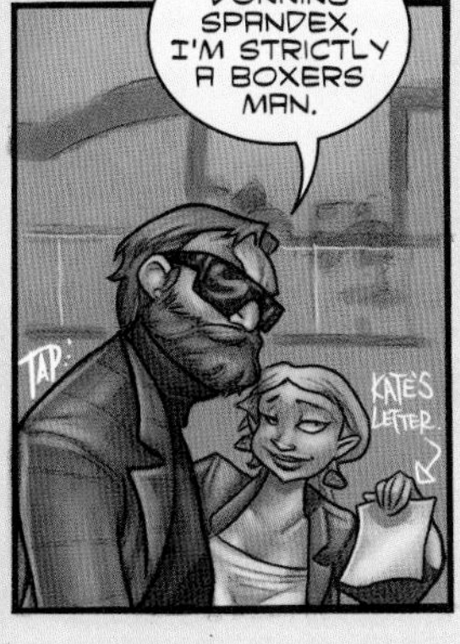
ACTUALLY, YES. WHEN I LOST MY SIGHT IN AN ACCIDENT, I BECAME BLESSED (OR CURSED) WITH MY SECOND SIGHT.
AS FOR DONNING SPANDEX, I'M STRICTLY A BOXERS MAN.
TAP
KATE'S LETTER

When Felicia comes to visit the Mars Corporation, you and she pass down a corridor full of doors with labels such as "Tessier-Ashpool" and "Umbrella." What goes on behind those doors? Are they all modeled to look like doctor's offices?

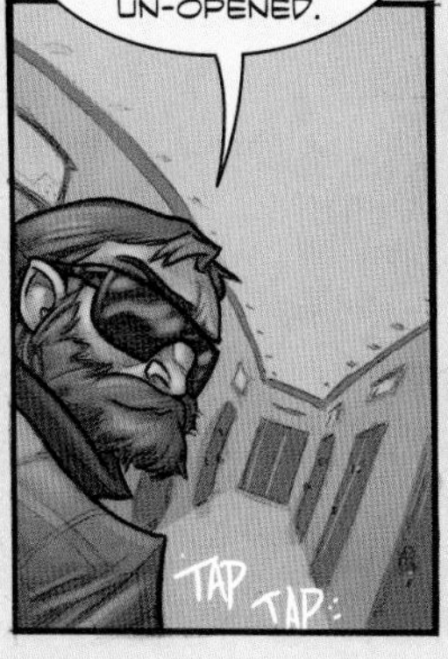
YOU KNOW, KATE, I NEVER BOTHERED OPENING ANY. I'VE LEARNED THE HARD WAY THAT SOME DOORS ARE BEST LEFT UN-OPENED.
TAP
TAP

Finally, what language are the sigils on the elevator buttons? Thanks!
Best, Kate, Edmond, OK

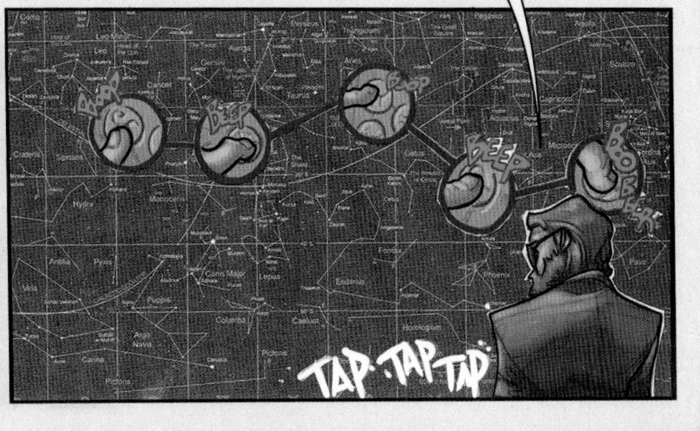
THOSE SIGILS ARE ACTUALLY ZODIAC AND STAR CONSTELLATION SYMBOLS. HOPE THAT HELPS. MAYBE WE'LL SEE YOU AROUND.
TAP TAP TAP

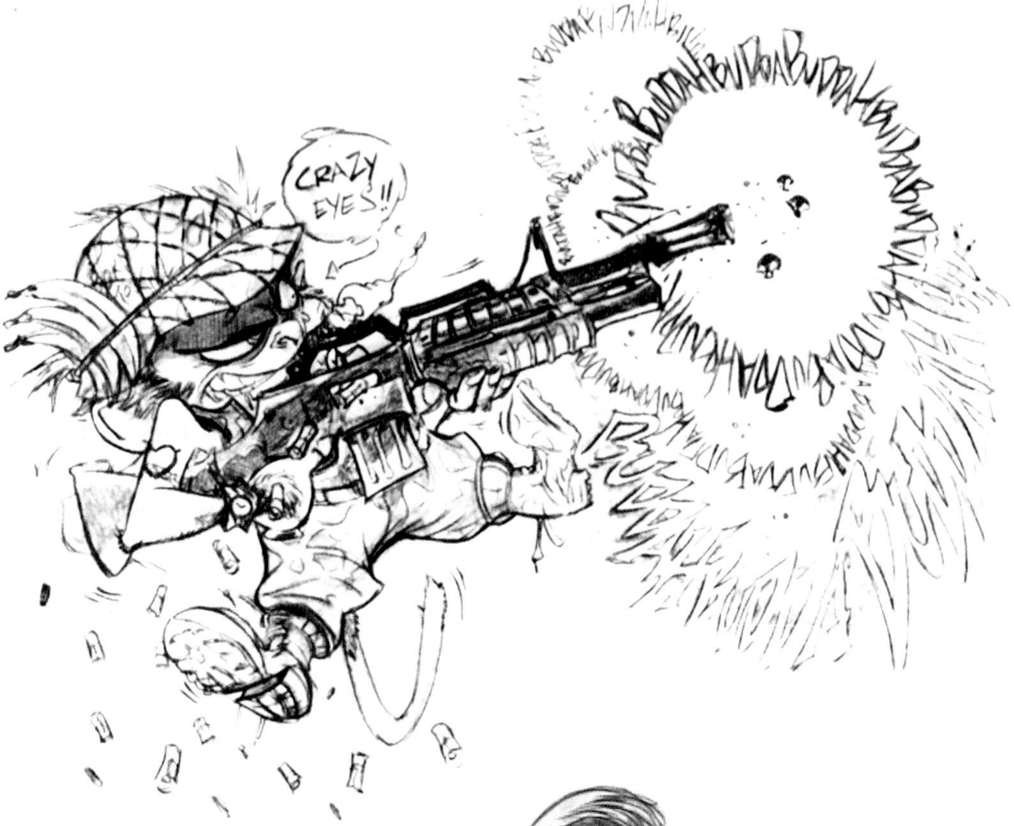
CRAZY EYES!!

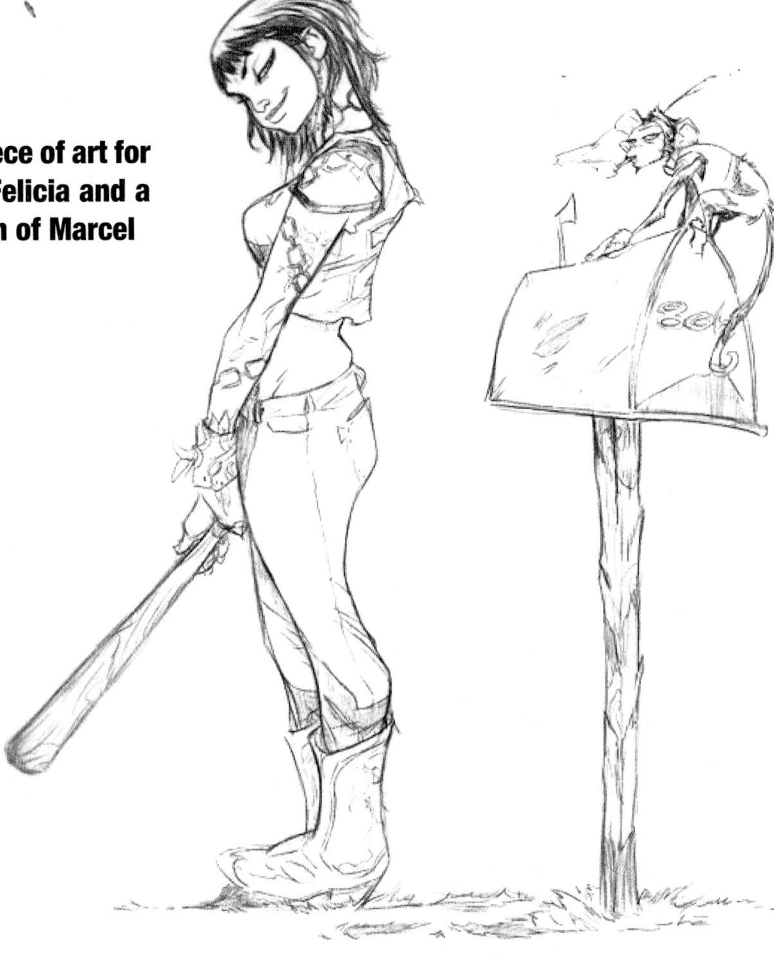

This is Mark's earliest piece of art for I Love Trouble, showing Felicia and a slightly different version of Marcel

THATCHER

OLLIE NORTH

These were sketches Mark did for the the photos on the walls of Ealing's office, a "rogue's gallery" showing him cozying up to some of the world's most notorious leaders and headline makers, from Ollie North to the Bushes. Unfortunately, when the scenes made it to print, it was pretty talk-heavy, and the dialogue balloons obscured most of his hard work.

GENERAL THAN YO.

GENERAL PETRAEUS

OMAR-AL BASHIR
IN THE
HIZZIE

FUCKIN' BUSHES.

MUAMMAR GADDAFI

PUTIN

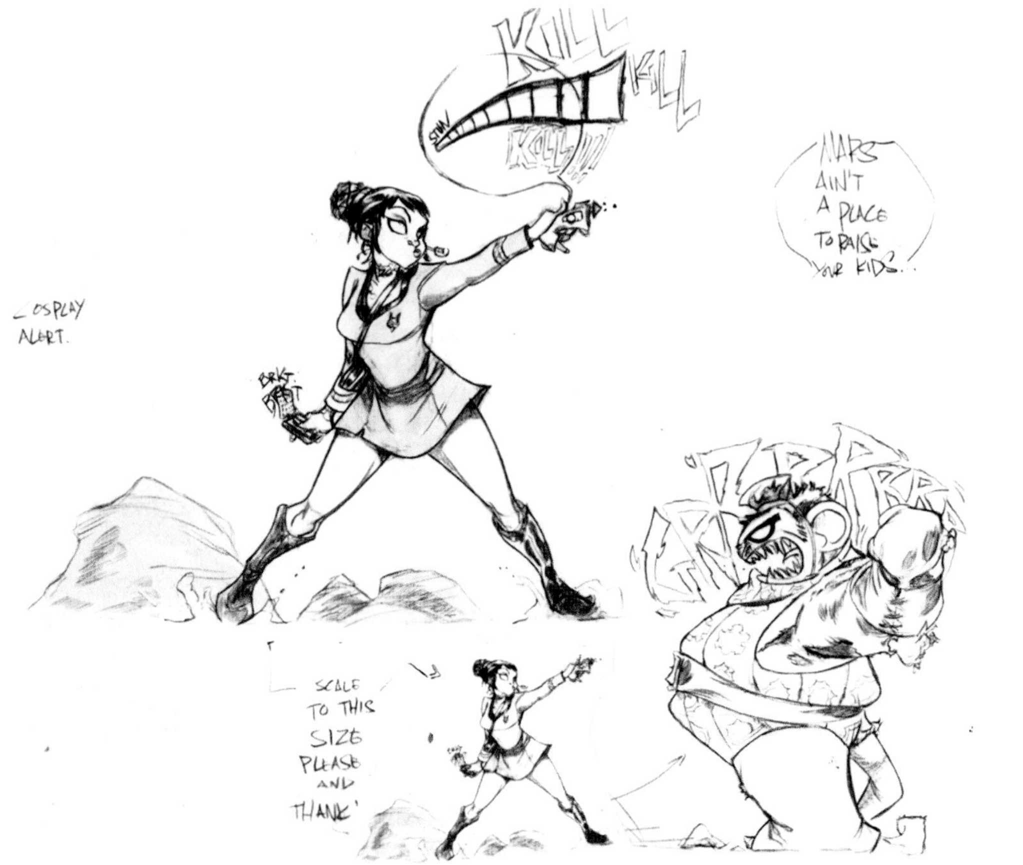
KILL
KILL
KILL
STUN
MARS AIN'T A PLACE TO RAISE YOUR KIDS...
COSPLAY ALERT.
SCALE TO THIS SIZE PLEASE AND THANK'

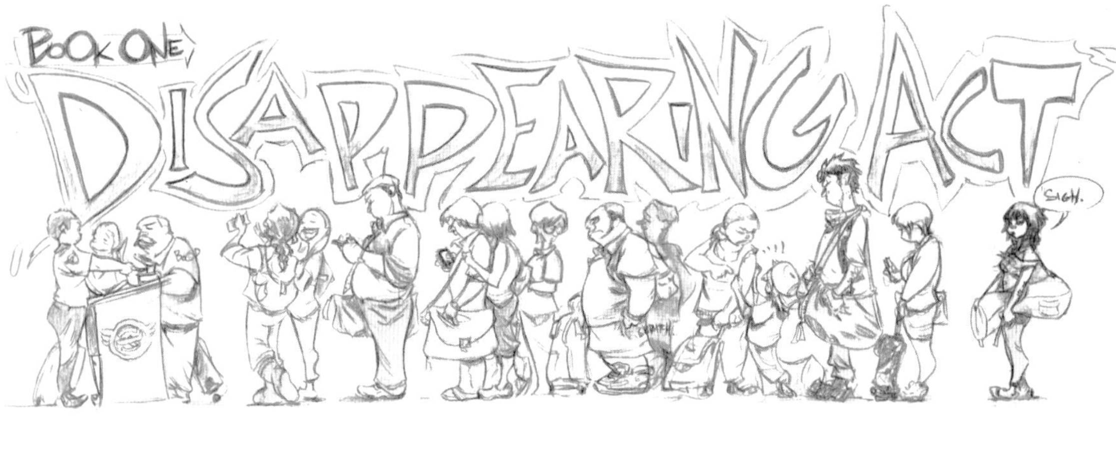
BOOK ONE
DISAPPEARING ACT
SIGH.

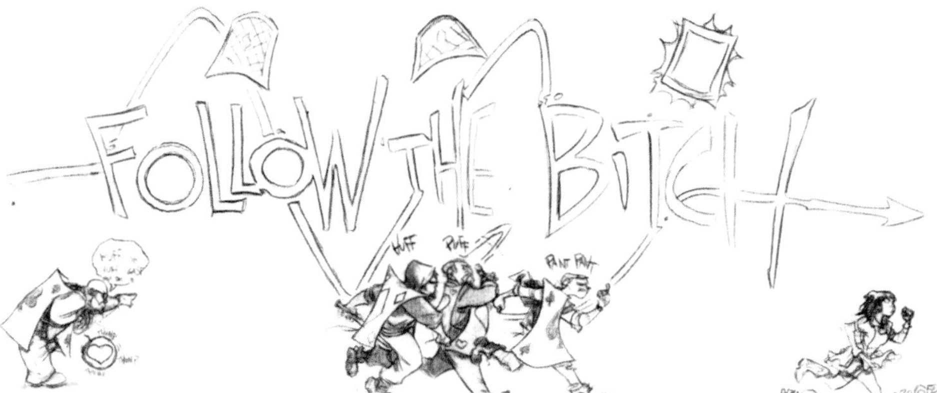
FOLLOW THE BITCH
HUFF
PUFF
PANT PANT

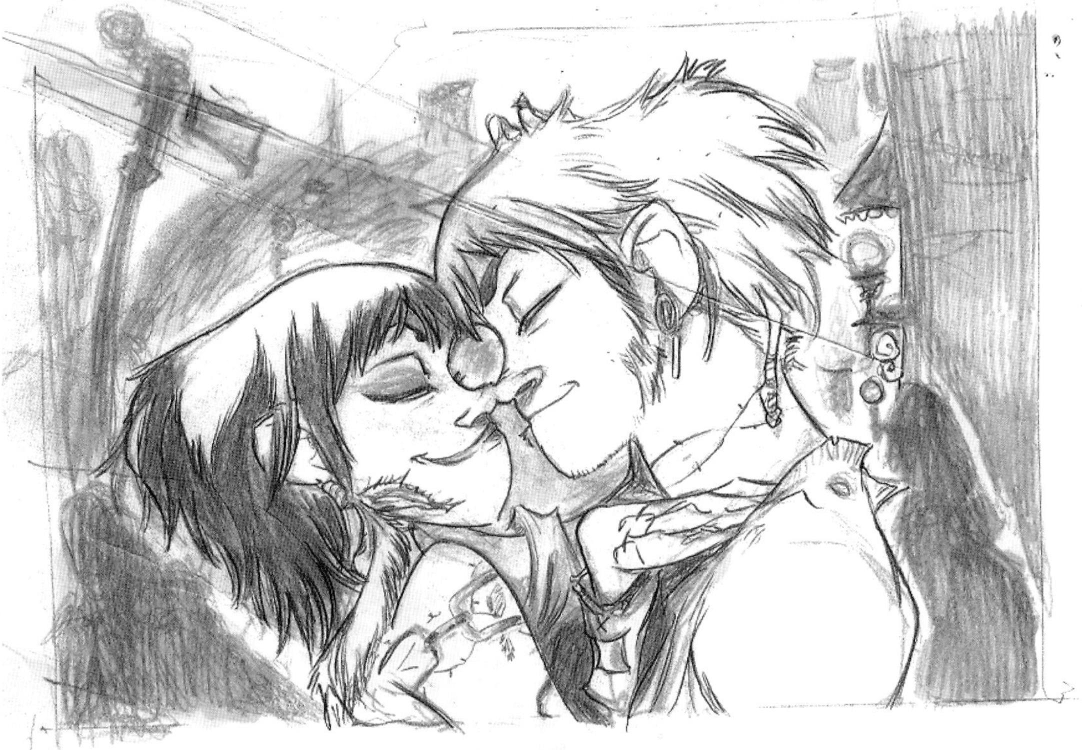

FRIDGE PHOTO

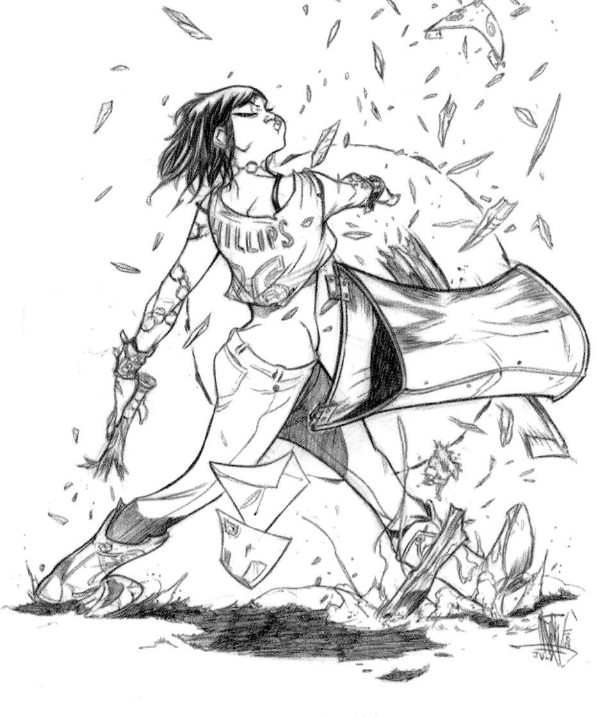
ILLIPS

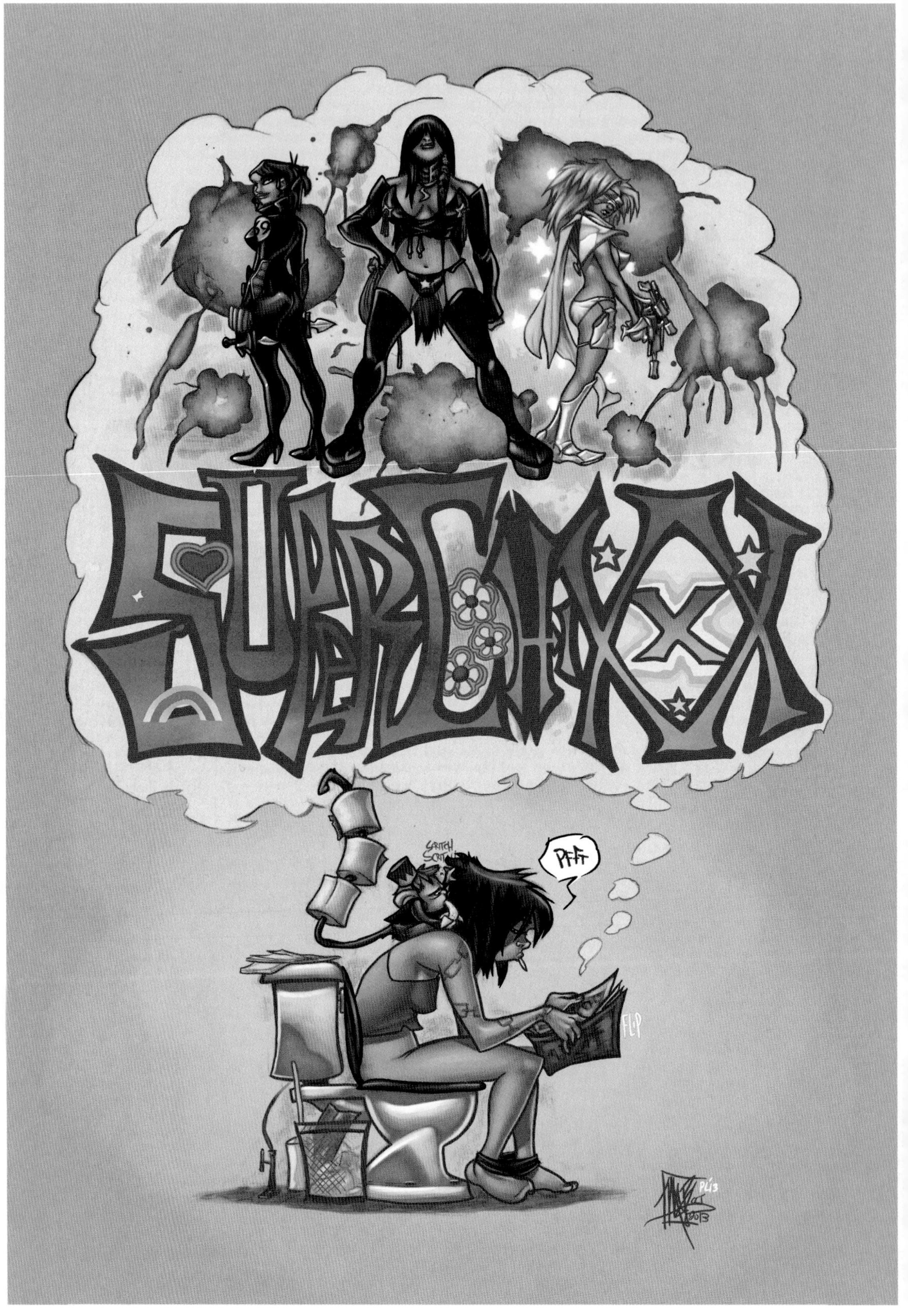
SCRITCH
PFFT
FLIP

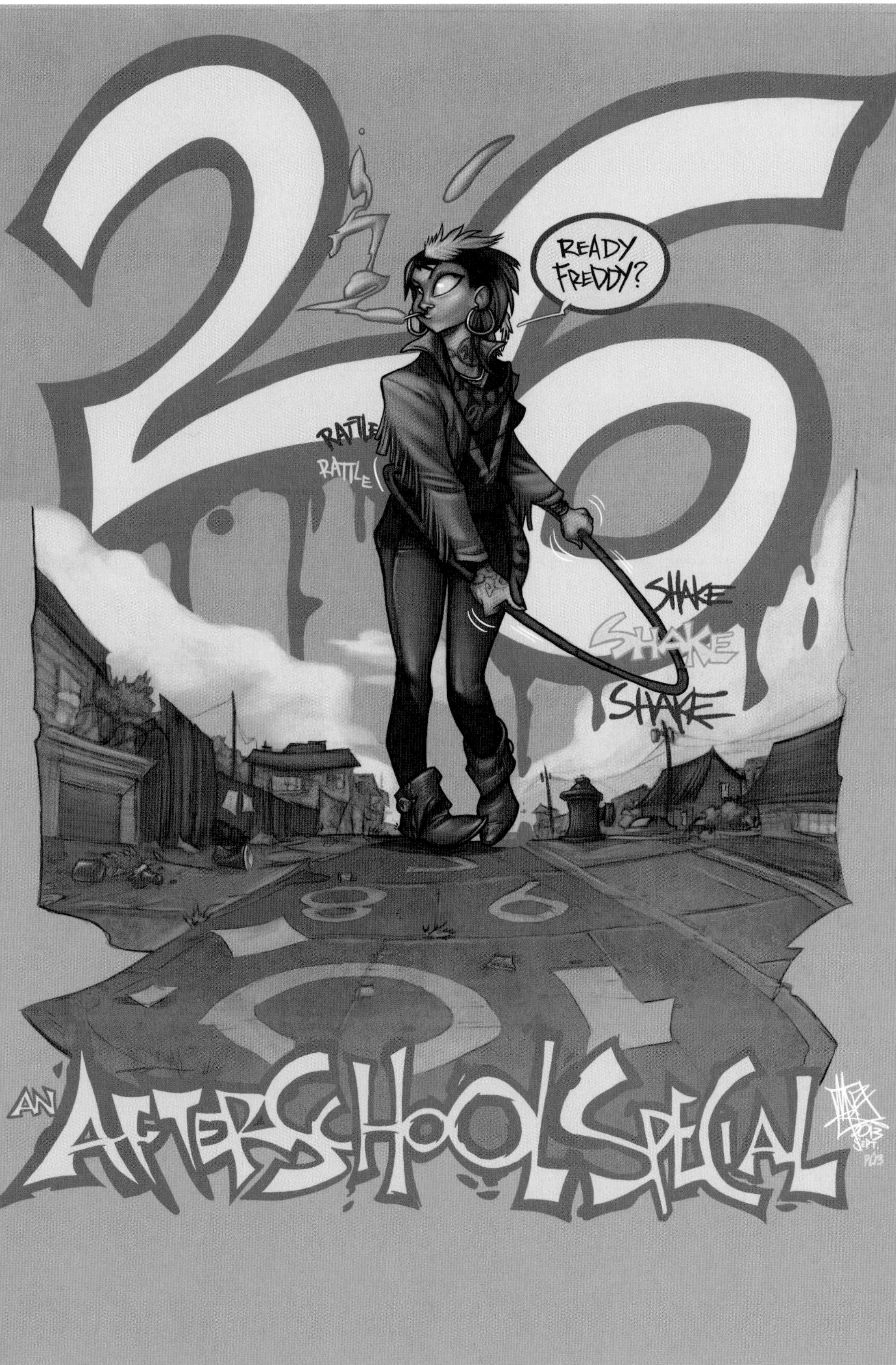
26
READY FREDDY?
RATTLE
RATTLE
SHAKE
SHAKE
SHAKE
AN AFTERSCHOOL SPECIAL

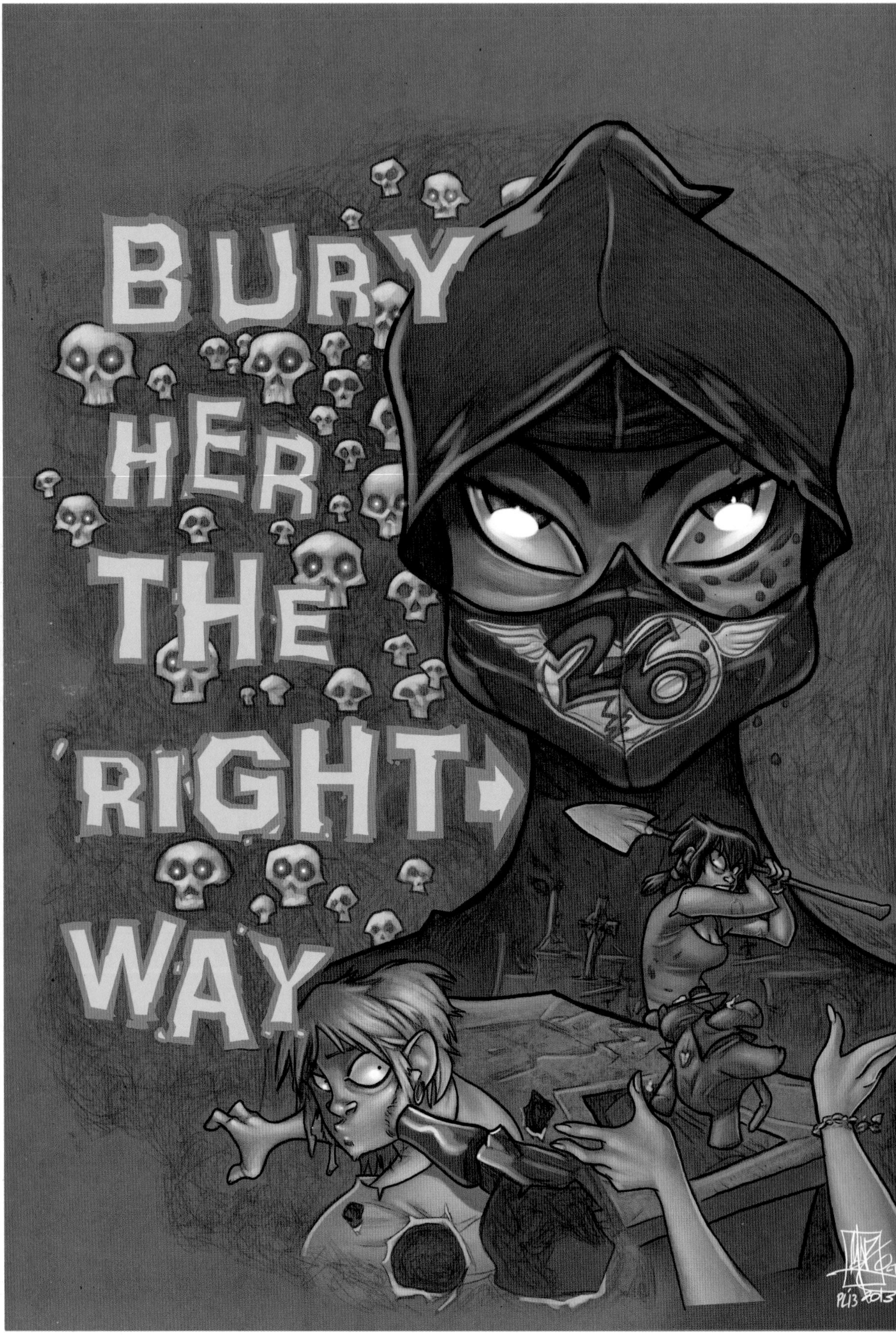
BURY
HER
THE
RIGHT
WAY
26